Transcultural Communication Through Global Englishes

This textbook introduces current thinking on English as a global language and explores its role in intercultural and transcultural communication. It covers how English functions as a lingua franca in multilingual scenarios alongside other languages in a wide variety of global settings, and the fluid and dynamic links between English, other languages, and cultural identities and references.

The implications for English language teaching (ELT), academia, business, and digital communication are explored. Contemporary research and theory are presented in an accessible manner, illustrated with examples from current research, and supported with discussions and tasks to enable students to relate these ideas to their own experiences, needs, and interests. Each chapter contains activities to help students orientate towards the topic, reflect on personal experiences and opinions, and check their understanding. Additionally, a detailed glossary of key terminology in Global Englishes and intercultural communication is provided.

Exploring in depth the links between Global Englishes, intercultural communication research, and transcultural communication research, this is key reading for all advanced students and researchers in Global or World Englishes, English as a lingua franca (ELF), and intercultural communication.

Will Baker is Director of the Centre for Global Englishes and an Associate Professor of Applied Linguistics at the University of Southampton. Publications include: co-editor of *The Routledge handbook of English as a lingua franca* (2018), author of the monograph *Culture and identity through English as a lingua franca* (2015), and co-editor of the book series "Developments in English as lingua franca" (2013–).

Tomokazu Ishikawa is an Assistant Professor at Tamagawa University's Center for English as a Lingua Franca, Tokyo, Japan, and a postdoctoral member at the University of Southampton's Centre for Global Englishes. He has published on ELF, mainly in relation to multilingualism, language attitudes and ideologies, and ELT.

Transcultural Communication Through Global Englishes

An Advanced Textbook for Students

Will Baker and
Tomokazu Ishikawa

Routledge
Taylor & Francis Group
LONDON AND NEW YORK

First published 2021
by Routledge
2 Park Square, Milton Park, Abingdon, Oxon OX14 4RN

and by Routledge
605 Third Avenue, New York, NY 10158

Routledge is an imprint of the Taylor & Francis Group, an informa business

British Library Cataloguing-in-Publication Data
A catalogue record for this book is available from the British Library

Library of Congress Cataloging-in-Publication Data
Names: Baker, Will, author. | Ishikawa, Tomokazu, author.
Title: Transcultural communication through Global Englishes: an advanced textbook for students / Will Baker and Tomokazu Ishikawa.
Description: Abingdon, Oxon; New York: Routledge, 2021. |
Includes bibliographical references and index.
Identifiers: LCCN 2020056687 | ISBN 9780367409364 (hardback) |
ISBN 9780367409357 (paperback) | ISBN 9780367809973 (ebook)
Subjects: LCSH: English language–Foreign countries. |
Intercultural communication. | English language–
Study and teaching–Foreign countries.
Classification: LCC PE2751 .B35 2021 | DDC 303.48/2–dc23
LC record available at https://lccn.loc.gov/2020056687

ISBN: 978-0-367-40936-4 (hbk)
ISBN: 978-0-367-40935-7 (pbk)
ISBN: 978-0-367-80997-3 (ebk)

Typeset in Sabon
by Newgen Publishing UK

Contents

Figures and tables

Figures

Tables

Preface and outline of the book

For many of us, intercultural and, as we propose in this book, transcultural communication is a part of our daily lives. Contemporary societies, especially in urban settings, are typically multicultural and multilingual. Higher-education institutions frequently have an international dimension with global connections to other institutions and staff and students from different countries. Our workplaces are often similarly intercultural due to an increasing number of multinational companies with branches and staff from around the world. International tourism is a billion-dollar industry, with many of us spending part of each year in 'another' culture for holidays or receiving tourists from other countries. At the time of writing this, international tourism has been severely curtailed by the COVID-19 pandemic but it has not completely stopped, and it seems likely to return in the near future. Even if our immediate physical environment is not especially intercultural, we are all familiar with cultural products from around the world which have become globalised in their reach, such as English football, Hollywood movies, Japanese manga and anime, K-pop, and Thai cuisine. The internet and digital communication has added another significant dimension to this, making connectivity across national and cultural borders instantaneous and easy. This digital dimension to intercultural and transcultural communication has become even more prominent since the physical travel restrictions brought about by COVID-19. Thus, we are constantly in contact with cultural 'others', including people, products, and practices.

Parallel to the increase in intercultural and transcultural communication, and indeed facilitating much of it, has been the rise in the use of English as a global language. The worldwide spread of English has now been well documented, with English an official language in a huge number of settings, including hundreds of countries and territories, educational institutions, multinational corporations, and political organisations. Even greater than its official role has been the expansion of English as a lingua franca (ELF), with billions of users of English as a second or additional language and the number of 'non-native' users of the language greatly outnumbering 'native' speakers (we will problematise the use of 'native' and 'non-native' to describe English speakers as regards Global Englishes but use it here for convenience). However, it is important to view this expansion of English from a multilingual perspective. Most users of English are multilinguals who will also be using other languages, and most settings of English use are similarly multilingual with other languages present. English is also not alone as a global language, with other 'big' global languages such as Mandarin Chinese, Spanish, and Arabic having a very wide reach. Increased mobility and digital connectivity also mean that many 'smaller' languages have extended their reach as well. So, for example, a 'national' language such as Vietnamese is present in many settings worldwide due to the migration of Vietnamese speakers and the connections between them, even if those speakers also use English. Therefore, in this book we will approach the use of English as a *multilingua* franca (EMF) as part of multilingual, intercultural and transcultural communication.

The need to recognise the changing understanding of the role of English as a global multilingua franca and the complexity of intercultural and transcultural communication is what has motivated us to write this textbook. Global Englishes research, and particularly ELF research, has in recent years adopted a more multilingual and translingual perspective. However, this has not currently appeared in textbooks. We think that a multilingual approach to understanding Global Englishes is crucial and should be part of our basic understanding of the subject. Similarly, intercultural communication research has taken an increasingly critical approach to culture and language, with complex and dynamic links between them now the norm in studies. The 'trans' dimension in which languages and cultures are seen as transcending boundaries and borders is a new but increasingly integral aspect of research. However, to our knowledge, this transcultural dimension has not yet become part of how the subject is taught. Given that the use of English as a multilingua franca for intercultural and transcultural communication is a normal part of many of our lives, we feel that it is important, and also hopefully of interest, to students of English and intercultural communication.

Another motivation for writing this book is that for us, as it probably is for many of you, transcultural communication through English as a multilingua franca is a part of our everyday experiences. It is not something exotic or strange but a very normal part of life. However, we did not see this reflected in textbooks, which often adopt a simplistic and sometimes stereotyped attitude to both English and intercultural communication. The first author of this book grew up in the south of England and is currently based at the University of Southampton in the UK. However, his job involves working with colleagues from around the world (this book being one example of that) and the majority of his students are international students for whom English is not a first language. Many of his research projects have been based in Asian settings (Thailand in particular) and he regularly travels around the world for research and conferences. Although COVID-19 has put a temporary stop to physical travel, he still frequently takes part in virtual online meetings, seminars, and conferences with colleagues from across the globe. Before studying and working in Southampton he was an English language teacher in Thailand and the UK for over a decade, again teaching students from around the world. Outside of work his family is bilingual, with English as his first language and Thai as his wife's first language. At home they speak a mixture of both these languages and their children have been brought up to be familiar with both Thai and English. School holidays are regularly spent in Thailand and Thai and English cultural practices (however we might define those) are a part of family life.

The second author of this book grew up in northern Japan and was on a music track. Composing classical music with technical terms (mostly Italian) and singing French, German, and Italian songs in preparation for a college of music, he ended up with a law major with an interest in international law. He did not enjoy studying law (apart from Latin terminology), and started teaching English and other subjects after graduation. When he came to the University of Southampton, his fiancée was studying in Paris, France, and thus he sometimes 'escaped' to Paris and stayed there. As such, using different languages has always been a part of his life, and he is currently teaching English at the Center for English as a Lingua Franca, Tamagawa University, Tokyo. His colleagues are 'American' (US), Australian, Brazilian, British, Bulgarian, Canadian, Chinese, Egyptian, Finnish, German, Indian, Irish, Italian, Japanese, Korean, New Zealand, Philippine, Russian, Sri Lankan, Thai, and Vietnamese – albeit he is usually not very aware of their original places or nationalities during interaction. Currently, he and his wife live in the metropolitan area of Tokyo, where multilingual and multicultural hybridity is the norm rather than the exception.

Throughout this book we will draw on our personal experiences of transcultural communication and Global Englishes as well as current research. You will notice that we return to some of our 'favourite' examples a number of times across the book. We think this is helpful in terms of continuity but also aids in illustrating the complexity and multiple levels of meaning and interpretation that can be adopted in understanding interactions in intercultural and transcultural communication through Global Englishes.

This book is structured around four parts divided into 15 chapters. In the first part we set out some of the core ideas, theories, and research in understanding culture, language, and Global Englishes. In Chapter 1 we examine how culture can be characterised and understood. In Chapter 2 we look at the links between culture and language.

Chapter 3 moves on to outlining global languages as part of a multilingual world. Chapter 4 turns specifically to the role of English as a global language and introduces the field of English as a lingua franca (ELF). In the second part we examine more critical approaches to culture, language, and global uses of English. Chapter 5 outlines current perspectives on intercultural communication, distinguishing them from earlier cross-cultural approaches, and considering the links with Global Englishes research. Chapter 6 focuses on identity as a core part of intercultural communication research and in understanding language and culture. In Chapter 7 we explore the issues of language ideologies and their relationship to English, especially as regards Standard Language and native-speakerism. In Chapter 8 we return to a discussion of English as a global language and emphasise the multilingual aspects of its use as a multilingua franca (EMF). In the third part we consider current approaches and domains of research and practice in culture, language, and Global Englishes. Chapter 9 provides an overview of the increasingly influential role of 'trans' theories such as translanguaging, transcultural communication, and transmodality in Global Englishes research. Chapter 10 contains a detailed overview and discussion of transcultural communication approaches and how they relate to Global Englishes. Chapter 11 explores digital communication and virtual spaces, such as social networking sites, as a contemporary and important domain of Global Englishes and transcultural communication. Chapter 12 delves into complexity theory and how it can help us understand global communication and particularly language attitudes and awareness. In the final part we draw the core themes of the book together in a discussion of the implications of Global Englishes and transcultural communication research for teaching and learning. Chapter 13 introduces EMF awareness and its relevance to teaching English and teaching *through* English in English-medium instruction programmes. Chapter 14 critically considers the core concepts in applied linguistics and intercultural communication of communicative and intercultural communicative competence, suggesting alternatives which are more relevant for transcultural communication and Global Englishes. Chapter 15 looks at intercultural education and language teaching and proposes intercultural citizenship, intercultural awareness, and transcultural education as key parts of a Global Englishes-orientated pedagogy in English language teaching (ELT).

The structure of the book builds from basic 'core' concepts to critical and current issues in Global Englishes, intercultural communication, and transcultural communication, and as such the chapters draw on and build on each other. However, each chapter is written in a way that means it can be read individually and there is no necessity to read the entire book to understand a chapter. Furthermore, cross-references are provided in each chapter to where key ideas are discussed in depth. Each chapter contains three activities to help orientate you to the subject of the chapter and to give you the chance to explore the concepts in relation to your own experiences and ideas. Summaries of core terms and ideas are provided to aid in checking your comprehension. A glossary is also provided, with important terms highlighted the first time they appear in the main sections of the textbook. At the end of each chapter we have included annotated suggestions for further reading if you would like to explore the topic further.

This textbook has been written for students in the areas of English language, intercultural communication, Global Englishes, ELT/TESOL (Teaching English to Speakers of Other Languages), and applied linguistics both at undergraduate- and postgraduate-taught levels. The book may also be of interest for students in business and management, communication studies, and cultural studies. We believe this book is innovative in a number of ways. First, it is the first textbook we are aware of that combines both intercultural communication and Global Englishes research. Second, the book introduces new theories and research in these fields especially as regards transcultural communication and English as a global multilingua franca, which have, to date, not featured in student textbooks. We hope you enjoy reading this book as much as we have enjoyed writing it!

Acknowledgements

We would like to thank the many students who have participated in our various courses on intercultural communication and Global Englishes over the years. Their enthusiasm and feedback have helped to shape much of the content of this book. We would also like to thank Eleni Steck at Routledge for her encouragement and guidance (and patience!) throughout the production of the book. Last, the insightful comments from reviewers at various stages of writing this book have been invaluable. Any mistakes or shortcomings, of course, remain our own.

Acronyms

AAVE	African American Vernacular English
ACE	the Asian Corpus of English
ALT	assistant language teacher
ASEAN	the Association of Southeast Asian Nations
BBC	the British Broadcasting Corporation
CA	cultural awareness
CAS	complex adaptive system
CEFR	the Common European Framework of Reference for Languages
CELF	the Center for English as a Lingua Franca (Tamagawa University)
CGE	the Centre for Global Englishes (the University of Southampton)
EAP	English for academic purposes
EFL	English as a foreign language
EIL	English as an international language
ELF	English as a lingua franca
ELFA	the corpus of ELF in academic settings
ELT	English language teaching
EMF	English as a multilingua franca
EMI	English-medium instruction
EMIC	electronically mediated intercultural communication
ENL	English as a native language
ESP	English for specific purposes
EU	the European Union
GA	General American (English)
GELT	Global Englishes language teaching
HE	higher education
ICA	intercultural awareness
ICC	intercultural communicative competence
ICE	the International Corpus of English
L1	first language(s)

L2	second language(s)
MEXT	the Ministry of Education, Culture, Sports, Science and Technology, Japan
MLA	the Modern Language Association of America
NES	native English speaker
NHK	Japan Broadcasting Corporation (Nippon Hōsō Kyōkai)
OBEC	the Office of the Basic Education Commission (the Ministry of Education, Thailand)
RP	Received Pronunciation
SA	study abroad
SLA	second-language acquisition
SNS	social networking site
STEM	science, technology, engineering, and mathematics
TEOS	Transcultural European Outdoor Studies
TESOL	Teaching English to Speakers of Other Languages
TIG	transient international group
UK	the United Kingdom (of Great Britain and Northern Ireland)
US	the United States (of America)
VOICE	the Vienna Oxford International Corpus of English
VoIP	Voice over Internet Protocol
WE	World Englishes
WrELFA	the corpus of written ELF in academic settings

Part I

Core issues in understanding culture, language, and Global Englishes

1 Characterising culture

Introduction

Culture is something we all feel we know something about, especially as most of us will claim membership of at least one culture, whether it be national, regional, ethnic, or any of the myriad of possible cultural groupings. Culture is something that we see and hear all around us in our everyday lives. It is debated in the media and politics, it is something we study at school, we often discuss it with family and friends, and we might even be asked to 'explain' it by visiting friends or colleagues from 'other' cultures. Yet, at the same time, culture is extremely difficult to define. As Raymond Williams has famously written, "culture is one of the two or three most complicated words in the English language" (2015: 86). When asked to define a particular culture, for example, 'Chinese culture' or 'Western culture', it is unlikely that any two people will agree exactly on what it is. We are, therefore, put in a dilemma when discussing culture, summed up neatly by the linguistic anthropologist Elinor Ochs: "while culture is considered important to fathom, it is obscure and difficult to analyse. You can't see it; you can't count it in any obvious way" (2002: 115).

While we cannot offer a single definition of culture, since the range of uses the idea is put to make this an impossible task, this chapter provides an introduction to the concept of culture and how it has been defined at different periods of time and in different disciplines. Given the aims of this book, we place a focus on linguistic approaches to culture and five different characterisations of culture are outlined. These are the traditional product approach, an interpretive **semiotic** approach, a **discourse** approach, a practice approach, and a critical ideological approach to culture. Two powerful **ideologies** that underlie current thinking about culture, nations and **globalisation**, are considered. We introduce the notion of **essentialism**, especially as related to product approaches to culture, and emphasise that this book follows a mixture of discourse, practice, and critical approaches to culture. We present three questions, drawn from Scollon and Scollon (2001), which underpin our perspective on culture in this textbook: "who has introduced culture as a relevant concept in interaction, with what purposes, and with what consequences?" Throughout the chapter you will be asked to reflect on your own understandings and experiences of different cultures.

Activity 1.1 Characterising culture 1

Brainstorm your ideas about what culture is. Add your ideas to the culture diagram below. A few examples have already been given. If you can, compare your answers to those of other people.

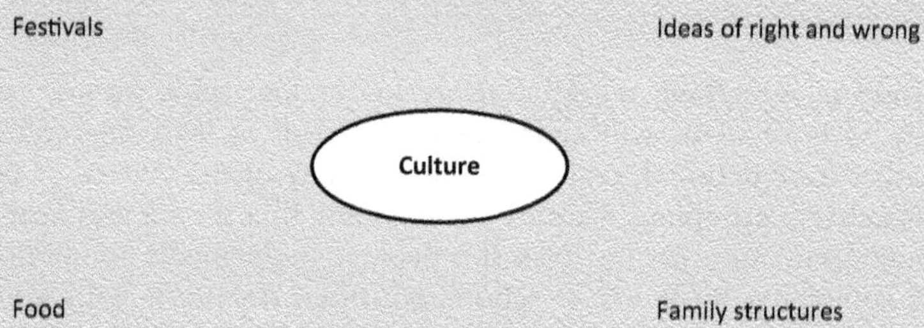

Based on what you wrote above, try to write a definition of culture here.

Feedback: *There are no right or wrong answers to these activities and there are many different things you may have chosen to include as part of culture. A few of the many things you might have chosen are language, clothes, food and drink, greetings, politeness, literature, education, religion, TV programmes, music, personal space, and gestures. This list could go on for pages and we still would not be finished. This illustrates the complexity and depth of culture, which we explore further in this chapter.*

1.1 Developing ideas of culture

The origins of the word culture come from the Latin word *cultūra*, meaning what is cultivated or grown, in contrast to *nāscere*, referring to what is born. In other words, culture is something which is learned and developed, not something we are born with. This idea of cultivation resulted in traditional perspectives on culture that associated it with civilisation. Thus, 'civilised' societies were seen as distinct from and superior to more 'primitive' or basic societies. Culture and civilisation were something to aim for and develop as societies moved forward. This understanding of culture was especially associated in the English-speaking world with the writer Matthew Arnold, who argued in *Culture and Anarchy* that cultural development would result in "an atmosphere of sweetness and light" (1869, cited in Bauman,

2011: 7) for all. Associated with civilisation and cultural development was the distinction between 'high' and 'low' cultures in which certain arts forms, for example, opera or literary fiction, and particular works of arts, for instance, a particular painting or poem, were viewed as superior and more 'cultured' than others. This was also extended to societies and cultures, with some societies viewed as more 'civilised', cultured, and superior to other 'primitive', less cultured ones. One of the most insidious results of such an essentialist, ethnocentric, and racist understanding of culture was the supposed justification it provided for the invasion and enslavement of people from 'lower' cultures under colonialism.

An alternative perspective on culture that developed in the nineteenth and twentieth centuries from a more anthropological perspective was the idea of culture as a way of life of a group of people, a well-known example of this being Edward Tylor's definition of culture as "that complex whole which includes knowledge, belief, art, morals, law, custom, and any other capabilities and habits acquired by man as a member of society" (1871: 1). While early anthropological approaches to culture, such as Tylor's, believed it was possible, and desirable, to continue to distinguish between 'high' and 'low' cultures based on their way of life, this changed in the twentieth century to less hierarchical perspectives. For instance, the United States (US) anthropologist Franz Boas (1911/1986), in his study of indigenous American cultures, rejected the ethnocentric hierarchical approach and instead adopted a cultural-relativist position, exploring cultures in their own terms with no association of superiority or inferiority between different cultures. The notion of culture as a way of life of a group of people and a cultural-relativist position are two features that continue in many characterisations of culture today.

1.2 Five perspectives on culture

In this section we will consider five current perspectives on culture: a product approach to culture (e.g., Hall, 1959; Hofstede et al., 2010); an interpretive semiotic approach to culture (e.g., Geertz, 1973/2000); a discourse approach to culture (e.g., Kramsch, 1998a); a practice approach to culture (e.g., Street, 1993); and a critical, ideological approach to culture (e.g., Holliday, 2011; Piller, 2017).

The product approach to culture

The product approach to culture sees culture as a *thing* which can be described and delineated. This is probably the most common understanding of culture outside of research and academia and is exemplified in the type of definition seen in dictionaries. For example, the *Oxford Advanced American Dictionary* defines culture as "the customs and beliefs, art, way of life, and social organization of a particular country or group".[1] A product approach is also frequently used in traditional **intercultural communication** research. For instance, Edward T. Hall, considered to be the 'father' of intercultural communication research, used the metaphor of an iceberg to describe culture. For Hall (1966), there are visible aspects of culture which can be clearly observed such as festivals, costumes, and food but, like an iceberg, most of culture is below the surface, such as beliefs, values, and thought patterns, and cannot be directly observed. Thus, for Hall, most of what we describe as culture is internalised in the mind and outside of our consciousness. Similarly, the cross-cultural psychologist Geert Hofstede (1991) uses the metaphor of the onion to describe the different layers of culture. Like Hall, Hofstede views culture as predominantly in the mind and characterises it as "the collective programming of the mind which distinguishes the members of one human group from another" (2001: 9). A product perspective to culture is also very common in English language teaching. For example, Tomalin and Stempleski (1993) distinguish between 'big-C' culture: history, geography, institutions, literature, art, music, and the way of life; and 'little-c' culture: culturally influenced behaviour, beliefs, and perceptions expressed mainly through language, but also including unconscious beliefs, values, customs, and habits. Such a perspective is still prevalent today, with a popular textbook on intercultural communication defining culture as "[t]he totality of that group's thought, experiences, and patterns of behavior and its concepts, values, and assumptions about life that guide behavior and how those evolve with contact with other cultures" (Jandt, 2021: 11).

An underlying theme running throughout these accounts of culture is the idea of culture as a thing or container into which the way of life of a particular group of people can be placed, both externally through observable products and behaviours, and internally through beliefs, values, and thought patterns in the mind. By approaching culture in this way it is possible to delineate and contain it and therefore distinguish between different cultures. In other words, groups of people can be differentiated from each other based on whether they fit into one cultural container or another. Within product-orientated approaches this is frequently done at the level of national cultures (e.g., Hofstede, 1991). So, for instance, statements about cultures often follow the pattern of, *people in culture X behave in this way and believe this, which is different from people in culture Y, who behave in this way and believe this*. Examples include Hall's notion (1966) of polychronic cultures (e.g., claims that in Mexico people have a more cyclical, fluid concept of time and are more likely to multitask and take time to interact with others rather than keep to a time schedule) versus monochronic cultures (e.g., claims that in Germany time is viewed in a linear manner and as a valuable resource that should not be wasted, and people are more likely to keep to time schedules and disapprove of lateness). Similar is Hofstede's (1991) conception of individualist cultures (e.g., US culture, in which the individual is more important than the group) versus collectivist cultures (e.g., Japan, where the group is more important than the individual). However, as will be discussed throughout the rest of this chapter, product approaches have been criticised for a number of reasons. These include claims that they take an overly simplistic view of culture that assumes individuals are synonymous with group characteristics. This can promote overgeneralisations about culturally based behaviour and hence lead to unhelpful **stereotypes** about people, when in reality groups of people, and individuals within those groups, are much more variable in their beliefs and behaviour than any cultural generalisations would suggest. Another criticism is that product perspectives on culture misrepresent culture as a static system, whereas it is actually a dynamic and constantly changing process, not a thing at all.

The interpretive semiotic approach to culture

An alternative approach to understanding culture is a semiotic, or symbolic, approach. The applied linguist Zhu Hua (2014; 2019) describes this as an 'interpretative approach', since, unlike the product approach, it does not attempt to provide an account of all the rules of a culture as part of a unified system, but instead interprets the meaning of individual events in their cultural context. As the ethnographer Clifford Geertz, the most well-known proponent of this approach, writes:

> man is an animal suspended in webs of significance he himself has spun[;] I take culture to be those webs, and the analysis of it to be therefore not an experimental science in search of law but an interpretative one in search of meaning.
>
> (1973/2000: 5)

A key part of Geertz's (1973/2000) approach to interpreting culture is to provide a 'thick description' of the particularity of individual events and then link them to the multiple layers of culture which give it meaning through ethnographic study (where the researcher becomes a part of the cultural group they study). This again contrasts with the 'thin descriptions' provided by the large-scale generalisations of product approaches such as Hofstede's (1991). Another important distinction between product and interpretative approaches is that culture is seen as created externally in interaction, not internally in the mind: "human thought is basically both social and public ... its natural habitat is the house yard, the market place, and the town square" (Geertz, 1973/

2000: 45). Last, under the semiotic approach, culture is conceived as primarily made up of learned patterns of meaning expressed symbolically; culture "denotes an historically transmitted pattern of meanings embodied in symbols, a system of inherited conceptions expressed in symbolic forms by means of which men communicate, perpetuate, and develop their knowledge about and attitudes toward life" (Geertz, 1973/2000: 89).

This semiotic and interpretative approach to culture has been very influential within linguistics since language is typically seen as the prime semiotic system. As the linguist Michael Halliday argues, language is a semiotic system that expresses the culture that we live in. The relationship between language, culture, and society is interrelated; language influences culture and culture influences language. Language as a social semiotic means "interpreting language within a sociocultural context, in which culture itself is interpreted in semiotic terms" (Halliday, 1978). In other words, there is a cyclical relationship between language and culture in which language is seen as the main way of constructing and representing culture, while at the same time language takes the forms that it does because of culture. This approach to culture has influenced many of the subsequent accounts of culture that will be presented later in this chapter, as well as thinking on the relationship between language and culture. However, while semiotic accounts are more interactive and dynamic in their characterisation of culture than product approaches, there is still concern about how they can account for the multiple meanings associated with symbolic systems in the highly diverse **multilingual** and **multicultural** environments we often find ourselves in currently (e.g., Pennycook, 2007; Blommaert, 2010), and this is particularly the case in relation to global uses of English (Baker, 2015).

The discourse approach to culture

The notion of culture as constructed in and through discourse has been influential in **applied linguistics** studies. Here, discourse is viewed from the perspective of Discourse, with a capital 'D' (Gee, 2015), in which discourse is understood as ways of thinking, talking, and writing about particular aspects of the world. For instance, we can discuss the discourse of 'gender' or 'education' or 'globalisation'. While discourse and language are closely linked, it is important to stress that they are not the same. So the same discourse can be expressed in many different languages, for example, globally relevant topics such as climate change and environmentalism. Influential scholars of a discourse approach to culture are Clare Kramsch and Ron and Suzie Wong Scollon. Kramsch defines culture as "1 Membership in a discourse community that shares a common social space and history, and a common system of standards for perceiving, believing, evaluating, and acting. 2 The discourse community itself. 3 The system of standards itself" (Kramsch, 1998a: 127). Furthermore, Kramsch sees cultural discourse communities as having three dimensions; first, the social dimension, in which the members of the community interact with each other; second, the historical dimension, in which the members draw on shared history and traditions; third, common imaginings, in which the members share imaginations of what their community and culture is, including the previous two dimensions. Importantly, Kramsch also introduces a critical dimension to culture, emphasising that what are viewed as shared standards, values, histories, traditions, and imaginings is a site of struggle and conflict. Thus, "culture, as a process that both includes and excludes, always entails the exercise of power and control" (Kramsch, 1998a: 8). The constant struggle to describe, or 'imagine', culture also means that culture is viewed as always heterogeneous and changing.

Scollon et al. argue that "culture is mostly too large a concept" (2012: 10) to be useful to researchers given the multiple interpretations of its meaning, as well as the dangers of stereotyping when discussing particular cultures. Instead, they propose the term 'discourse system', which is defined as:

> a 'cultural toolkit' consisting of four main kinds of things: ideas and beliefs about the world, conventional ways of treating other people, ways of communicating using various kinds of texts, media, and 'languages', and methods of learning how to use these other tools.
> (2012: 8)

Examples of discourse systems include nation, gender, generation, and profession, as well as more ideological systems, such as Confucian and Utilitarian discourse systems. While Scollon et al.'s explanation of these discourse systems is complex, Utilitarian discourse roughly equates to a 'global capitalist' perspective (2012: 114) and has its roots in Utilitarian philosophy in Europe. Key features are individualism and egalitarianism and in communication this translates to direct talk and the promotion of close, equal relations (Scollon et al., 2012: 121). In contrast, the Confucian discourse system has its origins in China and East Asia. Important aspects of this system are relationships between people, nature, and social harmony (Scollon et al., 2012: 124), which manifests itself in communication via respect for authority and maintaining hierarchical systems. However, Scollon et al. (2012) underscore that these two discourse systems should not be seen from an essentialist East/West divide. Confucian and Utilitarian discourse systems exist side-by-side in most modern East Asian societies and the European thinkers who proposed Utilitarian philosophies were heavily influenced by Confucian and East Asian scholarship (Scollon et al., 2012). Thus, by adopting this discourse system approach people are not reduced to one particular system, such as nationality or ethnicity, but are seen as simultaneously participating in multiple discourse systems. While it is debatable whether the term 'discourse' is any less broad or easy to interpret than 'culture', viewing people as participating in many different discourse systems and communities is very useful in capturing the complexity and diversity of people's identifications, cultural or otherwise, and helps to avoid the reification of stereotyped views of culture that reduce individuals to one dimension.

The practice approach to culture

Practice approaches view culture as something we 'do' rather than as something we 'have'. One of the most well-known formulations of this is the education and literary scholar Brian Street's (1993) notion of 'culture as a verb'. In other words, culture is not the static 'thing' that a noun suggests, but rather a process as associated with verbs. Culture is here viewed as subjective and constructed in interactions between individuals. Under this perspective culture is inherently intersubjective since it can only be constructed through and in interaction. Due to the situated nature of culture, this means that any characterisation of culture will always be temporary and partial. Culture is a constantly changing, dynamic and fluid practice which can be viewed from multiple perspectives and levels, or scales, such as global, national, regional, work, and family cultures. For the applied linguist Adrian Holliday, culture is seen as constructed social practices, "as ways of doing something which relate to particular cultural environments" (2013: 6). The most important cultural environments are what Holliday refers to as **small cultures**, defined as:

> cultural environments which are located in proximity to the people concerned. There are thus small social groupings or activities wherever there is cohesive behaviour, such as families, leisure and work groups, where people form rules for how to behave which will bind them together.
>
> (2013: 3)

Holliday believes that it is from these small cultures that all other cultural groups, such as national cultures, develop.

Another important dimension of practice approaches to cultures, highlighted by Holliday and others, is the historic dimension. The practices that form cultures are typically established through routines of behaviour which become social norms through repetition, often to the extent that they go unnoticed by the members of a culture. However, as culture is created intersubjectively in interaction there is always a degree of negotiation in the meaning of cultural practices between individuals. This results in a tension between the amount of freedom individuals have in negotiating and constructing social practices and the restrictions imposed by existing social norms or practices. Thus, for practice approaches to culture, as with discourse approaches, culture can be a site of conflict and power struggles between dominant and alternative practices.

The critical ideological approach to culture

A theme running through both the discourse and practice approaches to culture has been a critical perspective to culture in which the contested nature and power relationships in culture are recognised. This theme is explicitly dealt with in critical ideological approaches to culture. As the philosopher Madan Sarup writes, "Culture is not something fixed and frozen as the traditionalists would have us believe, but a process of constant struggle as cultures interact with each other and are affected by economic, political and social factors" (1996: 140). Thus, ideological accounts of culture focus on critically exploring how social structures are created in cultures, the factors affecting this, such as economics and politics, and the power relationships that emerge. The applied linguist Ingrid Piller sums up this position in the following way.

> Culture is an ideological construct called into play by social actors to produce and reproduce social categories and boundaries, and it must be the central research aim of a critical approach to intercultural communication to understand the reasons, forms and consequences of calling cultural difference into play.
>
> (2017: 10)

In other words, as researchers of intercultural communication we should not take culture for granted, but rather investigate how it is constructed and used in communication.

Here, ideology is understood as sets or systems of beliefs and ideas constructed by members of a community to make sense of the variability they encounter, often with a moral/political dimension (i.e., what is viewed as 'right', 'wrong', 'proper', 'standard'). All groups have their own ideologies and hence there is no neutral view; however, the ideologies of powerful groups are typically most prominent and influential (see, for example, Milroy & Milroy, 2012). In terms of culture and ideology, the discourse analyst James Paul Gee explains it as follows.

> Cultural models are not all wrong or all right. In fact, like all models, they are simplifications of reality. They are the ideology through which we all see our worlds. In that sense, we are all both 'beneficiaries' and 'victims' of ideology, thanks to the fact that we speak a language and live in culture. But we can – or at times are morally obligated to – interrogate our cultural models and replace them with others, sometimes even with explicit and well developed theories. Ultimately, these new theories are models too, but, we hope, better ones.
>
> (2008: 29)

Both Gee and Piller emphasise that it is the role of researchers to critically explore conceptions of culture and not take them for granted. However, it is also important to recognise that all perspectives on culture are ideologically informed, whether they be product, semiotic, discourse, or critical. It is the job of the researcher to recognise and be explicit about the ideology informing their perspective on culture. This approach to understanding culture is perhaps best captured in the following well-known quotation from the Scollons.

> [S]et aside any a priori notions of group membership and identity and ... ask instead how and under what circumstances concepts such as culture are produced by participants as relevant categories ... [w]ho has introduced culture as a relevant category, for what purposes, and with what consequences?
>
> (Scollon & Scollon, 2001: 544–545)

These are questions that will underpin the approach to culture and intercultural/**transcultural communication** throughout this book.

Summary

As you will have noticed from this discussion, culture is difficult to define. So, as the sociolinguist and cultural studies researcher Karen Risager explains, "there has been more or less a consensus that it is not possible to lay down an 'authorised' definition of culture" (2006: 42). We have, therefore, not attempted to provide a single definition, but rather presented five different perspectives on culture, all of which contain aspects that we think are useful in understanding culture. The five perspectives can be summarised in the Table 1.1 below.

From these five approaches to culture, a number of important themes emerge.

- First, culture can be seen as a system of shared products, symbols, discourses, practices, and ideologies among groups of people.

- Second, these shared products, symbols, discourses, practices, and ideologies and the groupings of people themselves that make up culture are contestable and sites of struggle.
- Third, the people and shared products, symbols, discourses, practices, and ideologies that make up cultures are constantly in process and changing and hence cannot be fixed and have no clear boundaries.

Thus, culture is complex and cannot be reduced to simple explanations. Indeed, we find the metaphors of **complexity theory** particularly helpful in understanding culture as a shared system, but a constantly changing system that is always in flux with no final end point. As one of the authors of this book has previously written:

> following a complexity perspective, cultural systems emerge from the interactions of groups of individuals but are not reducible to those individuals. Therefore, in contrast to simplistic, essentialist understandings of culture, individuals are not synonymous with the cultural systems or groups which they may identify or be identified with.
>
> (Baker & Sangiamchit, 2019: 2)

We will explore the idea of culture and language as complex emergent systems in more detail later in this book.

Table 1.1 Five perspectives on culture

Perspectives on culture	*Main features*	*Examples*
Product	Culture is a thing (festivals, food, folklore) possessed by groups of people typically at the national level	Hall (1959); Hofstede et al. (2010)
Interpretive semiotic	Culture is a symbolic (semiotic) system for meaning-making and interpretation; language is the prime semiotic system in culture	Geertz (1973/2000); Halliday (1978)
Discourse	Culture is a shared discourse system among groups of people	Kramsch (1998a); Scollon et al. (2012)
Practice	Culture is something we do (not something we have); culture is a process	Street (1993); Pennycook (2007)
Critical, ideological	Culture is a shared ideology; power imbalances between different ideologies mean that cultural characterisations are contestable	Holliday (2011); Piller (2017)

Activity 1.2 Characterising culture 2

Compare your earlier definition of culture with those below taken from the approaches presented here. What elements are the same or different? Which characterisations do you find most convincing? Would you like to change anything in your definition of culture after reading these?

Culture as product

"The collective programming of the mind which distinguishes the members of one human group from another" (Hofstede, 2001: 9).

"The totality of that group's thought, experiences, and patterns of behavior and its concepts, values, and assumptions about life that guide behavior and how those evolve with contact with other cultures" (Jandt, 2021: 11).

Culture as symbolic interpretation

"It [culture] denotes an historically transmitted pattern of meanings embodied in symbols, a system of inherited conceptions expressed in symbolic forms by means of which men communicate, perpetuate, and develop their knowledge about and attitudes toward life" (Geertz, 1973/2000: 89).

Culture as discourse

"1 Membership in a discourse community that shares a common social space and history, and a common system of standards for perceiving, believing, evaluating, and acting. 2 The discourse community itself. 3 The system of standards itself" (Kramsch, 1998a: 127).

Culture as practice

Culture is not something static, as suggested by its classification and use as a noun, but rather dynamic; "Culture is a verb" (Street, 1993); it is something we 'do', not something we 'have'.

Culture as ideology

"Culture is an ideological construct called into play by social actors to produce and reproduce social categories and boundaries, and it must be the central research aim of a critical approach to intercultural communication to understand the reasons, forms and consequences of calling cultural difference into play" (Piller, 2017: 10).

Critical approaches to culture

"[S]et aside any a priori notions of group membership and identity and ... ask instead how and under what circumstances concepts such as culture are produced by participants as relevant categories ... [w]ho has introduced culture as a relevant category, for what purposes, and with what consequences?" (Scollon & Scollon, 2001: 544–545).

Culture as complex emergent systems

Cultures are shared systems of products, symbols, discourses, practices, and ideologies among groups of people. However, these systems are constantly changing and in flux, with no fixed end point. Furthermore, cultural systems emerge from the interactions of groups of individuals but are not reducible to those individuals (Baker, 2015).

Feedback: *There are obviously no right or wrong answers to this activity. However, we would guess based on previous teaching experiences that many of your definitions were closer to the 'culture as product' and symbolic interpretations. Hopefully, you have now added some other dimensions to your definitions.*

1.3 Culture, nation, and globalisation

As we have seen, culture can be viewed at many different levels and in many different ways. Nonetheless, the influence of national conceptions of culture and the link to nation states remains very powerful and is frequently made use of in popular accounts of culture and in research participants' descriptions of culture. As Holliday explains, "it is a fact that people everywhere really do use, talk about, explain things in terms of, and present themselves with[,] national cultural profiles, despite their lack of scientific basis" (2013: 164). Two influential understandings of the processes by which ideologies of national cultures maintain their prominence are 'imagined communities' (Anderson, 2006/2016) and 'banal nationalism' (Billig, 1995). The political scientist Benedict Anderson explains imagined communities in relation to the nation state in the following way: "It is imagined because members of even the smallest nation will never know most of their fellow members, meet them, or even hear of them, yet in the minds of each lives the image of their communion" (2006/2016: 6). From this perspective, nations and national cultures are always socially constructed, rather than the 'natural' entities that they are sometimes portrayed as. However, this does not diminish the power of nations; rather, it emphasises the ideological nature of their construction. For Anderson a key part of the construction of a nation is its association with a shared national language. We can see the influence of this notion of imagined communities in Kramsch's (1998a) characterisation of culture as an imagined discourse community.

Connected to imagined communities, the sociologist Michael Billig introduced the concept of banal nationalism, which explores "the ideological means by which nation-states are reproduced" (1995: 6). Billig highlights the manner in which maintenance of nationalism and the nation is an everyday, but unnoticed (banal), part of our lives. Examples of reinforcement of the nation include maps that depict the nation and its borders, national flags, national images on coins and bank notes, and weather forecasts that are restricted to the national borders, as well as the idea of a national language. Through this constant reminder of nationalism the constructed nature of nation 'disappears' into the background of our lives and becomes normal and apparently natural. Piller (2017) highlights how uncritical approaches to culture and intercultural communication also reinforce this banal nationalism through reproducing the ideology of the nation and national cultures in describing the processes of intercultural communication.

Alongside nation, another powerful influence on culture in recent times has been globalisation. While globalisation has often been seen as undermining the role of nations in cultural ideologies, in practice the two frequently exist in parallel. Globalisation has been defined in many different ways, but here we will use the well-cited definition from the sociologist Jan Aart Scholte, as:

> the spread of transplanetary … connections between people. From this perspective, globalisation involves reductions in barriers to transworld social contacts. People become more able – physically, legally, linguistically, culturally and psychologically – to engage with each other wherever on earth they might be.
>
> (2008: 1478)

Under this concept globalisation is not in itself anything, but rather it is an umbrella term that covers a number of process as outlined in Scholte's definition. We will return to the concept of globalisation again in our discussion of global languages. The increased connections and engagement between people and communities at a global scale have had significant implications on how cultures are constructed and understood. The notions of **transnational** or **transcultural flows**, from sociology and anthropology (Appadurai, 1996; Hannez, 1996), have been proposed as a way to understand the relationships between globalisation and culture. These approaches emphasise the increasing scale and complexity of social networks and the flows of cultural practices and ideologies through these networks which result in an increased diversity of cultural practices and identifications. However, this global scale to culture is not viewed as a replacement to nation. Instead, the global scale is seen as existing alongside the national scale and many others in a multitude of cultural scales, identifications, and practices which are part of contemporary globalised societies. This transnational and transcultural perspective also rejects the idea that globalisation results in the homogenisation of cultures in which we become part of a unified 'global culture'. Instead, cultures are viewed as ever more diversified, with multiple layers, from the local, to the national and the global, interacting in dynamic and fluid ways.

In applied linguistics the notions of global flows of cultures and languages have been made use of extensively by Risager (2006; 2007) in her transnational paradigm and Alasdair Pennycook (2007) through transcultural flows. At the global scale, Risager (2006) envisages languages and cultures spreading across each other in networks of **linguistic and cultural flows**. Similarly, Pennycook employs the metaphor of flow to describe how:

> [t]ranscultural flows therefore refer not merely to the spread of particular forms of culture across boundaries, or the existence of supercultural commonalities (cultural forms that transcend locality), but rather to the processes of borrowing, blending, remaking and returning, to processes of alternative cultural production.
>
> (2007: 6)

For Pennycook, globalisation opens up new spaces for cultural creation and identification. However, again, he emphasises that the global dimension does not replace the local or the national scale. Instead, globalisation results in new ways in which local settings are connected in multiple ways, and the global flow and adaptation of cultural forms and practices across and through these interconnected localities. The idea of transcultural flows will be returned to throughout this book in relation to both language and culture and the notion of transcultural communication.

1.4 Cultural stereotypes, generalisations, and essentialism

The many different perspectives and layers of culture that we have presented so far illustrate that culture is complex and cannot be reduced to a single explanation. It is therefore important that we avoid overly simplistic accounts of culture if we want to have a better understanding of the diversity of our own cultural groupings and those of others. In intercultural communication literature these simplistic accounts of culture are typically referred to through terms such as stereotypes, essentialism, and **othering**. A stereotype is a belief about a group of people that is often not based on any personal experience, or an overgeneralisation based on a small amount of knowledge or experience. Stereotypes tend to be self-perpetuating in that people look for information that confirms their stereotype and ignore information that does not fit their stereotype. **Cultural stereotypes** typically link cultures and nations together, which as we have already seen is just one level of culture, and thus ignore the many other different scales of culture. We are all probably very familiar with national cultural stereotypes from the media and advertising, such as polite British people and shy Japanese people. Of course, there may be polite Brits or shy Japanese, but this does not mean that *all* British and Japanese behave this way, nor even that those that do behave this way do so *all the time*. It is especially problematic to assume that these behaviours or values are unique to a particular nation or even linked to the nation state at all. Other stereotypes may be even more detached from the everyday experiences of people in a particular culture. The first author of this book remembers being very shocked and surprised by an advert in Bangkok for a UK-based international chain of English language schools that featured a picture of a man dressed in a pin-striped suit wearing a bowler hat. In his experience he had never seen an English teacher, nor anyone else he knew in the UK, dressed in this way.

Closely linked to the notion of stereotypes is that of generalisations. Like stereotypes, generalisations may be based on a limited amount of knowledge or experience and are extended to a wider group of people. However, unlike stereotypes, generalisations are adaptable and change. When interacting with people in unfamiliar situations we need to begin somewhere and typically make use of our existing knowledge and experiences – what are often termed schemas (or schemata). Schemas are mental structures or patterns for interpreting the world and deciding how to behave (Holland & Quinn, 1987). Schemata shared by groups of people are referred to as 'cultural schemata' and it is these which enable people to behave in broadly similar ways and come to similar understandings of interactions. So, for example, we may have a schema for greeting work colleagues in the morning or for accepting a compliment from a friend. It is crucial, though, that when we use these schemata to make generalisations, they are adaptable and can change if our knowledge and experiences show them to be inadequate or mismatched (Sharifian, 2011; Baker, 2015). This is particularly important in unfamiliar interactions, such as intercultural communication, where our existing schema may not be relevant or appropriate. If we are not able to adapt and change our schemata when generalising, they can become stereotypes and hinder rather than help communication.

Understandings of cultures which are stereotyped and simplistic are often referred to as essentialist perspectives on culture. Holliday et al. define essentialism as "presuming that there is a universal essence, homogeneity and unity in a particular culture" (2017: 1). Essentialist perspectives on culture view it as a physical entity or thing, associate it with a particular place, typically a nation, see the world as divided into different and exclusive cultures with people belonging to only one culture, and believe that culture is the cause and explanation for people's behaviour (Holliday et al., 2017: 3–4). As with stereotypes, essentialist perspectives on culture are very common and are often found in advice on how to communicate or do business with people from particular cultures, as well as in many language-learning materials which present stereotyped images of 'other' cultures (Gray, 2010). A more sophisticated approach to culture, but still problematic, is what Holliday (2013) terms the neo-essentialist perspective. Neo-essentialism recognises the diversity of cultures and heterogeneity *within* cultures but still views the nation as the default culture that contains other aspects of culture. A distinction is still maintained between different national cultures, and deviations from 'national norms' are viewed as exceptions and sub-cultures. Again, this neo-essentialist perspective is frequently part of language-learning materials and approaches (Baker, 2015). Linked to essentialism is the notion of othering, in which people from cultures which are perceived as distinct from ours are viewed as always different and hence a cultural 'other' (Holliday, 2011). Othering will be discussed in more detail in relation to issues of **identity** later in this book. In contrast to essentialist views on culture is a non-essentialist approach in which any statements about culture are tentative and temporary (Holliday et al., 2017). As with the more critical approaches to culture outlined previously, cultures from a non-essentialist perspective are seen as complex, fluid, and multiple, with no clear boundaries. We will return to these themes of essentialism and othering, and how we might avoid the problems associated with them, in multilingual, intercultural, and transcultural communication throughout this book.

Activity 1.3 Cultural stereotypes

- List the stereotypes of your own culture and another culture you are familiar with. How many of these stereotypes do you think are true (if any)? How many of these stereotypes have you experienced personally?
- Has someone ever tried to explain your behaviour based on a cultural stereotype? How did it make you feel? Have you ever explained your own behaviour based on cultural stereotypes?

Feedback: *Your answers here will, of course, depend on your own experiences. You should have found that some of your stereotypes may be based on limited experiences, and others perhaps on nothing but media images and things other people have told you. We all make use of stereotypes and generalisations (the term we prefer to use)* *to help us make sense of the world and things that are new to us. However, it is important that these generalisations do not become fixed and applied to all people. If they are too static or we are not prepared to change our generalisation based on individual experiences, they quickly become unhelpful oversimplifications and stereotypes. These hinder rather than help intercultural communication.*

Chapter summary

In this chapter we considered a range of approaches to understanding culture. You should now be familiar with:

- a product approach to culture
- an interpretive semiotic approach to culture
- a discourse approach to culture
- a practice approach to culture
- a critical, ideological approach to culture

While we suggested that it is not possible to offer a single definition of culture that would be relevant in all settings and for all purposes, we identified a number of core themes in understanding culture. These were that, first, culture can be seen as a system of shared products, symbols, discourses, practices, and ideologies among groups of people. Second, these shared products, symbols, discourses, practices, and ideologies and the groupings of people themselves that make up culture are contestable and sites of struggle. Third, the people and shared products, symbols, discourses, practices, and ideologies that make up cultures are constantly in process and changing, and hence cannot be fixed and have no clear boundaries. In sum, culture is complex, multiple, fluid, and always in a process of change. However, we also saw that national conceptions of culture still form a powerful ideology in many people's understanding of culture. We examined the influence of globalisation on cultural practices and groupings and in particular focused on the notion of transcultural global flows of cultural practices and ideologies. Last, we considered the problems associated with simplistic, stereotyped views of culture – what is often termed essentialism – and contrasted this with more complex, non-essentialist perspectives on culture. The idea of transcultural flows and non-essentialist critical, complex perspectives on cultures will be themes returned to throughout this book.

Note

1 www.oxfordlearnersdictionaries.com/definition/american_english/culture_1 (accessed 30 September 2020).

Further reading

Baker, W. (2015). *Culture and identity through English as a lingua franca: Rethinking concepts and goals in intercultural communication.* Berlin: De Gruyter Mouton. Chapter three contains a detailed discussion of many of the theories of culture presented here, as well as an exploration of culture and complexity theory.

Geertz, C. (1973/2000). *The interpretation of cultures.* New York: Basic Books. A key text in understanding culture from a semiotic and ethnographic perspective. Written in a style accessible to a general audience.

Holliday, A. (2019). *Understanding intercultural communication: Negotiating a grammar of culture* (2nd edn). Abingdon: Routledge. A detailed discussion of critical perspectives on understanding culture, including Holliday's own 'grammar of culture' model.

2 Culture and language

Introduction

In the previous chapter, many of the theories of culture we looked at positioned language as a core part of an understanding of culture. But what is the relationship between language and culture? Is language a part of culture or vice-versa? Are they, as some have claimed, the same thing? What is the link between particular 'named' languages and cultures? So, for example, is the English language always linked to Anglophone (e.g., UK or US) cultures or can the two be separated? In this chapter, we provide an introduction to the complex relationships between language and culture. We underscore the close relationships between them but also emphasise that for us they are not synonymous. Indeed, we suggest that English can only function successfully as a **global lingua franca** if it can be adapted to a wide variety of cultural settings and practices.

We begin the chapter with an explanation of the influential Sapir-Whorf (1939) hypothesis and **linguistic relativity**, which proposes a strong connection between languages and our world view. We discuss both the strengths and weaknesses of the theory, including current versions of it such as that proposed by the anthropologist Daniel Everett (2012). We then present Risager's (2006; 2007) **language-culture nexus** approach to explain how language and culture can be linked but also separated. The idea of **cultural and linguistic flows,** which we introduced in the previous chapter, is considered in relation to the convergence of language and culture in communication. Next, the notion of language and culture as interacting **complex adaptive systems (CASs)** is explored. Finally, the notion of languages and cultures as resources and repertoires is briefly introduced as a topic to be expanded on later in the textbook. Examples from **Global Englishes** in different cultural settings will be given to illustrate these points and particularly the diverse range of links between languages and cultures. You will be asked to consider your own experiences of different languages and cultures and the possible links between them.

Activity 2.1 The links between language and culture

What do you think the links are between language and culture? Read the four scenarios below and decide which one matches most closely to your ideas. Think about the reasons for your choice.

1. A specific language is always linked to a specific culture and they are inseparable. For example, if you speak Japanese you will also be constructing or representing aspects of Japanese culture since it is embedded in the language.
2. Languages can be culturally neutral and do not have to be linked to any particular culture. For example, I can learn to speak French without learning anything about French culture or any other culture.
3. Language and culture are always linked in that language is a cultural practice. However, languages are not linked to any specific culture. For instance, I can use English to represent and construct any cultural practices or references that are relevant to the communication.
4. Languages are used to represent the culture you grew up in. So, for example, if you grow up speaking English in the United States (US), you will use English to represent US culture. Moreover, if you learn an additional language, you will still use it to represent the cultural practices of your original culture. So a US citizen learning and using French will be representing and constructing US culture through the French language.

Feedback: *Your answers will depend on your own experiences and opinions and all of these perspectives have been put forward by researchers of language and culture at some point. However, for transcultural communication through Global Englishes, scenario 3 is the most appropriate. We will discuss these different perspectives in more detail in the rest of this chapter.*

2.1 Linguistic relativity

One of the best known approaches to understanding the relationship between language and culture is linguistic relativity. This idea, formulated in the early twentieth century, is associated with the anthropologists and linguists Franz Boas (1911/1986), and Edward Sapir and Benjamin Whorf (1939). In its most basic terms it is the idea that through language we learn to categorise and make sense of the world and at the same time organise our thoughts. Hence, language and culture, as a world view, are seen as inexorably interlinked and a correlation is established between language, culture, and thought. This is most famously expressed through what is known as the Sapir-Whorf

(1939) hypothesis, which states: "the 'real world' is to a large extent unconsciously built up on the language habits of the group. No two languages are ever sufficiently similar to be considered as representing the same social reality" (Sapir, cited in Whorf, 1939). Following this hypothesis speakers of different languages will have different ways of interpreting and understanding the world; in other words, different languages mean different cultures. Perhaps the most well-known example of linguistic relativity is the claim that Eskimo languages have a large number of words for snow since it is an important part of their world and culture, whereas English has much fewer words as snow is less important in English-speaking people's cultures. However, as pointed out by Zhu (2014; 2019), research has cast doubt on the accuracy of this claim (English and Central Alaskan Yupik Eskimo in fact have a similar number of terms for snow) and, as we will see below, it is not clear that Boas or Sapir and Whorf ever seriously made this claim.

There are typically two interpretations of this hypothesis: the strong form of linguistic relativity and the weak form of linguistic relativity. The strong form, also known as linguistic determinism, is the idea that our language constrains and puts limits on how we understand the world and think. Thus, we are fixed into the world view and culture that we learn through our **first language** (L1). However, many scholars (e.g., Leavitt, 2015) argue that this is a misinterpretation of linguistic relativity and is not what Boas or Sapir and Whorf proposed. Indeed, both empirical evidence and theoretical developments have shown that such a deterministic correlation between language, culture, and thought cannot be true. If it were, it would be impossible to ever understand someone from another language and culture or to learn **additional languages**. Intercultural communication, translation, and interpreting would all be impossible. Research over many decades has clearly shown that all of these things are possible and successfully carried out by millions of people around the world on a daily basis. Furthermore, linguistic determinism is unable to account for people who grow up in or live in multilingual and multicultural environments, where communicating in multiple languages is the norm. Significantly, from the perspective of this book, linguistic determinism is also not able to explain how a global language such as English can function across so many different cultural settings.

The weak form of linguistic relativity proposes that the language we speak influences our thoughts and our understanding of the world but does not control or limit them. This interpretation has been much more influential in linguistics and has received extensive support from empirical evidence (for example, Deutscher, 2010). One of the main contributions of this understanding of linguistic relativity is the insight that there are particular things that a language *must* convey, while also recognising that this does not put a limit on what a language *can* convey (Leavitt, 2015). These take the form of grammatical categories such as tense and number in many Western languages (e.g., English), or marking of physical shape (e.g., Thai) or source of knowledge (e.g., Aymara) in others. Slobin (2003: 179) terms this the "anticipatory effects of language" (see also Slobin, 1996), whereby speakers need to pay attention to particular aspects of the physical world and organise their thoughts in certain ways in order to be able to express them through language. However, this is not seen as a fixed constraint and there is no suggestion that people cannot learn new ways of interpreting the world, organising their thoughts, or expressing them through their first or additional languages. Thus, while Thai may have two words for the colour blue, สีฟ้า ('see fah') and สีน้ำเงิน ('see nam nurghn') (roughly light and dark blue in English), and English only one, there is nothing to prevent English speakers learning to distinguish and use the two terms in Thai or for Thai speakers to learn to use the one word in English. Furthermore, as we will see when discussing Global Englishes, the extent to which any language *must* contain particular structures is debatable given the amount of adaptation and variety found in the use of global languages.

More recent support for the weak form of linguistic relativity has come from anthropology and especially the research of Michael Tomasello and Daniel Everett. Tomasello argues that language is a cultural practice that is learned, in the same way as any other cultural practice, through repetition of habitual group behaviour. He writes that:

> [l]anguage, or better linguistic communication, is thus not any kind of object, formal or otherwise; rather it is a form of social action constituted by social conventions for achieving social ends, premised on at least some shared understandings and shared purposes among users.
>
> (Tomasello, 2008: 343)

A similar argument is made by Everett, who claims that "language is in the first instance a tool for thinking and communicating and, though it is based in human psychology, it is crucially shaped from human cultures. It is a cultural tool as well as a cognitive tool" (2012: 19–20). Everett goes on to write that "Cognition + Culture + Communication = Language. This means that each normal human being has a brain, belongs to a community with values, and needs to communicate, and the confluence of these states results in language" (2012: 35). Thus, for both of these researchers the link between language and culture is strong. While they recognise the cognitive, internal dimension to language, language is primarily viewed as a cultural practice that emerges in response to the needs of the social group.

However, we need to be careful that we do not overgeneralise this link between language and culture to assume that particular cultures are embedded or fixed into particular languages. For example, it has been claimed that "the English language … carries with it values and beliefs which are hidden in linguistic codes but control from the depths the process of meaning making during human interactions" (Gu, 2009: 140); in other words, 'English' culture, under this view, is inseparable from the English language. This position has been most strongly argued by the linguist Anna Wierzbicka (1997; 2006), who proposes that different languages contain 'cultural scripts' (similar to the cultural schemata discussed in the previous chapter) which are inherent to those languages. In relation to English, Wierzbicka claims that even when it is used as a global language, for example, in the Association of Southeast Asian Nations (ASEAN), there is still "an internal cultural baggage" (2006: 312) to language so that "[t]he English that ASEAN has used from the outset as its only language … is, essentially, Anglo English, and it bears the imprint of the cultural history of the English language" (2006: 312). There are a number of problems with proposing such a strong link between a particular language and culture. First, from a theoretical perspective, as outlined in the previous chapter, this assumes an essentialist link between a national language and a national culture. Yet, as we have seen, culture exists at many scales or levels, with the nation being just one. Second, from an empirical perspective, evidence in Global Englishes research illustrates that although there may be aspects of the world that are normally conveyed in particular varieties of languages (e.g., British English), there is little that the language *must* convey. Most significantly, languages are also adaptable and changeable depending on the setting. In contrast to Weirzbicka's claim about ASEAN, the extensive research on ASEAN uses of English shows a great deal of variety with adaptation at all levels, including grammar, vocabulary, pronunciation, and pragmatics, often for the purpose of better representing local cultural practices and groupings. This may include non-marking of tense (e.g., yesterday I go to university), dropping of final consonant sounds (e.g., first – fir), locally relevant vocabulary and phrases (e.g., have you eaten yet? = how are you? (British English)), as well as extensive use of **accommodation, pragmatic**, and other communicative strategies (see Kirkpatrick, 2010a; Asian Corpus of English or ACE[1]).

2.2 The language-culture nexus

The previous discussion of linguistic relativity has brought up a number of difficulties in understanding the relationship between language and culture. On the one hand, we see that language and culture are closely linked. Indeed, many of theories presented so far view language as primarily a cultural practice. On the other hand, particular languages are not necessarily linked to particular cultures, i.e., the English language is not fixed in its connections to British or US culture. How can we explain this apparent dilemma? There are two ideas that prove helpful here. First, we can distinguish between different perspectives and locations of language. Second, we can closely examine how languages and cultures connect through the notion of the language-culture nexus (Risager, 2006; 2007) or more recently the language-culture interface (Risager, 2012; 2020). By distinguishing between different dimensions of language and communication, as a number of researchers do (e.g., Harris, 1998; Risager, 2006; Mauranen, 2012), it is possible to see how languages and cultures can be both connected and separated. The argument and theory around different levels of language, signs, and communication is a complex one that cannot be presented in full here, but a rough outline of the key ideas will help to illustrate the main points in relation to language and culture.

The first dimension to language is the psychological or cognitive perspective, which focuses on an individual's **linguistic resources**, that is, their mental or cognitive representation and processing of language and communication. The second dimension is the sociological (Risager, 2006) or microsocial (Mauranen, 2012) perspective, which focuses on linguistic practices: how individuals use linguistic resources in communication. These first two perspectives are what Risager (2006) calls the natural loci of language; in other words, these dimensions describe how linguistic resources are used in actual communication. In contrast, the third dimension to language is an artificial and ideological construct, which Risager (2006; 2007) terms the "system-oriented" point of view. This is the idea of language as a delineated and describable entity or 'system' and includes named national languages such as 'English', 'French', or 'Japanese'. Just as a national culture was seen as an ideological construct that could never be fully characterised, so too is the idea of a national language that can be described in its totality. However, again similar to national cultures, the constructed ideology of national languages is a powerful one that influences the natural cognitive and sociological dimensions to language.

By making use of these three dimensions of language we can now see how languages and cultures can be both linked and separated. At the psychological or cognitive dimension language and culture are always connected since linguistic resources are learned as part of sociocultural experiences and have an associated meaning for the individual. In other words, when we learn a word, phrase, or structure of language it always has a meaning or purpose for us related to the cultural setting in which it was learned. This type of connection between language and culture for individuals is often referred to as languaculture (Agar, 1994; Risager, 2006) or linguaculture (Risager,

2012; 2020). This means that there can be no such thing as a culturally 'neutral' language. All communication involves participants, contexts, and purposes, none of which are culturally neutral. However, in linguistic practices, the second sociological dimension to language, the link between languages and cultures is an open question and particular languages and cultures can be separated. This is because the meanings and purposes of linguistic resources will be based on every individual's life history and so meanings will be more or less similar depending on how much of a shared sociocultural history interactants in communication have. Thus, people who grow up in the same community and learn the same L1 will most likely share many similar interpretations of the language. So, for example, people who learn British English as their L1 and grow up in the UK may share many similar cultural experiences and references and so the links between the English language and 'British' culture will be close. In contrast, people using the same language, for example, English as a **lingua franca**, but with very different life histories and cultural experiences may have quite different interpretations of the language which are related to their own cultural contexts and, hence, are far removed for 'British' culture. So in this sense language and culture can be separated. At the ideological or system-orientated perspective national cultures and languages are again connected though powerful ideological links and are an important aspect of the banal nationalism that is a part of our everyday experiences of the nation state (see Chapter 1.3).

Risager (2006; 2007) makes another distinction, which further helps to explain how language and culture can be both linked and separable. This distinction is between the generic sense of language and culture, referring to the general phenomena of language and culture, and the differential sense of language and culture, referring to specific named languages (e.g., Japanese) and cultures (e.g., British). In the generic sense language and culture are always linked since, as Risager writes, "human language is always embedded in culture" (2007: 12). However, in the differential sense there is nothing inherent in a particular language (e.g., English) that links it to a particular national culture (e.g., Britain), as proposed in the strongest version of linguistic relativity presented earlier. Therefore, how particular languages and cultural practices come together is always an empirical question that must be investigated in each instance of communication and cannot be taken for granted. The coming together of language and culture is what Risager calls the language-culture nexus and involves the confluence of linguistic and cultural resources in a particular communicative event (2006; 2007). This confluence is highly variable, with languages being used to represent and create cultural practices in a myriad of different ways.

The example below illustrates how language and culture come together in complex and variable ways. This conversation is predominantly in English, but it is **English as a lingua franca** (ELF) since the participants are a Thai L1 speaker (Nami) and an L1 Belgian French speaker (Philippe). The conversation takes place in a café in a shopping mall in Bangkok (named MBK) and the subject is a cosplay (costume play, in which fans of Japanese manga, anime, and pop music dress up and role-play their favourite characters[2]).

Extract 2.1 Cosplay

01 Philippe:	oh ah just when I was waiting for you right there are like outside there is like this podium and girls dancing singing
02 Nami:	where outside of MBK it's a cos play right
03 Philippe:	I don't think so
04 Nami:	Japanese cos play
05 Philippe:	I don't think so
06 Nami:	oh it's not (cos play)
07 Philippe:	no it isn't cause my friend my student would be there they're are crazy about cos play
08 Nami:	yes, yeah my roommate too

(Baker, 2011: 40)

Note
(xxx) uncertain that word is correctly transcribed

In this example we see English used to refer to the Japanese, or in this case pan-Asian, cultural practice of cosplay (lines 02, 04, 06), with the conversation taking place in Thailand, with reference to a local setting (MBK; lines 01–02), and between speakers for whom English is a lingua franca. It is important to note that in this example English is not used at any point to refer to 'English' or Anglophone cultural practices or settings, or by speakers who would identify as part of an Anglophone culture. Rather, English is used to represent and construct a range of cultural practices that move across local, national, and global scales.

Activity 2.2 Reflecting on your own language learning and use and the links with different cultural contexts

Make a list of all the different languages and dialects you can speak. These do not have to be languages or dialects you can speak fluently; even if you can just use one or two words, add them to your list.

Questions

Q1 In what settings did you learn these languages (formal education, family, socially)?
Q2 Do you associate each language with any particular cultures or groups? How do you use each language and who do you use it with?

Compare your answers with others in small groups if possible.

Feedback: *There are clearly no right or wrong answers to this task. However, you should find that you speak a variety of languages to different degrees of proficiency, for different purposes, and with different groups of people, making the links between languages and cultural settings complex. You will probably also find that there is quite a lot of variety in the answers of your group.*

2.3 Language and culture flows

One way to think about how languages and cultures come together in the variable and complex ways described above is through the notion of linguistic and cultural flows. We have already introduced the concept of transcultural and transnational flows in relation to culture in Chapter 1 to describe the manner in which languages and cultures spread across each other in networks of linguistic and cultural flows (Risager, 2006; Pennycook, 2007). As Pennycook writes:

> English is a translocal language, a language of fluidity and fixity that moves across, while becoming embedded in, the materiality of localities and social relations. English is bound up with transcultural flows, a language of imagined communities and refashioning identities.
>
> (2007: 4–5)

Under this conception global languages, such as English, can be seen as moving through globally connected networks but being adapted and changed to local sociocultural settings and then passing on again in a constant 'flow' to new settings where the processes of change continue. Pennycook (2007) uses the example of hip-hop to show how hip-hop as a globally connected cultural practice is adapted and changed in each of the local settings in which it occurs and how the language used in hip-hop, English, is also adapted to local sociocultural contexts and linguistic practices (including the use of other languages). Thus, while hip-hop songs in New York or Tokyo are both recognisable as part of the genre, or cultural practice, of hip-hop music, they are not the same. One of the examples Pennycook presents comes from the Malaysian rappers Too Phat, whose lyrics are predominantly in English in this example but refer to a local setting, Ruja's, and local cultural practices, eating kuey teow (noodles) and roti canai (bread and curried chickpeas), as well as referencing their Muslim faith (dawn's last pray).

> If I die tonight, what would I do on my last day
> I know I'd wake early in the morn' for crack of dawn's last pray
> Then probably go for breakfast like I used to do
> Fried kuey teow FAM and roti canai at Ruja's with my boo
>
> (Pennycook, 2007: 3)

From the perspective of transcultural flows, then, the use of English across the globe does not lead to increasing similarity and homogenisation of cultures but rather is part of the process of change and complexification of cultures where, as Pennycook (2007) notes and shows in the hip-hop examples, new communities and identities are opened up connecting the local and the global. Blommaert sums up the position succinctly in arguing that "[s]ociolinguistically, the world has not become a village ... but rather a tremendously complex web of villages, towns, neighbourhoods, settlements connected by material and symbolic ties in often unpredictable ways" (2010: 1). However, we need to be careful not to over-emphasise the fluidity of language and culture and their links in transcultural flows. There are also influences which restrict the diversity of language. For a language to be understood by all participants there must be a degree of similarity or shared understanding of the language, and people are also not free to identify with any cultural group they wish, as will be discussed when we look at identity in Chapter 6. Therefore, there is a tension between the fluidity/adaptability and the fixity/sameness of language and culture and their connections. Pennycook goes on to propose that "[c]aught between fluidity and fixity, then, cultural and linguistic forms are always in a state of flux, always changing" (2007: 8).

2.4 Language, culture, and complexity theory

Complexity theory provides another view of the connections between language and culture which fits well with the idea of the language-culture nexus and cultural and linguistic flows. Complexity was briefly introduced in Chapter 1 in the summary of characterisations of culture. Complex systems, or complex adaptive systems (CASs), are systems in which the interaction of individual components or features gives rise to the emergence of more complex aggregate patterns which cannot be reduced or explained according to the individual features. As the complexity theorists John Miller and Scott Page explain it:

> [a]t the most basic level, the field of complex systems challenges the notion that by perfectly understanding the behavior of each component part of a system we will then understand the system as a whole. One *and* one may well make two, but to really understand two we must know both about the nature of 'one' and the meaning of 'and'.
>
> (2007: 3)

This means that in complex systems the relationships between parts of the system are crucial; we need to understand both 'one' as well as 'and'. It also means that you cannot understand the whole system by examining just one part of it. As already suggested in Chapter 1, this means that culture arises from the beliefs, behaviours, and interactions of individuals but is not reducible to any one individual, and also that no individual can be said to 'represent' all of a cultural system. The same points can be made in relation to language (e.g., Larsen-Freeman & Cameron, 2008). Language systems, such as 'English', arise out of the interaction of individuals who make use of the language in their communicative interactions. However, an individual's language use will not be the same as the description of the system since individuals vary in their language use and each person makes use of the linguistic resources associated with a language system in different ways.

By taking a complexity theory perspective on culture and language we can see culture and language as two interacting CASs which are influenced by and influence each other but are not synonymous. As the first author of this book has written:

> [t]hey [culture and language] can be seen as nested systems, systems within systems, which mutually co-evolve with each influencing and adapting to the other and with the boundaries between them fuzzy and blurred. Crucially, as with all complex systems, they are dynamic systems which are constantly in change and hence no fixed description is ever possible of them or the relationship between them.
>
> (Baker, 2015: 88)

However, it should be stressed that, as already noted in our discussion of the language-culture nexus, a view of language or culture as a system is an artificial view, which in this case is useful for researchers studying language and culture. This is not how language and culture are perceived in naturally occurring communication, where they will be used by participants in an integrated manner. The links between language and culture and how these come together in communicative practices can be represented in the figure below. In Figure 2.1 we see

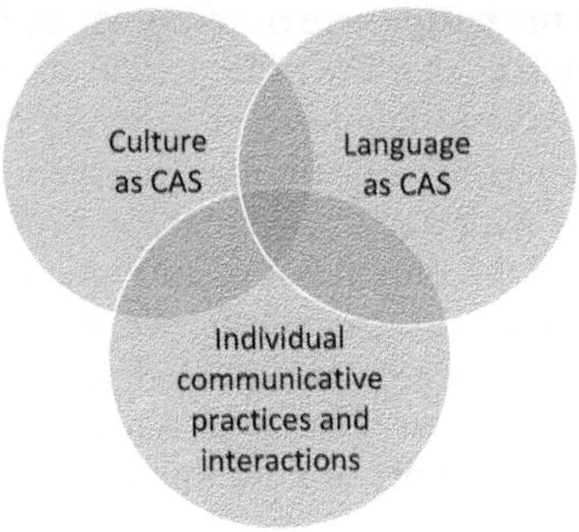

Figure 2.1 Culture and language as interacting complex adaptive systems

the links between language and culture as interacting CASs and how the two systems come together in individual communicative practices and interactions. We will return to complexity theory in understanding communication, language, and culture in Chapter 12.

2.5 Language and culture repertoires and resources

The fluidity and 'super-diversity' of intercultural and transcultural communication has led to the suggestion that the notion of 'a language' or 'the language' is no longer helpful. Likewise, neither is the notion of 'a culture' or 'the culture'. Instead, we would do better to consider participants in intercultural communication as making use of linguistic and cultural repertoires and resources that come together in the dynamic manner described under the language-culture nexus, global flows, and complexity theory (Canagarajah, 2013; Pennycook, 2007; 2010a; Blommaert, 2010; Baker, 2015). From this perspective, individuals are seen as having a range of linguistic (and other) resources for communication rather than possessing particular languages. The combination of all of an individual's linguistic resources is their **linguistic repertoire**. Therefore, if someone's linguistic resources are only those associated with one named language (e.g., English), then they would be viewed as having a monolingual repertoire. If someone has linguistic resources from various named languages (e.g., English, French, and Japanese), then they would be viewed as having a **multilingual repertoire**. It is also important to stress that individuals do not have to be 'proficient' in all areas of a named language for it to be part of their repertoires. For example, the first author of this book may be able to interact in a range of formal and informal **domains** in English (see Chapter 3.4) and have a high level of literacy but only be able to interact in social situations in Japanese and have no literacy (i.e., he cannot read or write in Japanese). From the perspective of resources and repertoires, people have linguistic resources that are often linked to the particular sociocultural settings in which they learned them, so the first author may have learned English as his L1 at home and then in education and in work and so have a wide range of resources as part of his repertoire. In contrast, he may have only learned Japanese as a **second language (L2)** in social situations with friends and work colleagues and so have a much more limited range of resources. This more limited range of resources is what Blommaert refers to as a truncated repertoire, which he argues is a common feature of multilingual repertoires.

> We never know 'all' of a language, we always know specific bits and pieces of it. This counts for our 'mother tongue' as well as for the languages we pick up in the course of a lifetime, and this is perfectly normal. I contend that such 'truncated' repertoires are a better diagnostic of what real multilingual competence means in an age of globalization[.]
>
> (2010: 23)

Furthermore, linguistic resources are viewed as just one set of resources alongside other semiotic and multimodal resources (e.g., images, gestures, tools and other external objects, place and positioning) which form part of people's communicative repertoires. These ideas are illustrated in the example below, from Pennycook and Otsuji (2015), which occurs in a French restaurant in Tokyo involving the restaurant manager, Nabil (L1 Arabic), as he squeezes past table A to serve the customers on table B. We see different linguistic resources employed as relevant to the context and activity, with French in relation to the restaurant and food, Japanese in relation to the location and customers, and English as a shared lingua franca.

Extract 2.2 A French restaurant in Tokyo

(With customer table A)

01 Nabil:	Sorry *Sumimasen, Gomennasai.* **hein**? *Chotto:: Chotto* Small place *dakara, kokowa na.* [Sorry, excuse me, sorry. It's a bi::t bit small space so, this place is.]
02 Customer:	*Daijōbu de::su.* [That's O::K.]

(With customer table B)

03 Nabil:	**Voilà.** *Yasai to* anchovy *kuro* olive sauce. [Here it is. Vegetable and anchovy black olive sauce.]
04 Customer:	*Ha::i.* [Ye::s.]
05 Nabil:	**Bon appétit!** [Bon appetit/Enjoy your meal!]

(Adapted from Pennycook & Otsuji, 2015: 78–79)

Notes

bold	French
italics	Japanese
plain	English [translation in brackets]
::	prolongation of the immediately prior sound

From this perspective, then, as with other approaches discussed in this chapter, the sociocultural settings of a particular interaction as well as the sociocultural history of the individuals involved are central in understanding communication. We will return to these ideas again in more detail throughout this book when we discuss **multilingualism**, **translanguaging**, and **multimodality**.

Activity 2.3 Petanque: Cultural and linguistic flows and convergence

The following example from Baker (2009a) is another extract from the conversation we looked at earlier in this chapter between Nami (L1 Thai) and Philippe (L1 Belgian French) in a café in a shopping mall in Bangkok. Here Nami and Philippe are discussing Nami's plans for her summer holiday in the south of France.

45 Philippe:	no Marseilles is really nice really nice city south of France close you have Nice Cannes it's really cool the food is amazing and they drink err Ricard
46 Nami:	Ricard
47 Philippe:	they play err petanque
48 Nami:	err
49 Philippe:	petanque
50 Nami:	petanque ahh petanque
51 Philippe:	yeah (?)
52 Nami:	there's some there's some people from my school that
53 Philippe:	you know that the French embassy they organise err a championship every year in Thailand
54 Nami:	yeah
55 Philippe:	I've been there a few times
56 Nami:	do you play
57 Philippe:	ah
58 Nami:	do you play
59 Philippe:	no. I'm shit
60 Nami:	((laughs)) you're really young ((laughs))
61 Philippe:	I know you have to be really old to play that game
62 Nami:	NO ((laughs))
63 Philippe:	maybe I'm not old enough
64 Nami:	no at school a lot of young students play petanque
65 Philippe:	maybe they think it's cool

(Baker, 2009a: 581–582)

Notes

(?)	inaudible
((laughs))	nonlinguistic features of the transcription
CAPS	strong emphasis

Questions

Q1 In what ways do the different languages and cultures come together here? You may want to think about who the speakers are, what languages are used, where they are during the conversation, the different places they refer to in the conversation and particularly the different interpretations and locations of the game petanque.

Q2 Can you think of any examples where you have used different languages to discuss diverse cultural practices and references?

Q3 When you have learned any additional languages, which cultures were the languages associated with, if any? Why do you think this was? Did it reflect your experience of using the language?

Feedback: *First, in terms of language use, this is a prototypical ELF interaction with English used as a contact language between two people who do not share an L1 in a non-Anglophone setting (Thailand). In relation to content and culture, the conversation begins with Phillippe providing information about the south of France for Nami. He offers a rather stereotyped, tourist brochure-type cultural image of interesting local places, food, drink, and a local custom – playing petanque. Nami also provides some information about petanque, saying that people at her school (university) also play this game, thereby suggesting an alternative to the solely French associations given by Philippe and an alternative localised association. Phillippe then goes on to discuss petanque played at the French embassy in Bangkok, introducing a global dimension or scale to the game, as part of the global flow of French cultural practices. The different interpretations appear to result in a misunderstanding, shown in lines 58 to 64. Nami says "you're really young" in what appears to be an exclamation of surprise that a young person should be bad at this game, as petanque is played by young students at her university. In contrast, Philippe interprets this as an excuse, saying that it is a game played by the old, following his earlier description of petanque in France. Nami rejects this interpretation twice, in lines 62 and 64, and suggests an alternative, saying "at school a lot of young students play petanque".*

As the first author of this book explains when originally presenting the example, "[This] shows two very different culturally based interpretations of a phenomenon expressed through English and the degree of interpretation and negotiation needed for successful communication. In this case, we have a French image of petanque as a game played by the old in the south of France and the alternative interpretation of petanque as a game played by young students in Thailand. It is significant that, although the language through which this is expressed is English, the cultural references are to France and Thailand rather than to English-speaking cultures. Moreover, petanque in this exchange ceases to belong to either one of these cultures but is rather in a third place between the two, where alternative cultural associations are competing and also perhaps creating new associations. Philippe now has the alternative image of petanque given by Nami, and Nami has also perhaps encountered for the first time the type of associations described by Philippe. However, neither of the participants seems to have produced a dominant characterisation. Although Nami does not reject Philippe's interpretation of petanque, she does refute it as the only interpretation, twice repeating that it is not a game played by the old. Similarly Philippe in the final line seems to be conceding that there may be alternative perspectives on the game when he says 'maybe they think it's cool'" (Baker, 2009a: 582–583).

In sum, in this example we can see how a cultural practice, petanque, is associated with multiple scales simultaneously in one interaction. We have the national scale with France, the global scale with the French embassy in Bangkok, and also two different local scales, the south of France and a university in Thailand. We also have Nami's and Phillippe's different interpretations of petanque, which coexist with neither appearing to be the dominant or 'correct' interpretation in this example. Crucially, all of this interaction takes place through English, or rather ELF, with varied and multiple cultural connections but none of them in any way associated with Anglophone cultures.

Chapter summary

This chapter explored the links between languages and cultures and emphasised that they are closely related but not synonymous or the same thing. We examined a number of approaches to conceptualising the connections between language and culture, which you should check you are familiar with. These were:

- linguistic relativity
- the language-culture nexus
- language and culture flows
- language, culture, and complexity theory
- language and culture as repertoires and resources

In particular, we considered the way in which languages can be used to both represent and construct different cultural practices and references depending on the participants, settings, and purposes of the interaction. We looked at examples from Global Englishes that illustrated how English can be used in highly diverse ways in a wide range of cultural settings and to refer to a multitude of cultural practices. This provided a counter-argument to the strong claims of linguistic relativity or linguistic determinism that propose that a language is 'inexorably' linked to a particular culture (e.g., English and Anglophone cultures). We also began to think about the way that English might act alongside other resources, both linguistic and non-linguistic, in the processes of communication.

Notes

1 http://corpus.eduhk.hk/ace/ (accessed 30 September 2020).
2 See, for example, https://cosplay.com/ (accessed 30 September 2020).

Further reading

Kramsch, C. (1998a). *Language and culture.* Oxford: Oxford University Press. An introduction to core approaches to understanding the relationship between language and culture with a more detailed explanation of Kramsch's own discourse perspective.

Pennycook, A. (2007). *Global Englishes and transcultural flows.* Abingdon: Routledge. An exploration of the fluid links between language and culture from a global perspective. The arguments are supported by examples of hip-hop from around the world.

Risager, K. (2006). *Language and culture: Global flows and local complexity.* Clevedon: Multilingual Matters. An in-depth exploration of the links between language and culture, including Risager's language-culture nexus and the languaculture approach.

3 Global languages in a multilingual world

Introduction

The book authors' first languages (L1) are English and Japanese, respectively. We are originally from the south of England and the northern part of Japan. You would say that English is a global language, but that Japanese is not. Then how would you describe Japanese instead? Japanese is the language used inside Japan, but rarely used outside by non-Japanese people. In this regard, it may be called a local language and you may think that *local* is antonymous with *global*. As you will see in Chapters 3 and 4, however, a global language can in fact be both local and global.

One certain aspect of global languages is that they have a large number of speakers. In this chapter we first examine global languages in terms of numbers of L1 speakers (see Chapter 2.2). By the term L1 we refer to people's strongest languages that they learn to speak as children. With more L1 speakers, languages are not just likely to survive in the future, but also likely to have an influence on global communication. We also explore the links between global languages and geography – in other words, the connections between languages and places. The chapter then considers global languages in terms of total numbers of speakers. In this multilingual world of mobility, many people function in their additional languages as well as L1. Therefore, total numbers of speakers do matter. Finally, we link this to English as a global language, or Global Englishes (Chapter 4), through a discussion of the possible future for English alongside other global languages. You will be given the opportunity to explore examples of global language use and reflect on your own experiences of global languages.

Activity 3.1 Global languages

Think about the questions below. Discuss your answers with others in small groups if possible.

Questions

Q1 What do you think are current global languages, or 'big beasts' (Ostler, 2010)?

Q2 What do you think about the 'big beast' metaphor for global languages?
Q3 Do you speak any of the following languages: Arabic, Chinese, English, French, Russian, or Spanish?
Q4 Do you think the above six languages as global? If so, in what way?
Q5 Who can claim "[t]he ownership of English" (Widdowson, 1994: 377) or other global languages?

Feedback: *Answers will vary, and some of your answers may change during the course of the study with this textbook. Just for your information, the six 'big beasts' cited in the third question are the official languages in the United Nations (United Nations, 2020).*

3.1 Global languages and L1 speakers

"We talk, therefore, we are" (Jensen, 1993: 33). This quotation is obviously likened to the seventeenth-century French philosopher René Descartes' dictum: "Cogito, ergo sum" or "I think, therefore I am". We not only think but also create and manipulate human communities through languages, which could serve as stronger proof of the existence of ourselves. Languages are of paramount importance for human lives, and virtually everyone across the globe has one or more L1.

It may be obvious to you what language has the most L1 speakers. According to the data provided by *Ethnologue*'s 22nd edition (Eberhard et al., 2019), Table 3.1 lists the five most spoken L1.

It is notable that Chinese has over three times more L1 speakers than English.

Table 3.1 Top five languages by numbers of L1 speakers

		Languages	*Speakers (millions)*
1		**Chinese**	**1,311**
2	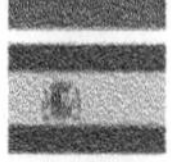	**Spanish**	**460**
3		**English**	**379**
4		**Hindi**	**341**
5		**Arabic**	**319**

Languages and nations

You may have thought of Table 3.1 as highly problematic. In this table, national flags are added to Eberhard et al.'s (2019) data. One day, while exploring Tokyo, Japan in 2019, we saw languages represented with national flags in advertisements for language schools, and we wonder whether you find such representations around you. On the very same day in Tokyo, we had a similar experience at a nationwide chain store selling electrical appliances. We talked to a staff lady with the Union Jack, the national flag of the United Kingdom (UK), printed on her name tag, but found that she was actually from Hong Kong. Like Table 3.1, the Union Jack was intended to show that she was able to communicate in English. Such being the case, several other staff members seemed to speak both Japanese and Chinese, given that the flags of Japan and the People's Republic of China were printed side-by-side on their name tags. These dual flags had nothing to do with their nationalities. More to the point, nations are one thing, and languages are another. What if another lady originally from the Canadian province of Québec, a Francophone region with many English speakers, were to work for the same store? She would perhaps have the flags of the UK, France, and Japan on her name tag so long as she speaks English, French, and Japanese, instead of the maple-leaf Canadian flag, also known as l'Unifolié.

Like most languages, the five languages in Table 3.1 are spoken in multiple countries. Even if we admit that the majorities of Chinese and Hindi speakers are from mainland China and India, respectively, these countries are not monolingual. Again, we cannot see a one-to-one correspondence between nations and languages. It is estimated that there are 305 languages in Greater China and 453 languages in India (Eberhard et al., 2019). While Mandarin Chinese is a **de facto** or virtually **official language** in the former, the Indian Constitution recognises 22 different languages, including the **de jure** or legally official language of Hindi (National Portal of India, 2020). English is not included in these 22 languages but is used for administrative purposes as a de facto official language. To give an example, the Lok Sabha or the House of the People in India has a bilingual English and Hindi website (Parliament of India, 2020). It should be added that English in India has a longer history than English in Australia, which you might think of as a traditional Anglophone country (Jenkins, 2015a).[1] For your reference, while official languages in the other flagged nations in Table 3.1 are Spanish in Spain (de jure), English in the UK (de facto), and Arabic in Saudi Arabia (de jure), the numbers of existing languages in the three respective countries are 34, 85, and 25 (Eberhard et al., 2019). You may find these numbers rather large. Now with the rising tide of immigration, multilingualism becomes even more salient in numerous nations. Put differently, multilingualism is largely the norm both domestically and globally.

Languages and language varieties

Table 3.2 is a reproduction of Table 3.1 without national flags and with major dialects as well as numbers of countries in which each language or dialect is spoken.

As seen in Table 3.2, both Chinese and Arabic have dialects or **language varieties**, documented in Eberhard et al. (2019). We will use the term language variety since some people might associate the word *dialect* with 'provincial' and 'vulgar' speech. Language changes over time, and develops into various local types (i.e., language varieties). Each variety has its primary geographical place to be used among the population, which is called a **speech community**. More precisely, each speech community develops its own conventions of language use through mutual interaction from generation to generation (Gumperz, 2009; Mauranen, 2018a). Generally speaking, it takes three or more

Table 3.2 Top five languages by numbers of L1 speakers

	Languages	*Speakers (millions)*	*Countries*
1	**Chinese**	**1,311**	**39**
	Mandarin	*918*	*13*
	Wu	*81.4*	*1*
	Yue	*73.1*	*13*
	Min Nan	*50.1*	*10*
	Hakka	*48.2*	*13*
	Jinyu	*46.9*	*1*
	Xiang	*37.3*	*1*
	Gan	*22.1*	*1*
	Others		
2	**Spanish**	**460**	**31**
3	**English**	**379**	**137**
4	**Hindi**	**341**	**4**
5	**Arabic**	**319**	**59**
	Egyptian Spoken	*64.6*	*1*
	Sudanese Spoken	*31.9*	*4*
	Algerian Spoken	*29.4*	*2*
	Moroccan Spoken	*27.5*	*3*
	North Levantine Spoken	*24.6*	*5*
	Sa'idi Spoken	*22.4*	*1*
	Mesopotamian Spoken	*15.7*	*4*
	Others		

(Adapted from Eberhard et al., 2019: 37)

generations for established language varieties to emerge (Mauranen, 2012). This is not the end of the story. People move from their original speech communities across their countries and beyond, and Chinese people are no exception. In Yokohama Chinatown, Japan, for example, it is not rare to hear different types of Chinese spoken in the same shop or restaurant, potentially influencing one another. In addition, given its de facto official status in Greater China, Mandarin Chinese is familiar to a vast number of Chinese speakers, thereby gradually influencing their local varieties and vice-versa. It seems almost impossible to keep each Chinese variety intact. In the first place, while there certainly exist distinct types of Chinese, it seems hard to tell exactly what features differentiate Chinese varieties. In other words, specifically what set of features cause people's use of Chinese to be Mandarin or non-Mandarin, for instance, and do Chinese speakers always agree on them?

Chinese is often said to be most difficult to learn, and so is Arabic. We both completed a PhD in Applied Linguistics at the University of Southampton (Baker, 2009b; Ishikawa, 2016a), where we met a growing number of Arabic-speaking students. Spoken Arabic appears to have ample variations. For instance, the second author of this book first wondered what language Egyptian students were speaking among each other. More accustomed to hearing the Arabic language spoken by his colleagues from Aleppo, Syria, he was a little surprised to know that they were speaking the 'same' Arabic. In their perception, they spoke 'standard' Arabic, unlike many of those in Upper Egypt. Meanwhile, he met a Maltese couple at the university, and to his ears their mother tongue was Arabic-like. It was called Malti or Maltese. He also remembers one Saudi Arabian student uttering that Hebrew was essentially the same language as Arabic, which is obviously arguable. While the same language has different varieties, some languages are similar to each other. Incidentally, during an international conference in Rome, Italy in 2013, he witnessed Spanish-speaking Chilean and Mexican colleagues managing to communicate with Italian-speaking waiters at a local hotel. Neither languages nor language varieties seem to be bounded – or, as it were, encapsulated – entities. You may wonder what **linguistic boundaries** or boundaries between languages or language varieties are like, if any. You may also wonder who has the authority to draw the boundaries, if ever, and in what way. We will explore these issues later in this book, especially in relation to **language ideologies** and English within multilingualism. Just for your curiosity, the next 15 most spoken L1 are shown in Table 3.3.

As seen in Table 3.3, and among an estimated 7,111 languages in the world (Eberhard et al., 2019), only 10 languages have more than 100 million L1 speakers.

Table 3.3 Top 6–20 languages by numbers of L1 speakers

	Languages	*Speakers (millions)*	*Countries*
6	**Bengali**	**228**	**4**
7	**Portuguese**	**221**	**15**
8	**Russian**	**154**	**19**
9	**Japanese**	**128**	**2**
10	**Lahnda**	**119**	**6**
	Western Punjabi	*92.7*	*2*
	Saraiki	*20.0*	*2*
	Pahari-Potwari	*3.54*	*2*
	Northern Hindko	*1.88*	*1*
11	**Marathi**	**83.1**	**1**
12	**Telugu**	**82.0**	**2**
13	**Malay**	**80.3**	**20**
	Indonesian	*43.4*	*1*
	Malay	*16.1*	*3*
	Minangkabau	*4.24*	*1*
	Banjar	*3.66*	*2*
	Musi	*3.10*	*1*
	Kedah Malay	*2.60*	*2*
	Central Malay	*1.59*	*1*
	Pattani Malay	*1.47*	*1*
	Jambi Malay	*1.00*	*1*
14	**Turkish**	**79.4**	**8**
15	**Korean**	**77.3**	**6**
16	**French**	**77.2**	**54**
17	**Standard German**	**76.1**	**28**
18	**Vietnamese**	**76.0**	**4**
19	**Tamil**	**75.0**	**7**
20	**Urdu**	**68.6**	**7**

(Adapted from Eberhard et al., 2019: 37–38)

3.2 Global languages and geography

English and Spanish, among others, are globally spoken languages. English does not solely belong to people in England, UK, and nor does Spanish to Spaniards. We know that there are different types of the same global languages, but how do we categorise them, if ever? You have probably heard of American English, British English, Indian English, and the like. It should be recognised that the term American English normally refers to the English spoken in the United States (US). Some people refer to the US as 'America', possibly without due regard to the fact that the Americas consist of the entirety of North and Latin America. Spanish may also be categorised at the national level, such as Argentinian Spanish, Chilean Spanish, Colombian Spanish, and Mexican Spanish. Intriguingly, online Spanish modules which are run by the collaboration of two Japanese universities include those of Mexican Spanish, or los módulos del español de México (KUIS, 2020). You see territorial boundaries clearly defined on a map, and different nations have different social systems. Cartographical boundaries at the national level are convenient for our conceptual control of languages and language varieties. At the same time, national languages serve for political unity and collective **identity**. Conversely, it would be harder for governments to engage citizens without having or naming national languages.

Spanish has spread over large areas and attained official-language status in 20 countries, either de jure or de facto. More specifically, along with Spain and Equatorial Guinea, Spanish is the sole or a major official language of the Latin American counties, except for Brazil. Likewise, the US Commonwealth of Puerto Rico designates both Spanish and English as official languages. In Latin America, Spanish is called either castellano or español, and in the linguistics circle, these terms are regarded as synonymous nowadays (Penny, 2002; Stavans, 2017).[2] However, people in general may name language rather arbitrarily. In 2019, the second author attended an international conference in Medellín, Colombia, a beautiful modern city with a historical atmosphere. On the first day at a hotel, a senior receptionist talked to him in Spanish. After some interaction, the gentleman let him know that the local language was castellano. A few days later, while talking with some Colombian undergraduates through English over lunch, he curiously asked them whether they spoke 'castellano'. A few responded by saying 'no', and immediately added that they spoke 'español'. One of them continued that they spoke 'different Spanish' and gave some vocabulary differences between Latin Americans and Spaniards as well as among Latin Americans. Their discussion went on to students from Argentina and thereabouts. Apparently, they were referring to the students' español rioplatense or Rioplatense Spanish, the Spanish language spoken around the Río de la Plata or the River Plate (Würth, 2020). For them, Latin Americans in different areas spoke different Spanish, which is called español, not castellano. Hochberg (2016: 16) offers a plausible explanation.

> I've encountered some Latin Americans who refuse to call their language *español*, hearing colonial overtones in the word, while others insist on *español* because to them, *castellano* can only mean the Spanish of Spain.

Whether it serves political purposes or not, again, our perception of language is linked to group identity, and we will come back to this issue later in Activity 3.2.

A geographical approach to language has been prominent in the academic field of **sociolinguistics** (Widdowson, 2015; Johnstone, 2016), which, as its name shows, enquires into the relationship between language and society. Even so, our conceptual categories of language do not neatly fit with geographical territories. For this reason, **perceptual dialectology** in sociolinguistics (e.g., Preston, 2018a) asks respondents "to label maps [in their own way] with where different dialects are spoken, or to rate various areas (e.g. each state in the US) on how 'correct' and 'pleasant' the language spoken there is" (Lindemann, 2005: 189). The respondents rely on their own perception and draw any line in this map task irrespective of borderlines (even when they are printed), or make comments on linguistic variations within and across the regions provided (e.g., states or provinces). Note that perceptual dialectology still constrains task-takers to respond geographically. It is therefore not entirely compatible with global communication, including cyber interactions (Ishikawa & Morán Panero, 2016; Ishikawa, 2021). As we have seen by now, the subjective and geographically oriented nature of human categorisation of language is prevalent in our lives.

Summary

So far we have referred to the following terms, and we do hope you are now familiar with all of them:

- first language (L1)
- de facto and de jure official languages
- language varieties and speech communities
- linguistic boundaries
- sociolinguistics
- perceptual dialectology

We have discussed global languages in terms of numbers of L1 speakers and in relation to nations, language varieties, and geography. Particular attention was given to the third aspect (i.e., languages and places) as it is so prevalent in people's perceptions of languages. In a nutshell, global languages are linked with all the three aspects subjectively.

Activity 3.2 "We're not Spanish"

In the following extract, international students are chatting at a party. After examining this example, give your answers to the questions below. Discuss the answers with others in small groups if possible.

S1: Austrian, female; S2 & S5: Argentinian, male; S3 & S4: Austrian, male [Translation in brackets]

01 S1:	You're always speaking Spanish so it doesn't work. @@@
02 S2:	Aún [But], ya que tenemos otra memoria y [that we have another memory and]. @@
03 S1:	But maybe I'll change the subject and write in Spanish or something like that.
04 S2:	Yeah, but actually we're NOT SPANISH.
05 S1:	Hh, yeah, but you're speaking.
06 S3:	Jetzt hast' ein problem [now you've got a problem]. @@@ @@
07 S2:	Ya [Yes], aún [but].
08 S1:	No, I don't know? Is it a Problem? When I say that you're Spanish?
09 S4:	Yes it's=
10 S1:	=But you're Spanish SPEAking.
11 S5:	Yeah, that's different.

(Adapted from VOICE, 2013: LEcon352; see Zhu, 2015: 79–82)

Notes

@	laughter and a laughter-like sound
CAPITAL LETTERS	emphasis
=	latched utterance

Questions

Q1 Do you see any problems with S1's perceptions of language and identity?
Q2 What does S2 mean by "we're NOT SPANISH" (line 04), and who does the word "we" refer to?
Q3 How would S2 refer to his L1 if asked by S1?
Q4 Apart from S5, both Austrians (S3 and S4) seem to sympathise with S2. Any thoughts?

Feedback: *Interspersed with laughter, the conversation in question is casual, and yet somewhat emotionally laden. To be specific, tension is created by S2's ironical use of Spanish (line 02), followed by S1's non-acknowledgement of his contribution (line 03), their emphatic modes (lines 04, 10), and S1's latched utterance (line 10) interrupting S4. Looking at S1's final two turns (lines 08, 10), you will see that she tends to correlate languages and nationalities uncritically. S2 makes it explicit that "we're not Spanish" or Spaniards (line 04), thereby speaking on behalf of S5 and other Argentinians, and possibly also Hispanophone speakers outside Spain. He might refer to his L1 as Argentinian Spanish, Rioplatense Spanish, or the like, and categorise it as español rather than castellano or the Spanish of Spain "to accentuate differences between themselves and others" (Zhu, 2015: 82). Meanwhile, S3 speaks German (line 06), thereby triggering attention from the fellow Austrians S1 and S4. These three Austrians use German or a German variety as the de jure official language of their* *home country, Austria, but obviously they are not German. Overall, there is no objective link between language and national, ethnic, or cultural identity, as expressed by S5: "that's different" (line 11).*

3.3 Global languages and total numbers of speakers

Language globalisation is, by definition, not just about L1 speakers. English is the best example since most of its users have different L1. In other words, English is their additional language or language other than L1 (e.g., L2 or L3). However, conclusive numbers of English speakers are hard to attain. In the first place, it is debatable who should be included as language users. To start our discussion, see the data in Table 3.4, provided by *Ethnologue* online (Eberhard et al., 2020).

Remarkably, only Chinese and English have more than 1 billion speakers.

Local versus global

Some of you may imagine a future when international publications like this textbook are written in Chinese. To the contrary, Honey (1997: 249) humorously remarks:

> English is the world language – at least for the next five hundred years, or until the Martians arrive. Whatever reasons may be given for their global spread, global languages have a large number of speakers as an obvious fact. Something like a quarter of the total population of the globe now speak, or are trying to learn English – a proportion without precedent in the history of the world.

Certainly, there are a vast number of Chinese speakers, especially those of Mandarin Chinese. However, this is because of the size of the Chinese population. If you look at both Tables 3.2 and 3.4, Chinese has 1.311 billion L1 speakers out of a total 1.512 billion (or more) speakers (86.7%), whereas English has only 379 million L1 speakers out of a total 1.268 billion speakers (29.9%). Simply put, Chinese is basically a local language in Greater China or a communal language for Chinese people around the world. On the other hand, English becomes a global language or global lingua franca, that is, a common language among people with diverse L1, including English.

Note that Table 3.4 is based on demographic figures. The first author, a British citizen, is counted as an English speaker, but the second author, a Japanese citizen, is probably not. Both authors use

Table 3.4 Top ten languages by total numbers of speakers

	Languages	*Speakers (millions)*
1	**Chinese**	**1,512+**
	Mandarin	*1,120*
	Yue	*85*
	Wu	*82*
	Min Nan	*49*
	Jinyu	*47*
	Hakka	*43*
	Xiang	*37*
	Gan	*22*
	Others	
2	**English**	**1,268**
3	**Hindi**	**637**
4	**Arabic**	**620+**
	Standard Arabic	*274*
	Egyptian Spoken	*68*
	Sudanese Spoken	*42*
	Moroccan Spoken	*33*
	Algerian Spoken	*33*
	North Levantine Spoken	*25*
	Sa'idi Spoken	*24*
	Najdi Spoken	*18*
	Mesopotamian Spoken	*16*
	Others	
5	**Spanish**	**538**
6	**French**	**277**
7	**Bengali**	**265**
8	**Russian**	**258**
9	**Portuguese**	**252**
10	**Indonesian**	**199**

(Adapted from Eberhard et al., 2020)

English for their professional lives, like our colleagues from around the world. It is more reasonable to count in all of them. In fact, already about a dozen years ago, Crystal (2008: 5) estimated the growing population of English users to approach "2 billion", and noted that "we have moved in 25 years from a fifth to a quarter to a third of the world's population being speakers of English". Now we even see this "2 billion", let alone "1,268 million" in Table 3.4, as a 'conservative' figure. In line with Jenkins (2015a), we project that more than 2 billion people regularly function in English to fulfill their lives.

Among the ten languages listed in Table 3.4, French and Indonesian also have more additional language users than L1 speakers. French does not enjoy such an extensive global reach as English, but apart from France, including its overseas regions, French plays a major role in continental Europe as one of the 24 official European Union (EU) languages,[3] also in Canada, especially its province of Québec, and moreover in former French colonies, largely within Africa. Back in 2012, the second author of this book was spoken to by a couple of ladies on an Orlybus, a bus from Paris Orly Airport to the Place Denfert-Rochereau, Paris, France. As far as he remembers, they said that they were from Casablanca, Morocco, and that they regularly used French although it was not their strongest language. Like these ladies, multilingual Africa is likely to have many French speakers for whom French is a regional lingua franca. It is unlikely to matter whether someone belongs to a particular Francophone speech community. In contrast, the same author clearly remembers his short stop at a café in Charles de Gaulle Airport, Paris, France in 2013, before going back to the UK. He asked a few questions, ordered some patisserie, coffee, and hot chocolate, paid money, and received his change. Throughout this process, the cashier clearly understood his English, but replied in articulate French. It looked as if French should be used as the language belonging to the local speech community instead of English as an international lingua franca. Intriguingly, you can take both internationalist and nationalistic approaches to the same global languages like French.

Indonesian is the de jure official language of Indonesia, and a regional language in Southeast Asia. Together with the other nine countries (i.e., Malaysia, Philippines, Singapore, Thailand, Brunei Darussalam, Viet Nam, Laos, Myanmar, and Cambodia), Indonesia belongs to the Association of Southeast Asian Nations (ASEAN).[4] Kirkpatrick (2012: 125) describes regional linguistic diversity as follows.

> The countries of ASEAN represent great linguistic and cultural diversity. In Indonesia alone, for example, with its population of more than 200 million, there are more than 300 ethnic groups and 700 languages. While not all the countries of ASEAN are as linguistically and culturally diverse as Indonesia, there are probably more than 1,000 languages spoken across the ten countries.

Clearly, Indonesian is all the more important as an **intranational** or domestic **lingua franca** for the citizens. With so many languages coexistent, the national language of Indonesian is inevitably an additional language for most Indonesians (Kirkpatrick, 2010a). Obviously, this means that English will be their L3 or even L4.

Global hegemony

English is not the first widespread lingua franca. Other historical 'giant' languages include Sanskrit, Greek, Latin, Arabic, and Portuguese

(Ostler, 2005/2006). Like past global languages, the present spread of English results from social and historical factors. World history has seen the colonial and industrial powers of the English-speaking UK from the seventeenth to the early twentieth centuries, followed by the ongoing political and economic power of the English-speaking US. Moreover, global languages have scientific and cultural bearings. Just for your interest, if you look at the 2021 edition of the QS World University Rankings (QS Quacquarelli Symonds, 2020), almost half of the top 100 universities are located in the US (n = *27*) or the UK (n = *18*). With academic institutions in other English-dominant regions, such as Australasia, Canada, Hong Kong, and Singapore, English is very often the default language of world research communities. Likewise, to take examples from popular culture, globally marketed Hollywood movies and Pixar Animation Studios films are both based in California, US.

As a language with more additional language users, French has been among popular foreign languages to be taught and learned at higher-education institutions. This seems to be the case even where French is not spoken and is generally not available as a school subject. It may be easy for you to find some colleges and universities offering French courses around your living places. We may say that the popularity of French has stemmed from cultural bearings. After all, both art (e.g., literature, fashion, dance) and cuisine from France are popular. To this effect, French in Japanese television commercials, for instance, stereotypically triggers association with "high elegance", "refined taste", "attractiveness", "sophisticated life style", and "fascination and charm" (Haarmann, 1989: 11). For another instance, some Lebanese recognise "French as a language of high culture" (Shaaban & Ghaith, 2002: 568) from the perspective of the product approach to culture (see Chapter 1.2). Indeed, English has adopted quite a few French-origin words. Just for your curiosity, below are examples of these words in their original French forms:

> *Apache (dance), baguette, ballet, bouillabaisse, brasserie, café, camouflage, champagne, château, chef, chic, corsage, coup d'État, croissant, cuisine, début, déjà vu, dessert, élite, ennui, en route, esprit de corps, étiquette, façade, fait accompli, fiancée, fricassée, garage, genre, gourmet, hors-d'œuvre, hôtel, liaison, limousine, marionnette, pâtisserie, pirouette, prestige, quiche, régime, rendez-vous, sachet, savoir-faire, silhouette, souvenir, vignette.*

Not all of these words may be familiar to you. Even so, you may have felt some of them to be no longer just French or 'foreign' words for non-French speakers.

3.4 Future of English as a global language

While both Chinese and English are 'giant' languages of our day, the former is not necessarily used globally across domains, or for purposes for which languages are used, such as academia, business, and in international organisations. After all, Chinese is notoriously difficult to learn, and it is estimated that over 430 million L1 Chinese people themselves speak English (Jenkins, 2015a). Therefore, English is more likely to be chosen in global communication with them. Furthermore, if we admit that the number of English users exceeds 2 billion, then the L1 Chinese speakers are outnumbered by those who use English as an additional language.

As with the case of L1 Chinese speakers, English is increasingly acquired by L1 Arabic speakers. A good example is the Arabic-speaking Gulf Cooperation Council states consisting of the United Arab Emirates, Bahrain, Saudi Arabia, Oman, Qatar, and Kuwait.[5] These Persian Gulf Arab states (except Iraq) have seen the steady rise of English use and education, due in part to an influx of expatriates and international businesses (Alharbi, 2018). Meanwhile, Hindi speakers are primarily found in India, where English is a de facto official language. More drastically, ASEAN grants English official status as the sole working language: "The working language of ASEAN shall be English" (ASEAN, 2008: 29). Seeing that so many of L1 speakers of 'major' languages, together with international organisations like ASEAN, use English as a communication tool, we suspect that English will stay as the world's lingua franca for the foreseeable future. This does not mean that English will stay the same as it is used by monolingual English speakers, as seen in Activity 3.3.

Spanish is another global language, but we would have to acknowledge its more limited domains of use at the global scale as well as its considerably smaller number of speakers than English. Having said that, the second author of this book remembers how useless his English and very limited Spanish was on streets in Lleida, Catalonia, Spain in 2016. In retrospect, the Lleida Museum (el Museu de Lleida) was especially worth the visit. If not Catalan, Spanish would have been helpful to enjoy this artistic museum to a full extent. Three years later, he visited a souvenir shop in Medellín, Colombia. Unforgettably, smartphone translation failed and led shopkeepers to laugh hard. It was so embarrassing, and how he wished he could communicate through Spanish!

To say the least, English is almost unrivalled as a global language. This historic lingua franca makes us question customary concepts. In particular, what is its **target speech community**, or the speech community in which we expect to participate? What is its **target culture**, or the culture with which we expect to familiarise ourselves? If we see no particular target speech community or target culture, then who are its

'native' speakers or indigenous speakers, and who are its **'non-native' speakers**? English as a global lingua franca, by definition, does not seem to go together well with local and regional thinking, and possibly with attachment to geography itself. The next chapter examines the above traditional concepts vis-à-vis the global spread of English.

Summary

We have additionally (re)introduced the following terms in this section:

- additional language
- global lingua franca
- intranational lingua franca
- domains (of language use)
- target speech community
- target culture
- 'native' and 'non-native' speakers (of English)

We have discussed global languages in terms of total numbers of speakers and in relation to local/global perspectives and global hegemony. Also, consideration was given to the future of English as a global language. In brief, global languages have local and global as well as historical and future dimensions to consider, together with academic and cultural implications.

Activity 3.3 "All busses were overfulled"

In the following extract, S1 is recalling her experience in France, where she encountered celebration occasions. S2 understands S1 without any problems throughout their conversation. After examining this example, discuss the questions below, if possible, with others in small groups.

S1: L1 German; S2: L1 Norwegian

01 S1: But really crazy. All busses were overfulled. All of the French one jump around and "Yeah!"
02 and sing their songs and
03 S2: <@>I see.</@>
04 S1: Yeah. It was really crazy.
05 S2: Yeah.

(Adapted from Hülmbauer, 2009: 228)

Note
<@>xxx</@> spoken laughingly

Questions

Q1 Paraphrase what S1 says in lines 01 and 02 in your own words.
Q2 Is there anything you do not understand in the above extract?
Q3 The word "overfulled" is not found in English dictionaries. What do you think it means? Why do you think this unconventional word is understood by S2?
Q4 Do you have any similar experiences with unconventional 'English' words?

Feedback: *S1 is describing "crazy" situations which she encountered in France. Lines 01 to 02 may be paraphrased as follows: "But it was really crazy. All busses were crowded with French people who all jumped around, shouted 'Yeah!', and sang their songs". You probably have no problem in understanding S1. Moreover, you would feel the original version as more vivid and authentic than the above paraphrase. Arguably, the word "overfulled" is more transparent than the word crowded even if both mean the same. It is easy to imagine that the busses were 'overly full'. Note that S1 presumably has the German word überfüllt in mind, and that S2's L1 Norwegian has a similar word overfylt.*

Chapter summary

In this chapter, our discussion of global languages identified some characteristic aspects of human language. Fundamentally, language is categorised subjectively and related to group identity, potentially as citizens. At the same time, languages cannot simply be correlated with nations. This is especially because multilingualism is largely the norm within and across nations. Global languages, in particular, have local varieties which emerge through mutual interaction over generations. However, boundaries between these language varieties and languages themselves are not concrete or categorical, but often associated with geographical territories.

We also saw that language globalisation accompanies social and historical factors and has scientific and cultural connotations. English is no exception. Nowadays, over 2 billion people may function in this language, and many of them use it as an additional language. In other words, English is the most prominent lingua franca among people with diverse L1, including English. It will stay as the world's lingua franca, involving L1 speakers of 'major' languages all the more so because other global languages are more regional and limited in domains of use. We indicated that this unprecedented spread of English requires a rethink of traditional concepts.

Notes

1 The next edition (4th edn) of Jenkins (2015a) will be available soon.
2 In Spain, the de jure official language is castellano (i.e., Spanish). As its name suggests, español in Spain may include not only castellano but also Basque, Catalan, and other languages of local origins (Hochberg, 2016).
3 https://europa.eu/european-union/about-eu/eu-languages_en (accessed 30 September 2020).
4 https://asean.org/asean/about-asean/ (accessed 30 September 2020).
5 www.gcc-sg.org/en-us/AboutGCC/MemberStates/Pages/Home.aspx (accessed 30 September 2020).

Further reading

Blommaert, J. (2010). *The sociolinguistics of globalization.* Cambridge: Cambridge University Press. The book offers conceptual underpinnings for studying complex social networks and mobility, along with associated unpredictable language change, in this age of globalisation.

Jenkins, J. (2018a). The future of English as a lingua franca? In J. Jenkins, W. Baker, & M. Dewey (Eds.), *The Routledge handbook of English as a lingua franca* (pp. 594–605). Abingdon: Routledge. An accessible chapter bridging the past development and possible future of the academic quest to comprehend global communication.

Morán Panero, S. (2018). Global languages and lingua franca communications. In J. Jenkins, W. Baker, & M. Dewey (Eds.), *The Routledge handbook of English as a lingua franca* (pp. 556–569). Abingdon: Routledge. A call for more investigation into the ontology (i.e., nature of existence) of both linguistic boundaries and 'English', targeting all involved in global communication.

4 Global Englishes in a multilingual world

Introduction

English is currently the most prominent global lingua franca. Even though Japanese people, for example, normally use Japanese among each other, they use English with others in numerous multilingual scenarios. For the sake of argument, if a Japanese student Skypes with a Taiwanese student, then it is likely that they will use English, while Chinese and Japanese resources will come into their English. It is quite possible that they will talk about 'Japanese' anime or 'Taiwanese' bubble tea, and understand each other by both talking mainly in English and texting Chinese-origin characters (called *kanji* in Japanese) as common resources.

In Chapter 4, we introduce the research sphere of **Global Englishes** (Pennycook, 2007; Jenkins, 2015a), which deals with the global spread of English. Global Englishes actually comprises two major research fields, **World Englishes (WE)** and **English as a lingua franca (ELF)** (Jenkins, 2015a), and the former is aligned with the appellation of **English as an international language (EIL)**, which can be regarded as another research field. WE and ELF accentuate, in their different ways, "the linguistic and sociocultural dimensions of global uses and users of English" (CGE, 2020). More specifically, the former features national or regional English varieties in the world, and the latter is concerned with communication among English users beyond geographical boundaries. This chapter first reviews WE and then turns to consider ELF. Both fields are important and complementary to each other, and their respective contributions and limitations as research fields are included in discussion. However, in accordance with the tenor of this textbook, later chapters will focus on ELF, an academic quest to comprehend global communication. Throughout the chapter you will have the opportunity to consider how English is used variably at a global scale.

Activity 4.1 Your English varieties

As a small group (or with your close friends), discuss what English varieties you think your group members are speaking and compare your ideas with their self-perceptions. In so doing, you may want to consider how important it is for you to associate yourself with a particular English variety.

Feedback: *There are no right or wrong answers. "We all live every day in virtual environments, defined by our ideas" (Crichton, 1994/2006: 446). After all, as in this quotation from a best-selling novel, our world is characterised by our ideas. We expect different ideas to come up from different groups, which in turn will help you understand your own perspectives on Global Englishes.*

4.1 World Englishes

As may be familiar to you, Braj B. Kachru (1985; 1992) introduced an influential three-circles model to provide a basis to understand how English is spread around the world (Figure 4.1). The Kachruvian model consists of **Inner, Outer,** and **Expanding Circles.**

Obviously, the Inner Circle is the smallest, and the Expanding Circle is the largest. We will refer to this prominent model in the discussion below.

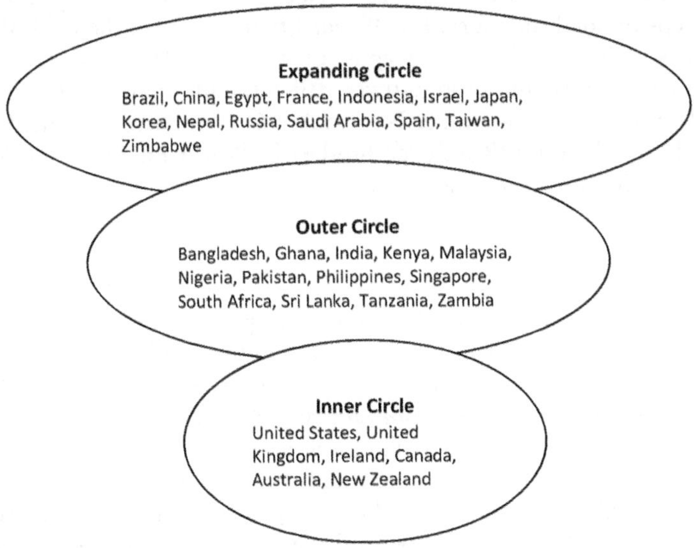

Figure 4.1 Kachru's (1992) three-circles model

(Adapted from Kachru, 1992: 356)

Profile of the field of WE

WE is an established research field in sociolinguistics, or, more broadly, in **applied linguistics**, which is commonly defined as "[t]he theoretical and empirical investigation of real-world problems in which language is a central issue" (Brumfit, 1995: 27). A major real-world problem for WE scholars is the relationship between the global spread of English and different local identities and cultures. Remember that the term WE stands for World Englishes (not the singular *English*) "to stress the diversity to be found in the language today, and to stress that English no longer has one single base of authority, prestige and normativity [i.e., standardised rules]" (Mesthrie & Bhatt, 2008: 3). In Braj B. Kachru's words:

> [t]he term symbolizes the functional and formal variations, divergent sociolinguistic contexts, ranges and varieties of English in creativity, and various types of acculturation in parts of the Western and non-Western world. This concept emphasizes "WE-ness," and not the dichotomy between us and them (the native and non-native users).
>
> (1992: 2)

Back in 1978, Braj B. Kachru and Larry E. Smith, widely known as the founding fathers of WE, organised the first international conferences in Hawaii and Illinois, US, respectively, later known as the International Association for World Englishes (IAWE) conference series. In 1981, they co-founded the journal of *World Englishes*. Also, the field of WE has a widely known major **corpus**, or a large collection of naturally occurring spoken and written texts, called the International Corpus of English (ICE) (Greenbaum & Nelson, 1996).[1] Moreover, this field now has the book series 'Routledge Studies in World Englishes' (2015–), with Ee Ling Low the series editor.

Geographical association

Fundamentally, WE approaches the global spread of English by looking at how English takes root in different countries and regions. In other words, this research field is primarily concerned with "the relationship between language and *community*" (Widdowson, 2015: 363; original emphasis). Examples include the national varieties of Nigerian, Kenyan, Indian, and Singapore Englishes, along with Black South African English and Southeast Asian Englishes (Filppula et al., 2017; Nelson et al., 2020). It may be said that the first author of this book speaks British English but not 'Euro-English' or English in continental Europe (Modiano, 2006/2009; 2017), and that the second author speaks an international variety of 'Japanese English' if his English expresses 'Japanese values' (Hino, 2012; 2018).

To be precise, tracing back to what Smith (1976) called English as an international auxiliary language (EIAL), or, more transparently, EIL,[2] WE research has analogised the internationalisation of English to its historical diasporas, namely the expansion of English from England to Ireland, Scotland, and Wales, followed by its further expansion to North America, Australia, and New Zealand (Kachru et al., 2006/2009; Kachru & Smith, 2008). This 'traditional' Anglophone world corresponds to the Inner Circle in Figure 4.1, where English is employed in all domains and the large majority of citizens speak English as their L1. WE scholars envisage further dispersion taking place. In the Outer Circle in Figure 4.1, mostly in former British colonies, 'new Englishes' (Pride, 1982) have developed as institutionalised and nativised varieties (Platt et al., 1984; Melchers et al., 2019). Being *new*, English was not spoken by the majority in a community. Being *institutionalised*, English is exploited for a range of social and political purposes. The language is also promoted through the educational system, usually with various degrees of **English-medium instruction (EMI)**, that is, teaching and learning of academic content through English. And being *nativised*, each English variety has developed its own local linguistic (e.g., phonological, grammatical, lexical, pragmatic, and discourse structural) features through mutual interaction over generations, involving populations with different L1. National identities are reinforced by **codification**, that is, documenting such local rules "in a grammar, a lexical or pronouncing dictionary, course books or any other type of reference manual" (Bamgboṣe, 1998: 4). Meanwhile, provincially, socially, and ethnically different subvarieties emerge, as most evidently seen in the US (Schneider, 2020). These subvarieties help "construct several, partially overlapping, identities" (Schneider, 2007: 32). In contrast, in the Expanding Circle in Figure 4.1, English serves mainly as an international, but not intranational, communication medium. Accordingly, "the forms and functions of English as an international lingua franca in the Expanding Circle have traditionally [been] featured comparatively rarely in World Englishes literature" (Saraceni, 2015: 80).

Taking a WE perspective, English varieties in the world have their local target speech communities and target cultures. As one example, Philippine English belongs to the Philippines and reflects cultural expectations there, thereby symbolising Filipino identity. To be sure, the users of Philippine English may not be seen as 'native' speakers of English as conventionally defined, since English is not always their strongest language or the language they learn to speak since birth. However, it is Filipinos who are the speakers or 'owners' of this nativised English variety and, to borrow the applied linguist Vivian Cook's words, they are therefore not "imitation or failed native [English] speakers" (1999: 195). As such, WE scholars advocate an egalitarian view summarised in this sentence by Roby Marlina: "We believe in and emphasise the importance of recognising the pluricentricity of English and the equal treatment given to all varieties of English and its speakers" (2014: 6).

4.2 Contributions and limitations of WE

WE contributes to raising awareness of global diversity in English use, especially in the Inner and Outer Circles (see Activity 4.2). To this effect, WE has offered evidence that local identities and cultures may result in local forms and functions of English, and argues that each English variety should be regarded in its own right. Kingsley Bolton states that "a pluricentric and pluralistic approach to the 'Englishes' or 'English languages' of the world has become so well established as to constitute something of an orthodoxy in contemporary English language studies and sociolinguistics" (2018: 7). Convincing as this statement is, the question remains how we identify plural centres and diversified English varieties by taking the "pluricentric and pluralistic approach". Simply put, in what way is English countable? On the one hand, cartographical boundaries are convenient for our conceptual control. On the other hand, national unity and identity formation are the basis of political communities. With these two perceptions combined, WE "places nationalism at its core" (Pennycook, 2007: 20) with "iconic badges like Indian English, Nigerian English, Malaysian English, and so on in their descriptions of local varieties of English" (Bhatt, 2017: 307). It looks almost like treating the spread of English as *inter*national (i.e., between nations), rather than global. In reality and by definition, global communication transcends national boundaries, involving people from across the three Kachruvian circles. In this age of mobility, and with so many English users from the Expanding Circle, enumerating the English language as geographically bounded entities does not seem to work to consider global communication.

The future development of Global Englishes requires more focus on the majority of English users today (i.e., those from the Expanding Circle), for whom English is primarily a global, not local or national, lingua franca. Ironically, WE alone may promote or reinforce the inadequacy of their English (Ishikawa, 2016b). For instance, there is no stable national speech community of 'Japanese English' or regional speech communities of, say, 'Greater Tokyo English' or 'Asian Pacific Englishes'. For this reason, these English 'varieties' are not, after all, comparable to 'new Englishes' in the Outer Circle as well as to 'traditional' Englishes in the Inner Circle. It is noteworthy that "the world's first undergraduate college of world Englishes" (D'Angelo,

2005: 329), in Chukyo University, Japan, ended its 18-year history in 2020, superseded by a more globally oriented college (Chukyo University, 2020). Frankly speaking, so long as it is categorised geographically, English in the Expanding Circle, compared to English in the Inner and Outer Circles, is either no more than a foreign language or an underdeveloped variety. Instead, global communication should be explained by "a theoretical framework which covers the dynamics of the Expanding Circle and of poststructural hybridity in global interactions" (Schneider, 2014: 28), or, more straightforwardly, by theories which go beyond geographically based thinking to capture "dynamic, variable and situationally dependent communication phenomena" (Ishikawa, 2017a: 34).

Summary

So far we have introduced the following terms, with which we hope you are now familiar:

- applied linguistics and Global Englishes: World Englishes (WE) and English as a lingua franca (ELF)
- English as an international language (EIL)
- Inner, Outer, and Expanding Circles
- corpus
- English-medium instruction (EMI)
- codification

We have reviewed the research field of WE in terms of its general profile, geographical association, and contributions, limitations, and future directions. In essence, WE describes national or regional English varieties in the world as institutionalised and nativised 'new Englishes'. In so doing, WE keeps with the twentieth-century sociolinguistic tradition of associating language with geographically bounded speech communities.

Activity 4.2 Indian English

In the online video clip available from http://labo.kuis.ac.jp/module/module/en_in.html#/en-01, two Indian speakers of English are greeting and introducing each other. After listening to their conversation (without a script) via this link, think about the questions below. Discuss your answers with others in small groups if possible.

Questions

Q1 Do you have any problems understanding their English?
Q2 Do you see any difference between your English and theirs?

Next, watch the same conversation with the script reproduced below and discuss the same two questions. Are your answers different this time? If so, in what way and why do you think they are different?

01 S1: Hi!
02 S2: Hi! Sanjay?
03 S1: Yes. How are you, Priya?
04 S2: I'm good. How are you? Long time no see.
05 S1: Yes, it's been a long time. I have been in Chennai for the past two years.
06 S2: Chennai? What are you doing there?
07 S1: I am doing B. Tech in Computer Science.
08 S2: Wow, that's great!
09 S1: How about you? What are you doing these days?
10 S2: I work for an MNC.
11 S1: That's good! What did you do after college?
12 S2: I did Master's in management from IIM Ahmedabad.
13 S1: IIM Ahmedabad, awesome! That's one of the top business schools! Should we go have coffee somewhere?
14 S2: Yes, that's a good idea.

(KUIS & TUFS, 2020)

Notes
MNC multinational company
IIM Indian Institute of Management

Feedback: *We guess many of you have discussed Sanjay's and Priya's pronunciation, which represents many Indian speakers of English. To be precise, their tongues are placed more inside for /t/ and /d/ (e.g., lines 04, 11, 13) and more frontally for the /l/ as in "schools" (line 13), and their lips are not rounded for the /w/ as in "work" (line 10). Similarly, and probably unlike most of you, they pronounce "great" /gre:t/ (line 08) and "Ahmedabad" /ˈemdəˌbɑ:d/ (lines 12, 13). Moreover, they place stress on the first letters of both MNC and IIM (lines 10, 12, 13) while both authors of this book would pronounce the last letters the strongest. Apart from pronunciation, "B. Tech" (line 07) is a local term for bachelor of technology. Note that no article is used for either "B. Tech" or "Master's" (lines 07, 12) even if you might prefer using the indefinite article in each case, i.e., a B. Tech and a Master's (or master's) (degree).*

4.3 English as a lingua franca

In the previous chapter (Chapter 3.3), we provided a general definition of a (global) lingua franca in relation to English: "a common language among people with diverse L1, including English" (p. 48). Even so, it is untenable to reify the global communication medium of English as *a* language or something like an 'object'. The research field of ELF has identified the gap between the established **English as a foreign language (EFL)** approach and the reality of prevalent social contacts for which English functions as a lingua franca at a global scale in various forms (Seidlhofer, 2011). More specifically, on the one hand, EFL takes a geographically bounded approach to the English used by L1 English speakers. On the other hand, although the acronyms are similar, ELF as a field of research has enquired into what an observable communicative use of English is like across geographical boundaries among English users who are often multilinguals and usually speak English as their additional language. This linguistic phenomenon in global encounters itself is also referred to as English (used) as lingua franca or ELF. ELF enquiry has long documented that English and **multilingual resources** are used dynamically and contextually for effective communication whether L1 English speakers are involved or not.

At its simplest, ELF as a linguistic phenomenon may be seen as multilingual contact. Mauranen (2012) introduces the notion of **English similect** or the contact language between an L1 and English as an additional language within individual minds. For the sake of argument, if an L1 Hungarian speaker and an L1 Japanese speaker talk in English, then they are supposed to use the Hungarian English similect and the Japanese English similect, respectively. In their minds, English and their L1 are contacting each other. To put it differently, their English use is always influenced by their L1 to varying degrees. More to the point, Mauranen (2012) argues that global communication is essentially about the **second-order language contact**. That is, contact languages, such as the Hungarian and Japanese English similects, are contacting each other during interaction.

Sharing the same L1, speakers of each English similect may use English in a similar way (thus called similect). Even so, their English is remarkably different from person to person, depending on individual experiences of encountering other English similects. Thus, any English similect is somewhat similar but actually diverse, there are potentially as many English similects as non-English L1, and two or more English similects do interact with one another globally as in Figure 4.2. It should be added that L1 English speakers of different origins may join this communication. The notions of similect and second-order language contact provide a shorthand explanation of how complex and rather amorphous global communication is. As a caveat, however, it is English users who contact or encounter across the globe rather than languages themselves (for more detail, see Chapter 8).

Until recently, this complex target of ELF research has most often been defined as "any use of English among speakers of different first

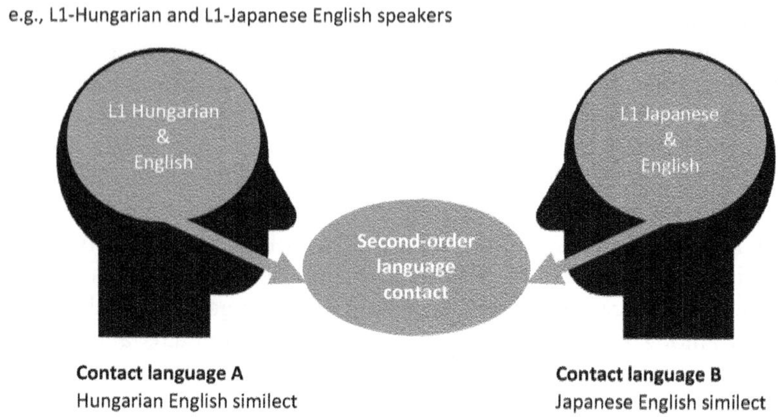

Figure 4.2 Mauranen's (2012) second-order language contact

languages for whom English is the communicative medium of choice, and often the only option" (Seidlhofer, 2011: 7; emphasis removed). Importantly, again, this definition focuses on the use or function of English as a global lingua franca among speakers with different linguistic backgrounds, including L1 English speakers of different origins. Useful as it is, this definition entails a couple of caveats (Ishikawa, 2017a). For one thing, the use of language is confined to English. However, the majority of English users today are multilinguals who interact with each other in different linguistic settings. As seen in Activity 3.2, English is not always chosen among these multilinguals, and we should not exclude this aspect from research. For another, the above definition does not include situations in which English is chosen among those who share their L1. This is a potentially interesting area of research, all the more so because some English language teaching and EMI classrooms in East Asia and beyond consist of an instructor and students from the same L1 backgrounds (Ishikawa, 2020a).

Along this line, while retaining the emphasis on function or communication, a currently prominent notion in the field, **English as a multilingua franca (EMF)**, stresses the inherent **multilingualism** of global encounters through English (Jenkins, 2015b). The working definition of EMF is "Multilingual communication in which English is available as a contact language of choice, but is not necessarily chosen" (Jenkins, 2015b: 73). Similar to the multilingual education scholar Jasone Cenoz's (2019) view of multilingualism, this new definition foregrounds multilingualism and backgrounds English and L1 status. As a corollary, it encompasses communication among English-knowing multilingual speakers of the same L1, and examples will be given in Chapter 8. In line with Jenkins (2015b), we will conceptualise our research target as English-within-multilingualism throughout this textbook.

In sum, ELF as a research field in applied linguistics "enquires into various aspects of the use of [language] among [English] speakers who [usually] do not share a first language" (Baird et al., 2014: 191). Accordingly, what features ELF as a linguistic phenomenon is the empirical evidence that "the best solutions [for mutual understanding] need not be the most standardised-like or native-like ... [or] even English" (Mauranen, 2018b: 114), and that global communication brings out multilingualism with varying degrees of overtness (Cogo, 2018) across different linguistic levels (e.g., phonology, grammar, lexis, pragmatics, and discourse structure). Again, we will explore the notion of EMF in great detail in Chapter 8.

Profile of the field of ELF

ELF is another established research field in sociolinguistics, or, more broadly, in applied linguistics. A major real-world problem for ELF scholars is global communication or how we communicate with each other beyond geographical boundaries. Unlike WE, cartographical territories are not foregrounded but considered to be among potential influences on communication. As evident in the first handbook of ELF (Jenkins et al., 2018), relevant domains are multifarious, including academia, business, international organisations, international migration, international families, and **digital communication**. Back in the 1980s, Jennifer Jenkins, then an English teacher, noticed that her students tended not to use the rules they learned in her classrooms when communicating among themselves. Tracing back to Jenkins (1996), the earliest publication that refers to ELF, her subsequent research has identified what is crucial in understanding each other as mutual accommodation, or more specifically **linguistic accommodation**, that is, adjusting and adapting language use according to the situation (Jenkins, 2000; 2014). The field of ELF documents various communicative situations in its major corpora: the Vienna-Oxford International Corpus of English (VOICE) (Seidlhofer, 2004),[3] the corpus of ELF in academic settings (ELFA) (Mauranen, 2003),[4] with an additional written corpus called WrELFA (Carey, 2013),[5] and the Asian Corpus of English (ACE) (Kirkpatrick, 2010b).[6] In 2008, Anna Mauranen organised the first annual ELF conference, and in 2012, Barbara Seidlhofer cofounded the *Journal of English as a Lingua Franca*, together with Jenkins and Mauranen; these three figures are often called the founding mothers of ELF. This field also has the book series 'Developments in English as a Lingua Franca' (2013–), with Jennifer Jenkins and the first author of this book as series co-editors.

Linguistic adaptability and multilingualism

ELF is sometimes misaligned with WE (Ishikawa, 2015; Ishikawa & Jenkins, 2019). To be specific, neither Jenkins' (2000) phonological Lingua Franca Core (LFC) nor Mauranen's (2012) aforementioned English similect can be related to linguistic varieties in the world. First and foremost, while Jenkins (2000) identifies phonological features, termed LFC, which would facilitate intelligibility among multilingual English users, she detects the use of LFC depending on specific interlocutors. In other words, LFC should not be considered separately from linguistic accommodation. Seeing that LFC refers exclusively to pronunciation, not to any other linguistic levels – and, in any case, is not a variety – what Jenkins (2000) demonstrates is how crucial pronunciation is within linguistic accommodation. Likewise, as seen above, Mauranen's (2012) English similect refers to contact language at the cognitive level, which has no stable speech community for mutual interaction, unlike any varieties. Thus, similect is idiolectal and should not be considered separately from parallel interaction, that is, second-order language contact.

At its simplest, ELF approaches the global spread of English by looking "into the relationship between language and *communication*, how linguistic resources are variably used to achieve meaning" (Widdowson, 2015: 363; original emphasis). Conversely, English serves as a global lingua franca because it is adaptable enough. Among many instances of variable use of English, corpus data has occasionally witnessed the countable usage of 'uncountable' nouns, such as *evidences*, *feedbacks*, *fundings*, and *softwares* (Jenkins, 2011: 929). You may say, for instance, *multiple evidences* rather than *multiple evidence*, and this additional *-s* will make your meaning clearer. Also, the corpus data has sometimes attested the regularised usage of 'irregular' affixation, such as ***conspirate***, ***examinate***, and ***pronunciate***, as well as ***approvement*** and ***increasive*** (Seidlhofer, 2011: 102–103). Considering the corresponding nouns ***conspiration***, ***examination***, and ***pronunciation***, the above ***-ate*** verbs are more coherent with other verbs of Romance origin and their derivative nouns (e.g., ***communicate*** and ***communication***). The adjective ***approvement*** takes the same formation of ***achivement***, as with the case of ***increasive*** and ***impressive***, for instance. While such consistent word formation may contribute to clear meaning-making, dictionaries list arguably more obscure words instead: conspire, examine, pronounce, approval, and increasing. Similarly, you can make conventional verbs more explicit with an additional word, as in the following examples: "reject **against** this idea", "return **back**", "answer **to** you", and "discuss **about** this" (Seidlhofer, 2011: 145–147). Again, dictionaries deem 'correct' only the economical usages of *reject this idea*, *return*, *answer you*, and *discuss this*.

Note that there is an inconsistency between *answer ~~to~~ you* and *reply to you* and between *discuss ~~about~~ this* and *argue about this*, for instance.

The above examples of variable use in grammar, or, more specifically, in word structure and arrangement (what is called morphosyntactic variability), are detectable irrespective of speakers' diverse L1 backgrounds. In fact, similar usages have been documented in WE research (Björkman, 2018). Meanwhile, as suggested in Activity 3.3, English in global communication is always influenced by other languages present at the moment. Moreover, again, English is not always chosen even when everyone present is an English speaker. We can even say that multilingualism, or, more precisely, multilingual influences and practices with English, is "the one single factor without which there would be no ELF" (Jenkins, 2015b: 63). To this effect, the notions of similect and second-order language contact represent conceptual simplifications (Mauranen, 2018a). On the one hand, again, global communication may involve L1 English speakers, including monolinguals. On the other hand, it is far more common to encounter multilingual English speakers. Due to accelerated mobility at the global scale, both authors of this book occasionally meet multilingual students who are not sure what their L1 are. In reality, then, our minds and global encounters are generally more multilingual than what Figure 4.2 illustrates. Also note that an individual's repertoire or the totality of individually available linguistic resources (Chapter 2.5) can be very different in each L1, including English.

Taking an ELF perspective, global communication does not have any particular target speech communities or target cultures. This does not mean that ELF researchers neglect either communities or cultures to which participants belong. To the contrary, ELF research eschews imposing communal or cultural frameworks before investigating what is actually going on during interaction. In the same vein, both what identity participants draw on and how important it is for them are empirical questions. So are power relations. To give an example, while migration and asylum-seeking domains are likely to involve power imbalances (e.g., Guido, 2018), it is premature to presume this inequity to affect communicative transactions in any way. Along these lines, unlike WE enquiry, ELF research would not 'naïvely' promote an egalitarian view or categorise the English used by Filipino participants, for example, into Philippine English, which in turn incorporates Filipino culture and reflects Filipino identity. Unless we make an inevitable link between English and geographical communities, no particular people can be 'native' or indigenous speakers of English as a global language. So long as linguistic accommodation is key to effective global communication, then multilingual English users will be more advantageous since they are likely to have more linguistic resources at their disposal.

4.4 Contributions and limitations of ELF

ELF contributes to opening up the possibility of understanding global communication more fully by moving beyond the sociolinguistic tradition of community-based thinking. As summarised below:

> ELF research has shifted away from associating language with geographical communities in the face of unprecedented global mobility … Accordingly, a global lingua franca, by definition, has no native or nativised speakers like those of communal languages or language varieties as conventionally defined.
>
> (Ishikawa & McBride, 2019: 334)

As the main limitation, ELF enquiry has been so exploratory and fast-developing that it does not constitute a simple, easy-to-understand paradigm. This is especially because "any attempt to understand communication in this complex, globalised world would always be partial and incomplete" (Ishikawa & Jenkins, 2019: 1).

Our current attempt to understand global communication coincides with Jenkins' (2015b) notion of English as a multilingua franca (EMF), which duly foregrounds the inherent multilingualism of global interactions through English. As implied in Chapter 2, EMF coincides with another notion of **transcultural communication**, which takes notice of how ambiguous cultural boundaries (e.g., gender and generation) and scales (e.g., local, national, and global) are in real-life interactions (Baker, 2015; 2018). Such situated meaning-making is usually transmodal, like an example to be shown later (see Activity 4.3). That is, yet another notion of **transmodality** or **transmodal communication** indexes how meaning is synergetically created and interpreted through multiple verbal and non-verbal modes, like emoticons, gestures and postures, images, and sounds (Murphy, 2012; Hawkins, 2018). If you are used to video chatting, texting, and social networking, then you may think that this is a commonly observable aspect of human communication. We argue that ELF theory comprises these three notions, all of which are conjoined by complexity theory (Larsen-Freeman, 1997; 2018; Baird et al., 2014; for introduction, see Chapter 2.4). Later chapters will unpack all the above theoretical foundations step by step in the hope of appreciating global communication.

Summary

Additional terms to be remembered from the ELF sections are:

- English similect and second-order language contact
- linguistic accommodation

- English as a multilingua franca (EMF) and multilingualism
- transcultural communication
- transmodality or transmodal communication

You will come across these terms in later chapters and learn about them in detail. So far we have overviewed the research field of ELF in terms of its general profile, linguistic adaptability and multilingualism, as well as its contributions, limitations, and future directions. As a relatively new field, ELF shifts away from cartographical and categorical thinking and highlights the multilingual nature of global encounters.

Activity 4.3 Democracy

In the following extract, three international friends, Diego, Ken, and Nikhil, are exchanging messages on Facebook about a cartoon (Figure 4.3) which has been posted by Ken. After examining this digital communication, give your answers to the questions below. Discuss the answers with others in small groups if possible.

Figure 4.3 A wolf in sheep's clothing

Diego: Colombian; Ken: Thai; Nikhil: Indian

01 Diego: Sometimes ...
02 Ken: Always.
03 Diego: Jajajaja. Unfortunately, you may be right.

04 Nikhil: Yayyy ... Look the speaker on the stage is a goat, just like us.
05 Ken: No ... We are more cute. 5555

(Adapted from Sangiamchit, 2018: 352)

Questions

Q1 How do you interpret the Facebook cartoon?
Q2 How would you read "Jajajaja" (line 03) and "5555" (line 05)?
Q3 What do Diego, Ken, and Nikhil think of the cartoon? How about you?
Q4 Compare the cartoon and text messages. Do you find a discrepancy between them? If so, does it have any effect on communication?

Feedback: *The Facebook cartoon is a satire on democracy in which a wolf and a flock of sheep represent a politician and the general public. The sneaky wolf manipulates a puppet sheep to obtain support from them for his own benefit. All the Facebook participants are amused by this depiction of democracy, and their meanings are created through the integration of the cartoon and text messages. Have you noticed that laughter is expressed as "Jajajaja" (line 03) and "5555" (line 05), both of which are pronounced as hahahaha in Spanish and Thai, respectively? It is possible that Ken and Nikhil read "Jajajaja" as such with no problem, owing to their experience of digital communication. Notably, Nikhil refers to the ruled animals as goats (line 04), and this different interpretation does not seem to cause any communicative problems. In India and thereabouts, goats are more common than sheep, and we can easily guess that the participants consider either goats or sheep to be symbols of the weak and dependent, as per their cultural backgrounds. All in all, this Facebook exchange serves as an example to consider the notions of transmodality, EMF, and transcultural communication.*

Chapter summary

In this chapter, our discussion centred on the research sphere of Global Englishes, which comprises two major fields: WE and ELF. English serves as a global language, thanks to its adaptability in word structure and arrangement. From a WE perspective, the global spread of English is understood as having national or regional English varieties in the world. These varieties are established over generations through extensive use in society, including education. They have unique linguistic features which may be documented as rules and which are expected to represent local identities and cultures. Accordingly, their target speech communities and target cultures are locally definable, frequently at the national level. However, we argued that such a nationalistic or a locally minded approach is not always helpful to consider global communication.

From an ELF perspective, the global spread of English is understood as multilingual contact, occasionally involving L1 English speakers of different origins. Relevant domains are manifold and beyond geographical boundaries, such as academia, business, and digital communication. Empirically, mutual understanding through this global language depends on the practice of adjusting and adapting its use in a situationally appropriate manner. Here, multilingual English users are likely to have more linguistic resources to adjust and adapt than monolingual counterparts. Meanwhile, it is not foreseeable what cultures, communities, identities, and power relations become relevant to each global interaction through available meaning-making modes. We suggested that ELF theory seeks to take a holistic approach to global communication as multilingual, transcultural, and transmodal. However, this approach is not always welcomed as it is complex and not easy to understand.

Notes

1 http://ice-corpora.net/ice/index.html (accessed 30 September 2020).
2 Smith (1976) is reproduced in the *Journal of English as a Lingua Franca*, Volume 4, Issue 1 (2015).
3 www.univie.ac.at/voice/ (accessed 30 September 2020).
4 www.helsinki.fi/en/researchgroups/english-as-a-lingua-franca-in-academic-settings/research/elfa-corpus (accessed 30 September 2020).
5 www.helsinki.fi/en/researchgroups/english-as-a-lingua-franca-in-academic-settings/research/wrelfa-corpus (accessed 30 September 2020).
6 https://corpus.eduhk.hk/ace/ (accessed 30 September 2020).

Further reading

Baker, W. (2018). English as a lingua franca and intercultural communication. In J. Jenkins, W. Baker, & M. Dewey (Eds.), *The Routledge handbook of English as a lingua franca* (pp. 25–36). Abingdon: Routledge. The chapter illustrates the complex and emergent nature of culture and identity in communication among multilinguals, as well as the associated awareness required.

Ishikawa, T. (2015). Academic rigour in criticising English as a Lingua Franca. *Englishes in Practice*, 2, 39–48. doi: 10.1515/eip-2015-0002. A short review of how ELF enquiry has been misrepresented and unjustifiably criticised by some scholars to meet their various needs.

Jenkins, J. (2017). ELF and WE: Competing or complementing paradigms? In E.L. Low & A. Pakir (Eds.), *World Englishes: Rethinking paradigms* (pp. 12–28). Abingdon: Routledge. The chapter explains both the contribution of WE to the development of ELF and the complementary nature of these research fields as constituents of Global Englishes.

Part II

Critical approaches to culture, language, and Global Englishes

5 Cross-cultural and intercultural communication

Introduction

The influential linguist Deborah Tannen once claimed that "[t]he fate of the earth depends on cross-cultural communication" (1986/2011: 43). At the same time intercultural communication (the term we prefer) is part of daily life for many of us. We live and work in societies in which many different languages and cultures are present (even if they are not always recognised). We may hear and see a diversity of languages and cultural practices in our workplaces, educational institutions, social and family lives. Therefore, intercultural communication, as it is understood in this book, is not something strange or exotic, but rather a normal communicative practice for many of us. Nonetheless, despite its everyday nature, understanding intercultural communication can be difficult. How do we decide what is considered intercultural communication and what is not? Do cultural differences help or hinder communication? How do we explore cultural differences without generating stereotypes? How can we account for the diversity of cultural groupings that people may identify with or make use of in communication? What can the global use of English as a lingua franca in a wide variety of cultural settings and with a huge diversity of users tell us about the processes of intercultural communication?

In the first section of this chapter we draw together the ideas presented so far in relation to culture, language, and Global Englishes and relate this specifically to answering questions about intercultural communication. We provide characterisations of intercultural communication, distinguishing between traditional **cross-cultural communication** approaches and intercultural communication approaches, and explore the differences between each. The problems with essentialism in cross-cultural communication perspectives, as well as the limitations of intercultural communication research in general, are discussed. You will be asked to consider the advantages and disadvantages of both cross-cultural and intercultural communication perspectives, as well as the dangers of essentialism in any intercultural approach. We focus on contemporary critical approaches to intercultural communication through core notions of **third places**, small cultures, **interculturality**, and transcultural communication, with examples provided for each approach. The links between Global Englishes research and intercultural communication are also considered. Finally, the notion of transcultural communication, as transcending rather than being in between cultural and linguistic boundaries, is introduced to be explored in more depth later in the textbook.

Activity 5.1 An intercultural story part 1

A young English teacher from the UK is in his first teaching job in a language school in Thailand. He enters his classroom to find 25 students. The maximum class size is supposed to be 15, and they do not really all fit in the room; it is very cramped, making classroom activities difficult. He teaches the class, but as soon as it is finished he goes to see the manager of the school, who is Thai. He explains the situation to the manager and the problems caused by the excess of students. Throughout this the manager listens with a smile on his face, saying nothing. At the end of the teacher's explanation the manager grins, but says nothing, and walks away. The young teacher is now rather confused and upset. The manager appears not to be taking his problem seriously. He did not acknowledge his problem or make any offer to remedy it. In fact, the teacher thinks his response was quite dismissive and the grin and smile on the manager's face reinforced this impression for him.

The next day, with some reluctance, the teacher returns to the class. However, on entering the class he is surprised to find 15 students there and the correct furniture arrangements. A new class has been started in the next room with the other 10 students. All of the teacher's concerns from the previous day have been addressed, leaving him rather confused. A colleague explains that a smile and a grin is a very normal response to a problem for Thai people, not a sign of condescension or dismissiveness. Furthermore, listening in silence is also an appropriate communicative response when someone is complaining. The English teacher has just learned an important lesson in intercultural communication.

(Adapted from Baker, 2015: 15)

Questions

Q1 How would you interpret what happened in this example of intercultural interaction?

Q2 Were cultural differences a factor in the apparent miscommunication?

Discuss your answers with others if possible, before reading the interpretation below.

Interpretation 1: *This is an example of miscommunication in intercultural communication. The participants have different expectations about how a particular interaction should proceed, which leads to misunderstanding on the part of the English teacher. We could explain this by examining the different expectations in the UK and Thailand for complaining/conflict and the role of smiles and silence in communication in each of these cultures. If the teacher is going to get along in Thailand, he is going to have to adjust his expectations of how communication proceeds and not presume the sort of responses he is familiar with from the UK.*

We will return to this example at the end of the chapter and provide a different interpretation of the interaction.

5.1 Characterising intercultural communication

Intercultural communication is a very wide field of study that cuts across many disciplines. For example, you may take a course in intercultural communication while studying anthropology, applied linguistics, business, cultural studies, education, nursing, management, and sociology, among others. Intercultural 'training' is also a feature of in-service education in many professional organisations. Therefore, as with concepts of culture discussed in Chapter 1, given its multidisciplinary nature a single definition of intercultural communication is not possible. However, again similar to culture, there are shared characteristics of intercultural communication as a field of research and education that can be identified. In this chapter, we will outline some of these key features with a particular focus on linguistic aspects of intercultural communication.

One way to understand intercultural communication is to examine the history of its development as a subject of study. Ingrid Piller suggests "that discourses of culture, cultural difference and intercultural communication arose in the historical context of the nineteenth and twentieth centuries as part of the processes of colonialism" (2017: 14). These discourses typically emphasised difference and otherness and were used to justify the supposed superiority of colonial powers and their 'right' to subjugate more 'primitive' others. As such, these approaches to intercultural communication made use of exotic and stereotyped views of 'other' people and did little to promote intercultural understanding. Looked at from a contemporary perspective they serve as a useful reminder of the power relations that are part of the process of constructing cultural characterisations. Karen Risager (2007) argues that at around the same time intercultural communication also took a more central place in language education with the idea of a language associated with a particular nation and culture becoming more prominent. This approach linking language, culture, and nation is still prominent in language education today. For instance, the rationale for learning French is typically that through doing this you will learn about the French nation, people, and culture. An important writer in intercultural communication studies has been Edward T. Hall (e.g., 1959) who is often described as the 'father' of cross-cultural and intercultural communication research. Hall's interest in intercultural communication began with military training in the Cold War period (1940s–1990s) and, unsurprisingly, also focused on differences between cultures at a national level. Within the field of business and management, Geert Hofstede (e.g., 1991) has been highly influential with a similar nation-based approach to intercultural communication in relation to business organisations.

As can be seen from this brief overview of the development of intercultural communication research, there has been an emphasis on comparing cultures at the national level and the correlation of language, culture, and nation. However, this approach has become increasingly criticised for taking stereotyped and essentialist perspectives on culture. Assuming cultural differences based on a person's nationality creates an 'us' and 'them' dichotomy which is more likely to hinder rather than help intercultural communication. As Piller writes, "some of the research that has come to centrally define the field is certainly cringe inducing in the ways in which it reproduces essentialist discourses of culture rather than questions them" (2011: 172). In order to avoid these "essentialist discourses", a more critical approach to characterising culture, language, nation, and the relationships between them and to individuals is needed.

5.2 Cross-cultural and intercultural communication

A way to help think about the differences between essentialist and critical approaches to intercultural communication is to make a distinction between cross-cultural communication and intercultural communication. While the terms are sometimes used synonymously, here they will be distinguished to illustrate the differences between the earlier cross-cultural approaches to intercultural communication, described in the previous section, and more critical intercultural perspectives. In cross-cultural perspectives, cultures are compared at a national level for supposed similarities and differences in behaviours. So, for example, a set of features may be identified as typical of Japanese people's communicative practices and another set of features identified as British people's communicative practices. The two sets of communicative practices will then be compared and similarities and differences identified. These in turn may lead to recommendations for communication between the two groups which avoid miscommunication or misunderstanding. Hofstede's research (e.g., 1991) into communication in business organisations is a well-known and well-used example of this approach. Hofstede identifies a number of dimensions of culture that can be used to compare differences between countries. One of these dimensions is 'uncertainty avoidance': "The extent to which the members of a culture feel threatened by ambiguous or unknown situations and have created beliefs and institutions that try to avoid these" (Hofstede et al., 2010). Comparing Japan and the UK on this dimension, a large difference is noted, and the following advice is given for Japan: "Managers ask for all the detailed facts and figures before taking any decision. This high need for Uncertainty Avoidance is one of the reasons why changes are so difficult to realize in Japan". And for the UK: "In work terms this results in planning that is not detail oriented – the end goal will be clear ... but the detail of how we get there will be light and the actual process fluid and flexible to emerging and changing environment".[1]

In contrast, intercultural communication perspectives are interested in "the study of distinct cultural or other groups in interaction with each other" (Scollon & Scollon, 2001: 539). This is a very different approach to comparing cultures at the national level. By focusing on the interaction, it recognises that individuals may act differently in *inter*cultural communication to *intra*cultural communication (communication between people from the same culture) and that cultural categories, similarities, and differences may be changeable and negotiable. It does not assume that cultural differences will necessarily be related to nations (although it does not deny that this can be an important difference) and it recognises people as individuals, not simply as representations of an assumed national culture. As Scollon and Scollon propose, in intercultural communication research "the analysis would not presuppose cultural membership but rather ask how does the concept of culture arise in these social actions. Who has introduced culture as a relevant category, for what purposes, and with what consequences?" (2001: 545). The differences between cross-cultural and intercultural approaches can be summarised as in Table 5.1.

It is important to note that this table is a simplification of the two approaches and many studies may have elements of both of these approaches. Furthermore, while the position taken here is generally critical of cross-cultural communication studies due to the essentialist perspective, there are times when comparisons of cultures at a national level or scale may be helpful, especially as regards people's beliefs and ideologies about culture. Indeed, national cultures, while only one level or scale of culture, are still a powerful cultural identification and reference. We also need to be careful not to over-simplify the distinctions between intercultural communication and intracultural

Table 5.1 Cross-cultural communication versus intercultural communication

Cross-cultural communication studies	*Intercultural communication studies*
The study of the communicative practices of distinct cultural groups independent from interaction (e.g., Chinese communicative practices versus German communicative practices)	The study of the communicative practices of distinct cultural or other groups in interaction with each other (e.g., Italians communicating with English)
Cultures are seen as separable entities	Cultures are not bounded entities with national borders, but fluid and dynamic with blurred boundaries
Cultures are viewed as relatively homogeneous	Cultures are heterogeneous, containing a great deal of variety among their members
Cultures are viewed at a national level	National cultures are one of many discourse communities which can be drawn upon in communication; others include gender, generation, profession, ethnicity, etc.
A priori assumption about cultural groupings	No a priori assumptions about the discourse communities, cultural or otherwise, that will be drawn on, with participants located in between adaptable and hybrid cultures
Experimental and quantitative research	Qualitative research using naturalistic recordings of instances of intercultural communication

(Based on Scollon & Scollon, 2001 from Baker, 2015: 22)

communication. People who identify with a shared culture can differ in many other ways related to class, gender, religion, profession, education, and so forth, which may be highly salient in understanding their communication. Likewise, people who identify with different cultures may share much else (for example, profession and educational background), meaning that communication is not especially influenced by their different cultural orientations. We will return to these issues when we examine language, culture, and identity.

We are now in a position to develop a more nuanced characterisation of intercultural communication compared to the essentialist cross-cultural definition that focused on comparing bounded national cultures. Our characterisation focuses instead on the level of individual interactions and the influence that cultural and linguistic identifications and differences have on this. As Zhu explains, "the field of intercultural communication is primarily concerned with how individuals, in order to achieve their communication goals, negotiate cultural or linguistic differences which may be perceived relevant by at least one party in the interaction" (2019: 210). To this definition, we would add that cultural and linguistic differences may also be perceived as important by researchers, with the caveat that their relevance needs to be empirically or theoretically justified and not simply assumed.

Finally, in cross-cultural communication research, cultural differences are seen as a 'problem' to be solved in 'difficult' communicative situations. In contrast, intercultural communication research views cultural differences as one of many differences in interactions which participants draw on, adapt, and negotiate. Differences are not necessarily seen as problems and much intercultural communication is viewed as successful with an interest in what makes the communication successful, rather than how 'difficulties' are overcome.

Activity 5.2 Cross-cultural and intercultural communication perspectives

Read the following description from Hofstede on the dimension of individualism ("the degree of interdependence a society maintains among its members" (Hofstede et al., 2010; emphasis removed)) in China and Germany.

> At a score of 20 China is a highly collectivist culture where people act in the interests of the group and not necessarily of themselves. In-group considerations affect hiring and promotions with closer in-groups (such as family) are getting preferential treatment. Employee commitment to the organization (but not necessarily to the people in the organization) is low. Whereas relationships with colleagues are cooperative for in-groups they are cold or even hostile to out-groups. Personal relationships prevail over task and company.
>
> The German society is a truly Individualist one (67). Small families with a focus on the parent-children relationship rather than aunts and uncles are most common. There is a strong belief in the ideal of self-actualization. Loyalty is based on personal preferences for people as well as a sense of duty and responsibility. This is defined by the contract between the employer and the employee. Communication is among the most direct in the world following the ideal to be "honest, even if it hurts" – and by this giving the counterpart a fair chance to learn from mistakes.
>
> (www.hofstede-insights.com/country-comparison/china,germany/)

Questions

Q1 Do you think these descriptions would be helpful for you if you wanted to communicate with someone from China or Germany? Why/why not?

Q2 If you have experience of communicating with people from these nations, does this match your experiences in all cases?
Q3 How might these descriptions be criticised from an intercultural perspective?

Feedback: *These characterisations of culture might help give you an idea of possible areas of difference between cultures and areas of misunderstanding or miscommunication. However, they are very generalised and simplistic and somewhat stereotyped. It is unlikely that these characterisations would apply to all people from these countries in all settings. As such, we need to be very careful when making cultural generalisations as they may hinder, rather than help, intercultural communication by setting up stereotypes of others.*

5.3 Critical approaches to intercultural communication

As highlighted in the previous section and the earlier chapters in this book, when trying to understand intercultural communication we need to adopt a critical approach to intercultural communication and to the terminology used. We need to recognise that languages and cultures are variable and negotiable, not fixed and static. They are constructed in interaction, not pre-given and established. We can only understand the links between languages and cultures by examining each instance of intercultural communication (see the earlier discussion of the language-culture nexus in Chapter 2.2) and we should try to avoid overgeneralisations that can result in stereotyped and simplistic representations. Just as culture itself was best described as a process and 'verb', rather than a noun, so intercultural communication should also be viewed not as a thing but as a process, or, as Ingrid Piller terms it, "a social practice in motion" (2011: 174).

However, it is equally important to acknowledge that people do not have complete freedom in constructing and negotiating language and culture choices, references, and links. The ideological dimensions and power structures present in intercultural communication must be recognised. While in voluntary and reasonably equal intercultural interaction there may be quite a large degree of freedom in how cultures are constructed and represented and the language choices made, in less equitable interactions the more powerful group may impose its interpretations of these categories on the less powerful group. Research on immigration interviews, for example, has shown how the imposition of particular characterisations of culture and language by more powerful government officials on less powerful immigrant groups can have negative and disempowering consequences for immigrants (Blommaert, 2010; Guido, 2012). In relation to the use of

English for intercultural communication the link between the English language and Anglophone cultures often works to the advantage of the Anglophone world, positioning Anglophone speakers as 'superior' or the 'norm'. In contrast, other speakers of English, who, as we have seen, are the majority of users of English for intercultural communication, are positioned as different and outside the 'norm' and, thus, deficient and in a less powerful position.

We also need to be careful that we do not adopt neo-essentialist perspectives in intercultural communication (Holliday, 2011). Neo-essentialism was introduced in Chapter 1.4 in relation to culture. Neo-essentialism approaches cultures as complex, made up of many different groups and with individuals identifying with a range of groupings. However, this complexity is typically seen as being *within* the bounds of a national culture. National cultures are still seen as the dominant norm, with other cultural groupings being different from this 'norm' and viewed as 'sub-cultures'. In relation to intercultural communication, neo-essentialism retains a clear distinction between one's 'own' culture and the 'foreign' other culture. Holliday describes this as the 'intercultural line', which is "an indelible line between Self and Other" (2011: 164). Such perspectives can lead to stereotyping or 'othering', which is more likely to hinder rather than help intercultural communication. We will return to issues of the 'self' and 'other' in the discussion of identity in Chapter 6.

Given the difficulties with terminology in intercultural communication research and the dangers of stereotyping and neo-essentialism, some scholars have suggested that we need new terms. In particular, Scollon et al. (2012) argue that culture has become too large and vague a term to have much value to researchers. Instead they recommend focusing on the level of discourse and discourse systems (see Chapter 1.2) and propose an 'inter-discourse' approach. Yet, many replacement terms, whether discourse or other alternatives, such as identity, also have the same problem as culture in that they refer to a large number of different phenomena and ideas, making them broad and rather vague in meaning (Baker, 2015). Moreover, due to the pervasiveness of culture as a category in intercultural communication it is difficult to ignore. As Zhu reminds us, "we also need to take care not to confuse the need to problematize the notion of culture at the conceptual level with the need for a working definition of culture for those disciplines and studies which investigate group variation" (2019: 199). Therefore, we believe that culture is still a useful term in understanding intercultural communication, but that we should approach it critically and not assume either its relevance or meaning in an interaction. Furthermore, in reviewing terminology, we will suggest later in this book that the 'inter' of intercultural communication is potentially problematic and requires further thought.

5.4 Intercultural communication and intercultural groups

In this section, we will outline five current approaches to understanding intercultural communication and intercultural groupings in applied linguistics which illustrate the more critical perspectives discussed previously. These are third places (Kramsch, 1993), **communities of practice** (Wenger, 1998), small cultures (Holliday, 1999; 2011), interculturality (Zhu, 2019), and transcultural communication (Baker & Sangiamchit, 2019).

Third places

The concept of third places or **third spaces** as used in applied linguistics is primarily drawn from the work of Clare Kramsch (1993) in language learning and teaching and Homi Bhabha (1994) in postcolonial studies. Both concepts share the idea of cultural adaptation and hybridity in multicultural spaces that mix elements of different cultures and differ from established 'national' cultures. From this perspective, cultural references and practices in intercultural communication are seen as occupying a space in between cultures but not the same as, or fixed to, any one culture. In this way, researchers argue, third spaces avoid the binary distinction of 'our' culture and 'other' cultures (Zhou & Pilcher, 2018). Kramsch's discussion in relation to second-language learning and use is particularly relevant to intercultural communication. She proposes a 'cultural faultline' (1993: 205) in which linguistic and cultural practices and products occupy a 'third space' (1993: 233) that is neither part of the language users' first language and culture (L1/C1) nor the target second language and culture (L2/C2). Instead, this third space allows for more liminal or dynamic linguistic and cultural practices that are created in situ.

The following example from a discussion at a Thai university between a group of Thai students (Oy and Nami), an Australian teacher (Chas), and the researcher (Will) illustrates how third places can help us to understand the way cultural practices are negotiated and constructed in interactions. In this extract the participants are deciding whether to end their discussion or not and negotiating who should make the decision.

Extract 5.1 The great up-to-you

01 Oy:	so carry on or drop it
02 Nami:	I hate saying up to you because I'm not really conservative type girl ((laughs)) don't like it
03 Oy:	err I don't like it either

04 Chas:	make a decision then ((gestures with hands to Nami and Oy))
05 Oy:	yeah you make it you're older than me ((gestures with hand to Nami))
06 Chas:	((laughs))
07 Will:	((laughs))
08 Nami:	[I think like. I think that's (?)]
09 Oy:	[a bit of respect] ((smiling and laughing))
10 Nami:	[thank you very much] ((places hand on Oy's shoulder smiling and laughing))
11 Will:	[that's very Thai] very conservative and Thai defer to the older person
12 Nami:	you used to be Thai ((places hand on Oy's shoulder laughs))
13 Oy:	((laughs))
14 Nami:	actually no I don't think so actually I have a lot of things to do
15 Chas:	ok
16 Oy:	oh ok right (I'll go as well)

(Baker, 2009a: 576)

Notes

((laughs))	nonlinguistic features of the transcription
[xxx]	overlapping or interrupted speech
(?)	inaudible
(xxx)	uncertain that word is correctly transcribed

Nami explains her interpretation of the exchange in a follow-up interview.

> *Nami:* oh that's the great up-to-you … yes that's because Thai people if you observe I think you observe that girls like to say they don't like to make the decision … everything is just man make a decision and girls aren't allowed to make a decision here in this society and I don't like it because I have my own right to do that too to do that too umm and so that's why I was like making it as a joke.
> (Baker, 2009a: 579)

But she goes on to make clear that she does not think that by rejecting this traditional Thai cultural practice of decision-making she is adopting Anglophone norms. Rather, she believes that it is important for 'new generations' to change cultures. Through learning and using

English she learns about different cultures and norms but she does not feel she is following those norms either. She feels she is adapting and adopting those cultural practices most relevant to her and as such can be seen as constructing a third space between cultures.

> *Nami:* ... yeah it's not not like a passion that I want to be like American people I want to be like British people it's not like that but it's just the way oh that's interesting ... you should develop your life yeah it's not just the Thai way but also the other way that you think that is good from that.
>
> (Baker, 2011: 208)

The notion of third places has been very helpful in going beyond some of the most simplistic interpretations of cross-cultural communication in which cultures and languages are bounded at the national scale and interlocutors are seen as communicating in a binary way associated with one culture or another. However, the concept has been criticised for establishing a new set of simplifications and stereotypes and in adopting a neo-essentialist perspective (e.g., Holliday, 2011; Baker, 2015). There is a danger that by using third places we are assuming that people in intercultural communication will be in between particular cultures. Yet, as we will see later in this book on transcultural communication, it is not always possible to identify the cultures participants are 'in between'. It is also possible for people to be many different things at the same time and identify with different cultures without feeling in between them. Nonetheless, while it is important not to allow third places to become reified and stereotyped, the ideas of cultural adaptation and hybridity are significant in understanding many aspects of intercultural communication. Furthermore, more recent concepts of third places have suggested different interpretations that open up discussions of the more transformative and transgressive nature of third spaces that go beyond binary distinctions between cultures (Kramsch, 2009; MacDonald, 2019; Zhou & Pilcher, 2018).

Communities of practice

In recognising that cultural groupings are associated with many different types of groupings beyond the national scale, such as ethnicity, gender, profession, religion, and generation, new frameworks for conceptualising cultural groupings are needed. One proposal has been the use of the communities of practice framework. This was originally developed by Lave and Wenger (1991) as a social theory of learning rather than in relation to culture or intercultural communication; however, as we will see throughout this chapter, it has been very influential in intercultural communication theory. The most well-known definition of communities of practice is given by Eckert and McConnell-Ginet as: "an aggregate of people who come together around mutual engagement in an endeavour. Ways of doing things, ways of talking, beliefs, values, power relationships – in short, practices – emerge in the course of this mutual endeavour" (1992: 464). Wenger (1998) went on to develop the concept and propose three core criteria for a community of practice.

1. Mutual engagement – in order to establish a community the members have to interact regularly with each other face-to-face and/or, more recently, virtually.
2. Joint enterprise – a goal or shared purpose that motivates community participants' regular interactions with each other.
3. Shared repertoires – a common range of resources that the members develop to negotiate and share meaning. This can include "routines, words, tools, ways of doing things, stories, gestures, symbols, genres" (Wenger, 1998: 83).

Communities of practice are something we see all around us in everyday life, for instance, in the workplace, social clubs, and virtual communities in social networks like Facebook (see Chapter 11).

As noted by Ehrenreich (2018), language plays a central role in both the shared practices and repertoires of communities of practice. Thus, this concept has been useful to ELF researchers in examining certain types of cultural groupings in intercultural communication through Global Englishes, such as the formation of multilingual and multicultural international students groups (Kalocsai, 2014; Ra, 2018), international business groups (Ehrenreich, 2009; Kankaanranta & Louhiala-Salminen, 2018), and virtual groups in digital communication (Vettorel, 2014). Yet, we need to be cautious in how we apply it since it is not applicable to all cultural groupings (see Baker, 2015; Ehrenreich, 2018). On the one hand, for many intercultural encounters the meeting will be too brief to establish the kind of links described in communities of practice (Pitzl, 2018a). On the other hand, cultural groupings may be more long-term but rather nebulous and changeable in their links, with no clear shared goals, for instance, groups of family or friends, as described in Holliday's (2011) small cultures below. Additionally, large-scale cultural groupings such as nations and ethnic or religious groups are much more diverse than the communities of practice framework encompasses.

Small cultures

The idea of small cultures is a perspective on culture introduced by the applied linguist Adrian Holliday (1999; 2011) as an alternative to essentialist, stereotyped nationalist accounts of culture (see

Chapter 1.2). Like communities of practice, small cultures focus on how cultures are constructed through interactions between small groups of people. These small cultures include everyday groupings such as families, groups of friends, neighbourhoods, work colleagues, classrooms, and leisure clubs. In small culture formation a sense of group cohesion is constructed through the building up of shared practices and discourses which become conventionalised and eventually reified (at which stage the conventions become 'invisible' and how they were constructed is forgotten; in other words, they are taken for granted). There is also a sense of the group as a distinct culture that is different from 'others'. It is important to stress that small cultures are not sub-cultures within larger national cultures. National cultures are viewed as one of many interacting factors that may, or may not, influence the formation of small cultures. Furthermore, we are all members of many different small cultures that we can orientate towards and interact with in different ways at different times. To illustrate this point Holliday (2011) draws on research from an ethnographic study of Southall, a cosmopolitan, multicultural suburb of London.

> The vast majority of all adult Southallians [each] saw themselves as members of several communities, each, with its own culture. The same person could speak and act as a member of the Muslim community in one context, in another take sides against other Muslims as a member of the Pakistani community, and in a third count himself part of the Punjabi community that excluded other Muslims but included Hindus, Sikhs, and even Christians.
>
> (Baumann, 1996: 5, cited in Holliday, 2011: 136–137; emphasis removed)

Despite the many similarities between small cultures and communities of practice, which Holliday acknowledges, he also states that small cultures are different and encompass more variable groupings due to having a much less instrumental or goal-focused orientation (2013: 162; 2019: 6). Most recently, Holliday has described "small culture formation on the run" (2013: 56) to emphasise that creating cultures is something we continuously do to help us make sense of and interact with society. This can include both the more permanent communities such as neighbourhoods and family groups but also more temporary encounters such as a conversation with a taxi driver during a taxi journey. Holliday suggests that, "on a daily basis we invent and perform routines and even invent small rituals as we engage, plan, solve problems, get used to things, move from one group to another" (2013: 56; 2019: 72). Small cultures offer a way of understanding how cultures are constructed in intercultural interaction that centres on what happens in the interaction itself rather than making use of essentialist pre-defined cultural categories.

Interculturality

As with other critical approaches in intercultural communication, interculturality attempts to avoid essentialist perspectives on culture through examining how cultural practices and identities are negotiated and constructed in interaction, rather than making a priori assumptions about cultural groupings (e.g., Young & Sercombe, 2010; Zhu, 2019). As Zhu explains:

> interculturality represents a line of investigation that departs from traditions of seeing cultural memberships or cultural differences, largely, if not always, as something 'given', 'static', or as something 'one either has or does not have'. Instead, it problematises the notion of cultural identities and emphasises the *emergent*, *discursive* and *inter-* nature of interactions.
>
> (2019: 219; original emphasis)

There is also a focus on identity as a central part of understanding the role of culture in communication and, again, we will return to the intercultural and identity later in Chapter 6. The overall approach to investigating interculturality is summarised by Zhu through the following questions.

1. Are cultural memberships always relevant to intercultural interactions?
2. What do participants do with cultural memberships?
3. How do participants do cultural identities?
4. What interactional resources are available for doing cultural identities?
5. Why do people bother with interculturality?
6. How far can participants go when doing interculturality? (2019: 220)

Again, in keeping with critical approaches, cultural practices and identities are seen as a process rather than an end product and are typically investigated through detailed analysis (frequently discourse analysis) of people's interactions and particularly the language used to construct and negotiate cultural identities. For example, Zhu (2010) investigates intergenerational talk in diasporic families in the UK. Her analysis of participants' talk about social, cultural, and linguistic practice illustrates how sociocultural practices and identities are made relevant to the interaction but also how the younger generation bring about changes in practices and develop new cultural identities. At the same time, interculturality researchers also highlight that we are not free to construct any cultural practices or identify with any cultural group that we wish. Issues around power and ideology are an important restraint on how we construct our cultural identities and how others perceive us. These are often related to issues of nationality and ethnicity including racism and othering (Zhu & Li, 2016). Zhu (2019) gives the following example to illustrate this point.

> Frank Wu, the first Asian American law professor at Howard University Law School, shared his experience about the *perpetual foreigner syndrome*, a problem facing many Asian Americans in everyday social interactions:
>
> '*Where are you from*?' is a question I like answering. '*Where are you really from*?' is a question I really hate answering ... For Asian Americans, the questions frequently come paired like that ... More than anything else that unites us, everyone with an Asian face who lives in America is afflicted by the perpetual foreigner syndrome. We are figuratively and even literally returned to Asia and ejected from America. (Wu, 2002, p. [14], Italics original)
>
> (Zhu, 2019: 226–227)

Transcultural communication

A recently emerging approach to understanding intercultural communication is transcultural communication. We will explore transcultural communication in detail later in the book but it would be helpful to introduce some of the central ideas at this stage. This perspective draws on the notion of transcultural and transnational flows outlined in Chapter 1.3 in relation to culture and globalisation (Appadurai, 1996; Hannerz, 1996) and Chapter 2 in relation to the complex links between languages and cultures (e.g., Risager, 2006; Pennycook, 2007). To recap, transcultural flows describe the expanding scale and complexity of social networks and the flows of cultural practices and languages through these networks which result in an increased diversity of cultural practices, identifications, and communication. In intercultural communication this means that the links between the languages used and the cultural references and meanings cannot be taken for granted. Instead, the connection is always an empirical question that must be investigated in each instance of communication (Risager, 2006). Risager (2012: 111; 2020: 120–121) outlines how these cultural flows can consist of different forms involving: linguistic flows of particular codes, such as

English; linguacultural flows of meanings related to a particular first-language use; discursive flows of meaning not associated with any specific language, such as the discourse of environmentalism; and other non-language cultural flows, such as music or images. Other researchers, such as Pennycook (2007), emphasise how these increasingly fluid and dynamic connections between languages and cultures made possible through transcultural flows open up new spaces for cultural practices and identifications.

More recently, similar claims have been made in relation to **translanguaging**, where participants in interactions "go beyond narrowly defined linguistic cues and transcend culturally defined language boundaries to achieve effective communication" (Li, 2018: 24–25). In other words, communication can be seen as going beyond named languages (such as Japanese and English) with interactants using whichever linguistic resources are necessary for effective communication. Likewise, Canagarajah (2013) investigates the relationships between the translingual practices of migrants and the construction of translocal spaces that combine and cross many different scales or levels of context and culture. While these perspectives underscore the inappropriateness of set language-culture correlations, especially at the national scale, they do not dismiss the national but rather approach it as one of many levels or scales. Most recently, transcultural communication approaches have questioned the 'inter' of intercultural communication. Instead of attempting to identify how participants are in between cultures or mixing elements of different named cultures and languages to create hybrid practices, a transcultural approach focuses on how participants move through cultures and languages, transforming and transcending linguistic and cultural boundaries in the process (Baker & Sangiamchit, 2019). We will return to explore transcultural communication in more detail in Chapter 10.

Summary

The five current approaches to intercultural communication and intercultural groups that we have outlined above all embrace a critical approach to culture where the focus is on investigating how cultures are negotiated and constructed in interaction. This means avoiding assumptions and preconceptions about the links between languages and cultures and the relevance of particular cultural categories and identifications. It also means that national cultures are viewed as just one of many cultural groupings that may, or may not, be relevant to intercultural communication. The five perspectives are summarised in Table 5.2.

Table 5.2 Five current approaches to intercultural communication and intercultural groups

Approach	*Main features*	*Examples*
Third places	Language and culture in intercultural communication occupy a 'third place' that is not part of the participants' first culture and language or a target culture and language. Culture and language become more free and liminal	Kramsch (1993); Zhou & Pilcher (2018)
Communities of practice	Used to describe groupings in non-essentialist terms with a focus on practices in which people come together around 'mutual engagement' in a 'joint endeavour' and in the process develop 'shared repertoires'. Limited to describing particular types of 'mid-level' groupings and not as relevant to larger- or smaller-scale cultural groupings and interactions	Wenger (1998); Ehrenreich (2009); Kalocsai (2014)
Small cultures	Cultures as constructed between small groups of people (e.g., families, classrooms, work) through shared practices and discourses. More relevant to understanding how people create culture in intercultural interactions than 'large' national cultural characterisations	Holliday (1999; 2011)
Interculturality	A focus on how culture and cultural identities are negotiated and constructed in intercultural interactions. It avoids pre-established assumptions about cultural identifications	Young & Sercombe (2010); Zhu (2019)
Transcultural communication	Drawing on transnational and transcultural flows, transcultural communication is particularly focused on how linguistic and cultural boundaries are transgressed and transcended in intercultural interactions, creating new sociocultural spaces, practices, and identities	Pennycook (2007); Baker & Sangiamchit (2019)

5.5 Global Englishes and intercultural communication

The use of English as a multilingua franca on a global scale (see Chapter 4.3, 4.4) is highly relevant in understanding intercultural and transcultural communication. In particular, ELF is by definition a form of intercultural communication since it involves users from different linguistic and cultural backgrounds. For example, Mauranen observes that "[a]s ELF gains ground in international communication, the intercultural perspective comes increasingly to the fore" (2012: 43).

Indeed, given the extensive use of ELF globally, it is likely to be the most common medium for intercultural communication. However, as we have already underlined in this book, it must be recognised that English in intercultural communication is used in a multilingual environment with other languages also present. The widespread use of ELF thus makes it a prime setting for investigating the complex and fluid links between language and culture in intercultural and transcultural communication. Though we are not claiming that there is anything unique about communication through ELF, what we observe in ELF is likely to be repeated in other forms of multilingual intercultural/transcultural communication. What is perhaps unique or different about ELF is the large scale on which it occurs, making communication through ELF an excellent source to observe and explore features of intercultural communication.

Global Englishes, and ELF research especially, have reported similar findings to the critical approaches to intercultural communication described previously. Intercultural communication is typically viewed as successful in ELF studies, with researchers interested in how participants achieve this, rather than the traditional cross-cultural focus on communicative difficulties and differences (Zhu, 2015). Language, identity, community, and culture are seen as constructed, variable, and negotiable with issues of power and ideology prevalent. The extensive data on intercultural communication through ELF provides ample evidence that communication through ELF is not culturally 'neutral', as has been claimed by some scholars (e.g., House, 2014). Moreover, as we have hopefully made clear throughout this book, language is always linked to culture in one way or another and to claim that there is a culturally neutral form of language is to misunderstand the nature of language and communication. While it may be true that at times there is nothing interesting or important for participants or researchers about culture, this does not mean that it is not present in communication. In cases where there are no significant cultural differences in communication, culture often becomes 'unnoticed' or 'invisible' to participants. Nonetheless, despite being 'invisible', culture is still crucial since without culture language would have no meaning or purpose.

Thus, participants in ELF studies have reported and have been observed using English to create and index multiple cultural resources and identities. Some of the key themes, which we will explore in more detail in Chapter 6, include:

- users of ELF moving between local L1 identities and more global orientations
- issues of ideology and power relationships in **cultural identity** construction and negotiation through ELF particularly as regards Anglophone 'native' speaker ideology

- the use of ELF as an important part of the construction of and identification with dynamic communities of practice in business, academia, and **virtual spaces**
- the construction of shared multilingual and multicultural identities in ELF interactions through the use of **code-switching** and translanguaging
- the role of adaptable, hybrid, and third-place identities with participants in ELF communication embracing being 'in between' and mediating between cultures or other groupings, as well as liminal and fluid identities

We believe that the fluid and emergent links between languages, cultures, and identities in ELF research challenge our understanding of the connections between these categories. Like intercultural communication research, in ELF studies the (super) diversity and complexity of languages and cultures highlights the difficulty and inappropriateness of attempting to establish set language-culture connections. The 'inter' of intercultural communication becomes problematic as it is frequently not clear in ELF research what cultures participants are 'in between'. This results, we argue, in the need for new thinking about intercultural communication such as that outlined in transcultural communication approaches.

Activity 5.3 An intercultural story part 2

A young English teacher from the UK is in his first teaching job in a language school in Thailand. He enters his classroom to find 25 students. The maximum class size is supposed to be 15, and they do not really all fit in the room; it is very cramped, making classroom activities difficult. He teaches the class, but as soon as it is finished he goes to see the manager of the school, who is Thai. He explains the situation to the manager and the problems caused by the excess of students. Throughout this the manager listens with a smile on his face, saying nothing. At the end of the teacher's explanation the manager grins, but says nothing, and walks away. The young teacher is now rather confused and upset. The manager appears not to be taking his problem seriously. He did not acknowledge his problem or make any offer to remedy it. In fact, the teacher thinks his response was quite dismissive and the grin and smile on the manager's face reinforced this impression for him.

The next day, with some reluctance, the teacher returns to the class. However, on entering the class he is surprised to find 15 students there and the correct furniture arrangements. A new class has been started in the next room with the other 10 students. All of the teacher's concerns from the previous day have been addressed, leaving him rather confused. A colleague explains that a smile and a grin is a very normal response to a problem for Thai people, not a sign of condescension or dismissiveness. Furthermore, listening in silence is also an appropriate communicative response when someone is complaining. The English teacher has just learned an important lesson in intercultural communication. If he is going to get along as an English teacher in Thailand, he is going to have to adjust his expectations of how communication proceeds and not presume the sort of responses he is familiar with from the UK.

(Adapted from Baker, 2015: 15)

Questions

Q1 Now that you have completed this chapter on intercultural communication, how would you interpret what happened in this example of intercultural interaction?

Q2 Would you make any changes to your previous interpretation?

Discuss your answers in groups if possible, before reading the interpretation below.

Interpretation 2: *If we follow interpretation 1, at the beginning of this chapter, we have already made a number of assumptions: first, that there is a cultural difference that gives rise to a 'problem' to be solved. An alternative interpretation is that the communication was actually reasonably successful. The teacher's concerns were clearly understood and addressed by the manager. Second, we have equated cultural difference with nationality, a British teacher and a Thai manager. Individuals identify with many different cultural, or other, groupings, with nationality being just one of them. In this example we should also consider that the participants' identities as teacher, employee, and manager are as relevant as being British or Thai. Linguistic issues are also important and should be included in our interpretation. The manager's proficiency in English is not particularly high and this may have influenced his responses. The employee has almost no ability to communicate in Thai. If the interaction had been in Thai, it might have been very different. Last, this is an intercultural interaction, both participants were aware of this, and it is likely that they proceeded accordingly by being flexible and open to different understandings. Indeed, the British teacher asked for clarification from a colleague, perhaps recognising that his communicative norms might not be appropriate in this situation.*

Q3 Was your interpretation closer to 1 or 2? Which interpretation do you find most convincing? Why?

Chapter summary

This chapter approached intercultural communication not as a problem to be solved, but as an everyday communicative practice for many of us. Intercultural communication was characterised as communication where cultural and linguistic differences are perceived as relevant to the interaction by participants and/or researchers. You should be familiar with the following approaches in intercultural communication:

- cross-cultural versus intercultural communication
- third places
- communities of practice
- small cultures
- interculturality
- transcultural communication

We explored the differences between traditional cross-cultural communication perspectives and more contemporary intercultural communication perspectives. In particular, we emphasised the danger of essentialism and stereotypes in cross-cultural communication approaches that often make use of static generalised national conceptions of culture. We contrasted this with more critical intercultural communication approaches that view culture as constructed, adaptable, and negotiable in interaction. Last, we looked at the links between Global Englishes, especially ELF studies, and intercultural communication. We suggested that the diversity and complexity of culture and language through English as a global lingua franca leads us to rethink some of the core concepts in intercultural communication, such as language, culture, and identity, and contributes to new ideas about transcultural communication.

Note

1 www.hofstede-insights.com/country-comparison/japan,the-uk/ (accessed 30 September 2020).

Further reading

Baker, W. (2015). *Culture and identity through English as a lingua franca: Rethinking concepts and goals in intercultural communication*. Berlin: De Gruyter Mouton. Chapter two contains a detailed discussion of intercultural communication and relates it directly to ELF research.

Piller, I. (2017). *Intercultural communication: A critical introduction* (2nd edn). Edinburgh: Edinburgh University Press. An accessible introduction to more critical approaches to intercultural communication.

Scollon, R., Scollon, S.W., & Jones, R.H. (2012). *Intercultural communication: A discourse approach* (3rd edn). Oxford: Wiley-Blackwell. A good discussion of critical and ethnographic perspectives on intercultural communication, including the Scollons' own discourse approach.

6 Culture, language, and identity

Introduction

Identity, like culture, is a subject that forms an important part of our everyday lives and is something we all have ideas and opinions about. Who we are (i.e., our identity) and which groups we belong to (i.e., our identifications) are fundamental questions for all of us. As the sociolinguist John Joseph (2004) notes, a simple response to the question of who we are might begin with our names; yet, how we define ourselves is typically more varied and complex than this. Most of us have many different identifications related to groupings such as gender, generation, ethnicity, profession, nation, region, family, and religion, among others. How these different identities interact and the role they have in culture and cultural identities is complex and constantly changing. Furthermore, the relationship between language and identity is a close and important one. Indeed, it is often suggested that in learning another language we are also learning a new identity. The role of English as a global language, which is no longer linked to any one nation or culture, brings up interesting issues of which groups we may, or may not, be identifying with through learning and using English.

This chapter begins with some core approaches to understanding identity with a focus on linguistic approaches that explain the relationships between language and identity. Essentialist and non-essentialist perspectives on identity are compared and we adopt a post-structuralist approach that emphasises the multiple and fluid identities we all have. Alongside this, the relationships between individual identities and group identities, including national identities, are critically explored, as well as notions of self-orientated and ascribed identities. The idea of cultural identities, as one of many identities, is introduced. Finally, we look at identity, and particularly cultural identity, in intercultural communication and Global Englishes. You will be asked to critically reflect on your own identities and consider issues of stereotyping and power relationships in intercultural communication.

Activity 6.1 Who do you think you are?

List all the different identities, identifications, or groups that you feel are part of 'who you are'. You may want to think of things such as gender, age, ethnicity, nation, profession, hobbies, family, class, etc. Include at least ten identities or groups.

Feedback: *You should find that the list is a very long one and you could probably keep adding to it! For example, the first author of this book wrote down: male, father, applied linguist, cyclist, Caucasian, British, middle-class, and middle-aged as just a few of the identities he ascribes to. Our identities are clearly multiple and complex things. Moreover, you will probably find that you adopt different identities in different settings and at different times. However, you may also feel that some identities are more fixed and stable (e.g., gender, ethnicity) while others are more flexible and changeable (e.g., professions, hobbies). You might also want to consider how much freedom you have (or don't have) in choosing identities.*

6.1 Characterising identity

Identities are typically described in applied linguistics as multiple, negotiable, and contested, and as a process rather than a fixed, unitary product or thing; nonetheless, within this approach there are a number of different perspectives. When discussing identity researchers may make distinctions between identity and **subjectivity** or **the self**. As Clare Kramsch explains, "Identity refers to identification with a social or cultural group, while subjectivity focuses on the ways in which the self is formed through the use of language and other symbolic systems, both intrapersonally and interpersonally" (2009: 25). In this book we will mainly focus on the external identification with social groups and the networks of groups we may orientate towards, or be associated with by others. While issues of subjectivity and the construction of the self are important, and there is much blurring between external identification and internal constructions of the self, the self will not be the main subject of discussion here. Yet, many of the theories of identity we draw on here have clear overlap with notions of the self, and subjectivity is a central issue in post-structuralist theories of identity (e.g., Norton, 2010). Furthermore, some scholars, such as the sociolinguist John Joseph (2004), argue that we cannot usefully distinguish between the internal construction of an individual identity and group identities.

Linked to the distinction between external identifications and internal constructions of self is the distinction between more stable, fixed 'core' identities and more flexible and changeable 'periphery' identities. The education scholar Phan Le Ha (2008) argues that cultural identities associated with nations and first languages are often viewed as core identities which are more permanent and central to a sense of self. In contrast, identities constructed through additional languages, such as Global Englishes, may be more peripheral and hence fluid and adaptable across time and space. Indeed, the extent to which identities are negotiable, changeable, or fixed has been an issue of concern and debate. Pavlenko and Blackledge (2004) put forward three types of identities: imposed identities (which are not negotiable), assumed identities (which are accepted and not negotiated), and negotiable identities (which can be contested and adapted by groups and individuals). This helps to highlight that we do not have complete freedom to choose or construct any identity we wish. For example, users of English as a lingua franca may regard themselves as competent *users* of the language but may be positioned by others as *learners* of the language (e.g., immigration officials, exam boards). Other identities which are more prestigious, such as being well-educated based on English proficiency, may be assumed and accepted with no negotiation. Finally, negotiable identities are those which can be contested and changed by groups or individuals. So, for example, the identity of a learner or user of English may be more negotiable in social interactions with other multilingual participants.

6.2 Identity and language

The link between language and identity is a strong one and, just as we discussed a language-culture nexus (Chapter 2.2) to illustrate the close link between the two concepts, we can discuss a language-identity nexus (Joseph, 2004) to highlight the close relationship of these two ideas. So, for example, the sociolinguist Bonny Norton writes that:

> [e]very time we speak, we are negotiating and renegotiating our sense of self in relation to the larger social world, and reorganizing that relationship across time and space. Our gender, race, class, ethnicity, sexual orientation, among other characteristics, are all implicated in this negotiation of identity.
>
> (2010: 350)

Joseph even goes as far as to claim that "the entire phenomenon of identity can be understood as a linguistic one" (2004: 12). While Joseph's claim may be slightly overstating the role of language in identity, there is general agreement that language is the main medium through which we construct and negotiate our identities and through which we perceive others' identities. Thus, when we speak or write we are engaged in a process of constructing our identities in the ongoing discourse. Additionally, others are forming opinions and ideas of who we are based on our speech or writing, just as we are of them.

The close link between language and how our identities are constructed and perceived by others in discourse underlines another important aspect of language and identity: power relationships. From the post-structuralist perspectives adopted in much applied linguistics research and in this book, languages, identities, communities, and cultures are viewed as heterogeneous and so sites of struggle and conflict. Thus, power structures and relationships are a key feature in understanding them. Much of this draws on the work of the sociologist Pierre Bourdieu (e.g., 1991) and especially the notion of social capital, which is the idea that some social practices have more social value and prestige, or 'capital', than others. In specific relation to language, we can discuss linguistic capital, in which certain forms of language have more linguistic and social capital than others. Therefore, if you speak with what is perceived as an 'educated' or 'standard' accent, vocabulary, and grammar, this may give you more social capital than another speaker who uses, for example, a local dialect, with a non-standard pronunciation, vocabulary, and grammar. Language use can, thus, be seen as one of the main ways in which a person's social position is constructed and represented. As Norton explains in reference to Bourdieu's work, "the value ascribed to speech cannot be understood apart from the person who speaks, and the person who speaks cannot be understood apart from larger networks of social relationships" (2010: 350).

However, it is important to point out that the relationships between languages, identity, and social status/power are not fixed in any of these aspects. For instance, while 'standard' accents may be perceived as better educated, regional accents may be considered more 'trustworthy'. Relationships also change over time, so in the UK there is no longer one 'standard' accent but rather a range of regional accents which are typically viewed at a similar status. Public media organisations such as the BBC have moved from a single standard (what was referred to as Received Pronunciation or RP) used by presenters in the past to a variety of accents now. Moreover, multilingualism and additional language learning and use adds a further level of complexity and fluidity to the relationships between language, community, identity, and power. In multilingual and multicultural settings and communities people may construct and negotiate variable identities which are not linked to any one community but are rather hybrid identities which mix cultures. Linked to this is the idea of third-place identities (discussed in Chapter 5.4), when people construct and negotiate identities which are not part of any one culture and community, but rather in between cultures (Bhabha, 1994; Kramsch, 1993). For example, in a study of urban multilingual communities in London, the sociolinguist Ben Rampton (1995/2018) identified what he described as 'liminal moments' when language users who are not part of a language community adopt and adapt the language of that community for their own uses and resist and subvert the dominant power structures. When they do this the language is altered by these new users to match their own purposes and needs. This, Rampton argues, illustrates the way in which linguistic and cultural identities are dynamic and interactive rather than "a set of reified ethnic units" which are fixed (1995/2018: 299). At the same time, people may not be 'in between' communities and cultures, but rather shuttling between multiple communities simultaneously without necessarily hybridising any of them (Canagarajah, 2007). As the education scholar Kumaravadivelu writes of his own experiences:

> [p]roponents of cultural hybridity would expect me to create a 'third culture', or a 'third space', without allowing either my inherited Indian culture or my learned American culture to fully determine my values and beliefs ... I do not believe I am dangling in cultural limbo. Instead I believe I live in several cultural domains at the same time – jumping in and out of them, sometimes with ease and sometimes with unease.
>
> (2008: 5)

Furthermore, learning an additional language opens up opportunities and spaces for the construction of new identities and we may feel that we are a 'different' person when we learn and use a new language. However, it is important to remember that while multilingualism illustrates the adaptable and fluid relationships between languages, identities, and communities, again, power issues are still present, and we do not have complete freedom to construct any identity we wish. We will return to the use of additional languages and its relationship to identity when we discuss Global Englishes and identity in more detail later in this chapter.

6.3 Identity, difference, and othering

A central part of our identity is that it is constructed as different to others at both the individual and group level. Our sense of self is as much about how we differ from others as it is about ourselves. This also applies to group identifications where the characteristics of any group we belong to are contrasted with the differing characteristics of 'other' groups. As the linguist Philip Riley expresses it: "In social terms, identity can, by definition, only be treated in reference with others, since others are its principal source. Discussing social identity as if it were an intrinsic property of one person makes about as much sense as discussing the sound of one hand clapping" (2007: 87). However, this results in a paradox in that we construct our identity through our *shared* identification with particular groups but at the same time we view ourselves as *different* from those groups and as individuals. Joseph describes this as a tension between 'identity-as-sameness' and 'identity-as-uniqueness' (2004: 37). Yet, these two aspects of identity are both crucial. It is our sense of sameness that enables us to identify with groups such as professions, nations, genders, or religions. Nonetheless, we can also decide to what extent we follow all the behaviours, beliefs, and values of a group. At the same time we are members of many different groups simultaneously. The constellation of identifications with many different groups and the different degrees of alignment with those groups will be unique to everyone and makes up our individual identities.

The process of excluding and differentiating other groups, while a core process of identification, is also a potential source of problems in intercultural communication. In particular, it can lead to stereotyping, essentialism, and othering, where members of 'other' groups are seen as inferior in one way or another to ourselves and members of our groups (see Chapter 1.4). The essentialism and othering of ethnic and cultural groups has been an important theme in post-colonial theory. One of the most well-known examples of this is Edward Said's (1978/2003) notion of Orientalism, in which a 'normal, superior Western' Self is constructed in dominant political and academic discourses and contrasted with an 'exotic, inferior Eastern' Other. This results in stereotyped, essentialist, and at times racist discourses of East versus West which Said argues have been present in much of the research and thinking about 'Eastern' cultures.

Critical approaches to intercultural communication have also been concerned with othering. For instance, Holliday has proposed a sequence by which 'our' identity and group are separated from the 'other', which leads to othering.

1. Identify 'our' group by contrasting it with 'their' group.
2. Strengthen the contrasted images of Self and Other by emphasising and reifying respective proficient and deficient values, artefacts and behaviours.
3. Do this by manipulating selected cultural resources such as Protestantism or Confucianism.
4. Position Self and Other by constructing moral reasons to attack, colonize or help.
5. The Other culture becomes a definable commodity.
6. The imagined Other works with or resists imposed definitions (2011: 70).

Holliday (2011) goes on to discuss how those being othered may also adopt dominant essentialist definitions of themselves as convenient explanations of their own behaviour and of existing inequalities. This is especially so in the case of essentialist East-versus-West discourses, despite the deficit position those identified as 'Eastern' are placed in by such discourses. For instance, the teacher-educator Ryuko Kubota discusses how *nihonjinron* (theories on the Japanese) are used to describe "group orientation, harmony, and homogeneity, which are often believed to be the central characteristics of Japanese culture" (1999: 21). She argues that this represents an essentialist view of Japanese culture which serves the interests of existing elites and power structures (for example, politicians and businesses). Furthermore, *nihonjinron* creates an image of a 'unique' and 'different' Japanese culture which can be contrasted with 'Western' values as part of a discourse of power struggles between Japan and 'Western' countries such as the US. In contrast, Kubota suggests that education can offer alternative non-essentialist perspectives on Japanese culture and cultural differences which support pluralism and criticality.

To conclude, othering is a process that we all engage in and is an unavoidable part of how we construct our identities, but it is important that we are reflective about this process and aware of how this can lead to stereotyping 'others' in intercultural communication. To counter this tendency to other, Holliday et al. (2017: 38) recommend that we avoid easy answers to explaining people's behaviour, and that everyone:

- [t]ake great care of connections they make between people, their behaviour and generalisations about the categories in which we place people – culture, gender and race being but examples[;]
- [be] disciplined in considering evidence which is not connected to these categories

Summary

So far we have looked at a number of key aspects of identity:

- identity as multiple, negotiable, contested, and a process (what is often termed a post-structuralist perspective), rather than a fixed, unitary product or 'thing'
- language as the main medium through which we construct and negotiate our identities and through which we perceive others' identities
- the close link between language, identity, and power, with language use seen as one of the main ways in which a person's social position is constructed and represented

- multilingualism leading to adaptable and fluid relationships between languages, identities, and communities; however, power issues are still present, and we do not have complete freedom to construct any identity we wish in different languages
- othering as an inevitable part of identity by which we identify with particular groups and differentiate ourselves from 'others', which can lead to stereotyping and essentialism

Activity 6.2 East/West divides

Read the description below from Kubota (2001) on how 'Western' (US) and 'Eastern' (Asian) classrooms are often described in applied linguistics research. Do you agree with the descriptions she reports or with her criticisms of them as essentialist and stereotyped? Does this match any of your own experiences?

> The intellectual qualities posed as ideal for U.S. students are independence, autonomy, and creativity, and students should ideally develop analytical, objective, and critical thinking skills. They are able to analyze, hypothesize, and evaluate in a rational manner. Their communication styles in classrooms are presumably assertive and direct, and, as contrastive rhetoric studies often claim, their written discourse style is linear, logical, analytical, and deductive (see Connor, 1996). They actively engage in classroom discussions by expressing their own opinions and questioning authority, whether it is a text, a teacher, or an established theory.
>
> These qualities are presented as diametrically opposed to the characteristics of Asian students, who are described intellectually as interdependent, inclined to preserve rather than create knowledge, reluctant to challenge authority, and engaged in memorization rather than analytical thinking (e.g., Ballard & Clanchy, 1991; Carson, 1992; Fox, 1994). Asian students allegedly plagiarize because they do not share the Western notion of text authorship that stresses originality, creativity, and individualism. In terms of oral communication styles, Asian students are described as reticent, passive, indirect, and not inclined to challenge the teacher's authority (Jones, 1999). Their written communication style is often characterized as indirect, circular, and inductive (see Connor, 1996). In short, Asian students are presumably inclined to respect authority and maintain group harmony and interpersonal relationships rather than to seek truth through analytical and critical thinking.
>
> Overall, this body of applied linguistics literature provides dichotomous images of U.S. and Asian classrooms. The images of U.S. classrooms are ideal but seem quite real. They foster the typical argument that Asian ESL students face a challenge in

> U.S. classrooms because of cultural differences between the East and the West.
>
> (Kubota, 2001: 14)

Questions

Q1 What does the idea of an East/West divide mean to you?
Q2 What are some of the problems it may lead to in intercultural communication?
Q3 Does the idea of an East/West divide have any value as a means of explaining individual or group behaviour in intercultural communication?

Feedback: *Your answers will of course depend on your personal opinions and experiences. Nonetheless, we would agree with Kubota that such dichotomies between 'East' and 'West' are essentialist and stereotyped and do not fit the complex reality of the use of Global Englishes in an intercultural and transcultural world. We think such simplistic divisions are particularly unhelpful in English language teaching, for many of the reasons Kubota (2001) explains.*

6.4 Cultural identity

In intercultural communication studies, perhaps unsurprisingly, one of the main focuses on identity has been cultural identity. As we have seen, cultural identity is just one of many identities, but in intercultural communication it is often one of the first identities and most prominent identities in the interaction. This is because cultural identity is frequently associated with race and ethnicity, which, alongside gender and generation, are immediately perceptible to participants in intercultural interaction. For instance, Zhu points out that "[a]lthough cultural identity is not only about ethnicity and race, ethnicity and race are central to cultural identity to the extent that ethnic or racial identities are often conflated with cultural identity in practice" (2019: 215). While a cultural identity is partly made up of ethnic and racial identifications, our cultural identity, as we have seen in previous sections, is much more complex than this. Another problem with conflating cultural identity with ethnicity and race is that it is typically a process of other-ascription, in other words, an identity imposed on us by others, rather than self-orientation, where we choose the identity ourselves (Zhu, 2019: 228). Therefore, ascribing a cultural identity to others based on ethnicity and race can easily lead to essentialism and stereotyping.

The effects of essentialist approaches to cultural identity based on ethnicity and race are vividly explained by Eljee Javier when describing her experiences as a Canadian-Filipino teacher of English in China. Her Asian ethnicity meant that many students initially thought that she was Chinese and questioned her authenticity as a 'native' English-speaking teacher, as Javier explains in the following example.

Extract 6.1 "I'm a native speaker"

New student:	So, you're not Chinese?
Me [Eljee Javier]:	No, not at all!
New student:	Your family is Chinese?
Me:	No, none of them are Chinese. Both my parents are from the Philippines.
New student:	But your English is so good!
Me:	Well, I'm a native speaker.
New student:	Of course.

> At this point I could tell she wasn't convinced of my English credentials. I felt myself grow increasingly frustrated and I found myself defensively saying the following:
>
> 'I' m from Canada.'
>
> Suddenly the light seemed to go on. Her face lit up in a smile and she thanked me for my time before sitting down, obviously pleased with the news.
>
> (2010: 99)

Javier's example provides a clear demonstration of the pervasive ideology in ELT that equates 'native' English speakers (NESs) with Anglophone Caucasians based on a stereotyped view of Anglophone cultural identities. However, in this case Javier is able to negotiate her cultural identity and draws on another central identification in cultural identity: nation. We will return to this example in more detail in Chapter 7.

While ethnicity and race are frequently initial means of categorising for individuals in instances of intercultural communication, in research (especially cross-cultural communication) nation is often prioritised in characterising cultural identity. As with race and ethnicity, there is again a danger that this can lead to essentialist characterisations of others based on stereotyped views of national cultures, as we discussed extensively in Chapter 1. The national scale is just one aspect or level of cultural identity and many other groupings at both local and global scales form part of our cultural identities. At the local scale, these can be small cultures (Holliday, 2011), as outlined in Chapter 5.4, such as families, groups of friends, and work places. At the global scale, these may include groupings that cut across national boundaries such as professional or religious groupings and also groups associated with global phenomena such as sporting events, music, and media. At other scales, people may also identify with regional communities and cultures. However, at the same time, we need to be careful not to ignore the importance of national identifications in many people's cultural identities. Participants in intercultural communication frequently make use of national explanations of culture to explain their own and others' behaviour and beliefs (Holliday, 2011; Baker, 2015). Furthermore, in many settings there has been an increased identification with national cultures and nationalism, often in response to perceived threats to cultural identity from globalisation. Nonetheless, while national identities may be an important part of people's cultural identity, equally they may not, and we should not assume that they are always relevant. Moreover, how people orientate to national cultures is variable and there are debates and struggles over what values and beliefs constitute a national culture, making national cultures constantly in process and never fixed.

Alongside more traditional aspects of cultural identity such as race, ethnicity, and nationality, globalisation has become increasingly influential in how people construct their cultural identities. As explained throughout this book, the fluid links between languages, communities, and cultures brought about through the increased interconnectivity associated with globalisation have resulted in new spaces, resources, and affordances for identity construction. The ideas of transcultural flows of linguistic and cultural practices are particularly helpful in understanding the influence of globalisation on cultural identity construction. In particular, Pennycook emphasises "the ways in which cultural forms move, change and are reused to fashion new identities in diverse contexts" (2007: 6). This is not a flow of cultural practices in one direction and a simple copying of cultural identities across global scales. Instead, it is a complex multidirectional flow in which local contexts, communities, and identities are adapted in response to globalisation but also, in turn, influence and adapt the global flows and their effect in other localities. As discussed in Chapter 2.3, Pennycook (2007) gives the example of different versions of hip-hop to illustrate how cultural practices are adapted to local and global contexts. Pennycook refers to such identities as *metroethnicity* and such practices as *metrolingualism*, and goes on to explain that: "As language learners move around the world in search of English or other desirable languages, or stay at home but tune in to new digital worlds through screens, mobiles and headphones, the possibilities of being something not yet culturally imagined mobilizes new identity options. And in these popular transcultural flows, languages, cultures and identities are frequently mixed" (2010a: 85). We will return to explore the relationship between English, globalisation, and identity in more detail later in this chapter.

However, just as with any other aspect of cultural identity, we need to be careful not to simplify or assume that globally orientated cultural identities are necessarily relevant to understanding participants in intercultural communication. For example, Canagarajah agrees with Pennycook (2007) that due to the fluidity of languages and cultures associated with the processes of globalisation, "we are able to enjoy identities that transcend our native language, ethnicity, or place of birth" (2013: 198). Yet, at the same time, he warns that we are not free to choose any identity we wish and existing social structures may limit our choices (as seen in Eljee Javier's example above). Additionally, Canagarajah suggests that members of minority communities and diasporas, which are frequently part of the multilingual and multicultural settings discussed in post-structuralist and critical approaches to intercultural communication, may see these dynamic and fluid theories of identity as a threat to their already marginalised heritage languages and identities. Canagarajah proposes that, while we need to recognise the constructed and ideological nature of heritage languages, communities, and identities, this does not necessarily have to undermine them. Instead, he argues that: "ideologies are not always evil or limiting; they are also enabling. One can marshal a diverse collection of semiotic resources and 'perform' one's identity and community through strategic practices" (2013: 200).

To explain how these different aspects of cultural identity are constructed and negotiated in intercultural communication, it is useful to return to the concept of interculturality as introduced in Chapter 5.4. Briefly summarising, interculturality approaches cultural identities as constructed and negotiated in discourse, rather than a 'given' and 'fixed' identity. Questions asked include: the relevance of cultural identities and memberships in intercultural interactions, how people construct cultural identities and the resources used to 'do' cultural identities, what people do with cultural identities, and why (Zhu, 2019: 220). Importantly, in emphasising that cultural identities are negotiated, Zhu (2019) underscores that we are again not free to choose any cultural identity. There may also be tensions between the cultural identity we wish to construct (self-orientation) and those that others impose on us (ascription by others).

In sum, cultural identity is one of the most prevalent aspects of identity in intercultural communication, both from the perspectives of participants and researchers. Key aspects of cultural identity are race, ethnicity, and nationality. However, as with all identities, cultural identity is more complex than this and may also involve identification with diverse groups such as local 'small cultures' (e.g., families, friends), regional, heritage, and diasporic groups, and other globally connected groups (e.g., professions). All of these groupings may be drawn on in highly variable ways in constructing and negotiating cultural identities. Recent research has explored the way in which globalisation has opened up new spaces for identification and identity construct that goes beyond traditional linguistic and cultural borders. Yet, it is also important to recognise that we cannot construct any cultural identity we want, and that others may ascribe us with particular cultural identities, which can be more or less negotiable in interaction.

6.5 Identity and Global Englishes

We outlined some of the relationships between Global Englishes and identity in Chapter 5.5, but below we recap and expand on the points made there.

- Pölzl and Seidlhofer (2006) document users of ELF moving between local L1 identities and more global orientations in a group of Arabic users of English who retained features of their L1 discourse styles in their English use.
- Issues of ideology and power relationships in cultural identity construction and negotiation have been explored in ELF interactions (Jenks, 2013; Zhu, 2015), with Anglophone 'native' speaker ideology a particular issue of concern (Jenkins, 2007).
- The use of ELF has been shown to be an important part of the construction of and identification with dynamic communities of practice, for example, Kalocsai's (2014) and Ra's (2018) studies of student communities, Ehrenreich's (2009) investigation of business communities, and Vettorel's (2014) research on virtual communities.
- Studies such as Klimpfinger (2009), Pitzl (2012), and Cogo (2012) report the construction of shared multilingual and multicultural identities in ELF interactions through the use of code-switching, creative idioms, and translanguaging.
- Research has illustrated the role of adaptability, hybridity, and third-place identities, with participants embracing being 'in between' and mediating between cultures or other groupings (Baker, 2009a; 2011; 2015).
- Most recently, ELF research has explored freer, liminal, and fluid identities and cultural practices that are not indexed to or 'between' any particular cultures or cultural identifications (Baker, 2015; Baker & Sangiamchit, 2019; Pitzl, 2018a).

In this section we will explore some of these issues in detail and provide examples drawn from current Global Englishes research. First, it may be helpful to restate a point made throughout this book that ELF is a not a culturally neutral form of communication (which is impossible), and so neither is ELF neutral as regards cultural identities. Given the dynamic links between language and culture in ELF communication, the connections between identity constructions and linguistic resources may be complex, but identity is present in ELF communication, as it is in all communication. What may be true is that there are many instances in intercultural communication through ELF where national cultural identities are not relevant to the interaction. As we have seen when looking at Global Englishes research, there are frequent examples when English is not linked in any obvious way to Anglophone national cultures, such as the US and the UK, or any other national culture. However, cultural identity is more than simply a national cultural identification and national cultural identities are just one possible level or scale among many in interpreting culture and identity.

One of the leading areas of research in Global Englishes and identity has been into the notion of 'nativeness' and identity. In particular, Jenkins (2007) undertook a global survey of English teachers' attitudes to their English use, ELF, and identity. Jenkins (2007) focused on issues of identity as they related to the prevailing ideology in ELT in which the English language is associated with NESs from Anglophone countries (as discussed in Javier's example above). Jenkins' findings illustrated contradictory identifications among her participants whereby they wanted their English use to be associated with a prestigious imagined 'native'-speaker variety of English, but at the same time they also wished to preserve aspects of their L1 identities expressed through their English accents. One of Jenkins' participants referred to this tension as giving rise to the feeling of being "linguistically schizophrenic" (2007: 214). These two positions are summarised by Jenkins as:

> NNS [non-native speaker] teachers may have very mixed feelings about expressing their membership of an international (ELF) community or even an L1 identity in their L2 English ... In most cases there was a strong sense that they desired a native-like English identity as signalled by a native-like accent, especially in their role as teachers. ... And yet most also expressed an attachment to their mother tongue and nationality, projected through their English accent, that they seemed reluctant to relinquish.
>
> (2007: 231)

However, as with all aspects of identity, we need to be careful not to oversimplify 'nativeness' as a category of identity in Global Englishes. As Baird et al. (2014) point out, what is indexed, or referred to, by 'nativeness' as an identity is contextually dependent. In other words, how the concept of an NES as an identity is constructed by participants in Global Englishes communication will vary. So, for example, in Jenkins' (2007) study, identifying with a 'native' variety of English was regarded as an aspect of professional identity as an English language teacher. In Kitazawa's (2013) research, among East Asian users of English, one of her participants described her admiration for a German speaker of English who had 'native-like' English. However, as Kitazawa explains, this does not entail a desire to adopt an NES identity, rather "what she evaluated highly was this 'achievement' accomplished by the German model, and not NS English itself" (2013: 196). In conclusion, 'nativeness' and the prestige of an idealised NES is a pervasive ideology in ELT and this in turn has an influence on Global Englishes users and their identifications with and through English use. Yet, we also need to be aware of the varied ways that 'nativeness' can be constructed and used as an identity. In many instances, users of Global Englishes do not wish to be identified as an NES so much as being identified with the prestige, achievement, and social capital of possessing a 'native-like' English. Equally significant, at other times, 'nativeness' may not be an especially relevant identity in intercultural interactions through English, as we will discuss in more detail below. It is, thus, important not to reify the notions of 'nativeness' and 'non-nativeness' and to create false dichotomies (see Baird et al., 2014).

Other studies have explored increasing identification with ELF rather than Anglophone Englishes, as well as the use of ELF to construct particular identities. For instance, Jenkins, Cogo, and Dewey (2011), reporting on the LINEE (Languages in a Network of European Excellence) project, note that for the majority of young Europeans in their research English is used as a lingua franca (although they may not use the term). They therefore "identify with their own use of English rather than with a standard NS variety" (2011: 307) and view English as a means of interacting with a globalised world. Kalocsai (2014) and Ra (2018) provide evidence for the role of ELF as a key part of a shared repertoire in forming communities of practices among international students. Kalocsai argues that ELF offers a resource "in building and maintaining locally relevant identities" (2014: 212). Furthermore, both Kalocsai (2014) and Ra (2018) illustrate the hybrid, multiple, and dynamic identifications that ELF opens up for their participants.

Due to the multilingual nature of Global Englishes and ELF, the relationship between English, other languages, and identity construction has also been a productive area of research. For instance, Klimpfinger (2009), making use of data from the VOICE corpus (see Chapter 4.3), has explored how code-switching can be used as an explicit index of cultural identities. She highlights a number of different ways this is done, including tags such as oui, oui ('yes, yes'), and specific cultural references which are linked to the speaker such as Roma rather than Rome. Klimpfinger (2009) and other researchers such as Cogo (2009) also suggest that participants in ELF communication may orientate towards shared multilingual and multicultural identities by switching into the L1 of other participants. The following conversation from Cogo (2009) between two colleagues (Daniela, L1 Italian, and Karen, L1 German) illustrates this point.

Extract 6.2 Conversation between two colleagues

01 Daniela:	(low) yeah
02 Karen:	yeah
03 Daniela:	ok
04 Karen:	e:h ok
05 Daniela:	grazie
06 Karen:	yeah ok ... grazie e:h danke: thank you for you eh how do you say thank you eh danke an dich
07 Daniela:	grazie a te
08 Karen:	(laughing) yeah

(Cogo, 2009: 266)

Notes

(low)	nonlinguistic features of the transcription
:	prolongation of the immediately prior sound
...	short pause (unmeasured)

Also based on data from the VOICE corpus, Pitzl (2009; 2012) has investigated the relationship between multilingualism, ELF use, and idioms and metaphors. Pitzl (2009) presents examples of creative language use through metaphors and idioms such as 'we should not wake up any dogs' (meaning to leave the situation as it is and not cause difficulties) and 'we have a lot of money in the sock' (meaning we have plenty of savings). Pitzl (2009) explains how these may be based on adaptations and translations of participants' L1 idioms or metaphors, adaptations of English idioms or metaphors, or new creative idioms. As regards cultural identity, as with code-switching, idioms and metaphors can serve as intentional displays of a particular L1 cultural identity, or as demonstrations of an awareness of other participants' cultural identities. Furthermore, Pitzl (2009) argues that they can be used to create more emergent identifications that "contribute to the interpersonal and interactional co-construction of local ELF intercultures" (2012: 47).

The notion of emergent identifications is explored in much of the research of the first author of this book. In Chapter 5.4 we already looked at the type of third-place identities that ELF users may construct which are not part of either their L1 culture or any fixed target language and culture. To return to the examples from the research participant in Baker (2009a), Nami, she suggests that English, and particularly ELF (although she does not use this term), allows for more 'open', fluid, and liminal identities.

> *Nami:* it's different because in English you you can express yourself more you you you it's also because of the cultural thing when when you umm yeah when you speak with the native speaker right they are more open because of their culture as well but even if you speak with the other people who isn't who are non umm English speaker err English is a kind of message containing something that it will make other people more open I don't know maybe I'm wrong but that is what I observe people people speak more people tend to forget their own culture for a while and they become more open.
>
> (Baker, 2009a: 580)

Other participants in the same study discussed the idea of taking on an identity as a mediator between different cultures. In the following example, Yim explains why she thinks she would make a good English teacher. She believes that 'native' English-speaking teachers and Thai students have different expectations for teaching and learning in relation to writing. Being a successful student in both Thai and English, Yim feels she is able to see both perspectives and mediate between them or "delete the gaps".

> *Yim:* ... when there is a way for me to help Thai people with the English language and if there is a possibility to do that I will want to do that because like I like I told you earlier that about like the teaching writing you know there is some spaces between the foreign teachers and the student ... and yeah and I think as I have had some experience with those problems and I should be able to you know to delete the gaps between yeah and solve the problem some of them.
>
> (Baker, 2011: 45)

At the same time, it is important to recognise that people do not have to be 'in between' and can identify with different communities simultaneously (Chapter 6.2). In the next examples, another participant, Oy, discusses adopting a British, or London, identification through her accent when speaking English, while simultaneously identifying with Thai culture.

> *Oy:* ... my friends ask me sometime they say can't you do it in Thai or in American accent and I say umm yeah but that would be funny

to me and I don't really like it ... I got a bit of a London accent as well

Oy: ... as I am a Thai woman or girl whatever you wanted to put it that way I still have to keep the culture with me.

(Baker, 2011: 45)

These examples illustrate how what might appear to outsiders to be contradictory identities do not necessarily feel problematic to the individuals themselves.

Adopting a perspective on identity that views it as emergent and fluid means that as researchers we need to pay close attention to the way that identity may be constructed and negotiated in interaction, as suggested in the theory of interculturality described earlier (Zhu, 2019). We will explore this in an example in the following activity in which we can see how different identities are negotiated and resisted in interaction and also how we need to be cautious about ascribing a priori identities to people.

Activity 6.3 Are you Chinese?

A group of students from a UK university and a Thai university are taking part in an online synchronous text chat discussion as part of a course they are doing (see Baker, 2015: 226–228). The participants are Sarah (L1 English, female), Ying (L1 Chinese, female), Som (L1 Thai, female), Wasana (L1 Thai, female), and Ana (L1 Portuguese, female). They are discussing both their use of English and where each of them comes from.

Read the extract and note the different languages, nationalities, and cultural identities in this example. When you have finished, compare your answers to the interpretation below.

01 Sarah:	I originally come from Canada, but grew up in Germany. So I consider myself to be inbetween a native and a non-native speaker.
02 Ying:	Actually, when I am with my friends who are from the same country as me, I always speak my mother tongue. But when I am alone, I speak English to myself.
03 Som:	wow that's really good.
04 Wasana:	Are you Chinese, Ying?
05 Ying:	Yes!
06 Som:	Ni Haw Ma?
07 Wasana:	Ni hao!
08 Ying:	Ni hao!
	[...]
09 Ana:	this is a real intercultural communication, uh? People from different backgrounds.

10 Som:	sorry i tried to say hi in chinese.
	[...]
11 Som:	what about you Ana?
12 Som:	where are you from?
13 Ana:	I am originally from Brazil
	[...]
14 Wasana:	My ancestors are Chinese.
	[...]
15 Sarah:	Wasana. Do you consider yourself multilingual then?
16 Ying:	Oh, nice to meet you! Perhaps that's why you say you are not talkative?
17 Ying:	For Chinese are sometimes overmodest. ...
	[...]
18 Wasana:	I don't consider that because I don't talk chinese when I was a child.
19 Wasana:	I just have taken some chinese courses and I don't speak it in my daily life.
	[...]
20 Sarah:	Wasana. Did you spend some time in China as well?
21 Ana:	Ying is a great teacher! She taught our class some mandarin the other day
	[...]
22 Wasana:	I never been in China, too.

(Baker, 2015: 227)

Notes

[...] Multiple conversations were taking place simultaneously in the chat session but for ease of reading they have not all been transcribed. "[...]" represents an untranscribed section.

... a section of dialogue not transcribed

Questions

Q1 What are the relationships between languages, nationalities, and cultural identities?
Q2 How are they negotiated in the interaction?
Q3 Are any identities rejected or resisted?

Feedback: *The first four lines of this example show how we should be careful not to make simplistic correlations between language and cultural identity. Although Sarah has Canadian nationality, she does not view herself as a "native" English speaker as she grew up in Germany and classifies herself as "inbetween". Ying also problematises correlations between cultural identity and language use, claiming that while Chinese is her "mother tongue" and the language she uses with Chinese friends, when she is alone she likes to speak English to herself. The proceeding interaction then goes on to illustrate how* *identities can be negotiated within the course of an interaction. On finding out that Ying is Chinese, Som and Wasana code-switch into a Chinese greeting (lines 06–08). In line 14 Wasana follows up her use of Chinese with the information that her ancestors are from China. This leads Ying to interpret this as an identification with a Chinese cultural identity and an explanation for Wasana's quietness in the discussion as part of her 'Chinese identity' (lines 16–17). However, this orientation to a Chinese cultural identity is rejected by Wasana (lines 18–19, 22) due to not speaking Chinese as a child, not using Chinese every day, and never having been to China. In sum, this example highlights the complex links between languages in general, ELF in particular, and the construction of identities, with Sarah, Ying, and Wasana all resisting simplistic correlations between the languages they use, 'nativeness', nationality, cultural heritage, and cultural identity.*

Chapter summary

In this chapter we explored the notion of identity and how it is, like culture, a core part of our everyday life, as well as crucial in understanding intercultural communication through Global Englishes. We considered how multifaceted the idea of identity was, with each of us having multiple identities related to the different groups we orientate towards and our sense of self. We looked at the key role of language in both representing and constructing our identity. Every time we speak or write we are engaged in a process of constructing and negotiating our identities. Based on our speech or writing our interlocutors are forming opinions and ideas of who we are, just as we are of them. Furthermore, learning an additional language, such as English, opens up opportunities and spaces for the construction of new identities. We may even feel that we are a 'different' person when we learn and use another language. We outlined a number of central concepts in understanding identity and language that you should now be familiar with:

- multiple identities
- identity and subjectivity/the self
- identity as external identification with groups
- fixed 'core' identities and flexible 'periphery' identities
- identity and power relationships including 'imposed', 'assumed', and 'negotiable' identities
- 'identity-as-sameness' and 'identity-as-uniqueness'
- identity and othering
- cultural identity, race, ethnicity, and nation
- identity and interculturality
- third-place and liminal identities

We also focused on the important role identity has played in research into Global Englishes and particularly ELF studies. We identified a number of strands in that research:

- ideology and power relationships in cultural identity construction and negotiation in ELF interactions with Anglophone 'native'-speaker ideology a particular issue of concern, especially in ELT
- the use of ELF that has been shown to be an important part of the construction of and identification with dynamic communities of practice such as multilingual and multicultural student communities
- the construction of shared multilingual and multicultural identities in ELF interactions through the use of code-switching, creative idioms, and translanguaging
- the role of adaptability, hybridity, and third-place identities in ELF interactions with participants embracing being 'in between' and mediating between cultures or other groupings
- liminal, fluid identities and cultural practices in ELF interactions that are not indexed to or 'between' any particular cultures or cultural identifications

A final point to remember is that our identities are constructed both in relation to others but also as different to them. This process of excluding and differentiating others, while an unavoidable part of identification, is also a potential source of problems in intercultural communication. In particular, it can lead to stereotyping and othering, where members of 'other' groups are seen as inferior in one way or another to ourselves and members of 'our' groups. It is important that we reflect on this process and are aware of how this can lead to essentialising 'others' in intercultural communication.

Further reading

Baker, W. (2015). *Culture and identity through English as a lingua franca: Rethinking concepts and goals in intercultural communication*. Berlin: De Gruyter Mouton. Chapter four provides a detailed discussion of identity, language, and English as a lingua franca in intercultural communication.

Holliday, A., Kullman, J., & Hyde, M. (2017). *Intercultural communication: An advanced resource book for students* (3rd edn). Abingdon: Routledge. The book provides a comprehensive and multi-level overview of identity and intercultural communication from a critical perspective.

Zhu, H. (2019). *Exploring intercultural communication: Language in action* (2nd edn). Abingdon: Routledge. Chapter twelve contains an in-depth discussion of language, identity, and interculturality.

7 Language ideologies surrounding Global Englishes

Introduction

We use language every day. We can find it in every corner of the world. Language is such a natural part of our lives that we tend not to give critical thought to its ideologies or taken-for-granted ideas and beliefs circulating in society to varying extents. As introduced in Chapter 1.2, these ideas and beliefs often connote moral or political values (e.g., 'right', 'proper', 'standard'). We are wondering what you have to say if we ask you who are the best speakers of English and what ideal English is like. Any answer to these questions would entail some ideologies of language, or, more commonly, language ideologies. This is all the more so because language itself has no power or intrinsic value, as described by the linguist Ruth Wodak: "language is not powerful on its own – it gains power by the use powerful people make of it" (2002: 10). Her words echo the sociolinguist James Milroy – "it is not difficult to argue that varieties of language do not actually have prestige in themselves: these varieties acquire prestige when their *speakers* have high prestige" (2001: 532; original emphasis).

This chapter examines the language ideologies of English vis-à-vis its current global status: **ideologies of native-speakerism** (Holliday, 2006; 2018), **monolingualism** (Blackledge, 2000), and **Standard English** (Milroy & Milroy, 2012). More specifically, we start with native-speakerism in English, most commonly in English language teaching (ELT), which presumes Anglophone speakers within the 'traditional' English-speaking world to be the custodians of English at the global scale. Native-speakerism results from the assumptions of their monolingual competence and its associated 'correctness' (Ishikawa, 2018a; 2020b; Seidlhofer, 2018). Accordingly, we explain the twinned ideologies of monolingualism and Standard English, with the latter as a special type of **Standard Language ideology** (Lippi-Green, 2012). Moreover, in line with Jenkins (2014), we elucidate why these twinned ideologies prevail against multilingual reality in reference to the linguistic anthropologist Kathryn Woolard's (2005; 2016) ideologies of **authenticity** and **anonymity**. Throughout the chapter, you will be given the opportunity to reflect on how English is positioned in society, for what purposes, and who benefits.

Activity 7.1 "In short, grammar is a sort of shibboleth"

As with other Standard Languages, Standard English is the abstract form of an English variety which is dominant and thus labelled as 'standard' in a country or state. According to the applied linguist Henry Widdowson (1994: 381), its grammar and spelling are most attentively protected for communal, rather than communicative, purposes. In reality, any Standard Language variety, including English, is not very stable and continues to change over generations, unlike Standard English in ELT. After reading this paragraph, think about your answers to questions 1 to 3 below, and discuss them in small groups if possible.

> [I]t is precisely because grammar is so often redundant in communicative transactions that it takes on another significance, namely that of expressing social identity. The mastery of a particular grammatical system, especially perhaps those features which are redundant, marks you as a member of the community which has developed that system for its own social purposes. Conversely, of course, those who are unable to master the system are excluded from the community. They do not belong. In short, grammar is a sort of shibboleth.

Questions

Q1 Have you ever thought that "grammar is so often redundant in communicative transactions" through English?

Q2 What linguistic (e.g., phonological, grammatical, pragmatic) features of English do you feel tend to express your own and your peers' social identities?

Q3 Do you agree with the statement that English "grammar is a sort of shibboleth [i.e., custom which is no longer important]", and why?

Feedback: *Answers will vary. Having said that, we are not sure how far English grammar is redundant across different settings, including academic. Also, you may have thought that pronunciation is "the aspect of language that most obviously expresses social identity and group membership" (Dalton-Puffer et al., 1997: 126). Note that in the linguistics circle, "it is generally conceded that standard English has no distinctive phonology" (Widdowson, 1994: 380). Widely acknowledged Received Pronunciation (RP) and General American (GA) English provide references in English pronunciation rather than a 'standard' to observe (Trudgill & Hannah, 2017). The former associates itself with* *the middle to upper classes in England, the UK, and the latter draws on similarities in North American English pronunciation. Nonetheless, Widdowson (1994) alludes to two important aspects in language use: who speakers represent themselves to be (i.e., the indexical function of language) and what they have to say (i.e., the referential function of language). We will discuss Standard English ideology in Chapter 7.2 and both indexical and referential natures of language in Chapter 7.3.*

7.1 Native-speakerism

On perusing academic job advertisements for applied linguists shortly before completing a PhD programme at the University of Southampton, the second author of this book made the following post on Facebook.

> It annoys me when academic job advertisements in Japan often use the term 'native speaker' synonymously with 'native English speaker'.
>
> (Ishikawa, 12 February 2016)[1]

One commonly observed issue in the present-day world is the synonymous use of the term 'native speakers' with 'native English speakers' (NESs). Surely, we can guess from context that someone is talking about a particular language. However, we would like to emphasise the truth: Everyone is a 'native' speaker of one or more languages. If 'native speakers' refers to NESs by default, then we, as it were, place English on top of the podium and the rest of the languages below. In other words, we assume English to be the default primary language in the world.

In the first place, we wonder why applicants for applied linguistics positions, most often in the case of ELT, should be NESs to be eligible for consideration. Indeed, native-speakerism has long been prevailing in the ELT industry (Kumaravadivelu, 2016), and, as Holliday (2018: 1151) defines:

> [n]ative-speakerism is an ideology that upholds the idea that so-called 'native speakers' are the best models and teachers of English because they represent a 'Western culture' from which spring the ideals both of English and of the methodology for teaching it[.]

It is assumed that NESs speak the 'best' English or 'genuine' and 'perfect' English, not interfered with by cultures outside their communities. Here language and culture, or presumed 'superior' culture, are naïvely linked with each other, which was problematised in Chapter 2. It is also assumed that NESs teach the language through 'superior' and systematic methods, in other words, implementing what Holliday (2005) calls English-speaking Western TESOL (i.e., Teaching English to Speakers of Other Languages). These methods typically rely on four skill categories (i.e., listening, reading, speaking, and writing), along with 'can do' statement checklists as in the Common European Framework of Reference for Languages (CEFR) (Council of Europe, 2001).[2] As one example, in terms of listening skills, what are called *Level A1* basic users in CEFR "[c]an follow speech that is very slow and carefully articulated, with long pauses for him/her to assimilate meaning" (Council of Europe, 2018: 55). We will explore pedagogy, including ELT, in the final part of this book.

It was "a distorted worldview that supports a particular vested interest" (Holliday, 2018: 1151), not just the synonymisation of 'native speakers' with NESs, which urged the second author to 'come out' on Facebook. For example, a Japanese institution stipulated the first prerequisite to apply for its ELT position in four words: "Be a native speaker" (T University, 10 February 2016),[3] which means NESs. For another example, at the time of writing, an ELT and EMI job opening at another Japanese institution says: "Applicants should be native English speakers" (S University, 24 January 2020). While there can be miscellaneous interpretations of the term NESs (Davies, 2013), these advertisements are likely to associate this category with L1 English speakers from the Kachruvian Inner Circle (Chapter 4.1), that is, from the UK, Ireland, the US, Canada, Australia, and New Zealand (Houghton & Rivers, 2013), or, possibly more narrowly, from the US and the UK (Jenkins, 2014; Holliday, 2018). To take a further example from Japan, the government investment called the Japan Exchange and Teaching (JET) Programme has recruited young overseas graduates largely as assistant language teachers (ALTs) of English at school, particularly from Japan's ally, the US (McConnell, 2000; Kobayashi, 2018). As of 2019, 2,958 (56.5%) of all the 5,234 JET Programme ALTs, mostly ALTs of English, are from the United States, and 1,721 (32.9%) are from the other Inner-Circle countries (CLAIR, 2020). Bluntly put, in places like Japan and beyond, perhaps including your locations, the term native speakers is likely to mean NESs who are indigenous to particular geographical areas. They are not just L1 English speakers but are also familiar with local conventions in 'traditional' Anglophone speech communities. The first author of this book would feel very uncomfortable if he were hired as an English instructor mainly because of his British nationality and L1 status (indeed, it was his early experience in ELT in which he was hired for these very reasons that led to his interest in Global Englishes), and the second author would feel discriminated against if he were not even considered to be a candidate because of his Japanese nationality and L1 status. In short, native-speakerism, we observe, can be both ignominious and discriminatory.

This observation brings us to another, arguably more fundamental issue: who can be the 'native' or indigenous speakers of this global language. In other words, we wonder at the appropriateness or even possibility of making a link between a language used by an ever-growing number of speakers at the global scale (Chapter 3.3) and a limited number of local geographical communities. The first author of this book is no exception. He is an indigenous speaker of a particular variety of British English, but this does not make him a 'native' speaker of English as a global language. As discussed in Chapter 4.3 and 4.4, so long as it is regarded as a global lingua franca, English is not "native to some and foreign to others" (Baker, 2011: 210). The aforementioned Facebook post continues as follows.

> But in the first place, why should we be so indigenous to any particular speech community in this age of multilingual and multicultural communication? My supervisor stated 16 years ago that "the word 'native' will return to its pejorative usage" [Jenkins, 2000: 229]. This seems to be happening around here [in Europe]. But what about my home country [Japan]?
>
> (Ishikawa, 12 February 2016)

Presumably, many L1 English speakers are more accustomed to using English as a local language than global, and have no experience of acquiring additional languages at the professional level. In this regard, the critical education scholar Glenn Toh wonders "whether one day, native [English] speakers will be employed as [English] teachers *despite* their native speaker status" (2016: 365; original emphasis). More straightforwardly, we wonder how many of you would like to learn a language from those who have never succeeded in learning another language themselves.

Many of us appear to fall into a conceptual trap by overestimating the role of local geographical communities even in communication beyond locality. They insist on an indigenous approach to the global language of English. It is worth exploring why this contradictory approach spreads widely. But before that, we will consider what underlies native-speakerism in the next section, namely, the coupling of monolingual and Standard English ideologies.

7.2 Ideologies of monolingualism and Standard English

Native-speakerism accompanies ideologies of monolingualism and Standard English. It is believed that NESs are 'best' since they are supposed to speak English 'genuinely' or monolingually without any interference from other languages, and thus 'perfectly' or 'correctly'. After all, Standard English in ELT is a monolingual construct. As a construct, this English is an idealised abstract entity. While we do not deny some usefulness of Standard English within the language classroom, we take issue with the view of, as it were, "English is English is English" (Seidlhofer & Jenkins, 2003: 141). That is, we problematise the danger of conflating English in its entirety with its perceived monolingual use, and then with Standard English in ELT or in the established English as a Foreign Language (EFL) approach more precisely. This approach entails teaching and learning English as originated from a national Standard Language of the 'traditional' English-speaking world, largely in the US and the UK.

Despite the fact that NESs are not necessarily monolinguals or experts in Standard English in the EFL approach, NESs as a whole tend to be associated with monolingual, Standard English. We will examine each of monolingual and Standard English ideologies below and the connections with native-speakerism.

Monolingual ideology

English is the most prominent global language of our day and an additional language for most of its users (Chapter 3.3). Obviously, they cannot become monolingual English speakers. Instead, they learn to become bilingual or multilingual English users. In addition, global communication usually takes place in multilingual settings, or, rather, scarcely ever consists of monolingual English speakers alone in a monolingual environment, let alone 'monocultural', however it may be defined. Thinking in this way, multilingualism is the norm at the global scale, "not the abstract language of monolinguals, as described by traditional usage books and grammars" (García, 2014: 2). In short, in agreement with the sociolinguist Adrian Blackledge (2000), we find the mismatch between the real-world objective of acquiring English and monolingual ideology.

It has been well known in sociolinguistics that language ideologies invoke conceptual bias and uniformity in association with particular social positions (Woolard, 1992; Woolard & Schieffelin, 1994; Milroy, 2001; 2007). This is exactly true of monolingual ideology, which imposes the universal value of perceived monolingual thinking and performance on the part of NESs even though they are not necessarily monolingual. More to the point, this ideology interprets learning additional languages as the acquisition of one bounded language after another with an individual's multilingual background held in abeyance. To borrow the applied linguist Vivian Cook's (2013: 37–38) words, each language is "treated in isolation, perpetuating the traditional monolingual conception of bilinguals as being two monolinguals

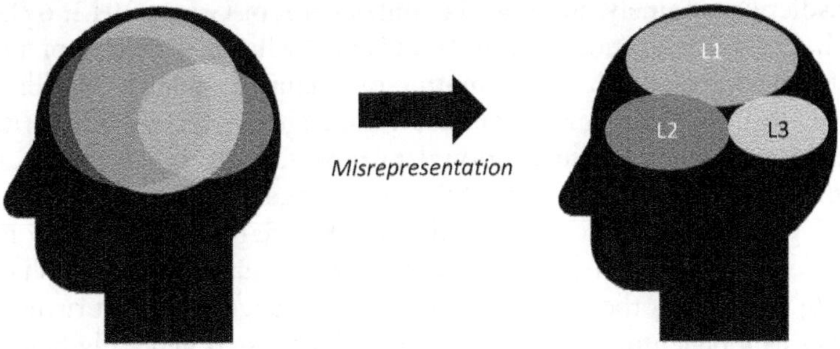

Figure 7.1 Plural monolingualism of an individual mind
(Adapted from Ishikawa, 2020b: 94)

rather than different people from monolinguals in L1". Similarly, Li Wei (2018: 16), another applied linguist, remarks:

> [t]he actual purpose of learning new languages – to become bilingual and multilingual, rather than to replace the learner's L1 to become another monolingual – often gets forgotten or neglected, and the bilingual, rather than monolingual, speaker is rarely used as the model for teaching and learning.

The attempt to compartmentalise an individual's multilingual repertoire (see Chapter 2.5), or what may be called the plural monolingualism of each individual mind, has no scientific justification based on current research.[4] While a multilingual repertoire is hard to illustrate schematically, we hope that the illustration in Figure 7.1 helps capture the differences between this and the artificial nature of monolingual ideology.

To sum up, monolingual ideology is unrealistic and irrelevant to most English users, for whom English is an additional language within their multilingual repertoires. It does not appreciate the obvious fact that they never become monolingual English users, unlike those who can only speak English.

Standard English ideology

Language ideologies, again, invoke conceptual bias and uniformity in association with particular social positions. In the case of Standard Language ideology, "an abstracted, idealized, homogen[e]ous" model, derived from the linguistic practices of the upper-middle class, is "imposed and maintained by dominant bloc institutions" in political jurisdictions, namely, states and countries (Lippi-Green, 2012: 67). As such, the identification of any 'standard' "will be a matter of institutional expediency", not a matter of linguistic quality (Seidlhofer, 2011: 46). In this regard, Standard Languages are essentially written varieties to serve for institutional purposes, such as education and administration (Widdowson, 1994). Language education and tests, in turn, play a major role in disseminating Standard Language ideology with 'correctness' attached to the Standard Language model (Shohamy, 2006; 2007). In other words, Standard Language in each jurisdiction serves as a benchmark so that 'non-standard' use is generally believed to be neither educated nor appropriate.

While Standard Language ideology is typical as regards most L1 (e.g., Japanese in Japan and British English in the UK), Standard English ideology is a special type of this Standard Language ideology since it manifests itself beyond national borders (Milroy & Milroy, 2012). It asserts "that a national standard language [in the Inner Circle, or, more narrowly, in the US and the UK] should be valid not only within a particular country but globally" as a variety with "a special and privileged status" (Seidlhofer, 2011: 42–43). In this assertion, the expansion of English to a multilingual world is interpreted simply as the distribution of an institutionalised L1 English variety within a couple of political entities (Trudgill & Hannah, 2017; Widdowson, 2003). In short, an insular authorised variety is deemed as turned into a global default.

Certainly, the concepts of "'[s]tandardness' and 'non-standardness' are ... deeply ingrained into sociolinguistic theory and methods" (Coupland, 2000: 632). However, it is difficult to define the 'standard' form of any language. After all, linguistic standardisation is an effort to stabilise otherwise unstable phenomena. Generally speaking, Standard Language in one generation is often different from that of another generation, and Standard Language within each generation tends to be used in a variable manner. This leads to the difference between Standard English in ELT originally from the UK and the US and Standard English varieties as actually observed in these countries now. Anecdotally, at English school, when a student submits the same paper to two teachers who are supposed to speak the same Standard English variety, their linguistic corrections of, say, articles, prepositions, and punctuations are often different and sometimes contradictory. We can find similar examples within the same individuals who work in higher education.

> For example, a Chinese PhD student's supervisor corrected the preposition 'on' to 'in' in the first draft of a chapter. The student duly made the various corrections required by the supervisor including changing the 'on' to 'in', and resubmitted his draft to the supervisor.

> He was amused but baffled when it was returned to him with the 'in' changed back to 'on'. I mentioned this incident to a Vietnamese participant who told me that the same thing sometimes happened to him.
>
> (Jenkins, 2014: 181–182)

In reality, natural languages, including their 'standard' varieties, are adaptable in linguistic features for the sake of communication. Put differently, language is not amenable to 'mechanical' standardization across **communicative contexts** (i.e., who interactants are, how they are interacting, in what circumstances, and for what purposes).

Travelling across Britain, you would easily find how diverse British English is in practice and also find it really hard to encounter someone who speaks Standard English as prescribed by widely commercialised textbooks in ELT. This applies not just to the UK but also to other 'traditional' English-speaking countries. At the same time, English is chosen for global encounters which can be for varying durations and hence lead to different amounts of negotiation and adaptation (e.g., Pitzl, 2018a). For example, you may use English with total strangers who ask directions at urban train stations around your living places. In such particular cases, a minimal amount of negotiation would take place between two parties, all related to an asking and telling transaction, motivated by "a clear pragmatic purpose which involves complementarity (one interactant demands and the other gives)" (Eggins & Slade, 1997/2004: 20). Unlike such one-off and pragmatic encounters, you may use English with your international friends or colleagues on a regular basis, both face-to-face and online. In such cases, various meaning-making resources would be used in linguistic accommodation (Chapter 4.3) among multiple parties in a more informal and humorous way (Eggins & Slade, 1997/2004; Jenkins, 2014). Whether global encounters are more transient or stable (Mortensen, 2013), you may want to foreground communicative purposes. As seen throughout this book, contextually appropriate resources are not limited to English, let alone Standard English. We would like to stress that in contrast with native-speakerism, the effective use of English and multilingual resources is not dependent on nationalities or L1. Ironically, monolingual Anglophones with a strong commitment to their national Standard English varieties and without any substantial communication experience with 'outsiders' of their countries may be the first to have trouble with global communication through 'English' despite the fact that this is their L1 (Sweeney & Zhu, 2010).

To wrap up, Standard English ideology assumes that nationally institutionalised English varieties, usually in the US and the UK, should become global 'standard'. However, it is one thing to serve communication in a multilingual world, and it is quite another to adhere to any national Standard Language variety at a particular time irrespective of communicative contexts, including Standard English.

Summary

Now that we have introduced the following terms, you should be able to explain native-speakerism with these relevant concepts:

- language ideology
- monolingual ideology
- Standard Language ideology
- Standard English ideology
- communicative contexts
- **indexical** and **referential functions of language** (see Chapter 7.3)

We have discussed native-speakerism together with monolingual and Standard English ideologies. It seems that native-speakerist ideas subscribe to the tripartite fallacy: (1) to compartmentalise individual multilingual development as if it were plural acquisitions of one language after another; (2) to equate a nationally institutionalised L1 variety at a certain period with the internationally used lingua franca of a multilingual world; and (3) to assume NESs from particular geographical territories to be monolingual experts in this 'standard' variety.

Activity 7.2 "I'm a native speaker"

You may remember the following narrative from Chapter 6.4, written by Eljee Javier (2010), a Canadian-Filipino who taught English in China and looked like a local. Read it again, then answer the questions below.

> On this particular day, though, I remember one of the new students approached me with the following question (in English):

New student: So, you're not Chinese?
Me [Eljee Javier]: No, not at all!
New student: Your family is Chinese?
Me: No, none of them are Chinese. Both my parents are from the Philippines.
New student: But your English is so good!
Me: Well, I'm a native [English] speaker.
New student: Of course.

At this point I could tell she wasn't convinced of my English credentials. I felt myself grow increasingly frustrated and I found myself defensively saying the following:

> 'I'm from Canada.'

Suddenly the light seemed to go on. Her face lit up in a smile and she thanked me for my time before sitting down, obviously pleased with the news. I had told previous classes that I was from Canada but this was the first time that I had used that fact as a deliberate way of validating myself as a native [English] speaker.

(Javier, 2010: 99)

Questions

Q1 Who did the new student believe to be the best teachers of English?
Q2 Do you see any problems with this student's perceptions of language and identity?
Q3 What do you think made Javier "increasingly frustrated"?
Q4 Any other thoughts?

Feedback: *This narrative was published about a decade ago, and we hope that the ELT environment is becoming free from racist and ethnicist attitudes around the world. It is clear that the new student believed NESs from the Kachruvian Inner Circle (Chapter 4.1) to be the best English speakers and teachers. She regarded learning from NESs as a matter "[o]f course", and the fact that Javier was from Canada made her pleased. It is also clear that this student not only identified 'good' English with L1 English but also dissociated it from local Chinese or Asian appearance, perhaps associating it instead with 'white' Anglo-Saxon appearance. This was evident from her utterance: "But your English is so good!". However, there is no inevitable link between people's L1, races, ethnic appearances, and geographical origins (for Javier's identity negotiation, see Chapter 6.4). In her reflection on this incident, Javier (2010) made explicit that she became frustrated in dual ways. On the one hand, she problematised the student's native-speakerist attitudes and felt uncomfortable adopting an NES identity as validating professional credentials. On the other hand, she had to take advantage of NES status for the purpose of countering the same student's racist and ethnicist attitudes. Her frustration is summarised as follows: "Yet, in asserting my foreignness [from local Chinese] as a way of validating my native [English] speaking status, I uphold the very system that I am fighting against [i.e., native-speakerism]" (Javier, 2010: 101). As you see, the above narrative illustrates that native-speakerism may involve racism and ethnicism, thereby making itself more problematic.*

7.3 Ideologies of authenticity and anonymity

At the time of writing, we find that one major language school chain based in Osaka, Japan is running online lessons. Students taking them can choose from any of the three types of English instructors as reproduced and translated into English in Figure 7.2.[5]

In resonance with the narrative in Activity 7.2, only the middle type of English instructors, represented by a white, blond-haired look, are associated with "real pronunciation and expressions" along with "proper and deeper understanding" of English. The photos of Japanese and Filipino instructors are laid aside, somewhat implying that they are 'second-class' English speakers. According to the website, the "native[-English-speaking] instructors" all have strong connections with the Kachruvian Inner Circle (Chapter 4.1), mostly the US and Canada. Of course, there is nothing wrong with learning English as a local language in the 'traditional' English-speaking world. However, given its global status, we wonder how we can claim that bilingual and multilingual English users outside the Inner Circle, like the aforementioned other types of instructors, fail to speak "real" English and understand it in a "proper and deeper" way. In other words, we wonder how relevant the quality of the "real", "proper", and "deeper" within particular locales will be to global communication.

This section discusses another set of ideologies: authenticity and anonymity. More specifically, while native-speakerism underlies monolingual and Standard English ideologies (Chapter 7.2), these twinned ideologies are undergirded by Woolard's (2005; 2016) ideologies of authenticity and anonymity (Jenkins, 2014). Both ideologies are applicable to other phenomena or objects (e.g., food), but our focus here is obviously on language.

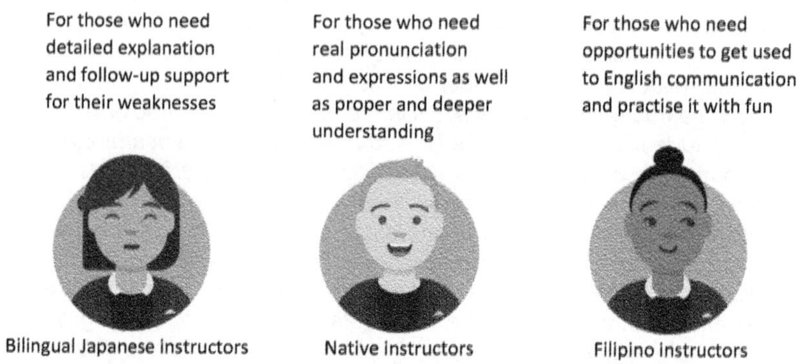

Figure 7.2 English online lesson website (originally in Japanese)

Ideology of authenticity

The ideology of authenticity or being real and true is concerned with how local and vernacular (i.e., associated with a particular group of speakers) a given language or language variety is. In Woolard's (2016: 22) words:

> [t]his ideology of authenticity locates the value of a language in its relationship to a particular community. Within this logic, a speech variety must be perceived as deeply rooted in social and geographic territory in order to have value.

For instance, having its own "system of sounds, word and sentence structure, meaning and structural organization of vocabulary items and other information" (Green, 2002: 1), African American Vernacular English (AAVE) should be grounded in identifiable local spaces shared by African American descendants. Otherwise, AAVE would lose its value according to this ideology. Speaking AAVE 'naturally', or as it is regularly used in shared speech communities, in turn represents or 'iconises' (Irvine & Gal, 2000) a particular social identity. What this ideology of authenticity emphasises is, then, the indexical, rather than referential, function of language (see Activity 7.1). To keep a language 'authentic', interacting with 'outsiders' or learning other languages or language varieties from outside may risk 'contaminating' its speakers' 'natural' language habitats.[6] In the same vein, the local language is perceived to be their property, and no outsider who studies it could really be an authentic speaker. Along this line, unlike the first author of this book, the second one would not be able to 'own' any types of British English as an outsider per the ideology of authenticity.

The ideology of authenticity has the potential to glorify the English spoken among those from particular social backgrounds within specific geographical territories. More precisely, in accord with ELT, this ideology attaches the value of English to the presumed, or rather imagined, Anglophone speech communities, especially in the UK and the US, consisting of white, upper-middle-class monolingual individuals. People categorised as having these attributes are supposed to speak national Standard English varieties without interference from external languages or language varieties. Like AAVE, it is such social and geographical peculiarities which lead to ideological authenticity.

Ideology of anonymity

The contrastive ideology of anonymity assumes that "hegemonic languages in modern society often rest their authority on a conception of anonymity" (Woolard, 2016: 25). In other words, authority resides in their perceived neutrality and universality as everyone's belongings, not as those of a limited group of individuals. Unlike the ideology of authenticity, what this ideology of anonymity emphasises is the referential, not indexical, nature of language. Language is perceived to be generic across communicative contexts. In this vein, nationalities and L1 are irrelevant to a hegemonic language like English since it is "denationalized" and "not the property of its mother tongue speakers" (Brutt-Griffler, 2002: 5). As such, this ideology dictates that there are desirable languages 'out there' for everyone to aim for and 'own'.

Notably, as Woolard (2005; 2016) observes, this ideology is beset with **méconnaissance** in the sociologist Pierre Bourdieu's (1977; 1991) sense, that is, 'ignorant misrecognition' (Ishikawa, 2020b). To be specific, the public fail to recognise the social, historical trajectory of the authority of dominant language use and instead 'recognise' authority as intrinsic in the language use itself. For this to happen, the arbitrary authorisation of linguistic conventions needs to be naturalised in a social sphere. In other words, citizens are made to believe that prestige is not a matter of political expediency but a matter of linguistic quality to the extent that they are unaware of an alternative order. In reference to the cultural theorist Raymond Williams (1973), Woolard (2016: 26) refers to this situation as the *saturation of consciousness*. Obviously, so long as people in general are unaware, they will sustain a taken-for-granted 'reality' (Bourdieu & Passeron, 1990). Put straightforwardly, if the whole society provides only one way of experiencing English or any given language, then the authority of its particular use eventually comes to appear, and becomes perceived to be, "self-evident and undisputed", in Bourdieu's (1977: 164) words. He calls this social condition "the *doxic* experience of the social world" (1977: 3; original emphasis). Prototypically, Japanese society generally gives the narrow set of representations of English in the direction of méconnaissance to glorify the ideological being of monolingual, Standard English (Ishikawa, 2016b; 2017b; see Activity 7.3). We could name a number of similar societies, and examples include Chile (Perez Andrade, 2019), China (Fang, 2015), Poland (Kiczkowiak, 2018), Saudi Arabia (Almayez, 2019), Thailand (Boonsuk, 2016), and Turkey (Karakaş, 2016).

It is such méconnaissance that connects the ideologies of anonymity and authenticity and allows them to work in collusion towards monolingual and Standard English ideologies. To borrow Jenkins' (2014: 78) words, "while the ideology of authenticity identifies certain local (native) varieties of English as the only genuine and valued ones, the ideology of anonymity presents these same local (native) varieties as unmarked and universal". Remarkably, "these same local (native) varieties" are, in fact, reified and commodified as Standard English in ELT, thereby not representing any existent speech communities.

Fundamentally, this Standard English is an idealised version of the language based on the intuitions of materials writers who are typically 'white', middle-class Anglophones, and different from the English they actually use for themselves (Leung, 2005; Hall, 2013). Bluntly put, while Standard English varieties in 'traditional' Anglophone nations serve for institutional purposes, the further abstracted versions of them in ELT serve for international commercial purposes in the EFL approach.

Summary

There are a few additional terms drawn on for discussion in this section:

- ideology of authenticity
- ideology of anonymity
- méconnaissance

We have discussed the ideologies of authenticity and anonymity. While the former affords the authenticity of language use to social, geographical peculiarities, the latter anonymises or 'deracinates' (Woolard, 2016) these peculiarities from the language use through méconnaissance. This méconnaissance is another fallacy: to misrecognise prestige as residing in linguistic features themselves while the social, historical reasons behind are consigned into oblivion in society. As a consequence, both ideologies (i.e., authenticity and anonymity) work together to buttress monolingual and Standard English ideologies.

Activity 7.3 *Doxic* experience within society

One of the authors of this book conducted research on attitudes towards individuals' own English use, involving 106 L1 Japanese university students from diverse disciplines who had received Japanese education (Ishikawa, 2017b; 2017c). After reading the following extract from the research findings, give your answers to the questions below, and share them in small groups if possible.

> The participants' attitudes were associated with two major issues inside Japan: concentration on 'correctness' without regard to communication purposes, and adherence to North American ENL [English as a native language]. Seeing that none of the participants who had encountered second-language English outside Japan saw it in its own right, overseas experience did not seem to exert much influence on their language attitudes.

Concerning the first issue, 47 questionnaire respondents (out of 95) and all the 18 interviewees made it clear that the school subject of English had marginalised oral communication, and focused on the knowledge of 'correct' grammar, and to some extent vocabulary and idiomatic expressions, in conjunction with reading and writing. In their view, this school English was in accordance with entrance exams. For instance, Interviewee 4 recalled that her upper secondary English oral communication (OC) class had actually been "a grammar class in the name of OC" and under the pretext of preparation for entrance exams. At the same time, the interview data suggested that there was no opportunity to see a normative approach to English challenged in Japanese daily life. A few interviewees explicitly noted that the normative approach was taken for granted in Japanese educational TV programmes, *eikaiwa* [i.e., English conversation (school)] commercials, or publications for Japanese learners of English. In addition, some questionnaire respondents and 11 interviewees problematised that university English modules made first-language Japanese users speak English among themselves. Interviewee 5, for example, repeatedly used the word "weird" to describe how she felt when English had to be used as a classroom language in Japan in the absence of non-Japanese speakers. Furthermore, apart from the English classroom, few participants seemed to have substantial regular opportunities to interact with non-Japanese in English either inside or outside university. A small number of questionnaire respondents claimed English in Japan to be either a symbol of effort or learned for knowledge, independently of its communication function.

With respect to the second issue, no participant doubted that North American ENL had predominated in the school subject of English along with entrance exams and other tests, albeit that some participants remembered having met non-North American ALTs, specifically those from the United Kingdom, Australia or New Zealand. It seems clear from the interview data that this predominance was supported by classroom materials. Interviewees 6 and 7, for example, remembered that Chinese and Indian or Kenyan characters had spoken North American ENL in lower secondary textbook CDs. Incidentally, Interviewee 8 similarly remembered that [US] presenters had acted Singaporean and other nationalities by using [North] American ENL in a Japanese educational radio programme series. In addition, both the questionnaire and interview data illustrated that the supremacy of ENL, mostly North American ENL, continued in the participants' university English modules, which were normally instructed by either a Japanese or an NES from North America, or to a lesser extent the United Kingdom or Australia. The same kind of supremacy was indicated by the participants who cited *eikaiwa* schools, foreign pop culture and some Japanese educational radio programme series.

(Ishikawa, 2017b: 250–251)

Questions

Q1 How well does the "concentration on 'correctness' without regard to communication purposes" resonate with the experience you had both inside and outside your regular schools before university? Is the situation different now if you have taken English courses at university or outside?

Q2 What about the "adherence to North American ENL"?

Feedback: *Obviously, your answers will depend on your personal experiences and opinions. As seen above, together with gatekeeping tests, Japanese English education concentrates on disseminating the knowledge of Standard (North American) English in ELT to a great extent. More to the point, there are hardly any opportunities to see the monolingual, normative approach to English challenged in Japanese daily life. The whole social experience, or rather "the doxic experience of the social world" (Bourdieu, 1977: 3), hinders Japanese citizens' critical thinking about what English as a global language is like, which will be the topic of the next chapter.*

Chapter summary

Particular language use becomes prestigious in our perception owing to language ideologies. In this chapter, our discussion has identified the intricacies of native-speakerism in English, especially ELT, which are schematised in Figure 7.3. This ideology favours NESs from the 'traditional' English-speaking world, especially from the UK and the US, as users of 'genuine' and 'perfect' English. What underlie native-speakerism are the twinned ideologies of monolingualism and Standard English. Those NESs are assumed to be the 'owners' of widely commercialised English varieties from the Anglophone world, or rather from imagined monolingual Anglophone speech communities. Originally, these varieties are domestically idealised as benchmarks of 'correctness'. As summarised in Chapter 7.2, native-speakerism, which logically subsumes monolingual and Standard English ideologies, entails the tripartite fallacy:

- to compartmentalise individual multilingual development as if it were plural acquisitions of one language after another
- to equate a nationally institutionalised L1 variety at a certain period with the internationally used lingua franca of a multilingual world
- to assume NESs from particular geographical territories to be monolingual experts in this 'standard' variety

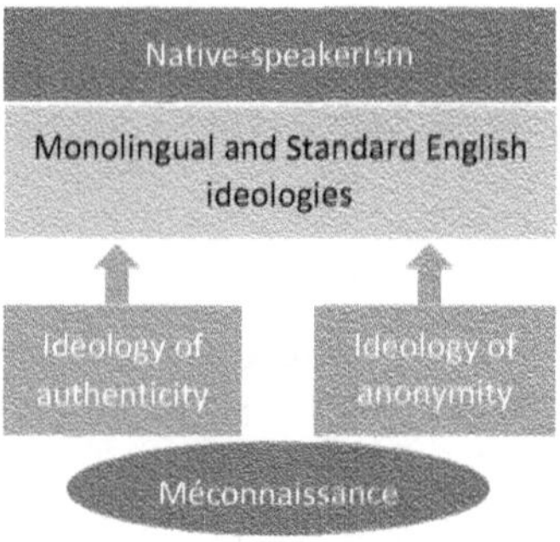

Figure 7.3 Intricacies of native-speakerism

After all, English as a global language should be adaptive across different communicative contexts, and essentialist ideas like this tripartite fallacy would not be helpful for effective global communication.

However mythical they may be, the ideologies of monolingualism and Standard English are still widely circulated in the world, as buttressed by the two contrastive ideologies of authenticity and anonymity. The former ideology (i.e., authenticity) values social and geographical peculiarities of imagined local Anglophone speech communities, the peculiarities inherent in the monolingual, 'standard' version of English. In contrast, the latter ideology (i.e., anonymity) values universalities, allowing the same English to become suddenly anonymous because it is believed to serve everyone's communicative purposes across contexts. As summarised in Chapter 7.3, this belief entails another fallacy, which eventually leads to native-speakerism:

- to misrecognise prestige as residing in linguistic features themselves while the social, historical reasons behind are consigned into oblivion in society

It is social experience both inside and outside education that confines or 'distorts' our perspective on language; in other words, it saturates our consciousness of language with the same old taken-for-granted 'reality'.

Notes

1 www.facebook.com/tomosoton (accessed 30 September 2020).
2 CEFR is a set of European-origin guidelines for describing language proficiency.
3 Academic jobs in Japan are searchable on the JREC-IN Portal website (Japan Science and Technology Agency, 2020).

4 The African Studies expert Sinfree Makoni's (2003: 139) "plural monolingualism" portrays multilingualism in South Africa, but here we refer to individual cognition, not to the societal level.
5 The avatars were generated on Avataaars Generator: https://getavataaars.com/ (accessed 30 September 2020).
6 Instead, multilingual hybridity can be the 'authentic' feature of a shared social space, as in the case of Multicultural London English (MLE), defined as "the overall range of distinctive language features used in multiethnic areas of London" (Cheshire et al., 2011: 154).

Further reading

Jenkins, J. (2007). *English as a Lingua Franca: Attitude and identity*. Oxford: Oxford University Press. Within the empirical research on ELT professionals' language attitudes and identities, chapter two makes evidence-based arguments about language ideologies surrounding an ELT environment.

Milroy, J. (2007). The ideology of the standard language. In C. Llamas, L. Mullany, & P. Stockwell (Eds.), *The Routledge companion to sociolinguistics* (pp. 133–139). Abingdon: Routledge. A concise, readable introduction to Standard Language ideology. Its discussion features English as a national Standard Language.

Seidlhofer, B. (2011). *Understanding English as a lingua franca*. Oxford: Oxford University Press. Chapter two discusses a backdrop of native-speakerism, and chapter three continues an extensive discussion in terms of Standard English and Standard English ideology.

8 Multilingualism in Global Englishes

Introduction

As the artist and writer Edmund de Waal has noted, "[w]ith languages, you are *at home anywhere*" (2010: 31; original emphasis). Imagine that you are enjoying your stay in southern Finland on a sunny day in June and drop by at a spacious pottery shop. In the shop you spot and stop at the KAHVI (coffee) sign and are offered free coffee. Looking to the left, you happen to find your South Korean friend who you last met more than a year ago in south-east England. You walk up to her with surprise. What an unexpected catch-up over coffee! You mention how generous it is that they offer free coffee and what a coincidence you both are there. You joke by saying that you feel exhilarated as if you were drinking caffè corretto (or Italian espresso with liquor). As a curious person she wonders whether there is any difference between this and Spanish carajillo and yet you don't know the exact answer. Throughout this conversation you feel at home, albeit that this is your first time to visit northern Europe.

You may have assumed the above conversation to be done through English. This example is based on a personal recollection of the second author of this book and English was actually the main medium of communication. At the same time multilingual influences and practices are features of their interaction, as duly foregrounded by Jenkins' (2015b) notion of English as a multilingua franca or EMF for short. As seen later, we can always find multilingualism in global communication to a varying degree. Thus, in this chapter we explore the notions of multilingual resources and repertoires and the role of English within multilingualism. You will also have the opportunity to explore examples of communication among English-knowing multilinguals, as well as considering your own opinions and experiences of English in a multilingual world.

Activity 8.1 Hunger is the best spice

What do you think each of the following underlined examples (1) to (4) means? When you have finished, compare your answers with the feedback below.

- After a long cycling we had a superb dinner. You know, (1)hunger is the best spice.
- We've developed a completely new design. I'll show it to you in a minute since (2)one look is worth a hundred words.
- Our company is always doing very well and going to acquire a large bank. It's like (3)adding wings to a tiger.
- That's not the case. Believe me. I can (4)"put my hands into the fire for it" (Pitzl, 2018b: 204).

Feedback: *Even without much contextual information each of the above four examples may well have triggered some plausible meaning in your interpretation. Instead of the first two you probably find the following equivalents in English dictionaries: (1) 'Hunger is the best sauce'; and (2) 'A picture is worth a thousand words' or the similar proverb 'Seeing is believing'. First, "Hunger is the best spice" is commonly found in at least two languages: Finnish 'Nälkä on paras mauste' and Swedish 'Hungern är den bästa kryddan'. As may be obvious the sauce and spice metaphors express how good food tastes when you are hungry. To be precise we are more likely to hear the metaphorical use of spice in Finnish and Swedish, but there is no inevitable link between these languages and the spice metaphor. Along this line you might not be surprised to hear Anglophones saying that hunger is the best spice rather than sauce. Next, 'A picture is worth a thousand words' or 'Seeing is believing' argues how convincing visual information is in comparison with verbal description. Its variant "One look is worth a hundred words" corresponds to Chinese 百闻不如一见 (bǎi wén bù rú yī jiàn) or Japanese 百聞は一見に如かず (hyakubun wa ikken ni shikazu), both of which literally say 'Hearing a hundred times is not as worthwhile as having one look'. As being a parallel non-English expression, example (2) is similar to "We should not wake up any dogs" (Pitzl, 2009, cited in Chapter 6.5), a variant of English 'Let sleeping dogs lie', which corresponds to German 'Wir sollten keine schlafenden Hunde wecken' (i.e., We should not wake up sleeping dogs) (Meierkord, 2012: 169).*

Unlike the first two you will probably not find equivalents for examples (3) and (4) in English dictionaries. Example (3) is a literal translation from Chinese 如虎添翼 (rú hǔ tiān yì) and corresponds to Korean 호랑이에게 날개 달기 (holangi-ehgeh nalgae dalgi) (i.e., giving wings to a tiger), both of which usually mean becoming even more powerful or stronger. Just for your reference the Japanese counterpart is 鬼に金棒 (oni ni kanabō), or, if translated literally, 'like a demon with a metal rod'. So long as you regard tigers and demons as mighty, the figurative sense of double advantage would not be difficult to recognise. Likewise, example (4) is almost the same as Dutch 'de hand voor iemand in het vuur steken' (i.e., to put the hand in the fire for someone) and German 'die Hand für jemanden/etwas ins Feuer legen' (i.e., to put the hand in the fire for someone/something). Arguably, the metaphorical image encapsulated in "put my hands into the fire for it" expresses the speaker's sincerity more emphatically than simply saying, for instance, 'guarantee it' or 'vouch for it' (Pitzl, 2009; 2018b).

Further discussion

- Can you think of any similar examples which you have used or may use in the future through English by exploiting your own linguistic and cultural backgrounds?
- What about other English users' similar examples which you remember having heard, if any?
- If possible, share your thoughts in small groups.

8.1 English as a multilingua franca

ELF research is essentially an academic quest to comprehend global communication among English users. As with cultures, the accelerated social connection at a global scale has had an impact on how languages are used for communication. To understand a currently prominent notion in the field of ELF (i.e., English as a multilingua franca or EMF), this section considers ELF as a linguistic phenomenon and refers back to globalisation, global linguistic and cultural flows, linguistic resources and repertoires as well as English similects. In so doing language use is viewed as that of "mobile [multilingual] resources" (Blommaert, 2010) across "dynamic multilingual repertoires" (e.g., May, 2014: 232). What multilingualism is like in the notion of EMF will be illustrated in the next section, where key ideas are emergent multilingual influences and practices, **covert multilingual resources,** and **multilanguaging** (Jenkins, 2015b; Cogo, 2018; Ishikawa, 2017a).

At the time of writing the world started suffering from a new pandemic virus. The Tokyo Metropolitan Government in Japan warned of a possible regional outbreak by citing the word *overshoot* or オーバーシュート (ōbāshūto). Reuters reported:

> Tokyo has seen a surge in coronavirus cases this week, reporting a record 47 cases on Thursday for a total of 259 [in Japan]. While not many for a city of nearly 14 million, experts have warned of a high risk of an "overshoot" – or explosive rise – given that more than half of the newest cases could not be traced.
>
> (Park, 2020)

This quoted word, "overshoot" or オーバーシュート (ōbāshūto), had caught on with the media and among Japanese speakers. Almost all Tokyoites, or the Japanese more generally, must have been familiar with the words *over* (オーバー) and *shoot* (シュート), which might have generated the strong metaphoric images of extensiveness (e.g., to spread *over*) and rapidity (e.g., to *shoot* ahead). Perhaps, they needed an impactful, and possibly also unusual, word to attract our collaborative efforts and prevent us from falling victim to the invisible enemy. In the future we could possibly see this use of *overshoot* (i.e., "explosive rise") more internationally now that major news sources including Reuters have reported it. After all, in this age of globalisation, words in particular settings and 'named' languages may easily move across to other settings and languages.

Globalisation is certainly not a sudden event. As one example, the management theorist Kenichi Ohmae (1995), currently the president of an online university (Business BreakThrough University),[1] ascribes the emergence and expansion of a global market to the historical development of the capitalist economy. In his view the territorial borders of economic activity have long become blurred and in flux and do not coincide with those of nation states, thereby referring to cartographical categories as "no more than an illusion" (Ohmae, 1995: 20). Obviously, human activities are not limited to economics or financial and business domains. As with the above local news reported globally in English, the internet and mobile technologies make global reach quite ordinary and ubiquitous. Then, globalisation is fundamentally about our increased spatial connections or "supraterritorial relations" along with territorial ones (Scholte, 2008: 1496). As mentioned in the opening chapter (Chapter 1.3), while territorial relations take notice of geographical locations and political dominions of the earth's surface, supraterritorial relations add the "qualities of *transworld simultaneity* (that is, they extend anywhere across the planet at the same time) and *transworld instantaneity* (that is, they move anywhere on the planet in no time)" (Scholte, 2008: 1480).[2] In other words, globalisation is not just about the shrinking of territorial space but also about the furthering of the complexity of social relations thanks to simultaneous and instant mobility. For example, it is possible that as with one of the authors of this book, a tremendous number of people across the globe are using MacBook laptops (with different keyboards) and drinking Starbucks coffee (with local variations) at this moment. Like both authors they may regularly exchange emails abroad. It is also possible that quite a few students and researchers in different parts of the world read this chapter like you, and that some students occasionally engage in online discussion of topics related to this textbook. In brief, globalisation is a qualitative transformation of social connections as well as quantitative.

As introduced in Chapters 1.3 and 2.3, what this quantitative and qualitative transformation accompanies are global or transnational flows across local, national, and global scales (Risager, 2006; 2007;

Pennycook, 2007). Along with the increased mobility of people, technology, finance, media, ideas, and values (Appadurai, 1996), among others, we are experiencing complex web-like linguistic flows across spatial borders. While global languages, such as English, are adapted and altered in these constant flows, what accelerates this change is multilingual contact in language use (e.g., Alim, 2009) or in "the two 'natural' loci of language" (Risager, 2006: 74) out of the three (Harris, 1997; 1998; Risager, 2006; 2007; Mauranen, 2012). As already discussed in Chapter 2.2, these three loci are: (1) linguistic resources and repertoires at the psychological or cognitive level; (2) linguistic practices at the interactional level; and (3) linguistic constructs at the ideological level. This final locus takes a "macrosocial" (Harris, 1997; 1998; Mauranen, 2012) or "system-oriented" (Risager, 2006; 2007) view towards real-world linguistic phenomena (e.g., Vetchinnikova, 2015), usually in the form of "politically named languages" (Li, 2016: 6) such as English and Japanese. Like Blommaert (2010), we use the term *linguistic resources* to refer to observable concrete linguistic forms or patterns, in contrast with abstractly defined 'objects' of *languages* at the ideological level. Linguistic resources become increasingly *mobile* due to globalisation and potentially have different indexical and referential functions (i.e., representing who speakers are and delivering what they have to say; Activity 7.1; Chapter 7.3) across different **communicative contexts** (i.e., who interactants are, how they are interacting, in what circumstances, and for what purposes; Chapter 7.2). In brief, "mobile linguistic resources" (e.g., Pennycook, 2011: 884) are specific parts of language ubiquitously deployed in and for each communicative context at a global scale. Below we would like to refer back to the example in Chapter 4.3 with additional information.

8.2 Mobile multilingual resources and dynamic multilingual repertoires

Imagine that L1-Hungarian and L1-Japanese doctoral students communicate through English at the University of Southampton, UK. At the psychological or cognitive level, each of them has their own multilingual repertoire, or the totality of individually available multilingual resources (Chapters 2.5, 4.3). More specifically, the former student learned Hungarian as his L1 at home in southern Hungary and then also English at school like many people around the world. After studying abroad in Catalonia, Spain with international students from Europe and South America and obtaining a master's degree in history in his hometown, he moved to London with family and started working at an international company with locals and immigrants. He took advantage of some literacy in Spanish in the business domain and felt comfortable with diverse English which he encountered in metropolitan areas every day. Now living in Southampton, he 'mixes' some Japanese in social situations, especially when he sees Japanese members at a local Hungarian society. On the other hand, the latter student learned Japanese as his L1 at home in northern Japan and then some Italian, German, and French in relation to imported scores and books at music school while adding English later in secondary education. At university he took a French course and studied abroad at a sister college in Cambridge with a particular interest in European Union law. As a law major, he found Latin terminology to be associable with modern European languages. After obtaining a master's degree in TESOL based on the Tokyo campus of a US university he moved to Southampton, where he shares residence with students from Austria, mainland China, Hong Kong, India, and Uganda. He takes advantage of some literacy in French and Chinese in academic and social domains, often finding himself involved in multilingual communication with his flatmates or with international students in Paris (which is within relatively easy reach from Southampton). As such, both L1-Hungarian and L1-Japanese students have rich multilingual resources in their respective repertoires, but this does not mean that they 'possess' each language separately in a full range of domains. At the same time, even though both have a good command of English and speak Japanese, their resources in these 'same' languages are different in quantity (for Japanese in particular) and linguacultural quality (i.e., cultural association with language for each individual; Risager, 2015; 2020). Moreover, English and other resources coexist within their respective repertoires for every making-meaning activity, whether consciously or subconsciously.

At the interactional level, these L1-Hungarian and L1-Japanese students regularly adapt and adjust their language use for communicative purposes (i.e., linguistic accommodation; Chapter 4.3). Simply put, as explained in Chapter 4.3, they use the Hungarian English similect and the Japanese English similect (i.e., the English influenced by either L1 Hungarian or L1 Japanese at the cognitive level) during this linguistic accommodation. Mauranen (2012) refers to this as *second-order language contact*. In reality, however, these L1 are not the only linguistic resources activated for meaning negotiation. The Hungarian student's language use is drawing variably on his multilingual resources from phonology to discourse, even if it appears English on the surface. This 'English' use in turn is accommodating to and accommodated by the Japanese student's 'English' use, which is similarly drawing on individual multilingual resources. In the first place, they have developed their own 'English' through such multilingual communication in their lives. As time goes by and the better the two students know one another, the less amount of linguistic accommodation becomes necessary to achieve mutual understanding. Incidentally, they increase their "multilingual resource pool" (Pitzl, 2018b), whose lexical items are not necessarily categorisable into one particular language. For example, they usually sit at the same corner of a study hall at their graduate school and start to call this corner Quartier magyar (or the 'Hungarian district'). Although the Japanese student is obviously not magyar (which means *Hungarian* in Hungarian), the use of the French-origin word *Quartier* symbolises his occasional visits to and affection for Paris. For another example, they occasionally use the word *gambatting*, which derives from the Japanese word 頑張る (gambaru) and takes the form of *-ing* to make it more conspicuous (Ranta, 2006) and English-like. The original Japanese word usually means 'keep working hard' and they use gambatting in this sense. They find this word to be friendly as well as funny, all the more so because the similar-sounding word *gambolling* means quite the opposite according to the Hungarian's British colleagues. Other lexical resources they occasionally use with international colleagues include *chidísimo*, or the superlative of 'Mexican' slang *chido*, *ppalli ppalli* or Korean 빨리빨리, and *undingable*, with Chinese 顶 (dǐng) embedded, which basically means the coolest, chop-chop, and unbearable, respectively.

Again, globalisation entails global linguistic flows. As with the above example of the two international students, these flows lead to unpredictable encounters with linguistic resources at a global scale (e.g., Blommaert, 2010). The fact that we each have a myriad of opportunities to deal with language and communication throughout our lives adds complexity to the linguistic flows. Even on a single day you might, for example, study classic literature in a library, browse and keep up with an online newscast, and socialise at an international nightclub. In sum, due to globalisation the linguistic resources we use and encounter become increasingly associable with multiple languages, rendering many individuals' repertoires variably multilingual. Put differently, it is more common that mobile linguistic resources are multilingual, and that individuals' linguistic repertoires are dynamically multilingual too. Despite this reality, however, at the ideological level languages are neatly separated into named categories (e.g., English, Japanese), normally at the national level and very often in association with national cultures and speech communities. Here languages are assumed to be bounded systems, but, as ideological entities, we cannot describe and delineate any of them to a full extent. As schematised in Figure 8.1 we face tremendous meetings or tensions between fixity at the ideological level and fluidity at the cognitive and interactional levels. The constructed ideology of national languages as fixed, systematic 'objects' remains powerful whenever we learn language and communicate. Even so, individual language development and use for global communication exploit linguistic resources as a fluid, messy process, as with the above international students. Together with cultural

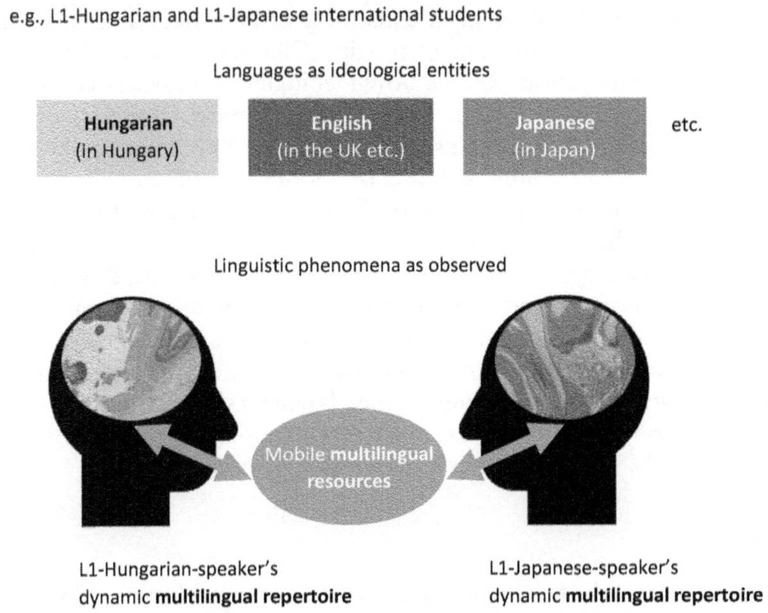

Figure 8.1 Languages and multilingual resources and repertoires

flows (Chapter 2.3), language does flow through social networks and mobility, and, again, to borrow Pennycook's words: "Caught between fluidity and fixity, then, cultural and linguistic forms are always in a state of flux, always changing, always part of a process of the refashioning of identity" (2007: 8).

On the one hand, national languages (e.g., Japanese as the de facto official language of Japan) or language varieties (e.g., British English as the de facto official language of the UK) are designated and their idealised norms are provided in the form of Standard Languages which in fact change over generations (Chapter 7.2). Each language or language variety has its own speech community defined geographically and imagined ideologically, most frequently at the national level (Chapter 1.3). As with English varieties in the world (Chapter 4.1), local or regional mutual interactions lead to different provincial, social, and ethnic language (sub)varieties. On the other hand, our world has already experienced roughly one generation of increased global mobility and associated linguistic flows, mainly thanks to the advent of digital communication. Our 'natural' linguistic resources are easily mobilised across communicative contexts and our repertoires do not necessarily fit with particular speech communities (Chapter 3.1) or even communities of practice (Chapter 5.4). Fundamentally, we are able to practise language beyond the membership of any pre-set communities. This is not to say that the ideological constructs of languages and language varieties, as well as language ideologies (Chapter 7), are irrelevant to global communication. Rather, how ideologies and associated power relationships play a role in communicative transactions is always an empirical question. Against this backdrop, ELF enquiry observes the dynamic and contextual use of mobile multilingual resources across multilingual repertoires, or, better put, dynamic multilingual repertoires which are constantly being affected by contact between English users at a global scale. In other words, in line with Blommaert, "[o]ur focus of analysis should be the actual linguistic, communicative, semiotic resources that people have, [develop, and make use of for global communication], not abstracted and idealized (or ideologized) representations of such resources [i.e., languages]" (2010: 102). Note that the term **semiotic resources** relates to meaning-making cues, signs, and symbols, with the linguistic as a prime example.

Summary

To understand the notion of English as a multilingua franca (EMF), we have revisited the terms:

- globalisation
- linguistic and cultural flows
- linguistic resources and repertoires
- indexical and referential functions of language
- communicative contexts
- English similects, multilingual resources and repertoires
- semiotic resources

Activity 8.2 "It's not breakfast food..."

In the following mobile phone texts, Hanako and Hanna (pseudonyms) at an English-medium college in Tokyo are discussing breakfast. They were born and raised in Japan and the US, respectively, and Hanako has study-abroad experience in the Midwestern US. Read their text exchange and then answer the questions below.

[Translation in brackets]

01 Hanako: i recommend はなまるうどんのサラダうどん (Hanamaru Udon no sarada udon)
[i recommend Hanamaru Udon's salad udon noodles]

02 Hanna: It's not breakfast food...

03 Hanako: its good tho

04 Hanna: What about Platform Café?

05 Hanako: 行ったことない (ittakoto nai)

	[I've never been there]
06 Hanna:	I'll go then
07	They have yummy breakfast food~
08 Hanako:	pictures
09	i think サラダうどん (sarada udon) is perfect breakfast tho lol [i think salad udon is perfect breakfast tho lol]
10 Hanna:	忘れた (wasureta) … just I got boiled egg and toast [I forgot … just I got boiled egg and toast]
11	それおかしいよ (sore okashii yo) [I think that's strange]
12 Hanako:	おかしくないよ (okashiku nai yo) [i don't think it's strange]
13 Hanna:	おかしい (okashii) [It's strange]
14 Hanako:	healthy healthy
15 Hanna:	I usually just eat a みかん (mikan) at breakfast, so I'm very happy to have breakfast food~~~ [I usually just eat a satsuma orange at breakfast, so I'm very happy to have breakfast food~~~]

(Ishikawa, unpublished data)

Questions

Q1 Hanako and Hanna hold different views concerning breakfast. How much tension do you find between them? What makes you think so?
Q2 What languages or linguistic resources can you see here?
Q3 What cultural orientations, references, and practices can you observe here?

Feedback: *Hanako names a chain udon restaurant and likes to have salad udon noodles there for breakfast (line 01). For her it is a "perfect breakfast" (line 09), all the more so because it is "healthy healthy" (line 14). However, Hanna regards it as "not breakfast food" (line 02) and strange (lines 11, 13). They are on parallel tracks, either making repeated pro claims (lines 03, 09, 12, 14) or contrary claims (lines 02, 11, 13). Even so you probably do not see any serious tension between them for a number of reasons. First of all, the topic of this text conversation is not sensitive. Also, they both slip into and out of Japanese and use friendly, colloquial language, including "tho" (lines 03, 09), "lol" (line 09), and "よ (yo)" (lines 11, 12). This suggests that they can share similar multilingual identities (Chapter 6.5). Moreover, while disagreeing, Hanna's effective use of semiotic signs, "…" (line 02), "~" (line 07), and "~~~" (line 15), mitigates disagreement and promotes a friendly atmosphere.*

While some of the language here is clearly identifiable with 'named' languages such as Japanese and English, other uses are less easily identified. For instance, the name of the restaurant is 'Platform Café' but is this English? Similarly, 'lol' is originally an acronym for the English phrase 'laugh out loud' but it is now a phrase in many other named languages. It may be that asking what languages are used is the wrong question. Better is to think about how particular linguistic resources are used to create meaning and affect in specific contexts such as this friendly exchange.

Last but not least, Hanako's and Hanna's breakfast practices represent the complex nature of food culture and more importantly, their equally flexible cultural orientations to food. Hanako recommends salad udon (line 01), and udon noodles have different variations across Japan. Made in mainland China and elsewhere, however, one particular type is somewhat popular globally. As Hanna claims, whatever type of udon noodles are used, salad udon is not popular for breakfast in Japan, at least, where boiled eggs and toasts are probably more commonly eaten as with abroad. Similarly, while みかん (mikan) or satsuma orange is originally from southern Japan, it is not unusual to have orange or orange juice in the morning at a global scale. As with this example, language, communication, and culture can be integrated in a complex manner in our everyday conversation.

8.3 Multilingualism in English as a multilingua franca

We introduced the research field of ELF in Chapter 4, which enquires into how communication takes place among English users, and especially what an observable linguistic phenomenon is like, in this age of "supraterritorial relations" (Scholte, 2008: 1496). In other words, the main target of ELF enquiry is the communicative use or function of language (Seidlhofer, 2011) in global encounters between English users. ELF as a linguistic phenomenon is thus different from a delineated language or variety of language for a certain speech community, and there can be no ELF phonology, grammar, or other linguistic codes universalised or hypostatised (e.g., Baker & Jenkins, 2015). A currently prominent notion is Jenkins' (2015b) EMF, which positions English used as a global lingua franca within multilingualism. More precisely, while multilingualism has always been a crucial part of descriptive work in ELF research (e.g., Hülmbauer & Seidlhofer, 2013; Seidlhofer, 2017), EMF foregrounds multilingualism as the theoretical raison d'être of the target linguistic phenomenon (Jenkins, 2015b). As such the ELF phenomenon is defined as "Multilingual communication in which English is available as a contact language of choice, but is not necessarily chosen" (Jenkins, 2015b: 73). Simply put, global communication is never immune to multilingualism, and English is not always chosen among English users. Here multilingualism takes its form by the use of mobile multilingual resources across dynamic multilingual repertoires (Figure 8.1). Empirical data, such as VOICE and ELFA (see Chapter 4.3), have attested that multilingual influences and practices are always emergent across linguistic levels (e.g., phonology, grammar, lexis, pragmatics, and discourse structure). We, thus, may argue that monolingualism in English is not the norm nowadays, and that multilingualism with English is "the one single factor without which there would be no ELF" (Jenkins, 2015b: 63).

EMF theory observes what English-knowing agents actually do around the globe. It addresses the empirical evidence that "the best solutions [for mutual understanding] need not be the most standardised-like or native-like ... [or] even English" (Mauranen, 2018b: 114). As it happens, you may observe non-English resources extensively employed among English users. In other words, multilingual practices are sometimes overt. The following example is taken from text exchanges on mobile phones between Japanese and Taiwanese students at an English-medium college in Tokyo. They are meeting up on a street.

Extract 8.1 Meeting up on a street
[Translation in brackets]

01 Student A:	セブンの隣ね (sebun no tonari ne)
	[so it's next to the 7(-Eleven)]
02 Student B:	我在インフォ (wǒ zài info)
03	的前面 (de qián miàn)
	[I'm in front of the info(rmation board)]

(Ishikawa, unpublished data)[3]

The Japanese language combines three different scripts: kanji (i.e., Chinese characters), hiragana (literally 'ordinary') phonograms, and katakana (literally 'fragmentary' but in effect 'foreign') phonograms, and both "セブン" (7) and "インフォ" (info) are written in katakana. Line 01 makes sense as Japanese, and lines 02 and 03 are largely Chinese. You might have thought of student A as Japanese and student B as Taiwanese. However, the opposite is true (i.e., student A: Taiwanese; student B: Japanese). Similar to the ELF and multilingualism scholar Alessia Cogo's (2016: 71) data, English-speaking interactants may use available resources from their communication partners' L1. Here what the Japanese and Taiwanese students engage in is clearly multilingual accommodation.

Not surprisingly, multilingual resources are often overt when participants share relatively similar languages. In the next example three Europeans are chatting together. Having been invited to a wedding in Paris, Jean (L1 French) is showing pictures on the wedding couple's website to Anna (L1 Italian) and Karen (L1 German).

Extract 8.2 French wedding

01 Jean:	it's nice but it's a bit=
02 Anna:	=too much eh?=
03 Jean:	=cheesy
04 Karen:	[YE::AH
05 Anna:	[YE::AH
06 Karen:	yeah a bit too much I think @@
07 Jean:	so (.) blue flower we say (.) fleur bleue
08 Anna:	why? (.) [to say that it's cheesy?
09 Jean:	[fleur-yeah (.) fleur bleue means (.) you know when you have these pictures with little angels of
10 Karen:	a:::h [yeah
11 Anna:	[yeah
12 Jean:	fleur bleue
13 Karen:	kitsch- [kitschig
14 Jean:	[kitschig yeah @@@

(Cogo, 2010: 301)

Notes

=	latched utterance
[	overlapping speech
CAPITAL LETTERS	emphasis
:	lengthened sound
@	laughter and a laughter-like sound
(.)	brief pause

Jean tries to express his impression of the pictures by "cheesy" (line 03) and then by "fleur bleue" (line 07). Cogo (2010) explains that he is reminded of old-fashioned wall pictures of angels with blue flowers as a symbol of protecting children in his hometown and elsewhere. As such, he may feel something trite when he adds "fleur bleue" (line 07). Remarkably, he gives its literal English translation first – "blue flower" (line 07) – to make sure that Anna and Karen will understand it. In other words, he pre-empts their potential misunderstanding or non-understanding of it. After the sequence of further explanation of this local expression (line 09) and confirmation (lines 10, 11), Karen brings another felicitous word to the conversation, namely, kitschy, but in its original German form (i.e., "kitschig" in line 13), simultaneously echoed by Jean (line 14).

Throughout this conversation they seem to share similar multilingual identities by co-constructing meaning with multilingual resources (Chapter 6.5).

Multilingual practices and resources may also be overt even among speakers of the same L1. In the following example, two Japanese exchange students in southeast Spain are texting on mobile phones.

Extract 8.3 Travel planning
[Translation in brackets]

01 Student C:	あとギリシャについてはギリシャ人から返信なんもこないので無視! (Ato girisha ni tsuitewa girishajin kara henshin nanmo konai node mushi!) [Re Greece there's no reply at all from the Grecian and so ignore it!]
02 Student D:	Valeee [okk]
03	I bought a dome case for the gopro dakara creo que podemos sacar buenas fotos!! ❤ [I bought a dome case for the GoPro; therefore, I think we can take good photos!! ❤]
04 Student C:	っしゃあああ! あざすあざす! (Tshaaaa! Azasu azasu!) [Woooooo! Thx thx!]

(Ishikawa, unpublished data)

At first glance they may not appear to adjust or adapt their language use to each other. However, they actually accommodate it in their different ways. Student C's pragmatic use of highly informal Japanese sets a friendly tone. While individuals' Japanese repertoires can be very different, both students share so much of its colloquialism as peer students. At the same time student D's flexible use of multilingual resources represents everyday situations they face and cope with together.

Apart from phonological influences with which you may be familiar from experience, multilingualism is often more covert, unlike Extracts 8.1, 8.2, and 8.3. In this regard covert multilingual resources in Cogo's term take notice of individuals' "knowledge and experience that shapes their language" (2016: 63) and "concern the influence of the user's multilingual resources on their communication, which nonetheless remains in English … on the surface" (2018: 358). Below is an example in which university lecturers S1 (L1 Japanese) and S2 (L1 Italian) are talking about their Japanese colleague who has just "passed messages" (line 03 below), or finished marking papers, passed them to S1, and left already.

Extract 8.4 "Don't step on the stones"

01 S1: so she's so relieved
02 S2: oh [all right that's goo::d
03 S1:   [that she passed messages
04 S2: mhm=
05 S1: =but I have to do that by Monday=
06 S2: =mhm=
07 S1: =it's ok so she's re-that's why I said don't step on the stones … cause so relaxed you-you might feel
08 S2: (chuckle)
09 S2: oh all ri:ght [I see
10 S1:   [yeah
11 S2: but is it just a Japanese:: eh:: way of saying?
12 S1: yeah and when we finish something
13 S2: mhm mhm
14 S1: sort of our concentration … will not be … ah how can I explain … not disturbed … we can't concentrate on something

(Cogo & Dewey, 2012: 131)

Notes

[	overlapping speech
:	lengthened sound
=	latched utterance
(chuckle)	nonlinguistic features of the transcription

On the surface this conversation takes place solely in English, but within this stretch of interaction S1's Japanese-origin expression "don't step on the stones" (line 07) is shared with S2. The saying 足元の石ころにつまずく (ashimoto no ishikoro ni tsumazuku), literally 'to stumble on small stones at your feet', probably comes to mind when S1 tells S2 the background of her thought to the effect of pre-empting S2's potential misunderstanding or non-understanding. That is, their colleague becomes "so relieved" (line 01) or light-hearted and needs some caution to avoid making some blunder. S2 does understand the expression in question through comprehension check and confirmation (lines 11, 12) and invites further explanation from S1 (lines 12, 14).

It should be added that by the term covert multilingual resources, Cogo (2016; 2018) does not aim to distinguish between covert multilingual influences and overt multilingual practices. This would be difficult and not very fruitful. For example, multilingual influences on pronunciation may be covert in individuals' cognition but perceived to be overt by their interlocuters (Cogo, 2016). Cogo's point is that multilingualism in EMF is not just about overt code-switching or translanguaging (see Chapter 9).

Multilingual influences may also be covert based on similarities across languages. In the extract below, international students are looking for a street in Vienna, Austria.

Extract 8.5 "Here on my card"
S1: L1 German; S2: L1 Italian; S3: L1 Greek

01 S1: so it's somewhere here (1) you have to look at the streets
02 S2: quite far from here?
03 S1: no (.) it's not THAT far (2) e:rm=
04 S3: =here on my card (1) sixteenth
05 S1: sixth (1) er district
06 S2: sixth?
07 S1: mhm

(Hülmbauer, 2009: 340)

Notes

(1), (2)	longer pauses (number of seconds)
(.)	brief pause
CAPITAL LETTERS	emphasis
:	lengthened sound
=	latched utterance

You may have noticed that S3 refers to her *map* when she says "here on my card" (line 04). S1's and S2's interpretation of S3's "card" is embedded in the actual presence of the map and their ongoing action to find the street. Indeed, we may say that communication is a transmodal activity with words not independent of other interpretive clues (see Chapter 9). At the same time, in this example, Hülmbauer (2009; 2013) reminds us of the local German-speaking environment and names the 'false friends' (e.g., Hill, 1982) of German 'Karte', as well as Italian 'carta' or 'carta geografica' and Greek 'χάρτης' (chártis). All these 'false friends' resemble the word card in form and the word map in meaning. It may be argued that S3's "card" (line 04) is a very apt word choice for the participants involved, given these similarities across German, Italian, and Greek. The same could possibly happen around southern Finland (mentioned in the opening section of this chapter) owing to the similar 'false friends' of Finnish 'kartta' and Swedish 'karta'. It appears to be the word map that is deviant from others. But perhaps this use of "card" would not be difficult for an L1 English speaker to understand given its association with 'cartography'. On a side note, this English word (i.e., cartography) is almost the same as French 'cartographie', and we can add another 'false friend' of map, French 'carte'.

All the participants in the above extracts function in multiple languages to fulfil their lives and English is their additional language. But L1 English speakers also have opportunities to use English as a global lingua franca. They will be exposed to multilingualism through English, however covert it may be. Mobile multilingual resources (Figure 8.1) are thus relevant to all English users irrespective of their ability in other languages. Even monolingual English speakers, in other words, English speakers with monolingual repertoires, will be able to learn "to engage in the dynamic exploitation of previously unfamiliar linguistic resources by adapting to a multilingual environment" (Ishikawa, 2017a: 38). Jenkins (2015b) would call this capability multilanguaging, that is, linguistic development through accommodation to mobile multilingual resources. This term itself derives from Hoa Nguyen (2012), who argues that it "helps elucidate the dynamic mechanisms of language use and reduce any possible association of multilingualism with an accomplished and perfectionist state" (Nguyen, 2012: 68, cited in Jenkins, 2015b: 78). We will use *multilingual(ism)* in this book to include *multilanguaging* (Jenkins, 2015b; Ishikawa, 2017a). Accordingly, we regard linguistic accommodation in global encounters as essentially *multilingual* accommodation.

Last, at the discourse level, even if the final product looks completely English, like this paragraph, its writing process and rhetorical embodiment may be more multilingual. For example, one student at the American University of Beirut in Lebanon describes herself as follows.

> I think in my trilingual head. Most of the time, I think in Arabic but my words fail me often and I have to recourse to English and French to save the thought. I find myself using English when I don't know the pronunciation of the same word in French and vice versa.
>
> (Quoted in Mullin et al., 2014: 158)

In addition, this student is familiar to a 'parsimonious' discourse in English for academic writing and an 'elaborate' one in Arabic and French. More specifically, she has often seen argumentative sentences full of rhetorical flourishes in Arabic and French, unlike a direct, straightforward style of argument which is conventionally taught in academic writing. When she renders what she has to write into English, she is likely to give careful consideration "about the 'elaborateness' that Western English conventions undercut and about rhetorical moves that might instead be effectively meshed with the parsimonious" (Mullin et al., 2014: 158).

As seen in all the above examples, multilingualism is observable to varying degrees, and the notion of EMF invites us to look at inherent multilingualism among English users, for most of whom English is an additional language. More precisely, global communication through English entails emergent multilingual influences and practices across different linguistic levels. They are emergent since the actualisation of multilingual resources depends on each contingent interactional environment and each constellation of the individuals involved, all of whom have their own social, linguistic, and cultural backgrounds (e.g., Ishikawa, 2020b). In short, "contextual embodiment is crucial" (Baird et al., 2014: 181) in understanding multilingualism in EMF. Accordingly, none of the above examples are meant to be generalisable. After all, we cannot fully understand any communicative use of language without specific contextual considerations, and contextual and methodological "multifariousness testifies to rich potentials and intricacies of ELF as an object of study" (Ishikawa, 2018b: 456).

Activity 8.3 The future of English as a multilingua franca

Read the following two quotations from Jennifer Jenkins and Anna Mauranen concerning how English might develop in the future and its place in a linguistically diverse, multilingual world, then answer the questions below. Discuss your answers in small groups if possible.

> This is how I see ELF developing at least over the next two to three decades: an ELF future that will become both increasingly multilingual, and increasingly contingent and fluid. This view has much in common with Pennycook's (2010b) notion of 'Translingua franca English', although it takes the argument still further by shifting the emphasis from multilingualism within English to English within multilingualism.
>
> (Jenkins, 2018a: 601)

> English will keep changing as it has done throughout its history, with second-language users as an increasingly important influence in the thoroughly globalised contemporary world. It is unlikely to supplant local languages in its function as a lingua franca, but to complement the linguistic diversity that lives on locally and regionally. The rate of change is harder to for[e]see – language change never takes place at even speed – but one might surmise that the magic number of three generations, which holds for a variety of

social changes including language shift might be something to go on in predicting major changes in the use and forms of English. At present, we are really talking about the first global generation of ELF, if we date it back to roughly the adoption of the Internet. *The one thing we can predict with certainty is that English will keep changing.*

(Mauranen, 2015: 49, cited in Jenkins, 2018a: 602 with emphasis added)

Questions

Q1 Do you agree that English use will be "increasingly multilingual" in the future?
Q2 Do you think, as Mauranen suggests, that future generations will also become more multilingual in their use of English?
Q3 How multilingual do you think your use of English is? Is the multilingualism (if there is any) covert or overt?
Q4 If you agree that English use will become more multilingual, what do you think the implications might be for understanding and teaching English?

Feedback: *There are no right answers to these questions. However, as we have discussed in this chapter, any use of English for intercultural and transcultural communication is likely to involve multilingual resources in one way or another, even if we are not always aware of it. We have also discussed the increasing speed and complexity of linguistic and cultural flows which adds further diversity to our communities and communicative practices. However, as pointed out in Chapter 3.1, multilingualism is not a new phenomenon. The implications for understanding and teaching English are many and we will discuss these implications in the final part of this book.*

Chapter summary

We reviewed that English as a multilingua franca (EMF) conceptualises the linguistic phenomenon of ELF within multilingualism and entails these ideas:

- mobile multilingual resources
- dynamic multilingual repertoires
- emergent multilingual influences and practices
- covert multilingual resources
- multilanguaging

As we stressed, global communication among English users is inherently multilingual. In the first place, many English users have rich multilingual resources in their repertoires with English as their additional language. Present-day social networks and mobility at a global scale enable us to bring these resources together ubiquitously, thereby guiding our repertoires to develop in unpredictable ways. L1 English speakers are no exception, even if they are considered monolingual. Through lingua franca communication they will exploit previously unfamiliar resources which are associable with different languages in an ideological sense. To conclude, no matter how distinct each language is at the ideological level, real-world linguistic resources are malleable and permeable, influencing or affecting English use and occasionally leading to overt multilingual practices. As such the hallmark of global communication through English is multilingualism as emergent for each communicative event.

Notes

1 https://bbt.ac/ (accessed on 30 September 2020).
2 Note that the word *transworld* is used interchangeably with *global* (and *transplanetary*) in Scholte (2008).
3 The unpublished data in this chapter (including the data in Activity 8.2) will be published soon in relation to the discussion of EMI (Ishikawa, 2021, in press).
4 www.futurelearn.com/courses/understanding-language/0/steps/21196 (accessed 30 September 2020).

Further reading

Cogo, A. (2018). ELF and multilingualism. In J. Jenkins, W. Baker, & M. Dewey (Eds.), *The Routledge handbook of English as a lingua franca* (pp. 357–368). Abingdon: Routledge. An accessible overview of the links in both practice and research between ELF and multilingualism.

Jenkins, J. (2015b). Repositioning English and multilingualism in English as a Lingua Franca. *Englishes in Practice*, 2, 49–85. doi: 10.1515/eip-2015-0003. This landmark article reflects on theoretical development in the field of ELF and proposes the notion of EMF. Before reading this article, you may want to visit a FutureLearn webpage, 'Next steps in research: English the "multilingua" franca'.[4]

Pitzl, M.-L. (2018c). Creativity, idioms and metaphorical language in ELF. In J. Jenkins, W. Baker, & M. Dewey (Eds.), *The Routledge handbook of English as a lingua franca* (pp. 233–243). Abingdon: Routledge. The chapter outlines how English-knowing participants in global communication tap into their multilingual repertoires and use creative idioms and metaphors to fulfil a range of interactional and ideational purposes.

Part III

Contemporary issues and domains in culture, language, and Global Englishes

9 Trans theories and Global Englishes

Introduction

You may remember that we began the previous chapter with the example of the second author's unexpected meeting of a friend from South Korea while drinking coffee in a shop in Finland. We emphasised that, although the main medium of communication was English, it was English as part of wider multilingual practices, or English as a multilingua franca (EMF), which, as explained in this chapter, can also be seen as part of wider translanguaging practices. However, communication is not just about language. You may have envisaged two people standing close to each other in a large, bright shop, full of the smell of coffee, while smiling and holding fancy china cups. Moreover, drinking coffee is a global phenomenon, or, better put, cultural practice, with different variations which can be interpreted variously and dynamically in transcultural communication. Thus, language is embedded in transmodal and transcultural meaning-making in which, as Li Wei explains:

> [t]he Translanguaging perspective does not aim to count how many different languages an individual or a society owns or how well they manage the different languages, but instead focuses on the dynamic process whereby multilingual language users mediate complex social and cognitive activities through strategic and creative employment of multiple semiotic resources to act, to know, and to be.
>
> (2016: 21)

In this chapter we explore what has been termed **the 'trans' turn** in applied linguistics (Hawkins & Mori, 2018). In particular, we examine translanguaging and the related concepts of code-switching and **languaging**. We provide an overview of current translanguaging theory and the similarities and differences with Global Englishes, and especially EMF. We also consider the links between translanguaging, EMF, transcultural communication, **translanguaging space**, and transmodal communication, which we will go on to outline in more detail in the following chapters. You will also have the opportunity to reflect on your own experiences and opinions of multilingualism, translanguaging, and Global Englishes.

Activity 9.1 Bilingual breakfast

Read the example below and then answer the three questions that follow.

The first author's household is a bilingual one in which English and Thai are spoken daily. The extract below is a typical example of the type of conversation that might occur in the kitchen at breakfast time.

> Will: หิว – who would like ไข่, croissants, and น้ำส้ม?
> (Translation: I'm hungry – who would like eggs, croissants, and orange juice?)

Questions

Q1 What languages can you observe here?
Q2 Why do you think the different languages are used?
Q3 What is the effect of using different languages here?

Feedback: *This is a little bit of a 'trick' question. From a perspective as a linguist we can distinguish clearly between two named languages: Thai 'หิว', 'ไข่', 'น้ำส้ม' and English 'who would like', 'croissants' (which, to add another level of complexity, is exactly the same as the 'French' word), 'and'. However, from the perspective of the participants (the first author's household) these would not be relevant distinctions. These are just the words, or linguistic resources, that are used to talk about and describe various things in the kitchen that all of the family are familiar with. When making this utterance the speaker is not thinking 'I will use a Thai phrase or word here and an English one here'. Rather the participants are thinking about making breakfast and communicating this, using the shared linguistic resources of the family. Of course, if you ask the speakers they know that ideologically the words and phrases are assigned to particular named national languages but this is not how they function in this instance. This perspective, which questions the relevance of distinctions between named languages, has become known as translanguaging, which García and Kleyn describe in the following way: "for us, translanguaging refers to the deployment of a speaker's full linguistic repertoire, which does not in any way correspond to the socially and politically defined boundaries of named languages" (2016: 14).*

9.1 The trans turn and Global Englishes

Against the backdrop of globalisation, we see terms with the prefix trans- more often in applied linguistics. Examples include transnational, transpatial, transcultural, transmodal, and translingual or translanguaging more commonly. The Latin preposition trans meant *across* or *over* and we usually use the prefix trans- to mean the same today. The opening article of the *Applied Linguistics* special issue *Considering 'trans-' perspectives in language theories and practices* defines the 'trans' turn as follows.

> 'Trans-' can be understood to mean crossing borders or boundaries, and this move toward a 'trans-' disposition signals the need to transcend the named and bounded categories that have historically shaped our thinking about the world and its inhabitants, the nature of knowledge, and communicative resources.
>
> (Hawkins & Mori, 2018: 1)

Global Englishes, and especially the notion of EMF, accords with this 'trans' turn in that it questions the fixed scope of named, bounded languages typically at the national level. The same is true of intercultural and transcultural communication and multimodality and transmodal communication, as seen later in this chapter and in Chapters 10 and 11.

On a personal note, a researcher on the ResearchGate website[1] whom we had never met discussed the notions of transcultural and transmodal communication with the second author of this book and criticised the use of the 'trans' terms in his papers (Ishikawa & McBride, 2019; Ishikawa, 2020b) as self-contradictory. This researcher argued that any 'trans' notion negates traditional boundaries and yet predicates its validity on the existence of the boundaries themselves. This concern is worth noting and is aptly expressed by the aforementioned article.

> In fact, these terms with the 'trans-' prefix at once advocate for the appreciation of fluidity and flexibility seen in contemporary society and underscore the very existence of categories, borders, and boundaries that are called into question. How should we grapple with this tension between innovations and traditions … ?
>
> (Hawkins & Mori, 2018: 1)

After all we cannot transgress boundaries unless they exist. To answer this question Global Englishes research in EMF does not dismiss the ideological categories of languages. At the same time, it embraces and places focus on real-world linguistic domains in which mobile resources are used across dynamic repertoires (Figure 8.1). Put differently, EMF explores the *interplay* between the ideological being of *multiple*, enumerable languages and fluid, flexible linguistic resources and repertoires. We may say that this is why the 'multi' is retained in English as a *multi*lingua franca even though ELF researchers do recognise the dynamic communicative process foregrounded by the term translanguaging. Globalisation does not diminish the relevance of named language categories but rather accentuates their existence as *ideological constructs*. It is our communicative practices that transgress and potentially transform the perceived boundaries of these constructs.

9.2 Translanguaging

It may be helpful to begin with a characterisation of translanguaging from the leading translanguaging scholar Li Wei, who defines it as "the fluid and dynamic practices that transcend the boundaries between named languages, language varieties, and language and other semiotic systems" (2018: 9). While this definition refers to communicative practices, Li Wei also characterises translanguaging as a theory of language and states that "Translanguaging offers a practical theory of language that sees the latter as a multilingual, multisemiotic, multisensory, and multimodal resource that human beings use for thinking and for communicating thought" (2018: 26). We will consider both the practice and theory of translanguaging in greater detail below. To explain translanguaging we will first outline its relationship with the relevant (although distinct) area of code-switching and earlier theories of languaging. We will also briefly look at translanguaging's roots in bilingual language education before turning to current translanguaging theory.

Code-switching and translanguaging

You may be familiar with code-switching, whose research has a longer tradition (e.g., Gumperz, 1964) than translanguaging. We hereafter use the term translanguaging as embracing code-switching (García, 2009; cf. Otheguy et al., 2015). As its name suggests, individuals who code-switch assume the involvement of perceived different codes. Examples include US lawyers' strategic switch between African American Vernacular English (AAVE) and 'standard' North American English (Fuller, 1993; Hobbs, 2003) as well as long-term international couples' "automatic code-switching" in everyday interactions (Pietikäinen, 2014). Again, linguistic accommodation in global encounters is *multilingual* accommodation (Chapter 8.3). It is no wonder that interactants occasionally have an explicit awareness of exploiting plurilingual resources to serve one or more communicative functions. These functions are, for instance, inclusion or exclusion, discourse-marking, conceptual understanding, signalling culture, and promoting solidarity (e.g., Klimpfinger, 2009; Cogo, 2010; Mauranen, 2014; Vettorel, 2014). An example from Klimpfinger shows how participants code-switch between English (lines 01, 02 below) when addressing the whole group (who are multilingual) and French (their shared L1) when addressing one another (line 03 below).

Extract 9.1 Specifying an addressee
S2 & S3: L1 French

01 S2: if you are interested er i let it <un> xx </un> and er via email send er er to you and=
02 S3: =<to S2> also the french version. </to S2>=
03 S2: =<to S3> <L1fr> oui oui oui oui oui {yes} </L1fr>

(Klimpfinger, 2009: 360)

Notes

<un> xx </un>	unintelligible speech
=	latched utterance
<to S2> … </to S2>	addressing to S2
<L1fr> … </L1fr>	utterances in the speaker's L1 French
{yes}	translation in English

While deemphasising this explicit awareness of different codes and emphasising the permeability of languages (and non-linguistic cues, signs, and symbols), translanguaging carries on code-switching research (Li, 2018; Auer, forthcoming). Certainly, it may be claimed that "code-switching preserves named language categories intact", and that translanguaging "takes up an internal perspective to describe the languaging of speakers who are said to be bilingual or multilingual" (Vogel & García, 2017: 5). However, available publications with discussions of code-switching, including the first handbook of ELF (Jenkins et al., 2018), suggest that individuals' language categories are subjective and variable rather than intact, and that their internal perspectives are not detached from 'external' named categories, linguistic or otherwise, but linked to them "through their interpretive filters" (Kitazawa, 2013: 264). In short, both code-switching and translanguaging are not necessarily at odds epistemologically. Nonetheless, translanguaging is concerned with a much wider range of communicative, educational, and social issues than code-switching, as seen later.

Languaging and translanguaging

The suffix -ing in translanguaging is as significant as the prefix trans-, indicating that it is about a dynamic process. The linguist Peter Doughty's (1972; 1979) term languaging as "a function of … innate ability" (1979: 67) has been widely known in the field of second-language acquisition (SLA), often through the definition of a prominent scholar in the field, Merrill Swain: "the process of making meaning and shaping knowledge and experience through language" (2006: 98). Like other sociocultural theorists she notes the language-mediated nature of human cognition and learning in society. Another linguist, Nigel Love, similarly takes a cognitive perspective and defines languaging as "the first-order activity of making and interpreting linguistic *signs*, which in turn is a real-time, contextually determined process of investing behaviour or the products of behaviour (vocal, gestural or other) with semiotic significance" (2004: 530; original emphasis). Unlike an abstract language as "a second-order cultural construct" (Love, 2004: 530), then, languaging refers to making use of situationally available multimodal resources under cognitive, biological, and sociocultural restraints (e.g., Thibault, 2017). From the plane of his own systemic functional grammar, Michael Halliday, mentioned in Chapter 1.2, adds that "the noun 'language' is … a grammatical metaphor" (2003: 192) for "a vast, open-ended system of meaning potential, constantly renewing itself in interaction with its ecosocial environment" (2003: 25). In sum, languaging is the situated act of exerting the meaning potential of linguistic and other semiotic resources to understand and interact with the world.

Bilingual education and translanguaging

Translanguaging has its roots in bilingual education research. This term itself derives from Colin Baker's (2001)[2] English translation of Cen Williams' (1994) Welsh term trawsieithu (Lewis et al., 2012) and marries with the above 'languaging' perspectives. Williams (1994) uses the term to describe pedagogic practices and values in the flexible use of both English and Welsh in bilingual secondary schools. Later, another bilingual education scholar, Ofelia García, posits translanguaging as follows.

> [B]ilinguals have *one linguistic repertoire* from which they select features *strategically* to communicate effectively. That is, translanguaging takes as its starting point the ways in which *language is USED by bilingual people as the norm*, and not the abstract

> language of monolinguals, as described by traditional usage books and grammars.
>
> (2014: 2; original emphasis)

At a broader societal level, this strategic use aims to revitalise minority language (e.g., William, 1994), reengage minoritised learners (e.g., García, 2009), or otherwise challenge sociopolitical conditions (e.g., Li & Zhu, 2013; Li, 2020). At school or university, translanguaging is a pedagogic strategy when an imposed medium of instruction is different from students' strongest languages. Citing García (2009) and Creese and Blackledge (2015), Li Wei observes the potential of translanguaging in education as follows.

> By deliberately breaking the artificial and ideological divides between indigenous versus immigrant, majority versus minority, and target versus mother tongue languages, Translanguaging empowers both the learner and the teacher, transforms the power relations, and focuses the process of teaching and learning on making meaning, enhancing experience, and developing identity.
>
> (2018: 15)

Whether inside or outside the classroom, "Translanguaging highlights the ways in which language users make use of the tensions and conflicts among different signs, because of the socio-historical associations the signs carry with them, in a cycle of resemiotization [i.e., continuous contextualisation] and transformation [of the functions of these signs]" (Li & Lin, 2019: 211). As such, translanguaging exploits available linguistic and other semiotic resources to understand, interact with, and challenge the existing social world.

Current translanguaging theory

Currently, the translanguaging lens aims to develop three strands: transcendent or transgressive, transformative, and transdisciplinary. To be specific, in line with García and Li Wei (2014: 3), Li Wei summarises the three as referring to:

- the fluid practices that go beyond, i.e., *transcend*, socially constructed language systems and structures to engage diverse multiple meaning-making systems and subjectivities;
- the *transformative* capacity of the Translanguaging process not only for language systems but also for individuals' cognition and social structures; and
- the *transdisciplinary* consequences of re-conceptualizing language, language learning, and language use, and working across the

divides between linguistics, psychology, sociology, and education (2018: 27; original emphasis).

The following example from Singapore presented by Li Wei (2018) serves to show both the types of interaction that translanguaging researchers investigate and why a translanguaging perspective is important.

Extract 9.2 Seetoh talking to her old friend
Seetoh: Aiyoh (discourse particle), we are all <ka ki nang> (自己人 = own people, meaning ‘friends’), **bian khe khi** (免客气 = don’t mention it). Ren lai jiu hao (人来就好 = good of you to come), why bring so many “barang barang” (‘things’). **Paiseh** (歹劳 = I’m embarrassed). ‘Nei chan hai yau sum’ (你真有心 = you are so considerate).

(Li, 2018: 13–14)

Notes

Italics	Singlish
In square brackets < >	Teochew (Chinese)
Bold	Hokkien (Chinese)
Underlined	Mandarin (Chinese)
In double quotation marks	Malay
In single quotation marks	Cantonese (Chinese)
Standard font	English
( )	annotation

As Li Wei notes, the complexity of linguistic resources here makes it difficult and perhaps inappropriate to try to establish which languages and language varieties are being used. However, most significantly, Li Wei argues that examples like this demonstrate the limitations of approaching communication through a sole focus on named language entities, national or otherwise, that do not correspond to how people make use of their linguistic repertoires.

9.3 Translanguaging and English as a multilingua franca

Within Global Englishes translanguaging concurs with EMF since it observes our fluid interactional practices in global encounters and associated cognitive and potentially also social development beyond linguistics. Indeed, similarities between EMF and translanguaging are striking, especially when it comes to the first strand (i.e., transcendent or transgressive; see Chapter 9.2). This strand heeds how interactants transcend or transgress the boundaries of named languages and semiotic modes. Within this particular strand, EMF "may be regarded as broadly conceptualised translanguaging ... which emerges across individuals, time and space" (Ishikawa, 2017a: 38). As explained later and as suggested in the chapter on EMF (see Chapter 8.3), the implications of the first strand may be seen in any global encounter and as the gross property of a communicative situation. At the same time, with regards the second strand of translanguaging (i.e., transformative; see Chapter 9.2), EMF also entails being politically active for social change and academic impact. In the past, one of the motivating goals of ELF research, or Global Englishes research more generally, has been to challenge the existing power structures that place Anglophone Englishes and native-speakerism as a core part of applied linguistics, especially ELT (see Chapter 7). While the place of 'native' English speakers (NESs) has changed in applied linguistics over a couple of decades, now EMF argues for multilingualism as the norm whether English is an individual's first language or not. Moreover, regarding the final strand (i.e., transdisciplinary; see Chapter 9.2), as a major research field in applied linguistics ELF is inevitably as transdisciplinary as translanguaging to engage in "[t]he theoretical and empirical investigation of real-world problems in which language is a central issue" (Brumfit, 1995: 27).

The parallels between the two fields are also recognised by translanguaging researchers. Li Wei notes in his discussion of 'Chinglish', translanguaging, and ELF in China as follows.

> The Translanguaging perspective that this article sets out to promote helps to highlight the creative and critical dimensions of this Post-Multilingualism phenomenon by simultaneously considering the structural and cognitive complexities of linguistic multicompetence and the historical, political, and ideological sensitivities and impacts of Chinglish. It connects well with ELF research which, over the last 15 years or so, has shared precisely these concerns[.]
>
> (2016: 20)

Similarly, Kimura and Canagarajah identify three central shared features between the two fields that they claim are, first, moving beyond 'nativeness' to an analysis of communication between any speakers of different linguacultural backgrounds; second, an emphasis on pragmatically motivated variable communicative practices, rather than a description of particular linguistic forms; third, a multilingual (re)orientation that "consider[s] ELF as variable manifestations of multilingualism, rather than a superordinate code" (2018: 300).

Nonetheless, there are a number of differences between Global Englishes, EMF, and translanguaging. An obvious distinction is that, while power relationships (e.g., Guido, 2012; Jenks, 2018) and pedagogic issues (e.g., Dewey, 2012; Bayyurt & Akcan, 2015) have been part of ELF research, translanguaging engages in a wider range of social issues around education in general and the place of language in society beyond ELT and English. García and Li Wei (2014: 3) expect that "orders of discourses shift and the voices of Others come to the forefront, relating then translanguaging to criticality, critical pedagogy, social justice and the linguistic human rights agenda". This more salient social transformational goal reflects the fact that the researchers involved have tended to observe the language use of unprivileged groups since Williams (1994). Other modest differences include that EMF takes the malleability and permeability of named languages at the cognitive and interactional levels as its *starting point* because it is immanent in *all* global communication (Jenkins, 2015a). Accordingly, while translanguaging tends to focus on overt multilingual practices, EMF potentially targets any global communication to enquire into situational multilingual influences and practices with varying degrees of overtness (see covert multilingual resources in Chapter 8.3).

In addition, as implied by the term "repertoires in flux" (Jenkins, 2015a: 76), multilingualism in EMF is the gross property of the individuals involved, along with local environments (Ishikawa, 2017a). Referring back to the opening episode of this and the previous chapters (a chance meeting in a shop in Finland between the second author and a Korean friend), even if so-called monolingual English speakers join the conversation, their language use will be affected by the Japanese and Korean interlocutors and perhaps also by a local multilingual environment. The linguistic resources each individual brings have different origins and development paths. The monolingual English speakers also need to accommodate and thereby *multilanguage* for the sake of effective communication (see multilanguaging in Chapter 8.3). With a focus on effective global communication and multilingualism, ELF enquiry in general has evidenced how crucial multilingual accommodation is, irrespective of an individual's ability in other languages (e.g., Sweeney & Zhu, 2010; Baird et al., 2014). Meanwhile, more drastically, and with more explicit focus on cognition, translanguaging "challenges the idea that different named languages, which exist as historical, political, and ideological entities, exist as cognitive entities in the human mind." (Li & Ho, 2018: 37).

Finally, again, EMF is concerned with "Multilingual communication in which English is available as a contact language of choice, but is not necessarily chosen" (Jenkins, 2015a: 73). The availability of English is different from multilingualism and translanguaging, both of which can dispense with English (e.g., Fei & Weekly, 2020; Pennycook, 2020). For this reason, the scope of EMF may be narrower than translanguaging. Even so, global communication would be more difficult without this currently most prominent lingua franca in the world (Chapter 3.3). It should be noted that as with translanguaging, the English in EMF is not equal to monolingually oriented Standard English in ELT, but rather the language always along with, and influenced or affected by, multilingual reality (Chapter 8).

Activity 9.2 EMF and translanguaging practices

Cogo (2012; 2016) investigated the multilingual practices of a small business with part of the focus on ELF and translanguaging. In the following example three employees are discussing what should appear in the content of an invoice. Read the example (we have removed the tags indicating languages) and answer the questions that follow.

H: L1 German; M & P: L1 Spanish

01 P: ah: ok ok yeah (aspiration) ah: (2.5) and then the netto (3) pfourteen (2) one two so the position is important one two (2) and then we have the euros (1) and then we have the the porcentage? (.) but has another name says usl
02 H: u u eh u s t ist umsatzsteuer
03 P: was ist dis?
04 M: betrag (.) betrag? como prefieres?
05 H: no betrag is whole amount Pedro
06 P: ah ok
07 H: betrag is amount
08 P: amount ok
09 H: and and taxes is u s t

(Adapted from Cogo, 2016: 71)

Notes

:	lengthened sound
(aspiration)	nonlinguistic features of the transcription
(1), (2)	longer pauses (number of seconds)
(.)	brief pause

Questions

Q1 What languages can you identify in the example?
Q2 Was it easy or difficult to assign each line or word to a specific language? Why?

Feedback: *You will probably have identified English and, depending on your familiarity with the respective languages, you may have identified German and Spanish. Here is the example again with the language tags now added – English is unmarked, de = German, and sp = Spanish.*

H: L1 German; M & P: L1 Spanish

01 P: ah: ok ok yeah (aspiration) ah: (2.5) and then the <LNde>netto<LNde> (3) pfourteen (2) one two so the position is important one two (2) and then we have the euros (1) and then we have the the porcentage? (.) but has another name says usl
02 H: u u eh <L1de>u s t ist umsatzsteuer<L1de>
03 P: <LNde>was ist dis?<LNde>
04 M: <LNde>betrag (.) betrag?<LNde> <L1sp>como prefieres? <L1sp>
05 H: no <L1de>betrag<L1de> is whole amount Pedro
06 P: ah ok
07 H: <L1de>betrag<L1de> is amount
08 P: amount ok
09 H: and and taxes is <L1de>u s t<L1de>

(Cogo, 2016: 71)

Notes

<LNde>...<LNde>	utterances in German, which is not the speaker's L1
<L1de>...<L1de>	utterances in the speaker's L1 German
<L1sp>...<L1sp>	utterances in the speaker's L1 Spanish

However, Cogo discusses the complexity of linguistic resources used here and the problems that this leads to if we try to analyse the extract from a traditional linguistic perspective which makes clear distinctions between named languages.

> *[T]hese resources are mentioned in such an intricately mixed way that it is perhaps impossible, and possibly unnecessary, to identify a specific function for every piece of multilingual resource used. From a methodological perspective, it is also rather difficult to assign a language, or tag the transcript with the language of origin, for every item used. [Line 03, i.e., "was ist dis?"], for example, is like an amalgamation of German, Spanish and English, and the use of the tag <LNde> is a simplification of what is really happening in the exchange and what P is doing with his repertoire of resources.*
> (Cogo, 2018: 364)

9.4 Translanguaging, English as a multilingua franca, and contemporary trans perspectives

It may be helpful to review the discussion of EMF in the previous chapter and that of translanguaging in the current chapter before introducing three related ideas. As detailed in Chapter 8, the notion of EMF foregrounds inherent multilingualism in English used as a global lingua franca. Real-world multilingual resources are malleable and permeable and individuals' meaning-making resources are contacted through social networks and mobility. As a result, multilingual influences and practices are always emergent with varying degrees of overtness from pronunciation to the organisation of talk. Over time and across space, individuals develop their available multilingual resources dynamically through continuous engagement in global communication. Like cultures and identities, how ideologies and associated power relationships become relevant to each participant in each interaction is unpredictable. So-called monolingual English speakers are no exception, and they will learn to exploit multilingual resources by adjusting and adapting their communication to each transnational encounter.

In this chapter, we have added translanguaging perspectives. Similar to EMF, translanguaging observes bilinguals' and multilinguals' situational exploitation of available meaning-making resources to understand, interact with, and challenge their society. During this process they transcend or transgress the boundaries of named languages and semiotic modes. EMF, in turn, underscores the interplay between such real-world dynamic communicative practices (foregrounded by translanguaging) and the ideological existence of multiple languages. This interplay may transform the perceived boundaries of linguistic and other categories. At the same time, EMF posits multilingual influences and practices as immanent in *all* global communication, however covert they may be. This is all the more so because it takes multilingualism as a gross property of each communicative situation rather than the property of individuals. Also, unlike translanguaging, EMF narrows down its research target to scenarios in which the currently most prominent lingua franca in the world (i.e., English) is available as a contact language of choice.

In this section we introduce the connections between translanguaging, EMF, and three current 'trans' perspectives: transcultural communication, translanguaging space, and transmodal communication. Translanguaging and EMF accord closely with the notion of transcultural communication, which questions the fixed scope of named cultures typically at the national level. Within translanguaging theory, the concept of translanguaging space(s) is especially relevant to transcultural communication. Li Wei defines this as "a space that is created by and for Translanguaging practices, and a space where language users break down the ideologically laden dichotomies between the macro and the micro, the societal and the individual, and the social and the psychological through interaction" (2018: 23). There are clear parallels here to transcultural communication, which, as a reminder, is characterised as "communication where interactants move through and across, rather than in-between, cultural and linguistic boundaries, thus, 'named' languages and cultures can no longer be taken for granted and in the process borders become blurred, transgressed and transcended" (Baker & Sangiamchit, 2019: 472). Crucially, in both translanguaging spaces and transcultural communication participants are not seen as *between* different languages and cultures but rather as breaking down and transcending the borders between languages, cultures, and other meaning-making resources. Thus, we would argue that translanguaging connects more appropriately with transcultural communication than intercultural communication, as the prefix inter-implies that communication takes place *between* different cultures.

To be sure, intercultural communication is still a useful term and ideological categories of cultures, including national ones, should not be dismissed. However, in EMF theory and research we see how participants' cultural understandings and orientations are various within and across different scales (e.g., local, national, global) as well as variable for each interaction (e.g., Pitzl, 2018b). Ideological national scales for languages and cultures are just among many. In the first place, it depends on an interactional context how much culture affects or influences meaning-making and what role other social differences, such as age, gender, and professional occupation, play in cultural interpretations. In the ELF field, the first author's research (e.g., Baker, 2015; 2018) in particular has depicted how cultural meaning is co-constructed, contested, negotiable, nebulous, and overlapping among multilingual English users. It is not too much to say that cultural resources in global communication are so amorphous that we cannot always envisage cultural boundaries in any clear manner.

The notion of EMF also accords with another significant aspect of translanguaging and transcultural communication, that is, multimodality and transmodal communication, which questions the separation or concentration on language as a semiotic tool. Linguistic resources coexist with other semiotic means, such as facial expression, gesture and posture, image, light, place and positioning, fragrance, and sound. Again, if you remember the example given in the introduction to the previous and present chapters, we included the sights, smells, sounds, and feel of the setting. Many of these features can be referred to as modes which are defined as: "a socially shaped and culturally given resource for meaning making. *Image, writing, layout, music, gesture, speech, moving image, soundtrack* are examples of modes used in representation and communication" (Kress, 2014/2017: 60; original emphasis). Multimodality, thus, involves the full range of communication forms for understanding communication and representation and attempts to counter the bias towards language as the only semiotic resource researched (Kress & van Leeuwen, 2001; Jewitt, 2014/2017). As Pennycook argues, "the separation of language from the complexity of signs with which its use is associated has limited our understanding of a broader semiotics" (2007: 49). Similarly, in the context of translanguaging, Li Wei remarks:

> [m]ultimodality is an integral part of human language evolution and essential to human communication. ... The recent expansion of new communication media has woken human beings' sense of multimodal communication once again and begun to shift the attention to other modalities of human communication [than language].
> (2020: 245)

As is probably familiar to you, the "new communication media" such as **social networking sites (SNSs)** and the internet allow us to use text, hyperlinks, images, animations, and videos to create meaning and affect online instantaneously, thereby accelerating global or transnational flows of language, culture, and identity. The term **transmodality** (often synonymously used with 'transmodal communication') is particularly useful in describing such *processes* where a range of modes are used simultaneously, with boundaries between modes blurring, and useful distinctions among modes not easily made (e.g., Sultana, 2016; Hawkins, 2018). If we attempt to analyse modes separately, we may lose a more holistic understanding of the communication. Therefore, like the distinction between interculturality and **transculturality** (see Chapter 10.2), transmodality is not a rejection of multimodality but instead a perspective that focuses on multimodal resources and transmodal processes that result in what the multimodal scholar Denise Newfield terms "the transmodal moment" (2014/2017: 103). Figure 9.1 provides an example of the transmodal possibilities of translanguaging with the use of text 'I', the heart symbol, and the flag of the People's Republic of China, all of which are combined to produce the phrase 'I love China'.

As with translanguaging, in the ELF field, EMF takes an interest in how real-world interactional practices defy and blur the boundaries of

Figure 9.1 A translanguaging sign
(Li, 2016: 6)

semiotic modes, including named languages. Individuals see these multiple modes generating meaning simultaneously and collaboratively in a given time and space (Dovchin et al., 2016; Baker & Sangiamchit, 2019). As seen in Chapter 11 in relation to Global Englishes, the notion of transmodality or transmodal communication indexes how meaning is experienced through the integration of multiple verbal and non-verbal modes. It emphasises how modes are integrated, not as the sum of each mode, but as one synergetic whole. Transmodality does not, of course, only refer to digital communication but to all communication. For instance, Canagarajah (2018) investigates how international STEM (or science, technology, engineering, and mathematics) scholars in a Midwestern American university make use of the meaning-making affordances provided by language, non-verbal artefacts, and context in communication. You will have the opportunity to explore transcultural communication and Global Englishes in more detail in Chapter 10 and transmodality and Global Englishes in Chapter 11.

Activity 9.3 What is English?

Throughout this chapter (and this book) we have critically considered how we can understand English in all its diverse uses as a global language. Through the discussion of translanguaging the very notion of a 'language' has itself been questioned. We have seen how people communicate in ways that do not correspond easily to categories of named languages and how communication also blurs boundaries between linguistic resources and other meaning-making resources (multimodality and transmodal communication). In relation to English, Barbara Seidlhofer has noted that although ELF researchers are agreed on the diverse functions of English as a lingua franca, "[t]he absolutely crucial question, of course, remains how the 'English' that functions as a lingua franca is conceptualized" (2011: 77).

Think about your own experiences of using and learning English and answer the questions below. If possible look at settings where your English use has been recorded such as social networking sites or emails.

Questions

Q1 What is English for you?
Q2 To what extent is your English the same or different to others' English?
Q3 How easy is it to separate your knowledge and use of English from other languages (or linguistic resources) as well as other modes of communication?

Feedback: *Your answers will of course vary according to your experiences and opinions. Nonetheless, we think it is unlikely that your 'English' is exactly the same as others; at the same time, there will also be many aspects that are the same. Baird et al. give the following explanation of how we might understand 'English' in ELF communication: "what is shared in ELF interactions that enables the participants to refer to the language as English is related to social experience rather than abstract rules. In many cases these shared experiences will be learning 'English' as a subject at school and then later engaging with wider communities which also make use of English. Thus, ELF users share overlapping repertoires of communicative practices and the associated conventionalised, but adaptable and variable, linguistic forms which form part of these practices" (2014: 182–183). However, this position, which follows an emergentist and complexity theory perspective, is not without controversy. We will return to complexity theory in more detail in Chapter 12.*

Chapter summary

You should now be familiar with **'trans' theories** in applied linguistics, including:

- translanguaging
- transcultural communication
- transmodality or transmodal communication

In addition, you should also be familiar with relevant ideas, and these are:

- code-switching and translanguaging
- languaging and translanguaging
- translanguaging space
- multimodality and transmodality

In this chapter, we provided an overview of how the above notions and ideas relate to Global Englishes, multilingualism, and particularly EMF. Overall, EMF accords with translanguaging, transcultural, and transmodal communication. In EMF scenarios participants cannot always envisage linguistic and cultural categories in a clear manner or experience meaning as a result of each distinct mode. Instead, multilingual resources are permeable, cultural resources are rather amorphous, and semiotic modes are synergetically integrated. To facilitate global communication among English users, then, **multilingual, transcultural, and transmodal accommodation** will be key, and all of these aspects pertain to translanguaging, whose spaces are increasingly available thanks to globalisation. Having said that, as seen in Chapter 7 (Activity 7.3 in particular), ELT tends to focus on idealised Standard English rather than how to use available meaning-making resources including learned Standard English. Pedagogic applications of EMF and 'trans' perspectives will be examined in the final part of this book. Before that, we will outline a theory of transcultural communication (Chapter 10), feature how Global Englishes, translanguaging, transcultural communication, and transmodality come together in digital communication (Chapter 11), and conjoin EMF and 'trans' theories through complexity theory (Chapter 12).

Notes

1 www.researchgate.net/ (accessed 30 September 2020).
2 Baker (2001) is currently available as Baker and Wright (2017).

Further reading

Kimura, D. & Canagarajah, S. (2018). Translingual practice and ELF. In J. Jenkins, W. Baker, & M. Dewey (Eds.), *The Routledge handbook of English as a lingua franca* (pp. 295–308). Abingdon: Routledge. A useful and concise overview of the connections and differences between translanguaging and ELF research.

Li, W. (2016). New Chinglish and the Post-Multilingualism challenge: Translanguaging ELF in China. *Journal of English as a Lingua Franca*, *5*, 1–25. doi: 10.1515/jelf-2016-0001. The article offers an early discussion of the links between translanguaging and ELF research with a number of interesting and entertaining examples of translanguaging and ELF from China.

Li, W. & Ho, W. Y. (J.). (2018). Language learning *sans frontiers*: A translanguaging view. *Annual Review of Applied Linguistics*, *38*, 33–59. doi: 10.1017/S0267190518000053. This accessible article covers the main arguments proposed by translanguaging and provides empirical examples from a study on self-directed, technology-mediated learning of Chinese.

10 Intercultural and transcultural communication

Introduction

In our previous discussions of culture, language, identity, communication, and Global Englishes we have highlighted the complexity of the relationships between them. In particular, we have problematised a simple or fixed correlation between any of these categories. Global Englishes and intercultural communication research has shown that English is used in 'super-diverse' settings for a wide range of purposes and with participants from many different linguistic and cultural backgrounds. How then do we account for all this super-diversity and complexity? What are the relationships between culture and language if there are no clear correlations? Is culture even a relevant concept in such communication? If it is relevant, what are the cultural groupings and references made use of and how do they relate to language(s) and identities?

This chapter outlines transcultural communication as one approach to answering some of these questions. Transcultural communication is a recent extension of intercultural communication theory which incorporates many of the features of the 'trans' turn in applied linguistics discussed in the previous chapter. Transcultural communication attempts to develop more critical approaches to language and culture within the field to better account for the complex and fluid relationships between languages and cultures in interactions, especially through English used as a global lingua franca (Baker, 2018). Differences between intercultural and transcultural communication are discussed and a number of perspectives on **transculturality** outlined. A key theme that we consider is the idea of transcending and transgressing cultural boundaries, as well as the notion of cultural practices that are not fixed to any particular named national or other culture (e.g., 'American' (US) or 'British' culture). As Baker and Sangiamchit write, "[a] transcultural perspective provides a significant new dimension to research in which borders between languages, communities and cultures are transcended, transgressed and transformed" (2019: 471). We then consider the relevance of transcultural communication to education and applied linguistics. Last, we explore the links between Global Englishes and transcultural communication and provide examples from recent research to illustrate the points and for you to explore.

Activity 10.1 Moon cake

The following extract in Baker and Sangiamchit (2019) comes from a private message exchange on Facebook between international students in the UK – North (Thai) and Ling (Chinese), both female. Read the extract and then answer and discuss the questions below.

North

01 My lovely daughter
02 Thank you for your moon cake
03 It's really delicious
04 I gave P'Sa and P'Yui already
05 and I'll give P'Beau on this Sat

Ling

06 U r welcome, and the mid-autumn festival is this Sunday, enjoy~
07 Can u tell P'Sa, she can get her bag back now~

(Baker & Sangiamchit, 2019: 481)

Questions

Q1 What is the subject of their conversation?
Q2 What culture(s) would you associate this subject with? Can it be linked to any specific named culture?
Q3 What languages are present in this extract?
Q4 Are the distinctions between different named languages always clear?
Q5 Are there any other modalities used?

Feedback: *North and Ling are discussing the mid-autumn festival and moon cakes, which are traditionally associated with Chinese culture. However, while Ling is Chinese, North is Thai but still seems very familiar with this cultural practice. Indeed the mid-autumn festival is celebrated throughout Asia and is not only Chinese. Furthermore, both these students are now in the UK and so are engaging in these cultural practices in that setting. Additionally, the exchange takes place in the virtual space of an online social networking site.*

In relation to language the majority of the exchange takes place through English; however, the use of 'P" as in "P'Sa" (lines 04, 07) is from Thai where 'P' (พี่)' translates as 'older sibling'. It is used when speaking to an older person in an informal situation in order to show respect and intimacy. Here the intonation marker from Thai (') is retained in the English orthography. The use of 'daughter' in line 01 is also for a similar reason of showing intimacy in informal conversation. These are originally Thai cultural practices but are used in an intercultural or transcultural interaction here. Also note that the use of semiotic signs "~" (lines 06, 07) promotes further intimacy (see Activity 8.2).

This example illustrates the complexity of the links between language and culture, where it is not possible to clearly attribute cultural practices to a particular language use or national culture.

10.1 From intercultural communication to transcultural communication

It may be helpful to begin with a summary of some of the ideas outlined so far in this book in relation to culture, language, and intercultural communication as a foundation for the discussion of transcultural communication. We emphasised that culture is complex and cannot be reduced to simple explanations but, nonetheless, there are core features of how we understand culture (Chapter 1, especially Chapter 1.2). First, culture can be seen as a system of shared products, symbols, discourses, practices, and ideologies among groups of people. Second, these shared products, symbols, discourses, practices, and ideologies, and the groupings of people themselves that make up culture, are contestable and sites of struggle. Third, the people and shared products, symbols, discourses, practices, and ideologies that make up cultures are constantly in process and changing and hence cannot be fixed and have no clear boundaries. In relation to culture and language, we have explored how culture and language are closely linked but that they are not synonymous (Chapter 2). We considered how languages can be used to both represent and construct different cultural practices and resources depending on the participants, settings, and purposes of the interaction. We discussed how cultural and linguistic practices can be seen as flows that come together in different ways in particular instances of communication. This provided a counter-argument to the strong claims of linguistic relativity that view language as inexorably linked to a particular culture (e.g., English and Anglophone cultures). We illustrated this with a number of examples from Global Englishes research that showed how English is used in diverse ways to construct and refer to a multitude of cultural practices in a wide range of cultural settings. We also explored the way that English is used alongside other linguistic and multimodal resources in intercultural communication (for further examples, see Chapter 11).

When outlining our approach to intercultural communication we made a distinction between cross-cultural communication research and intercultural communication (Chapter 5, especially Chapter 5.2). Cross-cultural communication approaches typically investigate cultures at the level of national language, culture, and identity correlations with the aim of making broad generalisations about national cultural groupings (e.g., Japanese people do this ..., German people do this ...). These have been criticised for taking an essentialist and stereotyped perspective in which individual differences within cultures are minimised and artificially rigid boundaries are created between cultures. Similarly problematic is the assumption that the national scale for cultural groupings is always the most relevant, given the many different cultural groupings we all belong to and identify with. In contrast, intercultural communication research focuses on communication where cultural and linguistic differences are perceived as salient to either the interlocutors or researchers in understanding the interaction (Baker, 2015; Zhu, 2014; 2019). Rather than making a priori assumptions about cultural groupings, national or otherwise, intercultural communication research has examined the construction and negotiation of cultural identities, references, and practices in situ. Intercultural communication approaches typically make use of data from individual authentic interactions rather than broad generalisations. Findings have underscored the multiple, hybrid, and fluid cultural groupings and identities people draw on and construct in intercultural communication.

One of the most recent approaches to understanding intercultural interactions is transcultural communication (Chapter 5.4). Just as intercultural communication research on authentic interactions highlighted the limitations and essentialism of cross-cultural communication perspectives, we argue that recent studies from Global Englishes and ELF perspectives have underscored the limitations of intercultural communication approaches. In particular, the 'inter' of intercultural communication becomes problematic since due to the complexity and diversity of languages and cultures in Global Englishes scenarios, it is often not clear what specific cultures participants are in between. Therefore, instead of attempting to identify how participants are in between cultures or mixing elements of different named cultures and languages to create hybrid practices, as in intercultural communication approaches, a transcultural approach focuses on how participants move *through and across* cultures and languages. These processes of communication, we propose, are best represented by the prefix trans- instead of 'inter'. Thus, transcultural communication is characterised as communication where interactants move through and across, rather than in between, cultural and linguistic boundaries, and named languages and cultures can no longer be taken for granted, and in the process cultural and linguistic borders become blurred, transgressed, and transcended. Yet, it is important to point out that this does not involve a rejection of intercultural communication perspectives. Instead, transcultural communication approaches represent an extension of critical intercultural communication research where the complexity and fluidity of cultural and linguistic practices becomes the starting point for investigations (Baker & Sangiamchit, 2019). Moreover, like critical intercultural communication perspectives, the ideological importance of national scales, identifications, and boundaries between cultures and languages is not ignored. However, national scales and borders are not assumed to be relevant (indeed as we will see later they are often not present in Global Englishes scenarios), and where they are seen as salient they are critically interrogated.

Having outlined the three approaches, cross-cultural, intercultural, and transcultural, we can now extend the table presented in Chapter 5.2 (Table 10.1).

10.2 Transculturality and transcultural communication

Although we believe that the approach to transcultural communication taken in this book is a new perspective in intercultural communication and Global Englishes research, as already discussed in Chapter 5.4, the notion of the transcultural and transculturality is not new and some explanation of how it has been used previously may be helpful. In Chapters 1.3 and 2.3 we looked at the idea of transnational and transcultural flows (Appadurai, 1996; Risager, 2006; Pennycook, 2007; see Chapter 8.1, 8.2) to account for the way in which languages and cultures spread around the globe through complex networks of connections. Through these flows, cultural and linguistic practices are adapted and changed by their use in different local, but globally connected, contexts and so are in constant processes of transformation. Transcultural flows account for the manner in which the local, national, and global are connected but also how, at the same time, new spaces are opened up for alternative cultural production and identification. Pennycook (2007) gives the example of hip-hop as adapted and relevant to different local settings but also globally connected. We could make similar claims for other popular cultural products such as movies, TV, clothing, and sport, as well as globally connected domains such as business, academia, and research. However, it is important to acknowledge that this does not mean complete freedom to choose any cultural identification or adapt linguistic and cultural practices in any way we wish. As we wrote in Chapter 6.4 and 6.5 when explaining interculturality, and in Chapter 7 in discussing language ideologies, there are still significant power imbalances and social restrictions on what can be changed or how we identify or are identified.

Table 10.1 Cross-cultural, intercultural, and transcultural communication

Cross-cultural communication	*Intercultural communication*	*Transcultural communication*
The study of the communicative practices of distinct cultural groups independent from interaction (e.g., Chinese communicative practices versus German communicative practices)	The study of the communicative practices of distinct cultural or other groups in interaction with each other (e.g., Italians communicating with English)	The study of communicative practices where cultural and linguistic differences are relevant to participants or researchers but not necessarily linked to any particular group
Cultures are seen as separable entities	Cultures are not bounded entities with national borders, but fluid and dynamic with blurred boundaries	Cultural and linguistic boundaries can be transcended and transgressed
Cultures are viewed as relatively homogeneous	Cultures are heterogeneous, containing a great deal of variety among their members	Cultures are heterogeneous and cultural characterisations are contestable
Cultures are viewed at a national level	National cultures are one of many discourse communities which can be drawn upon in communication; others include gender, generation, profession, ethnicity, etc.	National cultures are one of many scales, ranging from the local to the global, and participants move through and across scales rather than in between
A priori assumption about cultural groupings	No a priori assumptions about the discourse communities, cultural or otherwise, that will be drawn on, with participants located in between adaptable and hybrid cultures	Cultural practices and representations can be constructed in situ and emergent; participants are not in between any named cultures
Experimental and quantitative research	Qualitative research using naturalistic recordings of instances of intercultural communication	Qualitative research using naturalistic recordings of instances of intercultural communication

The notion of transcultural and transnational flows comes originally from sociology (e.g., Appadurai, 1996) and transculturation and transculturality have an even longer history in anthropology and cultural and post-colonial studies. One of the most well-known uses is from the post-colonial scholar Mary Louise Pratt, who introduced the term **contact zones** and linked this to transculturation (1992; 2008). As she explains it, contact zones are "social spaces where disparate cultures meet, clash, and grapple with each other, often in highly asymmetrical relations of domination and subordination" and also: "Transculturation is a phenomenon of the contact zone ... the concept of transculturation serves to raise several sets of questions. What do people on the receiving end of empire do with metropolitan modes of representation? How do they appropriate them? How do they talk back?" (2008: 7). As such, this conception of the transcultural is closer to third spaces, explained in Chapter 5.4, in looking at how different identifiable cultures come together and are adapted and hybridised. Contact zones and transculturation are especially important in underlining that these processes of cultural adaption are often unequal with more and less powerful groupings, but that less powerful groups do have agency and voice and can "talk back".

The anthropologist James Clifford (1992) proposed the idea of transnational, "traveling cultures" to explain how cultures can be both local and global, intercultural and native. He discusses the manner in which cultures *travel with people* and also how *people travel to* cultures and the influences this has on processes and conceptualisations of cultures. Echoing many of the issues of fluidity, hybridity, and tension discussed in later transcultural theories, he writes that:

> [a]nthropological 'culture' is not what it used to be. And once the representational challenge is seen to be the portrayal and understanding of local/global historical encounters, co-productions, dominations, and resistances, then one needs to focus on hybrid, cosmopolitan experiences as much as on rooted, native ones. In my current problematic, the goal is not to *replace* the cultural figure 'native' with the intercultural figure 'traveler'. Rather the task is to focus on concrete mediations of the two, in specific cases of historical tension and relationship.
>
> (1992: 101)

The term transculturality is introduced by the philosopher Wolfgang Welsch (1999) as a replacement for single cultures, multiculturality, and interculturality, which, he believes, are all problematic terms as regards how culture needs to be conceived for contemporary societies. While his critique of interculturality as preserving the idea of separate cultures interacting with each other is perhaps closer to how we have characterised cross-cultural, rather than intercultural, approaches, Welsch introduces some core features of transcultural perspectives. These include the idea of networks of cultural connections and groups and identities which transcend and 'pass through' traditional geographical and national cultural boundaries.

> [T]he description of today's cultures as islands or spheres is factually incorrect and normatively deceptive. Cultures de facto no longer have the insinuated form of homogeneity and separateness. They have instead assumed a new form, which is to be called *transcultural* insofar that it *passes through* classical cultural boundaries. Cultural conditions today are largely characterized by mixes and permeations.
>
> (Welsch, 1999: 4)

Interestingly, Welsch also proposes that transcultural groupings and identities are the most 'genuinely' cultural ones since they are "for the very first time, no longer complying with geographical or national stipulations, but following pure cultural interchange processes" (1999: 10).

More recently, Monceri (2019) has also approached transculturality from a philosophical perspective, arguing, in a similar manner to what we have proposed, that the prefix trans- opens up new ways of thinking about culture. Significantly, Monceri claims that transculturality goes beyond the intercultural ideas of links between identifiable different cultures and that it should also lead to questioning of the idea of culture itself. Monceri writes that transculturality "can also be understood in the meaning of 'going beyond', that is to say that it is able at least to evoke the possibility to 'trespass', or better 'transgress', the borders of the very notion of 'culture'" (2019: 87–88). Drawing on post-colonial studies, Monceri believes that this questioning is crucial since much current thinking on culture (and knowledge in general) is based on Western-centric notions which set up a false dichotomy between the 'West' and the 'Other'. She also proposes the transcultural-self as an alternative to current ideas of identity as "an individual who wittingly exercises her power to re-construct the world and its 'rules of the game', by selecting features different from those accepted until the present moment, but that are already existent in the environment, and simply discarded until now" (2019: 89). In other words, the transcultural-self is someone who is able to view the world and their place in it from multiple different perspectives and, as such, this links with ideas of **intercultural** or **global citizenship** which will be brought up later in the final chapter of this book.

Guilherme and Dietz (2015) offer an overview of the similarities and differences between many of the terms we have discussed so far, including conceptualisations of multicultural, intercultural, and transcultural. They point out, as we have shown in our discussion in this book, that these three concepts have been understood and used differently at different times, in different disciplines, and by different scholars, meaning that "it is impossible to establish fixed and stable lines between them" (2015: 1). Nonetheless, they also emphasise that when we use these concepts it is important to try to be as precise as we can in our meaning, a point which we fully agree with. While Guilherme and Dietz's discussion covers more perspectives than can be summarised here, there are a number of key points of relevance to this discussion. First, the transcultural is more than the translation of one cultural perspective to another (as sometimes suggested in post-colonial studies), since from transcultural perspectives there are multiple cultures and timescales simultaneously present with no clear borders (2015: 8). Second, notions of **intercultural** and **transcultural competence** need to be viewed not as prescribed 'recipes' for any intercultural context but as relationally and contextually dependent "professional habitus to be acquired, trained, and developed by teachers, social workers, and other 'intercultural mediators'" (2015: 9), an idea we will return to in Chapter 14. Third, all these perspectives are part of contemporary discourses in society in general, in academia and in the areas of interest in this book, Global Englishes and intercultural/transcultural communication, and so need to be accounted for in theory and research. As Guilherme and Dietz write:

> [a]ll these concepts whose definitions we have been attempting to discuss, and put into dialogue with each other, namely, 'multiculturalism', 'interculturalism'/'interculturality' and 'the transcultural,' are simultaneously ideologically loaded and culturally slippery. They are, however, unavoidable concepts in contemporary social and cultural studies, which need academic digging.
>
> (2015: 11)

10.3 Transcultural education and applied linguistics

One discipline where the transcultural is being applied, in both theory and practice, is in education, and particularly higher education (HE). The education scholar Janette Ryan (2011) argues that given the international nature of many universities that have students and staff from around the world, as well as global teaching and research connections, we need to move beyond local ethnocentrisms towards a transcultural approach. Ryan writes that "[t]ranscultural approaches encompass the creation of culturally inclusive teaching and learning environments at the level of the classroom, in curriculum design and pedagogical approaches, through to epistemological plurality of the knowledge base" (2011: 635). This approach involves universities engaging in dialogue about multiple different approaches to both knowledge and learning from many different settings. Ryan emphasises that this must involve a two-way process of mutual respect and learning between different settings, rather than the dominance of one setting over another, as is currently the case with the power of Anglophone and European universities (see Chapter 3.3). Similarly, the first author of this book has written about the "transcultural university" (Baker, 2016) in relation to recognising the 'super-diversity' of many international HE settings. Due to the globally connected nature of both staff and students, the national scale is only one scale at which universities operate, with institutions frequently functioning as part of global networks that transcend national boundaries. This means that we need to fundamentally re-think the way we educate students for mobility and study-abroad. Instead of preparing students to accommodate to and integrate into a 'local' language and culture, typically viewed at the level of national languages and cultures, students need to be ready to take part in multilingual and multicultural settings. So, for example, rather than preparing international students who are coming to study in the UK with British English and culture, as is typically the case, students should be prepared for using English as an academic lingua franca for intercultural communication in multicultural groups. This would better prepare students for the reality of studying in an international university in the UK where they are likely to be interacting with highly diverse groups of people with the local being just one scale. Indeed, studies such as Fang and Baker (2018), and Baker and Fang (2021) have shown that international students in the UK can be surprised by the diversity of the student population, the small numbers of 'local' students, and hence their lack of interaction with the 'local' population. International students frequently report feeling very underprepared for this diverse intercultural environment.

A number of alternative transcultural educational approaches have been explored in recent research. For example, Smith and Segbers (2018) present an empirical study of a HE programme hosted by three universities in three countries in a Transcultural European Outdoor Studies (TEOS) master's. They report on the benefits of such a programme where students are required to engage in different cultural settings and to undertake reflection on those experiences as part of their learning experience. Smith and Segbers also highlight the importance of language in transcultural learning, stating that "language skills cannot be underestimated" (2018: 80), including both English as the academic lingua franca of the programme and also local languages in the different university settings. They recommend that language education should be a formal part of **transcultural education** programmes. Language education and transcultural communication is dealt with in detail in studies by Thompson (2011) and Juan-Garau and Jacob (2015), although with the caveat that the transcultural is conceptualised in a way closer to how intercultural and third spaces are viewed here. Nonetheless, these studies show the value of integrating a complex and dynamic view of culture and language in language teaching. They illustrate the influence transcultural perspectives have on learners' awareness of critical understandings of cultures and cultural boundaries, as well as the development of both intercultural/transcultural competence and the ability to make use of linguistic repertoires, including English, in intercultural communication. These are the topics we will return to in detail in Chapters 13 and 14 when we discuss English as a multilingua franca and intercultural competence and awareness.

Turning specifically to education and applied linguistics, as presented in Chapter 9.1, a special issue of the journal *Applied Linguistics* (Hawkins & Mori, 2018) explicitly addresses the relevance of 'trans' theories in the discipline. Discussing the 'trans' turn in applied linguistics, Hawkins and Mori highlight a number of different terms which are now used, including "transnational, transcultural, translocal, transpatial, transmodal, translanguaging, and translingual" (2018: 1). Similar to the perspective we take in this book, Hawkins and Mori also suggest that "from a 'trans-' perspective, we must consider movement across nations and cultures, spaces and places, modes and semiotic resources, and autonomous named languages" (2018: 1), and that these processes involve transgressing and transcending these boundaries and borders. Yet, it is also important to acknowledge the power of names and labels for languages and cultures, and that researchers and educators need to engage critically with the power structures that naming creates (Hawkins & Mori, 2018: 6; see Chapter 9.1). Within the special issue, Li Wei outlines a theory of translanguaging, arguing that "Translanguaging Instinct drives humans to go beyond narrowly defined linguistic cues and transcend culturally defined language boundaries to achieve effective communication" (2018: 24–25). In an empirical study, Hawkins (2018) uses the notion of transnational and translocal to examine online educational exchanges between youth in Uganda and the US and how they utilise multimodal resources to make meaning across places and spaces where cultures may not be shared. Mori and Sanuth (2018) employ the concept of transcultural competence in relation to examining US study-abroad students in Nigeria. However, they are critical of the original definition of transcultural competence proposed by the Modern Language Association of America (MLA) as "the ability to operate between languages" (2007: 237) which makes multiple references to 'target' languages and cultures. Instead, they emphasise the importance of focusing on "multilingual speakers who make use of a variety of linguistic and other semiotic resources, crossing the boundaries of named languages" (Mori & Sanuth, 2018: 83). In these papers, and others in this special issue, there is an emphasis on holistic and complex understandings of meaning-making which integrate investigations of languages, modes, contexts, and cultures.

Summary

In the previous sections, we explored a range of perspectives on transculturality from different disciplines that have helped form our understanding of transcultural communication today. These have included:

- transnational and transcultural flows
- transculturation and contact zones
- transnational and travelling cultures
- transculturality as a social and philosophical idea

We have also considered the differences and similarities between terms such as multicultural, intercultural, and transcultural. Last, we have looked at the relevance of transculturality and 'trans' theories in general to education and applied linguistics as well as the links between transculturality, translanguaging, and transmodality.

Activity 10.2 Reflecting on transculturality

In this activity you will consider what some of different terms discussed so far mean to you. Read the characterisations of key terms below and then discuss the following questions: How many of these terms have you seen before? Where have you seen them and how were they used? How might they be translated into your first language (if it is not English)? What do these terms mean to you and do you agree with the characterisations given here?

- **Cross-cultural communication**. A perspective that focuses on comparisons between the cultural practices of distinct cultural groups typically at the national level, e.g., Japanese cultural characteristics compared to British cultural characteristics.
- **Multiculturalism**. A perspective that focuses on different cultural groups existing alongside each other within a society or nation, e.g., South Asian communities in the UK.
- **Intercultural communication**. A perspective that focuses on distinct cultural (or other) groupings in interaction with each other with the national scale viewed as one of many, e.g., Chinese and Saudi students interacting in an international university.
- **Transculturality**. A multidisciplinary approach that encompasses a wide range of perspectives but generally focuses on how individuals or groups cut across and through cultural borders and create new cultural spaces (similar to third places), e.g., hybridised and adapted cultural practices of diasporic and immigrant communities.
- **Transcultural communication**. A perspective that focuses on communication that passes through cultural and linguistic

boundaries and in the process transgresses, transcends, and transforms those boundaries. Similar to transculturality but the focus is on interactions where multiple cultures and languages are present simultaneously and participants are not necessarily in between or hybridising any identifiable cultural practices, e.g., transcultural, translanguaging, and transmodal communication in social networking sites making use of multicultural, multilingual, and multimodal resources.

Feedback: *There are obviously no right or wrong responses to this activity. However, we hope that through this chapter you have been able to think about the development of intercultural communication research from cross-cultural perspectives through to transcultural communication. We have also looked at a range of perspectives on transculturality and how they relate to, or are different to, multicultural and intercultural approaches.*

10.4 Transcultural communication and Global Englishes

While transcultural communication is a relatively new area of investigation, as outlined in Chapter 5.4, Global Englishes research has been concerned with many issues of direct relevance to transcultural communication. These include negotiation, adaptation, and hybridity in language and communication; language ideologies and power relationships; and identity, community, and culture (for overviews, see Galloway & Rose, 2015; Jenkins, 2015a; Jenkins et al., 2018). In particular, a number of researchers, including the authors of this book, have been interested in fluid and liminal cultural practices, identities, and groupings that are not linked to or between any specific cultures (e.g., Baker, 2009a; 2011; 2015; Ishikawa, 2017a; 2020a). Current ELF research aligns especially closely with a 'trans' perspective in general, and a transcultural perspective in particular, by approaching English as one of many linguistic and other resources that may be used in interactions. Indeed, in adopting this approach, Jenkins states that English as a multilingua franca is "used predominantly in transcultural communication among multilingual English speakers, who will make use of their full linguistic repertoires as appropriate in the context of any specific interaction" (2018a: 601). Due to the recent nature of Global Englishes and transcultural communication research, at present, there are a limited, although growing, number of conceptual and empirical studies (e.g., Cogo, 2016; Dovchin et al., 2016; Li, 2016; Baker, 2018; Baker & Sangiamchit, 2019; Jenkins, 2018a; Pitzl, 2018a; Lee & Canagarajah, 2019; Ishikawa, 2020a; 2020b) and we will review some of them here.

In an early study of Global Englishes, ELF, and translanguaging that also explores the sociocultural dimensions, Li Wei (2016) discusses 'New Chinglish'. Drawing on data illustrating translingual and transmodal processes, Li Wei proposes that translanguaging "transforms its users and their subjectivities, creating new spaces for social relations, social structures, and social cognition" (2016: 21). He analyses a number of different examples of 'Chinglish' from advertising, public signs, and various online domains. One such domain is 'Shitizen Chinglish' used to refer to the creative use of English and Chinese in online forums, with the term itself a playful and ironic mix of English and Chinese (Li, 2016: 15). Some of the examples given include:

- *freedamn* (freedom + damn) 中国特色自由 (the Chinese translation that goes with it says 'freedom with Chinese characteristics')
- *gunvernment* (gun + government) 枪杆子政权 (after Mao's famous saying, 'Government comes out of the barrel of the gun')
- *gambller* 干部 (deliberate ill-transliteration of the Chinese term for government officials, *banbu*) (Li, 2016: 16)

Li Wei argues that such creativity illustrates how through translanguaging users find "ways of expressing one's cultural values and sociopolitical views through a language or multiple languages that are traditionally associated with the Other or Others" (2016: 20). Importantly and closely related to the transcultural approaches outlined in this chapter, Li Wei also proposes that we need to go beyond notions such as hybridity in order to account for "the cultural-historical, linguistic-cognitive, and politico-ideological complexity and significance" (2016: 20) of such linguistic and communicative practices.

Dovchin et al. (2016) report on an ethnographic study of translingual Englishes in Mongolia and Bangladesh, in which English and other linguistic and cultural resources are in constant interplay in the interactions they observe. They propose that these "Translingual Englishes may be creative and playful but they are also associated with differences in one's unequal social class, wealth and power" (2016: 92). The following examples are taken from Facebook wall posts by two of the research participants.

Extract 10.1 Unequal translingual Englishes

Facebook text	Translation
(1) *Naidan:* Намрын налгар өдрүүдээ гэж…**ккк** – ☺ **feeling wonderful**.	Nice autumn day…kkk – ☺ feeling wonderful.
(2) *Dolgormaa:* **UB**-d **weather** tiim muu bgamuu, **flight** hoishlogdloo, **just wandering around, but saw an Absolute Hunk! Girls! *Wink wink***	Is the weather that bad in UB? My flight has been delayed, just wandering around, but saw an Absolute Hunk! Girls! *Wink wink*

(Dovchin et al., 2016: 99)

Notes
Bold English
Regular font Mongolian

The post shows a mixture of Mongolian and English as well as different scripts (Cyrillic in (1)), the onomatopoeic expression "kkk" (used to express a giggle in online communication), and multimodal resources, the emoji ☺ and the facial expression *Wink wink*. However, the researchers discuss how these examples also demonstrate unequal repertoires of linguistic and cultural resources. Naidan has infrequent access to and limited familiarity with digital communication and so is offline most of the time, only posting occasionally. Furthermore, his use of English is restricted to phrases and expressions pre-provided by Facebook with most of his posts in Mongolian. In contrast, Dolgormaa is frequently online and regularly posts in English. Her post begins with a reference to a local setting (the weather in Ulaanbaatar (UB)) but she quickly moves beyond the local scale. Her mention of "Absolute Hunk" refers to a global brand of vodka being advertised by a US TV star from the show 'Sex and the City' and she posts a photo of this for her female friends. Her references to and familiarity with global cultural products and practices, combined with the fact that she is posting while waiting for a flight, show her privileged access to transnational movement and resources. Dovchin et al. go on to suggest that "[b]oth speakers can access various forms of linguistic and semiotic diversity, although the complexity is shaped by the speakers' specific socio-economic backgrounds and access to resources", with Dolgormaa having a "wider range of cultural, media and linguistic resources at her disposal" (2016: 100).

Pitzl (2018a) focuses on translingual and transcultural spaces in the very common, but under-researched, phenomena of short-term groupings in which ELF use frequently takes place. As Pitzl remarks, many ELF groupings last no longer than an international business meeting, conference panel, or a visit to a local tourist attraction (2018a: 30). She uses the term transient international groups or TIGs to account for the social dimensions of such fluid and temporary groups and defines them as follows.

> Transient International Groups (TIGs) [refer] to groups of multilingual ELF users who interact for a particular purpose at a particular location for a certain amount of time. These groups are *transient* in the sense that a group forms, speakers negotiate and interact, and then the group dissolves again. Each TIG is therefore temporary. Multilingual ELF users who form a TIG will oftentimes be aware of the transient and temporary nature of their group during its existence (although they need not be). TIGs are *international* in the sense

> that the individual multilingual ELF users will (in most contexts) come from at least two different countries.
>
> (2018a: 30)

Pitzl argues that this is more appropriate than the speech communities (Chapter 3.1) or communities of practice (Chapter 5.4) frameworks used to characterise comparatively stable social groups. Due to the temporary nature of TIGs, and as noted in much previous ELF research, they are likely to be characterised by a high degree of negotiation of meaning, creativity, and accommodation with norms and conventions emerging in situ (2018a: 37). Pitzl believes that researchers need to examine how these conventions of shared translingual and transcultural territory are established. To support this she presents a case study of a four-person TIG in Malta (3 L1 Maltese speakers and 1 L1 Serbian speaker) and their use of the Italian idiom "fuma come un turco" (to smoke like a Turk) in an ELF interaction. Pitzl explores both "the transcultural complexity of this example, in which the speakers refer to multiple (regio-)cultural territories", as well as the "multilingual metaphorical creativity" (2018a: 39) in the use of an idiom in a language that is not the L1 of any of the speakers. In particular, she is interested in what happens in the participants' interactions before this point that allows them to establish the shared territory in which "such a complex translingual and transcultural remark can be made just like that, more or less in passing, by an ELF speaker and can be successfully interpreted by the ELF speakers addressed" (2018a: 39).

Lee and Canagarajah (2019) investigate the also under-researched area of transcultural and translingual practices in writing. They present a case study of Koky (L1 Czech, male, in his 40s), a student in an academic writing class that was part of an intensive language programme in a US university. Lee and Canagarajah seek to illustrate how through Koky's 'different' approach in producing an academic essay, Koky demonstrates his "transcultural disposition" which enables his translingual writing practices. A transcultural disposition in Lee and Canagarajah's term is characterised as "situating oneself in liminal social spaces and drawing from values and practices of diverse cultures to constantly reconstruct one's identity and social belonging" (2019: 16). This is closely linked to the idea of intercultural and transcultural competence, which will be discussed in Chapter 14. According to Lee and Canagarajah, it is this transcultural disposition that underpins successful translingual practices (2019: 18). This disposition allows Koky to resist the monolingual and monocultural ideology of academic writing in the US and express his own voice in a more liminal space. As they conclude, and very much aligned with the approach we have put forward in this book:

> transcultural and translingual approaches illuminate a co-constructed, emergent, generative nature of interculturality rather than treating culture as given, priori, and essentialized products. The approaches allow us to attend to how individuals negotiate multiple, and at times, conflicting expectations and norms in language and cultural practices for their own voice and identity beyond the limiting cultural categories and boundaries.
>
> (2019: 24)

The final example, involving one of the authors of this book and a research colleague from Thailand (Baker & Sangiamchit, 2019), deals specifically with the concept of transcultural communication and Global Englishes in online digital communication. Baker and Sangiamchit (2019) present an ethnographic study of a group of international students at a UK university with a focus on their cultural and linguistic practices in an online social network community. They make use of the perspective to transcultural communication outlined at the beginning of this chapter as "communication where interactants move through and across, rather than in-between, cultural and linguistic boundaries, thus, 'named' languages and cultures can no longer be taken for granted and in the process borders become blurred, transgressed and transcended" (2019: 472). This approach is explicitly linked to translanguaging and transmodal perspectives, as well as current ELF and Global Englishes research. Baker and Sangiamchit (2019) illustrate these themes with data from exchanges on the popular social networking site (SNS) Facebook, in which the research participants interacted with multilingual and multicultural groups of friends. We have already explored one example from this study at the beginning of this chapter (Activity 10.1) and we will look at another here.

Figure 10.1 Edited photo on Facebook

In this extract (10.2) Ken (L1 Thai, male) makes a post on his friend Hessam's (L1 Farsi, male) Facebook wall. It is the edited photo Figure 10.1 and text combining an image of martial arts film star Jet Li with text from another martial arts film star, Bruce Lee. Ken explained in an interview that he did this to tease Hessam because he knew Hessam was a fan of Jet Li and hated Bruce Lee.

Extract 10.2 Jet Lee

01 Ken:	Hope you like it. Good night ... Like · Share · 9 hours ago SM likes this.
02 Hessam:	you are a bastard Ken! I am gone kill you! :) 9 hours ago · Like · 1
03 Ken:	You are very welcome ;) 9 hours ago · Like · 1
04 Hessam:	the family name is also need correction! it should read "Li" instead of "Lee" 9 hours ago · Like
05 Ken:	OK Thanks That's gonna be the next version 9 hours ago · Like · 1
06 Hessam:	bastard! I really like this guy! and he was the true champion of china from the age of 11 to 19 for 8 consecutive years winning gold medals! now you are making joke with him ... I am gone show you the cannon feast punch tomorrow! 9 hours ago · Like · 1
07 Hessam:	just kidding of course! no need to move away from Southampton mate! 9 hours ago · Like · 1

(Baker & Sangiamchit, 2019: 482)

First, this example reveals multiple cultural scales or levels simultaneously. We have two globally recognised martial arts film stars and martial arts itself is a globally familiar cultural practice. At the same time both these film stars and martial arts are historically culturally associated with China, as seen in Hessam's comment in line 06. The interaction also refers to a local geographical place, Southampton (line 07), where the participants are physically located. Furthermore, the exchange itself takes place in the virtual space of an online social network community. Second, Hessam positions himself as the cultural expert in this exchange through his knowledge of martial arts, demonstrated in the discussion of Jet Li's achievements (line 06), the correct spelling of his name (Li/Lee, line 04), and the English translation of the Chinese martial arts term "cannon feast punch" (line 06). As an Iranian communicating through ELF, Hessam's position of expertise would not be predicted if we adopted a traditional national scale of cultural and linguistic identification. Third, these different cultural scales and identities are constructed through the use of English but in the fluid manner associated with ELF. See, for example, the different spellings of 'going to' as "gone" and "gonna" (lines 02, 05, 06). Moreover, the multilingual aspects of ELF are also highlighted through the discussion of the spelling of Chinese names 'Li/Lee' (line 04) and the translation of the Chinese martial arts term "cannon feast punch" (line 06; "feast" is presumably a misspelling of fist). Finally, the exchange is also multimodal or rather transmodal (see Chapter 9.4), with the use of image, text, and emoticons (lines 02, 03) intertwined. Indeed, the interaction and teasing relies on an interplay of image and text through the juxtaposition of an image of an admired person (Jet Li) with text from a disliked person (Bruce Lee) placed next to each other and then explicitly altered through the crossing out of "Bruce" and replacement with "Jet". We will return to this study of online transcultural communication in the next chapter when we explore culture and language in digital communication.

In sum, current studies of Global Englishes and transcultural communication, such as those described above, illustrate the close links between 'trans' theories in research and the importance of taking a holistic approach to understanding language, communication, identity, and culture. We see a complex range of cultural practices, references, and resources occurring at multiple scales simultaneously moving through and across local, national, and global levels and boundaries. Furthermore, the connections between languages, cultures, and identities are equally complex. Although English is the main language used in the examples studied here, it is the fluid and dynamic use of English related to ELF, rather than any particular variety or Anglophone-associated English. Moreover, alongside English other languages are also present, with participants typically making use of multilingual resources through translingual practices. However, as underlined throughout this book, issues of power and ideology are as much a part of transcultural communication through Global Englishes as any other kind of communication. In particular, Dovchin et al. (2016) highlighted the unequal access and resources (cultural and financial) that participants in transcultural communication may have. At the same time, studies such as Li (2016) and Lee and Canagarajah (2019) show how transcultural and translingual practices can be used to resist and provide an alternative to dominant monolingual and monocultural ideologies. We also see these transcultural and translingual practices taking place in a wide range of domains from oral interactions (Pitzl, 2018a), to advertising (Li, 2016), and even academic writing (Lee & Canagarajah, 2019). Most prevalent, though, has been research on digital communication (Dovchin et al., 2016; Li, 2016; Baker & Sangiamchit, 2019), due to both its ubiquitous nature and also the opportunities and spaces the digital domain provides for transcultural communication. Again, this will be the topic of the next chapter.

Activity 10.3 Transcultural groups

Think about all the different groups that you are part of (or have been part of in the past) where you use English. These can be face-to-face or online, friendship groups, classrooms, families, work, sport, or leisure. Make a list of them.

Think about how temporary or permanent these groups are. Are they short-term transient groups (like those described by Pitzl (2018a)) or more long-term and stable? Add some notes on this to your list. What are the shared resources of these groups? Add some further notes on this to your list. This can include:

- linguistic resources (e.g., English but also other shared languages, even if it is only a 'little' of another language)
- other multimodal resources (e.g., emojis, photos, gifs, videos, etc.)
- cultural resources (e.g., shared practices for things like greetings, sports, and games; shared cultural references to places, spaces, or events)
- anything else that you think is shared in the group

Based on the notes you have made, now consider if you think these groups are intercultural and/or transcultural.

Feedback: *Your answers to this activity will obviously depend on your personal experiences. We can guess that all of you identify with groups that are quite diverse in how permanent they are. It also seems very likely that you will have different sets of resources in different groups (i.e., family groups versus work or school groups). However, to what extent you feel any of the groups are intercultural or transcultural will be more varied.*

Chapter summary

In this chapter, we explored the notion of transcultural communication. We looked at how research on language and communication across cultures has moved from cross-cultural, to intercultural, and now transcultural approaches. Transcultural communication is characterised as communication where interactants move through and across, rather than in between, cultural and linguistic boundaries, and named languages and cultures can no longer be taken for granted, and in the process, cultural and linguistic borders become blurred, transgressed, and transcended. We also discussed the origins of transculturality and transcultural communication in different disciplines and a range of conceptions of these terms, including similarities and differences between them. We also gave more thought to the links between transcultural communication and other 'trans' theories such as translanguaging and transmodality. You should now be familiar with:

- a range of 'trans' theories including translanguaging and transculturality
- transcultural communication and how it differs from cross-cultural communication, intercultural communication, and **multiculturalism**
- transcultural communication, and its relevance to education and applied linguistics

In the final part of this chapter we turned our attention to transcultural communication and Global Englishes. We presented an overview of current research that, as in previous chapters, further highlighted the complex and multiple links between languages and cultures in Global Englishes use. This included recognition of the multilingual and multimodal resources that English use is often part of, as well as the multiple cultural scales that can be simultaneously present in transcultural interactions.

Further reading

Baker, W. & Sangiamchit, C. (2019). Transcultural communication: Language, communication and culture through English as a lingua franca in a social network community. *Language and Intercultural Communication*, *19*, 471–487. doi: 10.1080/14708477.2019.1606230. An in-depth outline of transcultural communication theory illustrated with data from a study of a multilingual and multicultural social network community.

Guilherme, M. & Dietz, G. (2015). Difference in diversity: Multiple perspectives on multicultural, intercultural, and transcultural conceptual complexities. *Journal of Multicultural Discourses*, *10*, 1–21. doi: 10.1080/17447143.2015.1015539. A challenging but detailed discussion and evaluation of a range of different perspectives to transculturality.

Hawkins, M.R. & Mori, J. (2018). Considering 'trans-' perspectives in language theories and practices. *Applied Linguistics*, *39*, 1–8. doi: 10.1093/applin/amx056. The introduction to a special issue of *Applied Linguistics* covering a variety of different approaches to 'trans' theories in applied linguistics research and thinking.

11 Culture and language in digital communication

Introduction

For many of us, online or digital communication is now an integral part of our everyday communicative practices and social interactions. We are guessing that for lots of you, just like for the authors of this book, digital connections and having daily access to the internet are considered an essential aspect of life in a similar way to electricity and other utilities. We use digital connections to read our morning news on websites, check the weather, traffic, train, and bus times on an app, send and receive emails for work, connect with friends and family on social networking sites (SNSs), stream movies and TV shows, shop online, and even study in virtual learning environments. Furthermore, digital communication has enabled us to instantly connect with anyone and anything anywhere in the world that is also digitally connected. Given this ubiquitous nature of digital communication and its global reach, this is also a prime site for intercultural interactions and communication. Indeed, the combination of digital communication and the use of Global Englishes are often seen as two of the key processes in the increasing spread and speed of intercultural connections and globalisation. As the sociolinguists Piia Varis and Xuan Wang propose, "[t]he Internet is the superdiverse space par excellence – a space of seemingly endless possibilities for self-expression and community formation" (2011: 71).

This chapter begins with an outline of the features of digital communication and the role of Global Englishes, alongside other languages, in this domain. We then turn specifically to intercultural and transcultural digital communication and particularly the features of **electronically mediated intercultural communication (EMIC)** (Sangiamchit, 2018), including the use of multimodal, multilingual, multicultural, and mobile resources in transcultural, translingual, and transmodal communication processes. We place focus on social media and SNSs, such as Facebook, given their current importance as social spaces. We consider how identity, community, and culture are constructed and represented in these digital spaces. Examples from recent empirical research are presented (e.g., Baker & Sangiamchit, 2019) to support the discussion. You will also be asked to consider your own use of digital communication and its role in intercultural/transcultural communication for you.

Activity 11.1 Your digital communication use

Make a list of all the digital/online communication devices (e.g., phones, tablets, PCs) and platforms (e.g., email, websites, social media, social networking sites, blogs, texting, searches) you use.

Think about the languages you use in digital communication. Do you use different languages in different platforms and for different purposes? Do you use any other resources (e.g., photos, videos, emojis)?

What are some of the subjects discussed/written/posted about? Are they different in different platforms? What is the cultural content, if any (e.g., national, local, global, something else)?

Feedback: *Your answers will obviously depend on your own experiences. However, you may have found that there is quite a lot of variety in your digital communication especially around modes such as language, emoji, video, etc.*

11.1 Characterising digital communication

There are currently estimated to be 4.54 billion internet users, which represents 59% of the world population (Kemp, 2020). This is obviously a very large number of users and so we can expect a lot of communication to take place on the internet, as we will see in the rest of this chapter. However, there are a number of important things to note about this number. First, while the internet may seem a common and taken-for-granted aspect of life for many of us, a significant part of the world population is still not connected to the internet (about 40%). Second, there is a lot of regional variation in percentages of the population who are internet users, as shown in Figure 11.1. For instance, it is 94–95% in North America and Western and Northern Europe, but falls to around 60% in Southeast and East Asia, and below 50% for most of Africa (Kemp, 2019). However, at the same time, given its population size, Asia accounts for over 50% of internet users, with Europe and North America less than 25% (Internet World Stats, 2020). Third, the internet and digital communication is a reasonably recent phenomenon. There are debates as to when exactly the internet started but public and commercial use began in the late 1980s and 1990s and there was a huge growth between the mid-1990s and early 2000s. The first author of this book can still clearly recall in the mid-1990s initially browsing the internet through Netscape (the

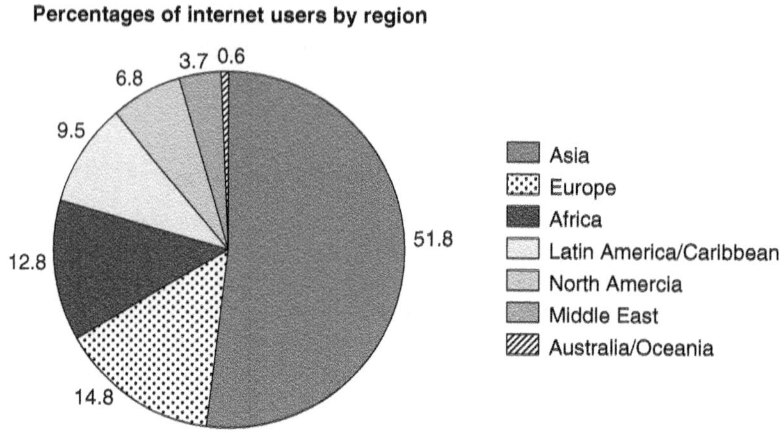

Figure 11.1 World distribution of internet users

(Based on data from Internet World Stats, 2020)

first popular browser) and sending and receiving his first email. This involved going to a university computer centre (almost nobody had a private internet connection where he was living) and making use of a shared email account (they were strictly controlled and rationed). This relativity recent growth of the internet means that there is a generational gap in internet use, with younger users outnumbering older users. For example, in 2019 in the UK 99% of adults aged 16 to 44 were internet users, compared with 47% of adults aged 75 years and over (Prescott, 2019).

For those who use the internet, digital communication is often a fundamental part of their daily communicative practices. The applied linguist Caroline Tagg defines digital communication as:

> interactions between people that are mediated by digital communications technology (tools which transmit information in digital form). In practice, this means communication over the internet or GSM (Global System for Mobile Communications, through which SMS text messages are sent), via a range of devices, including desktop computers, laptops, notebooks, tablets and smartphones; and on various media (Facebook, Twitter, Wikipedia).
> (2015: 5)

Tagg (2015) notes that many aspects of digital communication are not new but that, nonetheless, there are a range of prominent features. Digital communication can be synchronous (instant, as in Skype and live text chats) and asynchronous (delayed, as in email and posts on

SNSs) or a mixture of both. It takes place in a globally connected network of people and resources. Drawing on the work of the Microsoft researcher danah boyd (boyd & Marwick, 2011), Tagg outlines four key affordances that this globally networked digital communication provides. It is "*persistent* (information online persists indefinitely), *searchable* (it can be retrieved across different contexts) and *replicable* (it can be copied, linked to or reposted into new contexts) ... online posts have the potential for great visibility or *scalability* ... and that people cannot be sure who will access their posts" (2015: 7).

11.2 Digital communication, languages, and Global Englishes

As with other aspects of the global spread of languages discussed in this book, English has, unsurprisingly, also been prominent in its reach across digital communication and the internet. Figure 11.2 shows that English has the largest number of users on the internet, which includes those who use it as an L2 or additional language. However, it is also interesting to observe that Chinese is quite close to English in terms of users. Again, other large global languages such as Arabic and Spanish have a significant number of internet users. Thus, while English is certainly prominent in terms of internet users, other languages, and especially Chinese, are well represented, suggesting a multilingual internet

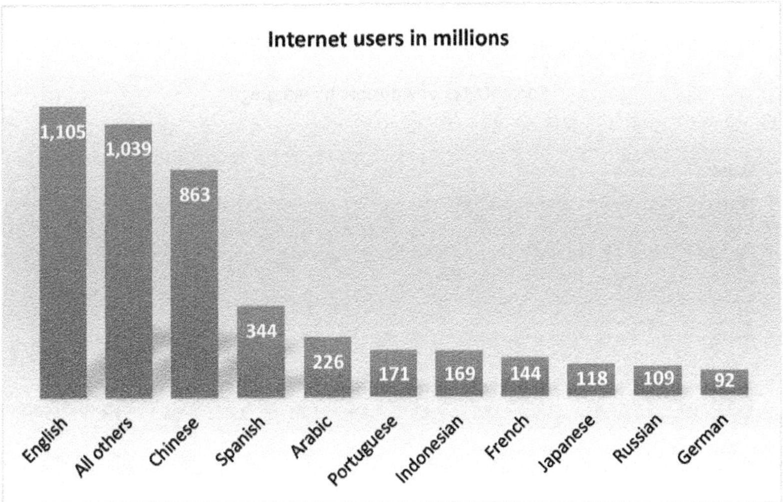

Figure 11.2 Top ten languages on the internet
(Based on data from Internet World Stats, 2019)

rather than an internet dominated by a single language. Nonetheless, again, the 'big' global languages dominate, with the world's 7000 or so other languages having fewer combined users than English alone.

Some things to consider about Figure 11.2 are that this data represents internet users and does not, of course, include those users of languages that may not have access to the internet. Moreover, although the number of users of Chinese is very high, the use of Chinese in website content is very low and decreasing, at between 2–1% of websites (W3Techs, 2020). In contrast, as shown in Figure 11.3, English is very dominant here, with over 60% of website content in English, and the next nearest language is Russian, with 8–9% (W3Techs, 2020). This may reflect the dominance of English-speaking Anglophone tech companies such as Microsoft, Google, and Facebook. However, given that the majority of internet users are not from Anglophone settings (remember, over 50% are in Asia), it also suggests that a lot of web content and English language use is both by and for non-Anglophone English speakers who are using it as a global lingua franca. Communication between users in SNSs is also not measured in these statistics and, as we will discuss later in the chapter, this can be highly multilingual. Furthermore, given that there are almost as many social media users (3.80 billion) as there are internet users (4.54 billion), it is a key domain of digital communication (Kemp, 2020).

It should also be pointed out that large numbers are not everything in relation to language use. Although many minority or 'smaller' languages make up a small proportion of internet use and websites, and

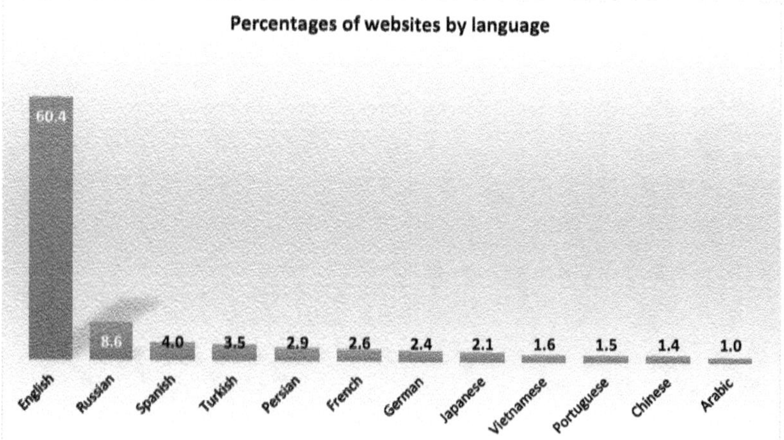

Figure 11.3 Top ten website content languages
(Based on data from W3Techs, 2020)

there are concerns about the speakers of minority languages having access to digital communication, the internet and digital communication have also presented a variety of opportunities. As Tagg (2015) notes, language-minority communities have managed to successfully use digital communication to maintain and promote their languages. Anyone with access to the internet can produce and access material in their chosen language, bypassing the traditional need for a 'top-down' authority (e.g., national or local government) to sanction and produce minority-language materials and literature. Furthermore, access to digital communication means that diasporas of minority-language communities can stay in contact in ways which were not possible before. Thus, their languages can still be used on a daily basis with other speakers around the world via digital communication even when living or working in environments where other languages dominate.

In sum, as with other aspects of globalisation, communication, and language use, digital communication provides a complex picture. We see a dominance of English in website content and prominence in terms of users. However, other 'big' global languages also have large numbers of internet users, suggesting a multilingual environment. Furthermore, many of the users of English on the internet and in digital communication are non-Anglophone users of ELF. Moreover, the statistics do not capture the more fluid and potentially multilingual uses of language in domains such as SNSs. Additionally, although the majority of the world's languages only represent a small proportion of the languages measured in these statistics, digital communication and the internet also provide opportunities to produce material and communicate in minority languages which did not exist, or were more restricted, before the growth of digital communication. Nonetheless, there are still concerns over access to digital communication for many minority-language communities and a sizeable minority of the world's population have limited or no access to the internet.

11.3 Digital communication and intercultural/transcultural communication

Given the global scope of digital communication and its multilingual and multicultural nature, it should be clear that much intercultural (and transcultural) communication takes place online. Indeed, as the first author of this book has written, drawing on research by Varis and Wang (2011), "the diversity of languages, cultures and communities present online gives rise to unprecedented opportunities for intercultural and transcultural communication and represents 'superdiverse space par excellence – a space of seemingly endless possibilities for self-expression and community formation'" (Baker & Sangiamchit, 2019: 474, quoting Varis & Wang, 2011: 71). However, we also need to recognise that such 'superdiverse' digital settings are not unusual and exotic but an everyday part of life for many of us, as the statistics for digital communication show. The Global Englishes and digital communication researcher Chittima Sangiamchit has proposed the term EMIC, or electronically mediated intercultural communication, which "involves online intercultural interactions through mediated digital devices" (2018: 345) to account for this phenomenon. Sangiamchit (2018) goes on to identify four aspects of EMIC: multilingualism and multiculturalism, multi-way communication, multimodality, and mobility. First, as already noted throughout this chapter, digital communication is highly multilingual and multicultural. Second, EMIC is multi-way in the sense of communication being synchronous, asynchronous, or a combination of both (as described previously). Third, much digital communication is multimodal, making use of text, emojis, images, sounds, videos, etc. Fourth, EMIC is characterised by a high degree of mobility and, as Sangiamchit notes, this is not just in relation to the mobility of users "but also objects (communication devices), symbols (for examples, information, images and videos), contexts and spaces" (2018: 347).

To these four aspects of EMIC we can also add the 'trans' dimension of the *processes* that users of digital communication engage in during interactions. These include translanguaging, transmodality, and transcultural communication. The features and processes of EMIC can be summarised as follows.

• multilingualism and multiculturalism • multi-way communication • multimodality • mobility (Sangiamchit, 2018)	• translanguaging • transmodal communication • transcultural communication (Baker & Sangiamchit, 2019)

Thus, we can see how participants in digital communication make use of their multilingual (different named languages such as English and Japanese), multicultural (different cultural references and practices such as local, national, and global references), and multimodal (text, emojis, and images, among others) resources through processes of translanguaging, transmodality, and transcultural communication. The extract below from Sultana's (2016) study of young Bangladeshis' online communication (Figure 11.4) offers a clear example of how these processes come together in digital communication.

This example illustrates the use of different languages, English and Bangla, as well as language specifically associated with digital communication, such as 'omg' (line 04) and 'haha' (lines 06, 09, 11, 14). We can see extensive use of emoticons or emojis (lines 02, 06, 09, 12,

dialogues engraved in the image and its translation: *Italics*

1.	Luna	*Oh no the tree trying to eat me!!*
2.	Ria	It already eatted ew ((grin emoticon))
3.	Luna	It dided.
4.	RA	Ehehehehheheh. omg! the tree eated u. ehehehe.
5.	AT	Adorable!
6.	Luna	haha i look scared for real though. thanks!! ((kiki emoticon))
7.	AR	Epic expression!!
8.	RA	 *maar dala — it killed me.*
9.	Luna	fazil ((Bangla word which means naughty)) haha
10.	YW	Mooney's bay!
11.	YW	I know where the tree is, ha ha
12.	Luna	((smile emoticon))
13.	SFE	And how come it able to diget ((digest)) u dear... ((gasp emoticon))
14.	Luna	it couldn't haha ((tongue emoticon))

Figure 11.4 Facebook conversation
(Sultana, 2016: 229)

13, 14). Images are also used in the first line and line 08. Furthermore, the use of English is, according to Sultana (2016), deliberately unconventional, e.g., 'eatted' (line 02), 'dided' (line 03), incorporating local Bangladeshi aspects of language use in a process of translanguaging. Finally, the references move across multiple scales with the first image from a park in Canada (Mooney's Bay) and the second image from a famous Indian film ('Devdas') with the title of a Hindi song, "*maar dala*" (line 08) (Sultana, 2016: 230). This example comes from the popular SNS Facebook and SNSs have emerged as an important area for understanding intercultural and transcultural communication through Global Englishes. We will explore transculturality, transmodality, and translanguaging on SNSs in more detail in the rest of this chapter.

11.4 Digital communication, social media, and social networking sites

Over the last decade or so we have seen the move from the internet as a source of easily accessible information, to be predominantly passively consumed, to the internet becoming a more interactive and creative platform – what is typically termed as Web 2.0. The digital communication scholar Susan Herring defines Web 2.0 as "web-based platforms that emerged as popular in the first decade of the twenty-first century, and that incorporate user-generated content and social interaction, often alongside or in response to structures or (multimedia) content provided by the sites themselves" (2013: 4; see also Herring, 2010). The most well-known examples of Web 2.0 platforms are social media (e.g., YouTube) and especially social networking sites (SNSs) (e.g., Facebook). Social media has proven to be very successful, with the majority of the world's internet users also making use of social media (3.80 billion out of 4.54 billion potential users; Kemp, 2020). Companies such as Facebook, YouTube, WeChat, and Instagram have grown hugely in a relatively short period of time and now have billions of users each, as demonstrated in Figure 11.5.

Ellison and Boyd offer well-cited characterisations of SNSs, as follows:

a networked communication platform in which participants

1) have uniquely identifiable profiles that consist of user-supplied content, content provided by other users, and/or system-provided data;
2) can publicly articulate connections that can be viewed and traversed by others; and
3) can consume, produce, and/or interact with streams of user-generated content provided by their connections on the site (2013: 158; emphasis removed)

They claim that these three features underpin all SNSs and provide a range of expanded interaction affordances in comparison to offline communication. A number of other significant features of SNSs can also be identified.

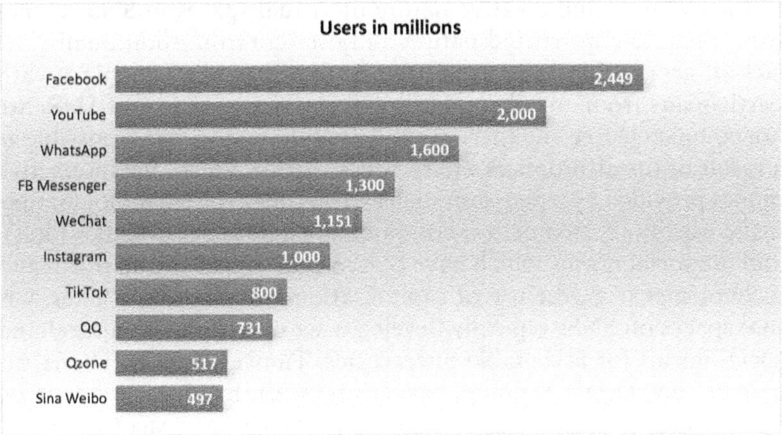

Figure 11.5 Social media platforms and users
(Based on data from Kemp, 2020)

As noted previously in relation to EMIC and digital communication, SNSs are typically multimodal in nature, with users able to make use of a range of resources when communicating. These include different languages, orthographies (i.e., Arabic, Chinese, Roman, etc.), emoticons and emojis, hyperlinks, pictures, video clips, animations, and sounds. In many cases, as we saw with the example above from Sultana's (2016) study, the communication involves a complex mix of these different resources interacting together to make meaning. The use of many different resources and modes in communication is traditionally seen as multimodality (Kress & Van Leeuwen, 2001), but recently researchers have also started to employ the term transmodality to describe the process of using a range of modes simultaneously where the use of different modes cannot easily be distinguished (see Sultana, 2016; Newfield, 2014/2017; Baker & Sangiamchit, 2019). This has been particularly relevant to SNSs where meaning and affect (emotional impact) are often created through the interaction of a variety of modes, for example, text, emoji, and video, where the boundaries between each mode become blurred. Scholars such as Pennycook (2007) and Li Wei (2018) have argued that to fully understand communication we need to adopt a more holistic approach in which we do not separate linguistic forms from the other modes of communication and semiotics in which they are typically embedded.

Another important feature is that SNSs are spaces rather than physical places. As Canagarajah (2013: 163–164) explains, spaces are social and co-constructed between participants, in contrast to places, which are based on physical geographical domains. Much of the dynamic and creative nature of virtual spaces in SNSs comes from their co-constructed nature and user control. Additionally, the lack of geographical constraint means that they can take place with participants from anywhere. However, the virtual spaces of SNSs are not completely free and there are still limitations on what is possible as a result of the affordances offered on a platform (e.g., the interactive modes provided by a platform such as YouTube), the technologies they make use of (e.g., templates, programming languages, graphics tools), and the social norms which have co-evolved around the platform and technologies (e.g., the use of capitalisation for 'shouting'). Thus, virtual spaces on SNSs typically develop a set of particular cultural and social norms for acceptable interactions (Pauwels, 2012). Therefore, as with any social grouping, tensions between freedom and control, fluidity and normativity, are also a part of virtual spaces on SNSs. An additional level of complexity between space and place is also added to SNSs such as Facebook in the links between the online and offline world. Tagg and Seargeant (2016/2020) point out that many Facebook users make friends through previous offline contacts rather than online connections. Furthermore, much of what is referenced and discussed in Facebook is users' offline activity, as we saw in the photo from the park that started the exchange in Sultana's (2016) research above.

Audience and the notion of "context collapse" (Marwick & boyd, 2011) are also significant aspects of social media. The audience for communication in social media is typically different in comparison to offline communication and in particular social media has a much wider audience. This process by which social media "collapse diverse social contexts into one" (Marwick & boyd, 2011: 10) is termed 'context collapse'. In other words, in social media different 'contexts' or social groups that would normally be separate in the offline world all come together. For instance, a Facebook user may have Facebook friends who are family members, old school friends, work colleagues, local friends, and acquaintances. Outside of rare occasions, such as weddings, these social groups would normally be separate in the offline world. However, in social media these groups are all the potential audience of any posting all the time. Thus, users have to manage different expectations, notions of appropriateness, and shared knowledge and history among these different groups. In terms of language, this can mean managing different expectations as regards levels of formality and register but also with the international and intercultural connections social media allows, different languages, and cultural norms. As studies such as Seargeant et al. (2012) and Androutsopoulos (2014) show, social media often leads to a convergence on English as a way to maximise the audience as it is a commonly shared language.

However, this is typically ELF and it is also a very multilingual and translingual use of English mixed with other languages from a user's repertoire. For example, Androutsopoulos' study shows that among a multilingual group of Facebook users in Germany, while an initial post might be in English, "a responding turn in German, the locally relevant conversational choice, is much more typical in the data than the uptake of English in online conversation" (2014: 72). This is illustrated in the extract below from Androutsopoulos (2014: 66).

Extract 11.1 Ingo's wall, December 2010
Translation in italics

01 Ingo n/a	Tones of snow in Hamburg!!!! I think it's enough but if we get school off?!...... keep snowing!☺
02 F1 16:19	Das ware ein bisschen toll :) Wann und wo wird das eig bestimmt? *That would be quite cool :) When and where is it being decided?*

Tagg and Seargeant (2016/2020) elaborate further on the nature of audiences in SNSs and especially Facebook. They adapt Bell's (1984) model of audience design for spoken interaction to audience design for Facebook and identify five parts of the potential audience.

- *Poster* of the status update or comment (the 'speaker' in Bell's model);
- *Addressee/s* (as in Bell's model, those to whom an update or comment is explicitly addressed);
- *Active Friends* (the people who someone typically interacts with on Facebook and who in some cases pertain to Bell's 'auditors', those not directly addressed but whose participation is ratified by the speaker);
- *Wider Friends* (the wider circle of social acquaintances, family, and professional contacts, who might in Bell's analysis be termed 'overhearers', those whose presence is known but for whom a post is not intended);
- *The Internet as a whole* (pertaining to Bell's 'eavesdroppers', those whose presence can in some circumstances become suddenly known to the speaker with implications for their language style and choice of utterance – seen in numerous cases on social media where ostensibly private messages are picked up on by the authorities or news media).

(Tagg & Seargeant, 2016/2020: 346)

These multiple audiences on Facebook mean that users must both consider the wider network of friends who may view a post and also choose strategies to include or exclude particular potential audience members. However, as the audience cannot be precisely known in advance (we cannot be sure who will or won't read a post on a Facebook page), Tagg and Seargeant argue that in effect Facebook users "are not so much targeting or responding to an audience as actually constructing it. Audience design entails drawing on what are perceived to be shared practices, and at the same time enacting and elaborating upon these practices (such as code-switching, or style-shifting)" (2016/2020: 347). In other words, to some extent, the users create the audience and community themselves on Facebook through the use of particular linguistic and cultural practices which are shared with other potential users. We will return to the relationship between audience, culture, and community on Facebook later in this chapter.

Finally, as Tagg and Seargeant explain, social media, with its focus on the participation and interaction of users and producers, has blurred "the dividing line between publishing or broadcasting and private or personal communication" (2016/2020: 341). Traditional broadcasting and publishing organisations now allow users to interact with their output through reactions, comments, and sharing, and many social media and SNSs have individually tailored news streams directly to private accounts. However, as cases such as Cambridge Analytica and its use of user data from Facebook to influence the 2016 US presidential election show, this blurring of private communication and news broadcasting has not been without controversy (Cadwalladr & Graham-Harrison, 2018). Other issues include the extent to which SNSs should be responsible for the content posted by individual users, particularly when they may have a harmful influence (for example, for children, young people, and vulnerable groups). Nonetheless, despite the controversies, social media is used by the majority of internet users and is now a daily part of life for many of us.

Summary

Some of the core features of SNSs outlined by researchers so far include:

- a visible network of connections between individual users by which they can both share and interact with user-generated content
- multimodal and multilingual content
- co-constructed virtual spaces rather than physical places but with strong links to offline activity for some SNSs (e.g., Facebook)
- wide audiences and 'context collapse' of different social groups

- audience design, in which the community is created through the users' shared practices
- the blurring of users and producers and private communication with publishing and broadcasting, resulting in a number of controversies

Activity 11.2 Social media, intercultural interactions, and understanding 'others'

Tagg and Seargeant begin their discussion of Facebook with the following quote, taken from a letter written by Mark Zuckerberg (the founder of Facebook).

> Personal relationships are the fundamental unit of our society. Relationships are how we discover new ideas, understand our world and ultimately derive long-term happiness. At Facebook, we build tools to help people connect with the people they want and share what they want, and by doing this we are extending people's capacity to build and maintain relationships. People sharing more – even if just with their close friends or families – creates a more open culture and leads to a better understanding of the lives and perspectives of others.
>
> (Zuckerberg 2012, cited in Tagg & Seargeant, 2016/2020: 339)

Think about your own use of social media and Facebook (if you use it). Do you agree with Zuckerberg's claims, e.g., that social media leads to more open cultures and a better understanding of others? In what ways can social media help with intercultural communication and an understanding of others? In what ways can social media cause problems in intercultural communication and understanding?

Feedback: *We agree that social media and digital communication open up new spaces for contact, and make communication across and through borders more accessible. But like any social setting there are also power issues and negative aspects. You may remember that we began this chapter with a quotation about the superdiversity of the internet from the sociolinguists Varis and Wang (2011). While the first half the quotation is positive, the second half is less so, and neatly encapsulates the possibilities and limitations of digital social spaces.*

> *The Internet is the superdiverse space par excellence – a space of seemingly endless possibilities for self-expression and community formation. Yet, online environments are not characterized only by happy heterogeneity: rather, we are able to see multiple layers of normativity in the form of self-, peer- and state-imposed*

> *norms. That is, though allowing for the continuous diversification of diversity, the Internet is also a space where diversity is controlled, ordered and curtailed.*
>
> *(2011: 71)*

11.5 Language, identity, and culture through digital transcultural communication

Now that we have explored digital communication, Global Englishes, EMIC, social media, and social networking, we should be in a position to draw together some of the central ideas and consider their influence on intercultural and transcultural communication, including core concepts such as identity, community, and culture.

Beginning with identity, much of the research into digital communication and identity has followed the post-structuralist approach to identity that has been outlined in this book (see Chapter 6) in which identities are seen as multiple, fluid, constructed, and negotiated in interaction. As the digital communication scholar Sage Lambert Graham (2016/2020) points out, many aspects of identity construction in the online world are similar to offline settings and the topics of research, such as multilingualism and multimodality, are not unique to online settings. Nonetheless, digital communication is of interest due to the scale at which it takes place, making it an important setting for social interaction and hence identity construction. Furthermore, while the identities participants construct through digital communication may not be unique to the online world, the resources and affordances provided in digital spaces are distinct from offline settings. Tagg and Seargeant suggest that in an SNSs like Facebook "the resources which people have at their disposal differ markedly from those typically associated with identity construction in face-to-face spoken contexts" (2016/2020: 343). These include the use of multimodal resources, for instance, emojis and photos, as discussed previously, as well as affordances such as hyperlinks and 'tags' to explanations of references and terminology, and even translation services. At the same time, other aspects of identity which are present in offline communication are absent, or much less prominent, for example, accent, tone, facial expressions, gestures, as well as elements of appearance such as age and gender. Furthermore, in SNSs people can be selective in how they construct their identities, choosing how they create their user profiles and the languages, texts, and images they link to these profiles. As danah boyd has famously noted, in SNSs "individuals must write themselves into being" (2008: 13). This gives people a degree of control and also freedom that may not always be present in offline interactions. As discussed in relation to globalisation and transcultural communication more generally, new social spaces, such as those provided by SNSs, offer new opportunities for identity construction that may not have been possible before. For instance, in Chapter 10.4 we saw how an Iranian international student in the UK was able to construct an identity as an expert in martial arts and martial arts film stars, including links to national 'Chinese' cultural references as well as global and local references. Indeed, as we will explore in more detail in this section, digital communication and SNSs have offered unprecedented opportunities for people to construct cultural identities which are not restricted by geographical or national boundaries and borders.

The following example from Tagg and Seargeant (2012) clearly illustrates the spaces SNSs provide for constructing multilingual and multicultural identities. This Facebook exchange takes place between a group of Thai friends who are internationally dispersed between Europe and Thailand. One of the members of the group, Dream, posts a selection of photos of desserts from a recent trip to Strasbourg and tags her friends, who respond below (see Figure 11.6).

In this example, we see English (line 01), Thai (e.g., line 02), and the use of French to describe some of the desserts (line 04). As Tagg and Seargeant (2012) suggest, the photos of these expensive-looking European desserts and the use of different languages to describe them serve to construct an identity for these Facebook users as cosmopolitan Thais. This also enhances the group's identity in terms of shared multilingual and multicultural resources, while at the same time possibly excluding those who do not share these multicultural and multilingual repertoires.

Yet, as also emphasised in earlier discussions of identity, participants do not have complete freedom in constructing identities. There are obviously the restrictions that come with the technology and platforms. So, for instance, Facebook only provides a certain number of ways to construct profiles and to interact with others (likes, posts, timelines, events, etc.). Resources and power relationships also influence identity construction, as shown in Dovchin et al. (2016), discussed in Chapter 10.4. Users may have different access to material resources, such as internet connections and mobile devices, and social resources, such as proficiency in English, which influences how they can construct their online identities. 'Authenticity' is also important in SNSs, and users' online identities, while not the same as offline identities, must to some extent match them (Tagg & Seargeant, 2016/2020). Finally, as outlined in the previous section, audiences are a crucial part of digital communication, and especially SNSs, and how identities are constructed will be influenced by the potential audience to a significant degree.

1 Aum: give me strawberry tart plsss:)

2 Beau: เง้ออ แกแก้แค้นชั้นเหรอออออออออ
[Issssss this your revenge?]

3 Tukta: กรี๊ดดด สวยงามมากดรีมจ้าาา...· · ·
[Greedd *(A screaming sound to express delight)* (It is) so beautiful, Dream.]

4 Tukta: Tiramisu Pomme et Tarte a la rhubarbe

5 Som รักในหลวง:: ทำแบบนี้นี่โกรธมากนะพี่ดรีม
ได้แต่นั่งดูเฉยๆเนี่ย >_<
[What you did makes me so angry Pee Dream.[4] (I) can only look]

6 Pooky: เมอแรงงงงแงๆๆๆ
ป.ล. พี่ดรีมคะ ปุ๊กกี้กลับมาจากค่ายแล้วนะคะ
[Meringueeee (เมอแรง is a loan word in Thai whose root is from meringue)
P.S. Pee Dream, Pooky came back from camping already]

7 Fah: น่ากินมากๆๆ เลยดรีม เผื่อด้วยนะ
[(It looks) sooo delicious, Dream. Eat some on my behalf]

Figure 11.6 Strasbourg desserts

Note: "Thai dialogue is translated below the utterance in which it occurs. The English translation aims to replicate the orthographic play in the Thai where possible. Short explanatory notes (in italics) are also embedded where necessary" (Tagg & Seargeant, 2012: 202)

You may remember that in Chapter 6.3 we emphasised that identity is not just about the construction of the self but also about identification with others (as well as distinctions from others). This obviously applies equally to online and offline settings and means that in order to understand identity construction in digital communication we need to understand the groupings or communities that users are identifying with. We have discussed the importance of audience in how identities are constructed in SNSs, with users having to negotiate multiple potential audiences simultaneously from varied social groupings such as family, friends, and work (i.e., "context collapse" in Marwick & boyd, 2011). Tagg and Seargeant (2016/2020) suggest that it is the notion of audience design that forms the link between individual identities and communities in SNSs as users shape and construct their identities in response to the potential communities they wish to interact with. Alongside context collapse, SNSs also differ from most offline communities in that being virtual spaces, rather than physical places, they are not bound by geographical constraints. This allows for groupings and communities that are diverse, flexible, dynamic, and emergent. Although, it should be noted that similarly 'superdiverse' communities have been described in contemporary sociolinguistic studies of urban settings (e.g., Blommaert, 2013; Pennycook & Otsuji, 2015). Even so, the ease by which links can be established between individuals with shared interest in online settings also means that many communities in SNSs are what the discourse analyst James Paul Gee (2004) refers to as "affinity spaces". This describes groupings which come together around a single issue (e.g., a political cause such as the climate emergency or human rights) or a shared interest (e.g., football club fans or fans of a particular anime series) but which often have little shared history or social interaction outside of the group and are, hence, a relatively transient group with weak social bonds. Again, though, it should be noted that such groupings also exist offline (e.g., sports and social clubs); however, SNSs have made it easier and quicker to join such groups and have given them a greater geographical spread.

Indeed, it is this removing of geographical constraints that perhaps leads to one of the most important aspects of communities and cultures in SNSs. Through their wide geographical spread SNS communities are able to involve participants from diverse settings and hence have a potentially very multicultural and multilingual membership. This has frequently been discussed in relation to the notions of transcultural and translocal (Chapter 10.3), with digital communication representing an expansion and acceleration of these processes already brought on through globalisation. The digital communication researcher Samu Kytölä writes: "a growing body of complex cultural phenomena emerge as translocal and transcultural in the first place, never 'produced' or 'consumed' – or meant to be consumed – in a national or local social context. In this cultural development, digital communication has played and continues to play a key role" (2016/2020: 373). As this quotation from Kytölä makes clear, it is not just the groupings that are translocal and transcultural but also the cultural practices that they engage in. These cultural practices might include popular cultural products and practices such as globally recognised music styles (e.g., hip-hop, as described by Pennycook (2007); see Chapter 2.3), global celebrities (e.g., movies stars, as in the example of Jet Li (Baker & Sangiamchit, 2019); see Chapter 10.4), or even online memes, such as the 'ice bucket challenge', none of which fit neatly into traditional cultural boundaries or borders.

At the same time, though, the local is still important; as Kytölä notes, a participant in an online community "is always writing from a particular location, which may have significant repercussions for how digitally mediated interaction chains and discourses emerge" (2016/2020: 375). In other words, cultural practices, even in digital communication, are still created and received in particular settings which will give them specific meanings and interpretations. Again drawing on the example of hip-hop, we can see how its form is changed and adapted to different localities (think about how Japanese hip-hop is both similar to and differs from French hip-hop or US hip-hop in language use, subject matter, and musical influences in social media such as YouTube). In this sense, then, digital communities and cultures can be seen as the connection of many different diverse localities, i.e., they are trans*local*. However, again, we should also be aware, as the quotation in the previous paragraph from Kytölä (2016/2020) suggests, that digital communication allows for emergent cultural practices, references, and identities that may not be 'local' or 'national'. As Canagarajah argues, we need to be more open to "the possibility that language norms may be renegotiated, or that spaces can be reconstructed by people in communicative situations" (2013: 156). Thus, we should recognise the multiplicity and complexity of scales or levels with practices and references not easily consigned to any one of them (local, national, or global) in digital transcultural communication (Baker & Sangiamchit, 2019).

These emergent cultural practices, communities, and identities have been the focus of much Global Englishes research in digital communication. We have already discussed a number of these studies in detail in this and other chapters (see especially Chapter 10.4), including: Tagg and Seargeant's (2012) study of the translocal and multilingual practices of a community of Thai users on an SNS; Androutsopoulos' (2014) research on English use, alongside other languages, on an SNS among multilingual youth based in Germany; Dovchin et al.'s (2016) and Sultana's (2016) studies of the translingual, transmodal, and transcultural practices of Mongolian and Bangladeshi youth online; Li Wei's (2016) discussion of translanguaging and English in digital communication in China; and Baker and Sangiamchit's (2019) study of transcultural communication among a group of international students on an SNS. Other notable studies include the ELF researcher Paola Vettorel's (2014) examination of the online blogging practices of young Europeans. She found bloggers making use of English alongside other linguistic resources to both represent local aspects of their linguacultural identities and also to identify with international groups with shared interests. In particular, Vettorel notes that there was extensive adaptation of English (and other languages), as well as frequent code-switching and translanguaging, using resources from both bloggers' L1 and also the L1 of other friends in their networks. These multilingual or translingual practices, Vettorel argues, were used to better represent local cultural references, establish and reference shared resources within the community, and to reference globally related interests of the group. Vettorel also suggests that all these different scales were present simultaneously, with no one level privileged.

From a slightly different perspective, Jenks (2013) examined the positioning and identification of a group of online English language users and found that although from a research approach the exchanges and users might be identified in terms of ELF, these were not categories used by the participants themselves. Instead, the participants identified themselves as 'foreigner', 'language learner', and 'non-native'. Jenks (2013) concludes that we need to be careful about a priori ascription of identities and recognise that participants and researchers may interpret identities in interactions differently. Turning to the educational domain, researchers such as Guth and Helm (2010) in Europe, and Ke and Cahyani (2014), Baker (2015), and Ishikawa (2020a) in the context of Asia, have explored the use of ELF in online educational exchanges. They have shown how experience of using English in online communication expands students' awareness of the use of ELF beyond Anglophone cultures and communicative norms, thus increasing students' confidence in using English as proficient multilinguals in intercultural communication. However, at the same time, like Jenks' (2013) study and earlier ELF research (e.g., Jenkins, 2007), the prestige of 'native'-speaker English and Anglophones is often still present (see Chapter 7). Many of these themes of language, identity, community, and culture related to transcultural communication, translanguaging, and transmodality are discussed in the study undertaken by the first author of this book and his colleague (Baker & Sangiamchit, 2019). We will explore another example from that research in detail now.

Activity 11.3 Cowboy iPhone

Read the extract below, adapted from Baker and Sangiamchit (2019), and then discuss the following questions. In their study a participant, Ken (L1 Thai, male) posted a YouTube clip on his Facebook wall of an ironic music video made on the launch of the latest iPhone in Thailand. The music video playfully mocks the excitement around the iPhone through both visual jokes (the actions and images in the music video) and a number of linguistic puns and jokes. The video is primarily in Thai and, as Ken explained in an interview, was posted for his Thai friends. However, the video also draws a response from Ken's friend Symeon (L1 Greek, male), who finds the video funny but does not understand Thai and so asks for further explanation.

ไหนพี่น้อง ขอดูโทรศัพท์หน่อยซิ?

See translation

Figure 11.7 Cowboy iPhone

	(คาวบอย – ไอโฟน Official MV) https://www.youtube.com/watch?v=J6Mmp8K86TQ
	Like · Share · Saturday at 17:15
	Woraluck likes this.
01 Symeon:	I'm not so sure for the purpose of this video ... but it makes me laugh ... What does he say? Saturday at 17:42 · Edited · Like · 1
02 Toh:	give me one pls. Saturday at 17:42 · Like · 1
03 Ken:	Symeon This guy names himself 'cowboy'. He is trying to mimic one of the most famous Thai band named 'Carabao'. The word 'Carabao' means 'water buffalo' in Tagalog language widely used in Philippine. Moreover, 'buffalo' is closely

	pronounced like 'fine' so 'I'm fine' has the close meaning to 'You are a buffalo' in Thai. That's the reason why you can see a lot of buffaloes in the music video. Saturday at 17:47 · Edited · Like · 1 Symeon Saturday at 17:49 · Like
04 Ken:	Are you fine? Saturday at 17:49 · Like
05 Symeon:	I'm flying on Wednesday and perhaps I'll come to the Uni ... So, I'll see you then Saturday at 17:50 · Like · 1
06 Ken:	'you are fine' means 'you are a buffalo' Saturday at 17:51 · Like · 1
07 Symeon:	haha ... and what's the relation to the iphone? Saturday at 17:54 · Like
08 Ken:	The name of this music is iPhone. The similarity of the pronunciation is played 'I-Phone' -> 'I-Fine'. The meaning of this music is pretty ironic. It's saying that 'Everyone has iPhone. if I don't have iPhone I will look like I-Fine (buffalo)'. ha ha Saturday at 18:01 · Edited · Like
09 Symeon:	Anyway ... it seems hilarious

(Baker & Sangiamchit, 2019: 478–479)

Questions

Q1 What are the multimodal/transmodal features of this example and how do they contribute to the interaction?
Q2 What are the multilingual/translingual features of this example and how do they contribute to the interaction?
Q3 What is the relationship between local and global cultures seen from this example? In what way is it an example of transcultural communication (if at all)?
Q4 Can you think of any examples like this from your own experiences of digital communication?

Feedback (adapted from Baker & Sangiamchit, 2019): *Starting the interpretation with cultural scales, from a traditional intercultural perspective we have a variety of national scales, with participants from Thailand and Greece, references to Thailand and the Philippines (line 03) in the text, as well as the US origin of the iPhone. However, the iPhone has now also become a global symbol of progress and prosperity. There are regional Asian references to buffaloes as slow and obedient, which is central to the ironic joke that those who unquestioningly follow the iPhone are like buffaloes (lines 03, 06–09). Additionally we have references to alternative groupings including class through* *the reference to the Thai singer "Carabao" (line 03), whose music was originally associated with working classes and political protest. The pun between the similar sound of iPhone and I-Fine (meaning a buffalo in contemporary Thai slang) (line 08) also provides a link to local youth cultures. Last, we have a reference to local physical places with the mention of "the Uni" (line 05) or university. Thus, we have multiple cultural scales simultaneously present with no one scale prominent or fixed but with participants moving through the different scales as described in transcultural communication.*

Turning to the use of English, other languages, and modes, we can see how these are all combined to construct multiple and fluid cultural scales and references to produce the joke that is the centre of the interaction. There are the images of the buffaloes, the singer dressing like a well-known Thai singer Carabao, who is associated with buffaloes, and the music in the song. Although the majority of the rest of the exchange is text-based, this text would make little sense without the video. Most of the written exchange is through ELF, and neither participant is a 'native' speaker of English or using 'standard' English. At the same time other languages are also present, including Thai in the original video, in the screen shot, and in text surrounding it, as well as "I-Fine" (line 08) in the comments and the use of the Tagalog word Carabao, highlighting the multilingual nature of ELF use. Again, as with the cultural scales, to fully understand the exchange it is necessary to take a holistic approach to the different languages and modes in which the distinctions between them are less important than the connections. Indeed we would argue that a complete understanding of this example requires a combination of transcultural, translingual, and transmodal competence that transcends the boundaries between named cultures, languages, and modes. Furthermore, "this example illustrates not passive acceptance of all these linguistic categories, cultural references and associations, but rather the participants being consciously transgressive in this playful critique of the iPhone and its socio-cultural meanings, as well as, playing with and transcending cultural and linguistic boundaries" (2019: 480).

Chapter summary

In this chapter we examined the growth in digital communication and its current global reach at over 4 billion users. We saw the central role that English plays in many domains of digital communication; however, we also emphasised that other languages are present and English is typically used as a lingua franca in multilingual environments. Given the global connections enabled by digital communication this is now an important part of understanding contemporary intercultural and transcultural communication. You should now be familiar with:

- digital communication
- Global Englishes and digital communication including the relationship between English and other languages in online environments
- EMIC (i.e., electronically mediated intercultural communication) including the use of multimodal, multilingual, multicultural, and mobile resources in transcultural, translingual, and transmodal communication processes
- social media and SNSs (i.e., social networking sites)
- identity, community, and culture in digital communication and social media

We suggested that the new social spaces opened up by digital communication, and especially social media, allow the construction and negotiation of dynamic and fluid identities, communities, and cultural practices that transcend traditional linguistic and cultural boundaries. However, as with any social practice there are also constraints related to technology, platforms, and digital cultural norms, as well as unequally distributed material and social resources.

Further reading

Baker, W. & Sangiamchit, C. (2019). Transcultural communication: Language, communication and culture through English as a lingua franca in a social network community. *Language and Intercultural Communication*, *19*, 471–487. doi: 10.1080/14708477.2019.1606230. An empirical study that explores many of the key themes in this chapter related to ELF, transcultural communication, translanguaging, and transmodality in digital spaces.

Sangiamchit, C. (2018). ELF in electronically mediated intercultural communication. In J. Jenkins, W. Baker, & M. Dewey (Eds.), *The Routledge handbook of English as a lingua franca* (pp. 345–356). Abingdon: Routledge. An overview of EMIC and its relationship to Global Englishes and ELF use and research.

Tagg, C. (2015). *Exploring digital communication: Language in action.* Abingdon: Routledge. A good introductory textbook to digital communication with sections specifically on English, identity, communities, and social media.

12 Complexity theory, language attitudes, and language awareness

> "When you know, to know you know [知之爲知之].
> When you don't know, to know you don't know [不知爲不知].
> That's what knowing is [是知也]."
>
> (Confucius)

Introduction

The authors have similar favourite quotations – one from Confucius, as above (see, e.g., Confucius, 2007: 22) and the other from Socrates (see Chapter 14). In the famous 論語 (Lúnyǔ) or *The Analects*, Confucius placed emphasis "not on knowledge as acquiring information to become more knowledgeable, but on developing awareness of one's knowledge" (Li, 2015: 52). The original version is 知之爲知之 (zhī zhī wéi zhī zhī), 不知爲不知 (bù zhī wéi bù zhī), 是知也 (shì zhī yě). With the first part omitted it is often said in Japanese that 知らざるを知らずと為す (shirazaru o shirazu to nasu), 是知るなり (kore shiru nari), i.e., "When you don't know, to know you don't know. That's what knowing is". What this version highlights is that knowing is being aware of one's ignorance. In order not to be trapped by essentialism and othering (Chapters 1.4, 6.3) or by provincialism and ideological monolingualism (Chapters 3.2, 7.2), we need to be prepared to reflect on the limitation of our knowledge. Only then, perhaps, will we be able to maximise our potential to communicate at a global scale.

If not a priori knowledge alone, then what will ensure effective global communication? This question is to be explored in the remainder of this book, based on the previous chapters and in relation to pedagogy. The current chapter focuses on language, followed by the next chapter about what we call EMF (English as a multilingua franca) awareness in EMI and ELT. In this chapter we begin with furthering the discussion of complexity theory (Chapter 2.4) to approach global communication more 'systematically' and comprehensively. Next, within a larger picture offered by complexity theory, we review Standard English in ELT (Chapter 7.2) and **communicative competence** (e.g.,

Canale, 1983/2013), twinned highly influential approaches to English communication in applied linguistics. Details of communicative competence will be discussed in relation to intercultural and transcultural communication in Chapter 14. Finally, in view of the constraints and opportunities derived from Standard English in ELT and complexity theory respectively, we problematise 'established' **language attitudes** to English. More specifically, we discuss one of the authors' research, a precursor of EMF awareness (Chapter 13), to examine language attitudes as they pertain to Standard English in ELT. You will have opportunities to give thought to both the limitations of a normative way of conceptualising English and the possibility of a holistic way of conceptualising 'English' communication, as well as reflect on your attitudes towards your own English.

Activity 12.1 Inconsistent grammatical correction

In Chapter 7.2, we quoted Jenkins (2014).

> For example, a Chinese PhD student's supervisor corrected the preposition "on" to "in" in the first draft of a chapter. The student duly made the various corrections required by the supervisor including changing the "on" to "in", and resubmitted his draft to the supervisor. He was amused but baffled when it was returned to him with the "in" changed back to "on". I mentioned this incident to a Vietnamese participant who told me that the same thing sometimes happened to him.
>
> (2014: 181–182)

- Have you ever had similar experiences when you wrote in an additional language? If so, how did you cope with them?
- Why do you think inconsistent grammatical correction in English sometimes happens?

Feedback: *Your answers and opinions will depend on your own experiences. Whatever your answers, you may have been reminded that no natural language is ready for decontextualised standardisation (Chapter 7.2). This is especially true for English as a global lingua franca, which by definition has no particular target speech communities (Chapter 4.3). Inconsistent grammatical correction in English as in Jenkins (2014) may stem from what Standard English is like in ELT materials. It is fundamentally an idealised version of the language within the intuitions of Anglophone materials writers and irrespective of how they use it for themselves (Leung, 2005; Hall, 2013) or what their generations learned as standard in their own local communities (Chapter 7.2).*

12.1 Complexity theory and global communication

Back in 2016, when the second author of this book was preparing for the doctoral viva voce (oral examination), one of the postdoctoral members at the University of Southampton's Centre for Global Englishes told him humorously that the best answer to virtually all the questions would be: "it's complex". The author did not use this tempting answer during his viva voce but, to be sure, anything related to global communication is rather complex. You may wonder how this complexity is to be understood.

Complexity theory provides a metaphoric heuristic to understand the mechanism of changing process during and beyond human lifespans (e.g., Baird et al., 2014; Blommaert, 2016). It is a **metatheory** or a theory about theories or notions (e.g., Larsen-Freeman, 2017). Its major limitation, accordingly, is that it requires theories or notions which refer directly to the empirical world for the purpose of grasping target phenomena. To this effect, we have introduced a currently prominent notion in the field of ELF: English as a multilingua franca or EMF (Chapter 8). EMF is akin to another notion of translanguaging in heeding how our social practices transcend or transgress the boundaries of ideologically named, multiple languages (Chapter 9.2, 9.3). At the same time, EMF and translanguaging accord closely with the notions of transcultural and transmodal communication. The former questions the fixed scope of named cultures which interactants move through and across (Chapter 10), and the latter indexes the simultaneous and collaborative use of meaning-making modes, often including language, as prominent in digital communication in particular (Chapter 11).

Fundamentally, complexity theory is about autonomous complex adaptive systems (CASs), or emergent and ever-changing 'systems', influencing each other in accordance with a diachronically and synchronically variable ecology (e.g., Larsen-Freeman, 1997; 2018). Unlike other systems, CASs by definition are never clear-cut or independent, but emergent from collective social activity, dynamically adaptive, and thus endlessly changing. We reframe language, culture, and mode as CASs below to rethink the aforementioned three notions (i.e., EMF coupled with translanguaging, transcultural, and transmodal communication).

Complexity theory allows us to envisage the interplay within and across language, culture, and mode. In a broad and rough scope, language, culture, and mode themselves are interacting with each other with fuzzy boundaries. They are working in relation to the social context. Figure 12.1 is a simple representation. We should immediately add that an attempt to view language, culture, or mode as a system is artificial for the purpose of helping researchers to study

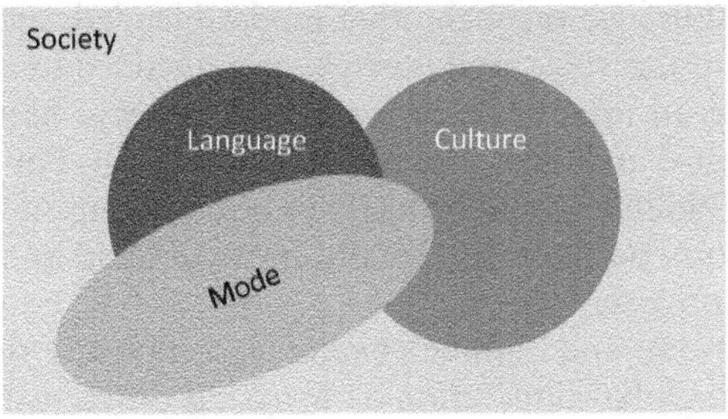

Figure 12.1 Language, culture, and mode as interacting CASs
(Adapted from Ishikawa, 2020b: 101)

communication (Chapter 2.4). In the first place, again, complexity theory is a metatheory to lend a hand to analysis of real-world phenomena rather than depict how the real-world is actually perceived.

If zoomed in, language as a CAS in Figure 12.1 comprises thousands of named languages or an even greater number of language varieties and provincially, socially, and ethnically different subvarieties (Chapters 3.1, 4.1) as smaller CASs. All these CASs are the result of an aggregated amount of interaction, and none of their changes is reducible to specific individuals or interactive instances at a certain moment. Also, the boundary of any of these CASs is, again, blurred and unstable. Likewise, both culture and mode consist of multiplex (i.e., multicultural or multimodal), multi-layered, and non-categorical CASs. It follows from this understanding that multilingual, multi-layered, and non-categorical CASs operate with an equally complicated constellation of cultural CASs through similarly intricate modal CASs over the course of our collective social practices.

In a particular communicative instance we integrate the affordances of these CASs. To illustrate this point, let's go back to one of the earliest examples in this book, Activity 2.3, which is based on the first author's data (Baker, 2009a) and one of the second author's favourite classroom activities (Ishikawa, 2020a). Nami and Phillipe are drawing on linguistic resources from multiple named languages, English, French, and Thai, and the game of petanque could be written in *pétanque* or *เปตอง*. While their conversation appears to be in English on the surface, we could imagine that these three languages are permeated with each other in phonology and beyond (for covert multilingual resources, see Chapter 8.3). Also, their cultural interpretation surrounding petanque is made by simultaneous reference to French, south French, and associated elder cultures as well as Thai, Bangkok, and associated youth cultures, thereby reaching a nuanced understanding of this game at a global scale within a short space of time. Moreover, language and culture are most likely to be connected not only through spoken mode but also through other modes blended, such as laughter, facial expression, gesture, and posture, as embedded in a casual, lively atmosphere of an urban café in Nami's hometown, Bangkok. All the relevant 'systems' are taken together subconsciously. For example, neither Nami or Phillipe would be likely to be conscious of exploiting the system of gesture or, more specifically, those of hand and arm gestures during their conversation.

As seen in Nami and Phillipe's example, complexity theory requires us to see each global interaction as invoking different linguistic, cultural, and modal CASs to different degrees. In turn, each communicative instance is a source of the 'energy' for triggering potential change in these CASs. Put differently, cross-sectionally speaking, complexity theory captures malleability across named languages and cultures in EMF scenarios, with English most often involved and Anglophone cultures more often irrelevant. Here, meaning-making modes are entangled to 'bridge' over language and culture. Longitudinally speaking, emergent norms across the globe are continuously entrained into named languages, cultures, and modes as change catalysts. Gleick states that "the act of playing the game has a way of changing the rules" (2008: 24). So long as we communicate, named languages and cultures will continue changing, with modes continually developing as well. The changing speed of the CASs can be markedly fast, given today's accelerated globalisation (Chapters 1.3, 8.1).

What complexity theory stresses is, then, the spatial and temporal uniqueness of each global interaction (see also the language-culture nexus and language and culture flows in Chapter 2.2, 2.3). It captures singularity in the flow of a collective evolutionary process with no fixed end point. In this regard, the theory would "emphasise the importance of viewing language from multiple dimensions, in which its contextual embodiment is crucial, and its isolation and compartmentalisation is problematic" (Baird et al., 2014: 190). Meanwhile, complexity theory expects that what emerges from each global encounter is **non-linear** or not fully predictable from the analysis of any antecedents (Jenkins, 2015b; Larsen-Freeman, 2018). As an extrapolation of this view to language use, it would be impossible to make a decontextualised distinction between an innovation and an error "because both are contingent upon the speakers' perception of, and acting on, the affordances in the context to create meaning" (Larsen-Freeman, 2018: 56). Conversely, complexity theory warns of a priori demarcation of any global interaction (e.g., the demarcation of the English language). This is because "in drawing boundaries, certain aspects of a multidimensional process are foregrounded, with the result that other dimensions are backgrounded" (Larsen-Freeman, 2018: 58), which leads to partial and possibly speculative claims. To this effect, the repositioning of English within multilingualism in the field of ELF, known as EMF

Table 12.1 Complexity theory and relevant notions of language, culture, and mode

Theories/notions	*Main features*	*Examples*
Complexity theory	Autonomous complex adaptive systems (CASs) influencing each other and thereby changing in accordance with variable ecologies; language, culture, and mode as CASs indicating that our communication is a non-linear, dynamic social practice	Larsen-Freeman (1997; 2018); Baird et al. (2014); Baker (2015); Ishikawa (2020b)
English as a multilingua franca (EMF)	Observing emergent multilingual influences and practices among English users at the global scale; underscoring the interplay between real-world fluid, flexible linguistic resources and ideologically bounded languages	Jenkins (2015b; 2018b); Ishikawa (2020a)
Translanguaging	Focusing on how bilinguals and multilinguals understand, interact with, and challenge society; questioning the existence of enumerable languages at the cognitive level	García (2009); Creese & Blackledge (2015); Li (2018)
Transcultural communication	Observing emergent cultural interpretations and frames of references during interaction; questioning the fixed scope of named cultures and the in-betweenness of them	Pennycook (2007); Baker (2015; 2018)
Transmodality/ transmodal communication	Indexing the simultaneous and collaborative use of meaning-making modes, often including language; underscoring the synergetic effect created through and across the boundaries of modes	Newfield (2014/ 2017); Baker & Sangiamchit (2019)

(Jenkins, 2015b; Chapter 8), has been an important step forward. In brief, complexity theory encourages those who are interested in global communication to take a more coherent and holistic approach to target phenomena. Complexity theory as a metatheory and subsumed theories or notions are summarised in Table 12.1.

12.2 Complexity theory, Standard English, and communicative competence

As argued in the previous section, complexity theory offers a meta-lens to conjoin EMF, translanguaging, and transcultural and transmodal communication while illustrating the non-linear, dynamic, and emergent nature of global communication. Within this larger picture we now review the global role of what has long characterised English communication in applied linguistics, namely, Standard English in ELT and communicative competence.

Standard English in ELT

The real-world objective to acquire L2 English is "to become bilingual and multilingual, rather than to replace the learner's L1 to become another monolingual" (Li, 2018: 16) in a particular locale. Even so, for the sake of practicality in language teaching, widely marketed Standard English in ELT (Chapter 7.2) represents a monolingual, provincial fiction as an idealised verbal being. More specifically, it emanates from an imagined Anglophone speech community among affluent speakers with monolingual repertoires at a certain point of time. Also, it seeks to enshrine a fixed set of their conventions independently of a global milieu. Moreover, it separates language as if it were a sole communication mode, thereby not giving full attention to how meaning is created and interpreted during interaction. All these points seem rather enigmatic in the light of complexity theory. As is hopefully clear by now, complexity theory goes against hypostasising language use in an essentialised, fixed social environment. It goes against prescribing and applying one-size-fits-all rules, linguistic or otherwise. Instead, this metatheory sees communicative norms as contextually embedded and subjectively mediated, and therefore as emergent rather than predetermined.

We argue, however, that the crux of the argument is "the danger of conflating the convenient fiction of 'standard' English with English in its entirety and thereby ignoring multilingual reality" (Ishikawa & Jenkins, 2019: 6). Standard English in ELT can be regarded as one single CAS out of many. As a caveat, its intactness and stability is still highly questionable since CASs are open systems, being always contestable and changeable. The prevalence of Standard English for global communication among English users becomes clear when it is viewed as a CAS. As Hall (2018) contends, on the one hand, Anglophone speakers only become familiar with national 'standard' language through schooling, which is more or less similar to Standard English in ELT. On the other hand, most English learners are exposed to this English as their additional language. In either case, Standard English never stands alone in anyone's mind but probably constitutes our 'shared' meaning-making resources.

Along this vein complexity theory is not a rejection of Standard English in ELT. After all, global communication through English is contact between multilingual and multilanguaging speakers (for multilanguaging, see Chapter 8.3), and "these contact situations are likely to involve Standard English among many non-clear-cut, dynamically adaptive, and thus endlessly changing systems"

(Ishikawa & McBride, 2019: 338). Conversely, there is no reason why Standard English learned in education cannot find its place in global communication.

Back in 2018, when the second author of this book was invited to Aichi University, Japan, to talk about the complexity of communication through Global Englishes and its pedagogic applications (including the petanque activity mentioned above), one of the participants asked him whether he had ever considered replacing Standard English in ELT with 'Japanese English'. Given the artificial nature of a system-oriented view of language, it might be possible to assume 'Japanese English' to be among these CASs, even if this 'variety' is hardly ever used among Japanese people themselves (Chapter 4.2). In fact, a good number of World Englishes (WE) scholars may envisage the future crafting of 'Japanese English' as a pedagogic model (e.g., Hino, 2018; for an overview of WE and related research in the Japanese context, see D'Angelo, 2018; see also Chapter 4.1). Certainly, it might serve as an alternative convenient fiction for ELT in Japan. However, in the light of complexity theory, it would always be one of many potential CASs to be drawn on for global communication. Moreover, the 'convenience' of this alternative fiction would be questionable, given the idiolectal nature of the Japanese English similect (Chapter 4.3), along with a degree of intra-individual flexibility across different situations at the global scale.

Communicative competence in applied linguistics

One of the most influential notions in the history of applied linguistics, including sociolinguistics, is communicative competence (Hymes, 1972), which subsumes grammatical, sociolinguistic, strategic (Canale & Swain, 1980), and discourse (Canale, 1983/2013) competences. A detailed review and historical development of this notion is given in Chapter 14. It will suffice to mention here that communicative competence deems social, linguistic, and cultural elements of English communication to be stable and predictable, unlike an ever-changing process and non-linearity in complexity theory. As with Standard English in ELT, this traditional notion predicates itself on idealised local Anglophone speech communities and concentrates on monolingual language use with non-verbal modes viewed as compensation strategies. In brief, communicative competence is not only essentialist but also imbued with "the 'lingua bias' of communication" (Li, 2018: 15; Chapter 9) and monolingual ideology (Chapter 7.2).

While the metatheory of complexity theory aligns with a dynamic view of language or the thinking of language as mobile multilingual resources and dynamic multilingual repertoires, it does not ignore the ideological take on language (Chapter 8.2). More precisely, the empirical theory of EMF suggests that language takes form and changes through the interplay of ideological fixity and interactional fluidity. What complexity theory with EMF stresses is, then, the limited usefulness of communicative competence or any static competence based on monolingualism and an exclusive focus on language. In line with translanguaging, EMF and complexity theory would not propose that present-day education maintain either an intensive or an extensive focus on traditional communicative competence. In this regard, what Vivian Cook (1991; 2002) calls **multi-competence** or the knowledge of multilingual (and multicultural) resources is far more appropriate, and we would advocate supplementing this cognitive competence with the affective and communicative needs of individuals. As metaphorised by complexity theory, global encounters are full of unexpectedness and unpredictability. This contingency requires individuals to employ meaning-making resources in a flexible and adaptive manner and keep the motivational attitudes to do so (Baker, 2015; Ishikawa, 2020a). We will use the term awareness in a broad sense for pedagogy to embrace the attitudinal, cognitive, and practical aspects of communication. EMF awareness in the subsequent chapter features language and meaning-making modes more than culture. In accord with the thesis of this book, the awareness of culture in global interaction will be elaborated in great detail in the final two chapters.

Summary

In the first section of this chapter we have explained the following terms:

- metatheory (of complexity theory)
- complex adaptive systems (CASs)
- non-linearity

We have characterised complexity theory as a metatheory, or a theory about empirical theories or notions, and as consisting of CASs which are emergent, ever-changing, and non-categorical. We have viewed language, culture, and mode as interacting CASs to explore global interactions, each of which, in turn, is a different blend of language, culture, and mode within a social environment. As a CAS, language, for example, cannot be considered to be an independent 'system' but as among interactive, nested 'systems'. What complexity theory vividly captures in global communication is, then, non-linearity. That is, each instance is unique and not fully predictable from the analysis of any previous cases.

Also, in the second section we have added the following concepts:

- Standard English in ELT and communicative competence
- multi-competence

In agreement with Seidlhofer and Jenkins, we disagree with the narrow view of "English is English is English" (2003: 141) in Chapter 7.2 or the view that English refers only to standardised English supposedly belonging to monolingual Anglophones. Nonetheless, we can also say that Standard English in ELT is one widespread type of English or a variety within English, and that English exists within multilingualism. In other words, it can be part of what Vivian Cook calls multi-competence. As such, this particular English is still useful as potentially shared meaning-making resources. In complexity theory terms it can be one single CAS out of many. Thus, the crux of the argument is that complexity theory highlights the limited role of any 'standard' model or competence.

Activity 12.2 Do you like your own English?

A foundational publication on language attitudes in the field of ELF is Jenkins' (2007) global study targeting English language teachers and English accents. Since then there has been a plethora of research on this topic. As a founding editor (2012–2019) of the *Journal of English as a Lingua Franca*, Barbara Seidlhofer recalls that "[a] theme that commonly recurs in discussions of the educational and pedagogic implications of ELF is that of attitude" (2019: 17). In this journal, Galloway and Rose's (2013) paper, entitled "They envision going to New York, not Jakarta", tells of established attitudes towards English in ELT on the part of English instructors – English not in Jakarta but idealised monolingual competence associated with Anglophone settings (New York) to be emulated.

Without substantial exposure to multilingual scenarios, students are likely to judge their English by traditional communicative competence and Standard English taught in the classroom. Below are some of the respondents' comments in Ishikawa's (2016c) open-ended questionnaire study, translated from Japanese to English. This study investigated Japanese university students' attitudes towards their English.

Questions and respondents' comments

Q1 What is positive or negative about your own and your peers' English?

- "As for their weakness, having been made to cram grammar into their heads too much, Japanese people worry about grammatical mistakes and become obsessed with perfect sentence structure when speaking English." (respondent 1)
- "The weaknesses include the tendency not to be able to avoid Japanese-influenced English words and sentence structures." (respondent 2)

Q2 What word(s) would you use to describe the English in question?
- "For the purpose of studying, but not using." (respondent 3)
- "Proof of effort!" (respondent 4)

Q3 What do you think about US people's English?
- "absolute authority" (respondent 5)
- "real English" (respondent 6)
- "the English generally accepted in the world" (respondent 7)

(Ishikawa, 2016c: 90–91)

Are there any comments which match your perceptions about your own English (Q1, Q2) or about US people's English (Q3)? What would you answer for Q1 to Q3 above? Discuss your perceptions and answers in small groups if possible.

Feedback: *Answers will vary depending on individual experiences and opinions. Even so, you may have thought that "perfect sentence structure" (respondent 1) depends on communicative settings or contexts (Chapter 7.2) and modes (Chapters 9 and 11), and that the malleability and permeability of named languages, including "Japanese-influenced English" (respondent 2), is what features global communication among English users (Chapter 8). It is ironical if respondents 3 and 4 studied English as an academic subject and for the purpose of achieving high scores in language tests mainly to prove how much effort they had made rather than to use English for intercultural and transcultural communication. At the same time, their comments imply that tenacious adherence to linguistic knowledge may not facilitate actual communication. Meanwhile, we argue that respondents 5 to 7 conflated idealised English and monolingual competence with US people's English in general. Other studies also show that Japanese university students highly evaluate the English spoken by educated people from the US (McKenzie, 2010; Evans & Imai, 2011; McKenzie & Gilmore, 2017). However, whether you go to New York or Jakarta or anywhere, you will see and hear how diverse real-world English is.*

12.3 Language attitudes and awareness

Before introducing the pedagogic intervention of EMF awareness in the next chapter, we would like to discuss language attitudes and awareness, or, more precisely, **language awareness** in a narrow sense. EMF awareness is linked to previous language attitude studies (Ishikawa, 2016c; 2017b; 2017c), which involved Japanese university students' attitudes towards Standard English in ELT as well as their awareness of English used as a global language.

Language attitudes

Like culture, we use 'attitudes' as both academic and general words. The authors of this book may casually say, for example, "what are your attitudes towards this textbook?". While we hope that your experience of reading it is a positive one, you may wonder exactly what is meant by the term attitudes. This is true of language attitude research. Indeed, what psychologist Gordon Allport observed 85 years ago (at the time of writing) could still be the case.

> As might be expected of so abstract and serviceable a term, [attitude] has come to signify many things to many writers, with the inevitable result that its meaning is somewhat indefinite and its scientific status called into question.
>
> (1935: 798)

However, even though the concept of attitudes (or language attitudes more specifically) is problematic, we still need a working definition for the purpose of rigorous research.

Unfortunately, despite the long research tradition (see, e.g., Giles & Billings, 2004) and the intensive research interest of many ELF researchers (see, e.g., Baird & Baird, 2018), language attitudes lack a widely agreed definition to this date. In the first place, it is not clear whether it is necessary or beneficial for researchers with different research focuses to have one single definition of language attitudes. At a broader level, language attitude research in the ELF field has favoured a study of contextualised, non-experimental, and discursive accounts and has analysed how they are expressed (Ishikawa & Morán Panero, 2016; Ishikawa, 2021). At a more specific level, it would be the remit of researchers to characterise language attitudes for their own studies.

We live with attitudes, whether consciously or subconsciously. Every day we bring our various evaluative concepts (e.g., beautiful, well-educated) to what we encounter, including language. Put differently, everyone has developed "a reservoir of beliefs and concepts" (Preston, 2010: 9) about language through life experiences. Accordingly, so long as language attitude research would like to include non-specialist views, the researcher may want to regard everyone as a folk, whether linguists or non-linguists, in line with a sociolinguistic approach called **folk linguistics** (Niedzielski & Preston, 1999/2003; Preston, 2018b). In this approach the research aims to explore people's evaluative repertoires formed and expressed through everyday life. This was exactly the aim of the second author's research (Ishikawa, 2016c; 2017b; 2017c), and his research was also informed by three key denominators of (language) attitudes thus far proposed mainly in social psychology: (1) evaluative – in other words, favourable or disfavourable (e.g., Petty et al., 1997); (2) dispositions formed through experience (e.g., Campbell, 1963); and (3) directed to a language-related psychological target (e.g., Garrett, 2010). As such language attitudes cannot be directly identified or observed (e.g., Eagly & Chaiken, 2007). Instead, they have been conceptualised as triggering, rather than constituting, people's affection, cognition, and behaviour (e.g., Rosenberg & Hovland, 1960; Ryan et al., 1982; Bassili & Brown, 2005/2014) and as inferable from discursive accounts from context to context (e.g., Perloff, 2021). All in all, language attitudes may be defined "as being identified with a reservoir of evaluative dispositional concepts, directed to a linguistic phenomenon as interpreted through social experience, and underlying observable responses which are constructed situationally" (Ishikawa, 2017b: 243).

There has been a debate over whether language attitudes emerge anew in each occasion "as temporarily constructed judgments" (Wilson & Hodges, 1992: 38) or remain stable to a varying degree per "the standard view of attitudes" (Banaji & Heiphetz, 2010: 357). Empirically, both are possible (Ishikawa & Morán Panero, 2016), and the researcher should therefore refrain from taking it for granted that participants always have stable evaluative repertoires of a given psychological target (e.g., Potter & Wetherell, 1987; Hyrkstedt & Kalaja, 1998; Morán Panero, 2019; Ishikawa, 2021). There is another important aspect of language attitudes. Whatever the stability of language attitudes may be, the processes of developing and expressing them "are inseparable from both ideological beliefs and indexical meanings surrounding a society" (Ishikawa & Morán Panero, 2016: 96). After all, the same psychological target may be interpreted differently through its different representations (e.g., Potter, 1996; Coupland, 2007). In turn, an individual's dispositions may exist only in relation to the socially available representations of any given object or phenomenon. This leads to a nuanced understanding of the longstanding issue of 'non-attitudes' (e.g., Converse, 1970; Krosnick et al., 2002). That is, it may be impossible to detect any stable attitudes not only towards an unfamiliar linguistic phenomenon but also towards unfamiliar ways of representing a familiar linguistic phenomenon. In this regard, English and its global spread are likely to be familiar to all English users, but its representation as a global multilingua franca in a multilingual world is not likely to be so. In fact, some of you might have had nothing to say about English through the lens of EMF (Chapter 8) before reading this textbook. A broadened scope of global communication as envisaged in complexity theory provides the potential to form or develop new attitudes towards the unfamiliar representations of the familiar language. To illustrate this point, we will discuss the second author's research below.

The awareness of English as a global (multi)lingua franca

The second author explored the language attitudes of L1 Japanese undergraduates from diverse disciplines by way of an open-ended questionnaire (*n* = *95*) (Ishikawa, 2016c; see Activity 12.2) and conversational interviews (*n* = *18*, 20 h. 11 min. in total) (Ishikawa, 2017b).[1] All the participants had received Japanese education, and all the interviewees had an interest and investment in global communication through English. The findings from this research are manifold, with the conversational interview study largely corroborating the open-ended questionnaire study. Two major findings across both methods are as follows.

- Participants had prevalently negative attitudes towards their English in comparison with Standard English in ELT and 'standard' pronunciation (see Activity 7.1).
- The *doxic* experience (Bourdieu, 1977) or taken-for-granted 'reality' of everyday life probably hindered grounding these attitudes on their own critical thinking as well as valuing their English communication ability for intercultural and transcultural communication (see Activity 7.3).

In Bourdieu's words, the term *doxic* refers to what is naturalised in a social sphere to the extent that it appears, and is perceived to be, "self-evident and undisputed" (1977: 164).

More specifically, some participants in Ishikawa (2016c; 2017b) had ambivalent attitudes, similar to prior studies, such as Matsuda (2003) and Sasayama (2013). However, their positivity towards their own English was clearly limited as against Standard English in ELT, and ambivalence was not evident among the many participants, for whom other issues were more significant. After all, as the data collection methods were totally open-ended, participants were free to decide what to address. In addition, Ishikawa's (2016c; 2017b) participants considered English in education to be in harmony with how English was positioned outside the classroom. More straightforwardly, Standard English in ELT appeared to be seen, in the whole society, as the only English to be acquired, tested, and necessary to become communicatively competent, however this competence may be defined. It would have been different, however, if English was used daily as an intranational lingua franca in Japan, like Ranta's (2010) Finnish and Tokumoto and Shibata's (2011) Malaysian contexts.

Nevertheless, the conversational interview study (Ishikawa, 2017b) served as virtually the very first opportunity for all the interviewees to reflect on their global communication experiences and review their

English as a global multilingua franca. Even though the researcher did not try to explain what the field of ELF or the notion of EMF was like, he frequently posed questions, such as "Whose English was more understandable to you?" and "How would you define communicative success in those situations?" and occasionally gave a summary of a perceived contradiction in what he had heard. Most of the interviewees approved of Global Englishes perspectives quite readily, especially those of ELF (Chapters 4 and 8). There were two commonalities across what they had to say.

- Commonality 1. Interviewees were unfamiliar with new global perspectives in the ELF field, which they tended to wonder why they had not recognised before.
- Commonality 2. Most interviewees perceived the global perspectives as important and valuable in their different ways while tending to show positive feelings overtly.

The two interview extracts below are our translations from Japanese (for the original Japanese version, see Ishikawa, 2021: 267–269). As an example of the first commonality, interviewee 1 criticised her previous view of English as in Extract 12.1. While the researcher initiated the topic of an obsession with 'correctness' at the expense of communication, this topic was first suggested by the interviewee well before the start of the extract, in relation to exchange students from overseas.

Extract 12.1 "That's all prejudice"
R: researcher, I1: interviewee 1

01 R: you say "deviant" or "mistaken" a lot [today
02 I1: [hmm
...
05 R: presumably deviant from the so-called standard usage of grammar and vocabulary from the United States or the United Kingdom. [deviant pronunciation
06 I1: [<quiet>hmmmmmm. ahhhh</quiet>
07 R: well it is deviant and thus [not good
08 I1: [<quiet>deviant. not good</quiet>
09 R: and
10 I1: <quiet>and</quiet>=
11 R: =shameful in the international [arena
12 I1: [hmm. hmm=
13 R: =er
14 I1: I've been thinking so haven't I

15 R: but. actually we can't communicate if obsessed with [that
16 I1: [hmmmm。 pro[bably having such an obsession itself is
17 R: [is that
18 I1: shameful isn't it. @@@@
19 R: I see
20 I1: phew
21 R: having such an obsession may in [fact be shameful
22 I1: [indeed somehow it's shameful
23 R: is that [now
24 I1: [that is all prejudice
25 R: wh. when did you get to think so
26 I1: well quite recently
27 R: @[@@
28 I1: [yeah. just now. @@[@
29 R: [now
30 I1: <louder and high-pitched>I didn't realise that</louder and high-pitched>
31 R: I [see
32 I1: [probably。 before having this interview opportunity

(Ishikawa, 2017b: 252–253)

Notes

[	overlapping or interrupted speech
=	latched utterance
xxx.	the end of a perceivable block of utterance
xxx。	significant pause
@	laughter and a laughter-like sound, approximating the syllable number (e.g., ha ha ha = @@@)
<quiet>xxx</quiet> etc.	spoken with specified features

After registering the researcher's remark ("hmmmm" in line 16), interviewee 1 started seeing the obsession with 'correctness' as "shameful" (line 18). Remarkably, after the checking and resolving sequence (lines 21, 22), she left the researcher's probing (line 23) unresolved, and appended the fairly strong words "all prejudice" (line 24), thereby criticising her normative way of thinking about English. She then acknowledged that she had probably never looked at English from wider global perspectives (lines 26, 28, 30, 32), and her louder, high-pitched voice (line 30) might have implied how novel they were. Just for your reference, the above terms *registering*, *checking*, *resolving*, *probing*, *unresolved*, and *append(ing)* come from Eggins and Slade's (1997/2004) speech functions analysis framework, but we believe that all these words are straightforward in meaning. (The same applies to *supporting replies*, *initiat(ing)*, and *expanding* in Extract 12.2 and Activity 12.3.)

As for the second commonality (above), interviewee 2, for example, discussed multilingual and transcultural accommodation (Chapters 8.3, 9.4; see also Chapter 13) in relation to human development.

Extract 12.2 "Our development as human beings"
R: researcher, I2: interviewee 2

01 I2: uh. making what you say easier for your interactants to understand is perhaps not limited to English
02 R: mmm
03 I2: isn't it. it connotes consideration for your interactants. It's like. when people with different positions in society. or rather. people with different upbringings
04 R: mmm=
05 I2: =people with different backgrounds. people with different first languages talk with each other. whether we can give our sympathy to those differences. in communication really。 has something to do with our development as human beings [I think
06 R: [ah. I really agree. I almost feel like that's why we have English edu[cation
07 I2: [hmm
08 R: but now it seems like our education is taking a different course of action=
09 I2: =oh dear. interesting. ah. oh dear really interesting

(Ishikawa, 2017b: 254)

Notes

[	overlapping or interrupted speech
=	latched utterance
xxx.	the end of a perceivable block of utterance
xxx。	significant pause

Interviewee 2 stressed the importance of having "sympathy" (line 05) for those with different social, linguistic, and cultural backgrounds in terms of human development. For him, communicative effectiveness in this globalised world was "not limited to English" (line 01) or not a purely linguistic issue but a matter of social, linguistic, and cultural sensitivity. He made a set of supporting replies in an excited tone to the researcher's discussion of Japanese English education (lines 08, 09). This appeared to reflect his keen interest in the interrelationship of multilingual and transcultural accommodation and human development.

To sum up, on the one hand, Standard English in ELT provides convenience and practicality in language teaching. On the other hand, students may not be able to have positive attitudes towards their English so long as English is identified only with this convenient fiction. Complexity theory and relevant notions in Table 12.1 help them develop attitudes towards new, much broader representations of communication through 'English'. Given that they are unlikely to have had any previous attitudes towards these unfamiliar representations, their language awareness is not to change old attitudes but to form or develop new attitudes. Reported positive attitudes in this section are promising and more likely to encourage students to engage actively in global encounters. However, we argue that the new understanding of English communication and associated positive attitudes are not enough by themselves. Fundamentally, communication is social practice, and the cognitive and attitudinal development should be conjoined with actual practice (see Chapters 13 and 15).

Activity 12.3 "like mathematical theorems or something like that"

In Ishikawa (2017b), discussed above, only two interviewees did not approve of Global Englishes perspectives. Interviewee 3 was one of them, and the following extract was taken from the same author's unpublished thesis (Ishikawa, 2016a). Immediately before this extract, the researcher showed his concern that Japanese school English education might not place a premium on communication process and diverse communication scenarios. Interviewee 3 registered his concern and took it in another direction.

R: researcher, I3: interviewee 3

01 I3: it's like. there is a fixed. notion of English. for [example
02 R: [hmm
03 I3: like. mathematical theorems or something [like that
04 R: [hmm
05 I3: already. like there's been something fixed and it's like school classes just show it to us right?
06 R: hmm
07 I3: so mathematics is. uh. it's said there's only one correct [answer
08 R: [hmm
09 I3: ah. well. I'm not very familiar with mathematics [though
10 R: [hmm

11 I3: like secondary school mathematics. or something similar to it. we are told something like this is correct English. therefore you should be able to learn it

(Ishikawa, 2016a: 147)

Do you agree with this view of the English language? Why? Discuss your answers in small groups if possible.

Feedback: *Interviewee 3 compared school English with school mathematics in the above extract. To summarise this extract, she initiated the topic of the fixed norms of English, presumably Standard English in ELT, in Japanese school English classes, and continued expanding it while likening these norms to "secondary school mathematics" (line 11). She most probably cited mathematics mainly because it had single correct answers (line 07). It is likely, then, that she presumed or was made to believe the existence of monolithic English norms to be acquired, irrespective of contexts and modes. As we have seen, this is exactly what complexity theory problematises and what hinders many students from having positive attitudes towards their English.*

Chapter summary

In this chapter we discussed:

- complexity theory and global communication
- Standard English in ELT
- communicative competence
- language attitudes
- language awareness

We problematised both hypostasised Standard English and essentialised communicative competence in view of complexity theory. More precisely, we argued that these traditional approaches are still relevant to global communication among English users, but that complexity theory leads us to regard them as just one CAS among many, not as the reflections of real-world ambiguity.

The hypostasised and essentialised view of global communication has implications for our language attitudes which may simply be defined as (1) evaluative, (2) dispositions, (3) towards a language-related psychological target. Language attitudes are inevitably affected by socially available representations of a target phenomenon. If the whole society provides the aforementioned traditional approaches alone for English communication, then students are likely to have difficulty having positive attitudes towards their English for intercultural and transcultural communication. However, complexity theory and relevant notions (i.e., EMF, translanguaging, and transcultural and transmodal communication) provide critical, holistic representations of 'English' communication. Moreover, the empirical research cited in this chapter evidences the positive attitudinal effect of students' practice or experience of global communication if accompanied by critical reflection on it. We propose that language education focus on communication process as envisaged by complexity theory and broaden the scope of language and cultural awareness to integrate attitudinal motivation, cognitive or notional understanding, and practical experience outside the classroom. We will detail pedagogic applications in Chapters 13 and 15.

Note

1 As seven initial interviewees were recruited from the questionnaire respondents, there were 106 participants in total.

Further reading

Baird, R., Baker, W., & Kitazawa, M. (2014). The complexity of ELF. *Journal of English as a Lingua Franca*, 3, 171–196. doi: 10.1515/jelf-2014-0007. An earlier discussion of the links between complexity theory and ELF research which casts doubt on differences and dichotomies which are sometimes accentuated in the field.

Ishikawa, T. (2017b). Japanese university students' attitudes towards their English and the possibility of ELF awareness. *Journal of English as a Lingua Franca*, 6, 237–263. doi: 10.1515/jelf-2017-0012. The article illustrates the close link between social representations and language attitudes to consider language awareness in the field of ELF.

Ishikawa, T. & Morán Panero, S. (2016). Exploring language attitudes in ELF research: Contrasting approaches in conversation. *Englishes in Practice*, 3, 74–109. doi: 101515/eip-2016-0004. The article examines the ontology of language attitudes from two different perspectives of their stability and researchability. It is written for students and researchers who would like to conduct language attitude research.

Part IV

Teaching and learning culture, language, and Global Englishes

13 Awareness of English-within-multilingualism

Introduction

"[W]e cannot predict what the learners will know or want to do next, what their goals, dreams and ambitions will be, or where their learning may take them" (van Lier, 2007: 52). Echoing Stenhouse (1975), van Lier (2007) calls for decentring predictability and testability in education and centring human agency and action instead. As with the notion of languaging (Chapter 9.2), students each learn language and make meaningful connections with the world in their different ways. Perhaps it is not teachable how every individual ought to "link the personal self to the new worldly demands presented by the new language" (van Lier, 2007: 62) for the sake of him/herself. But we believe teachers can assist in this endeavour by what we call English as a multilingua franca (EMF) awareness in this chapter and the pedagogic applications of **intercultural awareness (ICA)** and transcultural English language teaching (ELT) in the final two chapters.

The current chapter starts with theoretical underpinnings of **EMF awareness** by drawing together the previous discussions. More specifically, the first two sections summarise some of what has been offered so far in this book as a foundation for the discussion of EMF awareness. We review, first, a monolingual construct of Standard English in ELT (Chapter 7) vis-à-vis multilingual, translanguaging, transcultural, and transmodal reality (Chapters 8 and 9) and, second, social representations of English and language attitudes (Chapter 12). Next, we introduce the pedagogic intervention of EMF awareness and illustrate its efficacy with empirical data from university students in English-medium instruction (EMI). We also consider the applications of EMF awareness in ELT by citing the English as a Lingua Franca programme at a Japanese university as an example. You will have opportunities to consider both internationally marketed standardised English language tests and the possibility of EMF awareness in the light of your own experiences.

Activity 13.1 Standardised English language tests

You are probably familiar with one or more large-scale commercialised tests, such as TOEFL (Test of English as a Foreign Language), TOEIC (Test of English for International Communication), and IELTS (International English Language Testing System). TOEIC seems to be highly popular in Japan and South Korea, although the exact number of test-takers worldwide is not officially available (ETS, 2020a; 2020b). Likewise, many higher-education institutions around the world use TOEFL and IELTS to determine which students they will accept. In this regard, these tests are high-stakes globally. Read the claims below from Jenkins and Leung (2019) that we need an alternative to the monolithic, "all-purpose, large-scale 'fit-for-all' model of assessment" (Leung et al., 2016: 69) to take due notice of situated language and literacy.

> The principal line of argument is that we need to promote multiple assessment constructs (and designs) to reflect the diverse language and literacy practices that exist in university. This diversity has been clearly and unambiguously demonstrated by long-term research data in academic language and literacy studies and actual accounts of student experiences (e.g., McNamara et al., 2018). In addition, ... validation studies investigating the predictive power of the large-scale standardized academic English tests for test-takers' subsequent performance in university have yielded only low to moderate correlations. The case for further development is clear.
>
> (Jenkins & Leung, 2019: 14)

Do you agree with their call for further research and a new assessment method?

Feedback: *Your answers and opinions will depend on your own experiences. From students' perspectives it would be fair to say that the high-stakes tests in question are expensive. It costs more to take a single TOEFL or IELTS test than to buy a number of copies of this textbook. It may take time and perhaps also money to prepare for the test as well. Even so, from both students' and teachers' perspectives, high scores on these generalised tests do not necessarily predict high linguistic performance in academia, as indicated by Jenkins and Leung (2019). In other words, by relying on the fit-for-all model of globally marketed standardised English language tests universities may fail to select students who will be capable of academic tasks at their institutions. From administrators' perspectives it is handy to have a single benchmark across departments and faculties and assume that students with certain scores will not have any linguistic problems after enrolment. On a side note, while both authors graduated from the same university in the UK, only the second author had to take* *one of these tests before starting the doctoral programme. He had obtained an MA from an English-medium university (i.e., Columbia University in the City of New York), but his nationality was 'problematic', i.e., non-Anglophone. As with Harding and McNamara (2018), he wondered why Anglophones were exempted from the tests, all the more so because "[a]cademic language is ... no one's mother tongue" (Bourdieu & Passeron, 1994: 8).*

13.1 From a monolingual construct to multilingual, translanguaging, transcultural, and transmodal reality

Research in Global Englishes, and ELF in particular, has observed what a communicative phenomenon is like among English users at the global scale (Chapter 4). They are often multilinguals, and our world is by default multilingual both domestically and globally (Chapter 3.1). Alongside this, globalisation has been both shrinking geographical distances and networking across spatial borders (Chapters 1.3, 8.1), especially through digital communication (Chapter 11). With this increasing mobility, we are experiencing complex web-like multilingual flows (Chapters 1.3, 2.3, 8.1, 8.2, 10.2). In reality, therefore, English exists within multilingualism. It is no wonder if English "is available ... but is not necessarily chosen" (Jenkins, 2015b: 73). Also, it is no wonder that we can always detect multilingual influences from pronunciation to the organisation of talk even when interaction "remains in English ... on the surface" (Cogo, 2018: 358). After all, as captured by translanguaging enquiry (Chapter 9), we communicate through our whole linguistic resources as one unified repertoire. As theorised in EMF (Chapter 8), we adjust, adapt, and thereby develop our linguistic repertoires over the course of continuous global encounters. Anglophone interactants with monolingual repertoires are no exception. They need to translanguage, or more narrowly multilanguage, i.e., learn and exploit *previously unfamiliar* multilingual resources as communicatively effective. Multilingualism in the notion of EMF includes this multilanguaging, and EMF coincides with translanguaging.

Monolingual construct

The reality of English language use at a global scale as described above is very messy and hard to teach in the language classroom. In contrast, the Standard English that we see in ELT materials offers practicality in teaching and learning. It reifies our diverse, situational linguistic practices as if they were composed only of English and predictable

(Chapter 7), thereby making the subject of the English language testable. Nonetheless, in the first place, no Standard English stands alone in anyone's mind (Chapter 12.2), and Standard English in ELT does not even represent any existent speech communities (Chapter 7.3). It is based on an idealised monolingual speech community, usually imagined within the US or the UK. As may be familiar, this hypostasised version of English is commodified and marketed internationally, together with standardised English language tests, such as TOEFL, TOEIC, and IELTS (Activity 13.1). Back in 2013 when the second author of this book was writing a chapter on English in Japan for his doctoral thesis, he criticised TOEIC as virtually the Test of English for International *Commercialisation* to make money mainly in Japan and South Korea but also in other places under the name of 'International Communication'. As you could expect, he was advised not to include this dark humour in the thesis.

Certainly, the monolingual construct of Standard English facilitates ELT. Also, it is widely taught and thus serves as potentially shared meaning-making resources. What we really problematise is the danger of conflating this convenient fiction (Widdowson, 2015; Ishikawa & Jenkins, 2019) with English in its entirety (Chapter 12.2). It is convenient as an abstracted fiction so long as we take notice of multilingual reality. As envisaged by complexity theory or the metatheory of complex adaptive systems (Chapter 12.1, 12.2), Standard English in ELT (or of any type) should be recast as always contestable and changeable. At the same time, it should be viewed as just one 'system' among interactive, nested 'systems' to be drawn on in global encounters. As such, English, or language more broadly, culture, mode, and social context at a global scale all do matter in our actual communicative processes. In line with Table 12.1, below we will revisit multilingual reality which EMF captures and coincides with translanguaging, followed by transcultural and transmodal reality.

Multilingual reality

EMF as a currently prominent notion in the ELF field illustrates what English-knowing agents actually do around the globe (Chapter 8). As with translanguaging (Chapter 9), EMF highlights how malleable and permeable English and other named languages are. In other words, it gives "more importance to emergent multilingual influences or practices and dynamic repertoires than the English language itself and L1 status" (Ishikawa, 2020a: 409–410). As a corollary, it includes communication among English-knowing multilingual speakers of the same L1. Remember that "multilingual" here includes multilanguaging, and EMF also includes, again, 'multilingual' Anglophones even if their repertoires are monolingual. You may feel that ELF research often does not include Anglophones. This is simply because Global Englishes are used widely in various domains irrespective of interactants' L1 and whether there are L1 English speakers or not (see, e.g., Ishikawa, 2015).

EMF also highlights the tension between real-world fluid, flexible linguistic resources and ideologically named enumerable languages, such as English and Japanese (Chapter 9.1). No matter how dynamically multilingual our actual linguistic practices are, languages are neatly separated into named categories usually at the national level in an ideological sense. This constructed ideology of languages as fixed, bounded 'objects' is prominent whenever we learn and use language. Amid both the ideological fixity of languages and the inherent fluidity of linguistic resources, our global interaction depends on each social setting and each constellation of the individuals involved, all of whom have their own backgrounds, linguistic and otherwise. After all, globalisation does not diminish the relevance of multiple named languages but rather accentuates their ideological existence. This is why EMF by name retains 'multi' (i.e., English as a *multi*lingua franca) while appreciating the dynamic meaning-making process foregrounded by the term translanguaging.

ELF research over the past two decades has evidenced that "what is distinctive about ELF lies in the communicative strategies that its speakers use" (Seidlhofer, 2009: 211; Seidlhofer & Widdowson, 2009: 37–38). In particular, the pragmatic strategy of mutual linguistic accommodation (i.e., adjusting and adapting the way we use language according to the situation) is identified as crucial for securing understanding, irrespective of an individual's ability in other languages (Chapters 4.3, 8.2, 8.3). It is natural that linguistic resources among multilingual English users are multilingual, and it is thus inevitable that linguistic accommodation is multilingual accommodation. The other pragmatic strategies documented are more commonly found in any communication. While we will review these pragmatic strategies in detail in the next chapter, it will suffice here to mention that Pietikäinen (2018), for instance, cites the following examples of strategies: clarification questions (e.g., where?); incomprehension tokens (e.g., huh?); self-repeating and repeating (e.g., the meeting starts at 5 pm today – 5 pm?); self-paraphrasing and paraphrasing or reformulation (e.g., so you mean ...?); discourse organisation or reflection (e.g., in other words ...); and confirmation checks (e.g., really?).

Transcultural and transmodal reality

You may have experienced that effective communication is not just about language. EMF is fundamentally concerned with intercultural communication. In the research field of intercultural communication, an updated notion of transcultural communication problematises the fixed scope of named cultures, coupled with the essential in-betweenness of different cultures (Chapter 10). As you may have experienced, no simple assumption of cultural 'us' and 'others' would facilitate communication (Chapter 6.3). In reality, cultural understandings and orientations are various within and across different scales (e.g., local, national, global) and variable over the course of each interaction (Chapters 2.5, 10.4, 11.3, 11.5). In the first place, it depends on each interaction how far culture affects or influences meaning-making as well as what role other social differences (e.g., age, gender, geographical origin, professional occupation) play in cultural interpretations (Chapters 5.5, 6.5). Multilingual accommodation should thus accompany transcultural accommodation, which may be equated with the first author's term intercultural awareness or ICA, defined as:

> a conscious understanding of the role culturally based forms, practices and frames of reference can have in intercultural communication, and an ability to put these conceptions into practice in a flexible and context specific manner in communication.
>
> (Baker, 2015: 163)

The notion of ICA will be featured in Chapter 14.

At the same time, you may easily recognise that meaning-making resources are not limited to language. Global contact among English users is no exception. Put differently, language coexists with other modes, or cues, signs, and symbols. Examples include image, facial expression, gesture and posture, place and positioning, fragrance, light, and sound. Our real-world, real-time interactions and interpretations blur the boundaries of these modes by using them simultaneously and collaboratively, i.e., transmodal (Chapter 9.4, Chapter 11). In other words, meaning is synergetically created through and across multiple modes and is not reducible to individual modes as if they were independent (Chapter 12.1, 12.2). Multilingual accommodation should thus accompany transmodal accommodation or the conscious understanding and situated appropriation of available meaning-making modes during communication.

As EMF accords with transcultural and transmodal communication, mutual accommodation in EMF scenarios should be defined broadly as adjusting and adapting the way we use meaning-making resources and modes according to the situation (i.e., multilingual, transcultural, and transmodal accommodation; Ishikawa, 2021 in press). Again, it entails our conscious understanding of linguistic and cultural roles and effects on interaction as well as meaning-making affordances beyond language. It also entails our flexible, situationally appropriate interactional practices based on this understanding. The assumption here is that we keep the motivational attitudes in these practices, or, put differently, positive feelings and curiosity towards accommodation.

13.2 Social representations of English and their implications for language attitudes

Again, multilingual, translanguaging, transcultural, and transmodal reality is different from how English is portrayed in ELT and its materials (see, e.g., Leung & Lewkowicz, 2018; Galloway, 2018). This issue is exacerbated if "there was no opportunity to see a normative approach to English challenged in [students'] daily life" (Ishikawa, 2017b: 250), as if the whole society endorses only the idealised monolingual version of the language. In other words, students would be deprived of the opportunity to become aware of any alternative approach or to develop their attitudes towards a different representation of this global language. Below we will revisit social representations of English and their implications for language attitudes.

Social representations of English

As detailed in Chapter 7, monolingual and Standard English ideologies circulate in many societies so pervasively that citizens are not very conscious of how real-world English is different from English in ELT materials. Ideologically, English should be spoken without any interference from other languages, based on the abstracted version of a national standard of the traditional English-speaking world at a particular time. Language policies are usually vague and not explicitly aware of the thesis of this book, thereby allowing the above ideologies to serve as "a de facto language policy" (Shohamy, 2003: 283). This is especially true of counties like Japan, where there exists no national guideline for language education or language use in education at university (MEXT, 2014). We indicated throughout Chapter 7 that monolingual and Standard English ideologies inhere in a number of fallacies:

- to compartmentalise individual multilingual development as if it were plural acquisitions of one language after another
- to equate a nationally institutionalised Anglophone variety at a certain period with the internationally used lingua franca of a multilingual world
- to assume Anglophones from particular geographical territories to be monolingual experts in this 'standard' variety
- to misrecognise prestige as residing in linguistic features themselves while the social, historical reasons behind are consigned into oblivion in society

None of these essentialist ideas is context-sensitive and would facilitate the actual global use of English. This set of ideological forces often circumscribes a society and constitutes symbolic violence (Bourdieu & Passeron, 1990), or "the violence which is exercised upon a social agent with his or her complicity" (Bourdieu & Wacquant, 1992: 167). In other words, individuals unwittingly 'accept' the above fallacious values despite the existence of other, more beneficial ways of conceptualising English (see Chapter 13.1).

Language attitudes

Language attitudes may simply be defined as (1) evaluative, (2) dispositional concepts, (3) directed to a linguistic phenomenon, and we form and express our evaluative repertoires through everyday life (Chapter 12.3). As dispositions or mindsets, language attitudes are assumed to be inferable from our discursive responses. The crux of the argument here is that language attitudes are mediated by socially available representations of a psychological target. Put differently, in the case of English, language attitudes are inevitably affected by how this language is represented in social experience.

Despite multilingual, translanguaging, transcultural, and transmodal reality, if such holistic representations of English as a global communication tool are not available in society, students will find difficulty having positive attitudes towards their English (Chapter 12.3). Understanding EMF and relevant notions will offer new representations of English – in other words, the unfamiliar representations of the familiar language. A precedent language attitude research (Ishikawa, 2016c; 2017b; 2017c) evidences that global communication experience and critical reflection on it are likely to enable university students to reconsider English according to those broadened representations and develop positive attitudes towards their English, as well as global communication.

13.3 EMF awareness

Unlike in multilingual communication scenarios today, instructors and students can share their mother tongue in ELT and EMI in some contexts around the world. Indeed, when the second author of this book first taught an EMI module at a university in Tokyo in 2017, he was a little surprised to find that everyone spoke Japanese as their strongest language. They could have used Japanese resources almost exclusively to understand each other. It was no wonder if some students thought of this situation as "weird" (Activity 7.3). However, again, "EMF includes communication among English-knowing multilingual speakers of the same L1s or L1 varieties" (Ishikawa, 2020a: 410), and ELT and EMI classrooms are no exception if accompanied by EMF awareness.

In the ELF field the term awareness has been used in relation to either the development of students' language attitudes (e.g., Wang, 2013; Galloway & Rose, 2018; Fang & Ren, 2018) or ELF-oriented teacher training and development (Sifakis, 2014; 2019; Sifakis & Bayyurt, 2018; Sifakis et al., 2018). Nonetheless, the term awareness in EMF awareness is used in relation to an empirically researched pedagogic intervention. Similar to the awareness in ICA in the next chapter, we use this term in a broader sense than usual to index the integrity of attitudinal motivation, cognitive or notional understanding, and communication experience in and outside the classroom. Given that communication is a social act, we believe that the cognitive and attitudinal development should be consistent with actual communicative practices. To be specific, EMF awareness does not only aim to raise students' awareness (in a narrow sense) of the roles and effects of language and culture in communication and nurture confidence as English users. It also aims to enable students to connect this conscious understanding to their own transcultural and transmodal communication by appropriating English and multilingual resources in a flexible, situationally appropriate manner. Through EMF awareness we hope that students will continue developing the capability to communicate through actual experiences and reflections on them.

In accordance with the precedent research (Ishikawa, 2016c; 2017b; 2017c), EMF-aware modules should be designed according to two principles (Ishikawa, 2020a).

- **Principle 1** (individual experience). Providing students with experiences of EMF scenarios.
- **Principle 2** (collaborative reflection). Encouraging their critical thinking about language and culture in reference to their experiences and in reference to published research.

Certainly, it is challenging to provide multilingual experiences (principle 1) when students share their L1. However, an instructor can opt for:

- working with international students on campus
- running a module in collaboration with a classroom abroad through a research network
- scheduling a module in association with students' study-abroad programmes in which they will meet other students from different parts of the world

In the third case students can prepare and reflect on their communication experiences during sojourns in their local classrooms.

To encourage critical thinking about language and culture (principle 2), an instructor can give mini-lectures on ELF research, including multilingual, translanguaging, transcultural, and transmodal reality as recapitulated above (Chapter 13.1). Meanwhile, he or she can encourage proactive discussion, debate, or presentation about language and culture based on students' individual experiences as well as communication extracts from publications, such as those found in this book, namely:

- Extracts 2.1, 2.2, 5.1, 6.1, 6.2, 8.1, 8.2, 8.3, 8.4, 8.5, 9.1, 9.2, 10.1, 10.2, and 11.1
- Figures 11.4 and 11.6
- Activities 2.3, 3.2, 3.3, 4.3, 5.1, 5.3, 6.3, 7.2, 8.2, 9.2, 10.1, and 11.3

A challenging example will be given below in Activity 13.2, which features a hip-hop song (for similar examples, see Pennycook, 2005; 2007).

The cachet of EMF awareness is its focus on the appreciation of communicative *processes* rather than linguistic or other *products*, thereby taking an emergent, holistic approach to language in contrast with a prescriptive, essentialist representation of English in society (Chapter 13.2). It is thus in line with a processual approach to culture, language, and communication, such as Kramsch's (2009; 2011) **symbolic competence**, Canagarajah's (2013) **performative competence**, and much intercultural communication research to be explained in later chapters. Accordingly, an instructor should help students continuously practise and reflect on their multilingual, transcultural, and transmodal accommodation in the face of multilingual, translanguaging, transcultural, and transmodal reality (Chapter 13.1). As may be familiar to you, whether you like it or not, Standard English and the associated four-skill approach to language acquisition (i.e., reading, listening, writing, and speaking) are normally dealt with extensively in the ELT classroom at the global scale. This is very different from culture, which is often 'relegated' as a 'fifth' skill (Kramsch, 1993; 1995). While it is effective to introduce diversity in Global Englishes to students (e.g., Hino & Oda, 2015; Galloway, 2013; Galloway & Rose, 2018), any English variety is, after all, a linguistic sample which is not necessarily relevant to all students. No ELT instructor would probably like to 'bombard' students with linguistic information of many different varieties of English around the world, as an alternative or in addition to materialised Standard English. In the first place, English as a global lingua franca is not associable with any particular varieties (Chapters 4.3, 8.3). Therefore, we propose spotlighting students' practical capability to cope with unpredictability and unexpectedness in global communication as envisaged in complexity theory (Chapter 12.1). The knowledge of globally marketed Standard English would certainly be helpful, but its adaptative use in collaboration with other meaning-making resources would actually be the key for effective communication (Chapter 12.2). After all, Standard English in ELT is a monolingual construct, and it is our communicative practices that bridge this convenient fiction with multilingual reality.

It is the remit of each instructor to decide how far and in what way to implement EMF awareness within a situated academic setting and programme. In the rest of the chapter, we will show examples from the second author's EMI modules in which EMF awareness was featured for the purpose of assisting students' future academic and professional lives (Ishikawa, 2020a) and then a university-wide English programme under development in the direction of EMF awareness (Ishikawa & McBride, 2019).

Summary

So far we have drawn together previous arguments as a foundation for EMF awareness and outlined what EMF awareness is like. The convenient fiction of Standard English in ELT is often represented in society as if it were a universal code. However, effective communication in a multilingual, mobile world depends not on adhering to a particular English variety but on adjusting and adapting the way we use meaning-making resources and modes according to the situation. As you have seen, we are not entirely rejecting current approaches or proposing a radical alternative in ELT. By EMF awareness we are seeking to bridge between essentialist knowledge for teachability and emergent practices for communicability or effective communication. For this purpose, EMF awareness has two principles with which you should now be familiar. These are:

- individual experience of multilingual, transcultural, and transmodal accommodation
- collaborative reflection on individual experiences and published research

We do hope English language education meets the cognitive, affective, and communicative needs of individuals for global encounters. We also hope it encourages students to continue actively engaging and critically reflecting on their communication experiences through EMF awareness.

Activity 13.2 'Doctor'

The following extract is taken from the lyrics of 'Doctor' by rapper/singer CHANMINA. In this song she becomes sick of the overflow of similar trends. The word "niki" (line 07) is a cyber slang word from the Japanese word 兄貴 (aniki) or bro(ther). This word is used for someone respectable and reliable. After examining this extract, discuss the questions below.

[Translation in brackets] (The singer's pronunciation in parentheses)

01	聴き飽きたんだよもう全部	(Kikiakitan dayo mō zembu)
	[I've got so tired of listening to all that]	
02	見飽きたんだよこのブーム	(Miakitan dayo kono būmu)
	[I've got so tired of seeing this boom]	
03	This is no flavor syndrome	(This is no flavor syndromu)
	[This is No-Flavor Syndrome]	
04	お前らじゃ味がしないんだよ, hey	(Omaera ja aji ga shinain dayo, hey)
	[I do feel no flavour from you guys, hey]	
05	Help me doctor 変なんです	(Help me doctor; hen nan des)
	[Help me doctor; it's strange]	
06	味がしない死にそうです	(Aji ga shinai; shini sō des)
	[I'm gonna die feeling no flavour]	
07	ニキニキニキニキ doctor	(Niki niki niki niki doctor)
	[Niki, niki, niki, niki, Doctor]	
08	プリプリ please help me	(Puli puli please help me)
	[Plea, plea, please help me]	

(CHANMINA, 2018)

Q1 How is the rhythm created by language? If possible, watch the online video clip, available from www.youtube.com/watch?v=xIX8EzRdMI8.

Q2 What do you think she means by "This is no flavor syndrome" (line 03) and "Help me doctor" (line 05) or "doctor … please help me" (lines 07, 08)?

Feedback: *This extract starts with similarly structured sentences (lines 01, 02) which end with two-syllable words "全部" (zembu) and "ブーム" (būmu). Here the "japanesified" word (Hyde, 2002: 14) būmu fits better than the one-syllable word boom to create a unified* *rhythm. In the next line, CHANMINA makes the second segment of "syndrome" (i.e., -drome) 'japanesified' as "dromu" to rhyme with the words zembu and būmu. Likewise, English and Japanese words collaboratively alliterate in lines 04 and 05: "hey", "Help", and "変" (hen). Possibly, the end rhyme "です" (des) in lines 05 and 06 connotes the similarly pronounced word death. Towards the end of this extract, both "ニキニキ" (niki niki) and "プリプリ" (puli puli) are used rhythmically (lines 07, 08), and the latter rhymes with "please". Overall, the rhythmic flow is created across linguistic boundaries. This can be said for the repetitive /ɪ/ sound, especially at the beginning of several lines: 'Japanese' "Kikiakitan" (line 01) and "Miakitan" (line 02), 'English' "This is" (line 03), 'Japanese' "Aji ga shinai" and "shini" (line 06), the cyber slang word "Niki niki niki niki" (line 07), and the onomatopoeia "Puli puli" (line 08).*

English words in Japanese pop music have functioned as poetic devices (e.g., Stanlaw, 2004). CHANMINA appears to take advantage of this tradition by her term "no flavor syndrome" (line 03) and the English sentences in line 05 onwards. In her opinion, people in contemporary societies face the danger of becoming faceless and impersonal, and their originality and uniqueness are suppressed in the name of fashion. As one possible aspect of today's technologically connected world, the overflow of similar trends could lead us to feel as if we were living in a world of Doppelgänger, the word which CHANMINA actually uses in a different part of this song. She calls for a ニキ (niki) 'doctor' or someone who is respectable, reliable, and capable of 'curing' such a situation. On a side note, プリプリ (puli puli) usually signifies something resilient and fresh, the quality which she may feel is much needed now.

13.4 EMF awareness in English-medium instruction

The second author's open-ended questionnaire study on EMF awareness (Ishikawa, 2020a) is among the first few studies to investigate EMF in relation to pedagogy and, more specifically, whether and how exposure to EMF scenarios affects students' views of their communication outside the classroom. This study targeted undergraduates who had selected his semester-long sociolinguistics module on global communication, which was given at both University A's humanities faculty in Tokyo and University B, an institution of foreign studies in the suburbs of Tokyo. The module was EMI, and everyone's strongest language was Japanese in both classes. Technically speaking, EMI refers to teaching and learning of academic content through English (Chapter 4.1). However, students educated in Japan, at least, tend to take EMI as the opportunity to learn language (Murata & Iino, 2018). For this reason, "EMI has the potential to promote more active and purposeful language use through stimulating and fascinating content" (Ishikawa, 2020c: 67).

In total, 91 students (out of 108, from Years 1 to 4) and 15 students (out of 15, from Years 3 and 4) from respective universities participated and filled in the questionnaire, and all these 106 participants were English majors. Remember that there are two principles in EMF awareness (Chapter 13.3). The following is relevant to principle 1 (individual experience).

- University A. The faculty in question consisted almost exclusively of Japanese students. However, the class was run in collaboration with an international university in Taiwan. Students on both sides studied a similar syllabus and exchanged ideas via Skype during three in-class video conferences followed by individual discussions at home.
- University B. This institution attracted exchange students from Asia, Australasia, the Americas, and Europe on its small campus. All the 15 students had regular contact, mainly in English, with exchange students on their own initiative.

Meanwhile, according to principle 2 (collaborative reflection), at both universities, the second author did the following:

- gave an occasional mini-lecture on the advancement of ELF research (see, e.g., Jenkins, 2015b)
- provided a regular classroom activity about language and culture to facilitate sharing students' individual experiences during the semester and discussing them reflexively
- used published extracts as sample EMF scenarios (see the list in Chapter 13.3) to encourage extra small-group exchanges of views, followed by class discussion

Towards the end of the semester the second author administered the following questionnaire in each classroom at Universities A and B.

> Reflect on one or a few recent intercultural communication opportunities you had.
>
> Q1 Is there anything you would learn from your own experience?
>
> Q2 What does English mean for you as (future) English users?
>
> Q3 What do you think a capable user of English is like in the twenty-first century?

Note that the term intercultural communication was used as a generic term for his modules. The three open-ended questions (Q1–Q3) encouraged participants to reflect on their own most memorable communicative experiences, which they had shared already with peers in class. In this section and Activity 13.3, a participant's ID (P01–P18) and university (Univ. A or Univ. B) are given parenthetically after every quotation.

While more detailed findings are available elsewhere (see Ishikawa, 2020a), the major findings are as follows.

- Q1. Participants learned multilingual and transmodal accommodation as key for both perceived success and more active engagement in communication.
- Q2. Participants expected English to let them join a globalised world as well as serve career purposes.
- Q3. All the participants would agree that capable English users were not judgemental of who interactants were, but were experienced in multilingual and transmodal accommodation to embody an interest and respect for what interactants had to say.

Conversely, accommodation would not always be practical "if we stick to English only" (Q3, P01, Univ. B) and would be more likely to fail "if we stick to stereotypes of other cultures" (Q3, P01, Univ. B) or "kind of prejudice or stereotype to English ... by non-English or American people" (Q3, P02, Univ. A). Indeed, participants at University A would text in Chinese characters as a "quick method" (Q1, P03, Univ. A). More drastically, participants at University B recalled that they often slipped into Indonesian, Korean, or Spanish whether consciously or subconsciously. One of them remarked that even when Korean was suspended, "I can get her English because I know her English is influenced by Korean" (Q1, P04, Univ. B). To borrow one participant's words:

> I feel that today's societies focus on boundaries. To give an example, we tend to distinguish English [from other languages] and then we often prefer American or British English to other English. [But] we should produce new communities, ideas and customs by using English in multilingual environment.
>
> (Q3, P05, Univ. A)

For this participant, then, flexible use of English and multilingual resources would lead to achieving a new, broader understanding of language and the world.

At the same time, participants at both universities would use image or voice translation on smartphones "to support communication" (Q1, P06, Univ. B) as necessary, or find facial and bodily expressions so indispensable as to say, for instance:

> I learned what [my Skype partner] thought about intercultural communication ... and how difficult to communicate without using *full body language.*
>
> (Q1, P07, Univ. A; emphasis added)

As such, participants' meaning appeared to be embedded in multiple modes blended for communication either via Skype or face to face. It is notable that what participants did not mention was any cultural misunderstanding. This finding coincides with the first author's empirical claim that eschewing essentialist accounts of cultural 'differences' and 'problems' in pedagogy is crucial (Baker, 2015). It also adds empirical support to the second author's argument that cultural differences as obstacles to achieving meaning are not always clear in transcultural communication (Ishikawa, 2017a).

Inside the classroom, a discussion of multilingual experiences appeared to create another EMF scenario by itself when students disassociated English from monolingualism via their multilingual repertoires. We would suggest that an L1-shared classroom can be an authentic site for present-day communication in which multilingual and multicultural influences and practices are emergent by way of transcending linguistic and other meaning-making boundaries.

As another example, after the completion of the above study (Ishikawa, 2020a), but not in the form of pedagogic intervention research, the same author taught a similar but more intensive elective sociolinguistics module at University A's EMI faculty. His students were 57 undergraduates (from Years 2 to 5) with diverse social, linguistic, and cultural backgrounds, originally from Asia, the Americas, and Europe. Regarding principle 1 (individual experience), multilingual practices were part of their everyday lives both on and off the campus. Therefore, in accordance with principle 2 (collective reflection), pedagogic efforts were concentrated on encouraging their critical thinking about everyday communication experiences. A typical three-hour class consisted of:

- a lecture on ELF research to facilitate the reflection of their own and peers' communication experiences (see, e.g., Jenkins et al., 2018)
- a group of students' presentation on one chapter from *The Routledge handbook of English as a lingua franca* (Jenkins et al., 2018)
- a follow-up lecture on the same chapter

Lectures were interspersed with group and class discussions, and students' presentations often involved discussion opportunities. Towards the end of the semester each student gave a final presentation on a topic of his or her choice, and many presentations cited personal digital communication experiences, including Extracts 8.1, 8.3, and that of Activity 8.2. Here, again, students shared and reflected on their own everyday experiences to substantiate their understanding of EMF and relevant notions.

EMF awareness advocates shifting away from decontextualising and delineating language, culture, and meaning-making modes. This is simply because global communication is not reducible to any particular languages, cultures, or modes. Its effectiveness relies on multilingual, transcultural, and transmodal accommodation, in other words, the dynamic, adaptive, and reflexive use of communicative resources and modes in context from moment to moment as foregrounded by translanguaging enquiry. We would like to stress that the capability to continue learning from such actual interactional experiences is indispensable for those concerned with globalised EMI. We would also like to claim that EMF awareness helps students to gain this very ability by bringing to the fore the value of learning from out-of-class communication experiences.

As you may have noticed it is easy to feature EMF awareness if the content of EMI is sociolinguistics, particularly on global communication, as was the case in the modules presented in this section. It would be interesting to explore how far and in what way EMI can be undergirded by EMF awareness across disciplines. This is all the more so because multilingual resources are likely to facilitate comprehending abstract notions in academia and elsewhere (Mauranen, 2014; Dafouz & Smit, 2020). Perhaps, more straightforwardly, higher-education institutions could make similar EMF-aware sociolinguistics modules widely available to students across faculties and departments at an earlier stage of academic curricula. The objective is to support future EMI in many different fields, or effective 'English' communication in international academia more broadly. Alternatively, similar interventions might be arranged in ELT. One possible place is an English for academic purposes (EAP) programme commonly offered at university. There is a potential for developing such programmes towards EMF awareness, to which the discussion will turn.

13.5 EMF awareness in English language teaching

EMF awareness in ELT is a relatively new topic, and we will cite one innovative example in this section. To our knowledge, Tamagawa University's Center for English as a Lingua Franca (CELF) in Tokyo, Japan is among the world's first centres to apply ELF research to teaching EAP. Even though native-speakerism and associated provincialism (Chapter 7.1, 7.3) are strongly ingrained in Japanese society (Houghton & Rivers, 2013; Ishikawa, 2018a), CELF has valued diversity on a global scale in the communication experiences of its teaching staff (Oda, 2018a; 2019). They are originally from Asia, Australasia, the Americas, Europe, and Africa at the time of writing. Whether full- or part-time, new applicants are scrutinised for scholarly appreciation and pedagogic application of ELF research and intercultural background, along with academic qualifications and teaching experience (Oda, 2018b; CELF, 2020). It is irrelevant whether applicants are Anglophones or not. Instead, the founding director of CELF, Masaki Oda, clearly states that "monolingual English-speaking teachers would not meet the needs of our ELF program" (Oda, 2019: 265).

The implementation of EMF awareness at CELF is made possible as follows.

- Principle 1 (individual experience). There is no monolingual policy throughout the CELF programme and facilities. Every time students take new classes, different instructors are assigned. If they take four courses, for example, they will be taught by four different instructors with different social, linguistic, and cultural backgrounds. Also, each student is encouraged to take the initiative on how to use multilinguals' free tutoring service. Moreover, there are diverse study-abroad programmes offered by either university departments or the Center for University International Programs.
- Principle 2 (collaborative reflection). It is true that at present, widely circulated textbooks are used in the classroom, and that graded readers are available in the university library. However, each class has plenty of time to go beyond specified units of the textbooks, and any commercialised materials are appropriated based on individual instructors' initiative. As instructors should be able to use approximately half of the class time without a textbook, they can take advantage of this time for students' critical reflection on meaning-making both in and outside the classroom. To support the ideas of such class activities, CELF holds monthly faculty development workshops, in addition to the annual teacher orientation session and CELF Forum for English Language Teaching.

In fact, the first author of this book was invited to the 2019 CELF Forum for English Language Teaching, cosponsored by the Japan Society for the Promotion of Science Kakenhi (科研費) Grant (no. 19K20794).

Currently, the producing of activity-based, interdisciplinary textbooks at CELF is under consideration to assist in maximising teacher creativity. At the same time, CELF faculty do not see any textbooks, however ELF-oriented they may be, "as materials to be used uncritically or without thought as to how they might be modified, developed, supplemented, and extended in accordance with the needs and interests of local learners" (Ishikawa & McBride, 2019: 340). In addition, even though Japanese students in general are keen on TOEIC for job-hunting purposes (Kubota, 2011; Taguchi, 2013), believing that they may benefit by obtaining high scores, CELF is now working to exclude from its programme TOEIC or any other internationally commercialised English test that does not reflect global communication. In keeping with observations made by Jenkins and Leung (2019), CELF already took action in 2020 to replace student placement by TOEIC Bridge (i.e., a short, simplified version of TOEIC Listening and Reading) with student self-assessment. A new website will be created in the near future to facilitate this self-placement process.

Activity 13.3 "now I can fly!"

In this chapter we cited Ishikawa's (2020a) open-ended questionnaire study. Below are more comments from its participants.

Q1 Is there anything you would learn from your own experience?

- "I never thought that Japanese words are used as Taiwanese between teenagers. So, a plenty of languages exist in the world and affect each language?" (P08, Univ. A)
- Multilingual communication is the norm because "it gives us affinity" (P09, Univ. B), "a sense of familiarity" (P10, Univ. B), and "deeper understanding" (P04, Univ. B).

Q2 What does English mean for you as (future) English users?

- English "is a tool for expressing *our own* identities" (P11, Univ. A; emphasis added), "the greatest bridge that [can] combine cultures" (P12, Univ. A), and thus "the brighting [sic] star for me!" (P13, Univ. A).

Q3 What do you think a capable user of English is like in the twenty-first century?

- "Our differences [in social background] are characteristics and identities, so ... to want to know and understand them is important." (P14, Univ. A)
- "I think [accommodation] is one of the ways to show my respect to others and show my feelings to want to know more about them and to be close to them." (P15, Univ. B)

Other comments included the following.

- "These days, I use English more actively even outside [this] class because I learned that important is negotiating without hesitation." (Q1, P16, Univ. A)

- "I was really afraid of making mistakes but I've become not scared to use other languages [than Japanese]. ... Now I have many foreign friends." (Q1, P17, Univ. A)
- "I got more confident in my English ... I learned a lot and now I can fly! Thank you! ☺" (Q3, P18, Univ. A)

(Ishikawa, 2020a: 413–415)

Are there any comments which resonate with your feelings and thoughts about global communication? How would you answer Q1 to Q3 above in the light of your own global communication experiences? Discuss your ideas in small groups if possible.

Feedback: *Answers will vary depending on individual experiences and opinions. Whatever your answers, you may have noticed that the participants cast doubt on the discreteness of linguistic boundaries in Q1. In this regard, P08 was inclined to extrapolate her observation to different languages in the world. You may also have noticed in Q2 that participants foresaw substantial and far-reaching benefits from English as a communication tool so long as it was conceptualised within multilingualism and as a lingua franca, and therefore not linkable to any particular groups, cultural or otherwise. Meanwhile, the participants quoted in Q3 indicated the importance of being curious and respectful interactants when accommodating to each other. Comments like theirs echo an interviewee's claim in Ishikawa (2017b: 254) that accommodation contributes to "sympath[etic]" human relationships and even "our development as human beings" (see Extract 12.2). The other comments suggest that EMF awareness functioned as a catalyst for more active communicative participation. In fact, in Q1, over 40 per cent of the participants from University A (n = 39 out of 91) described how multilingual Tokyo was since they found opportunities to communicate either in cyberspace or with students, residents, and visitors from abroad. Perhaps P18's metaphoric thank-you notes with a final emoticon expressed how crucial he felt accommodative practices were in such multilingual contact.*

Chapter summary

In this chapter we reviewed:

- Standardised English language tests
- monolingual construct of Standard English in ELT
- social representations of English: monolingual and Standard English ideologies

vis-à-vis:

- multilingual, translanguaging, transcultural, and transmodal reality
- development of language attitudes

A critical, holistic approach to communication made possible by EMF and relevant notions offers the unfamiliar representations of the familiar linguistic phenomenon of English as a global language, to which students are likely to develop more positive attitudes. EMF awareness seeks to integrate these empowered attitudes with emancipated communicative practices through the conscious understanding of meaning-making processes among multilingual English users.

EMF awareness has two principles which should be implemented in consideration of each educational context:

- individual experience of multilingual, transcultural, and transmodal accommodation
- collaborative reflection on individual experiences and published research

EMF awareness is not the entire rejection of a monolingual and standardised approach to English but the bridge between this convenient fiction for efficient pedagogy and multilingual, translanguaging, transcultural, and transmodal reality for effective communication. We presented practical examples in EMI and ELT towards the end of this chapter. We also noted that, as predicated on the convenient fiction, globally commercialised standardised English language tests do not reflect the current reality. It is, thus, questionable to use them for high-stakes entry assessment.

Further reading

ELT Journal, volume 74, issue 4 (2020): Special issue on the relevance of ELF to ELT. As is always the case with *ELT Journal*, all the articles in this special issue are accessible and relatively short. Among them, Ishikawa's (2020a) research paper and Jenkins' (2020) opinion piece are especially relevant to this chapter. The former ('EMF awareness in the Japanese EFL/EMI context', doi: 10.1093/elt/ccaa037) regards students' EMF experiences as essential classroom 'materials', and the latter ('Where are we with ELF and language testing? An opinion piece', doi: 10.1093/elt/ccaa045) calls for the replacement of standardised English language tests with self-assessment.

Ishikawa, T. & McBride, P. (2019). Doing justice to ELF in ELT: Comments on Toh (2016). *Journal of English as a Lingua Franca*, *8*, 333–345. doi: 10.1515/jelf-2019–2026. A practice-based example of the impact of ELF research on a university-wide English programme.

Sifakis, N.C. (2019). ELF awareness in English language teaching: Principles and processes. *Applied Linguistics*, *40*, 288–306. doi: 10.1093/applin/amx034. A detailed discussion of the construct of ELF awareness in the form of an English for specific purposes (ESP) approach mainly to support teacher training and development.

14 From communicative competence to intercultural awareness: Intercultural awareness and transcultural communication through Global Englishes

> [A]lthough I do not suppose that either of us knows anything really beautiful and good, I am better off than he is – for he knows nothing, and thinks that he knows. I neither know nor think that I know.
>
> (Socrates in Plato's Apology)

Introduction

The quotation above (see, e.g., Plato, 1999) is one of the first author's favourites, in which the philosopher Socrates, as reported by Plato, suggests that to be truly wise and knowledgeable we need to be aware of what we *do not know* more than what we know. We discussed a similar quotation from Confucius in Chapter 12, which happens to be a favourite with the second author. The quotation in Chapter 12 highlighted the importance of awareness, not just knowledge. In the same way, the quotation from Socrates has been chosen here as it clearly represents one of the key factors in successful intercultural and transcultural communication, which is not knowledge or facts about other cultures and languages (although they still have a role). Instead, what is crucial is being prepared for the unexpected and unknown through openness to difference and change, as well as awareness of our own limitations (i.e., neither knowing nor thinking that I know).

In this chapter we draw together many of the key themes previously discussed to explore what competences (attitudes, skills, and knowledge) are needed for intercultural and transcultural communication through Global Englishes. We begin with a consideration of competence in communication (e.g., Hymes, 1972) and provide a brief overview of the concept and its central role in applied linguistics, intercultural communication, and language teaching and learning. We then move on to an expansion of **communicative competence** to **intercultural communicative competence** (ICC) (e.g., Byram, 1997) as a more relevant concept for *inter*cultural rather than *intra*cultural communication. Next we discuss recent approaches to competence and awareness in intercultural communication that approach language, identity, community, and culture as constructed, negotiable, and contested. Finally, the notion of **intercultural awareness** (ICA) (Baker, 2011; 2015) is presented as a way of conceptualising the knowledge, skills, and attitudes needed to successfully negotiate intercultural and *trans*cultural communication through English used as a global multilingua franca. You will be given the opportunity to consider your own experiences of intercultural and transcultural communication and Global Englishes and how they relate to **intercultural competence** and awareness.

Activity 14.1 What makes for successful intercultural and transcultural communication?

In this book we have discussed the dynamic and complex nature of intercultural and transcultural communication through Global Englishes. At the same time research shows that many of these interactions are successful. So how do participants manage this fluidity and complexity? What knowledge, skills, or competences do participants possess or make use of that enable meaningful and satisfactory intercultural and transcultural communication? Make a list of the knowledge, skills, and attitudes that you think are needed for successful intercultural and transcultural communication. If possible, compare and discuss your list with others.

Here are some further issues you might like to consider. How important is language to successful communication? How important are other (non-linguistic) factors? What is the influence (if any) of feelings and attitudes? What are the differences (if any) in competences needed when communicating with someone who speaks the same L1 or a different L1?

Feedback: *There are no correct answers or responses to these questions. However, you may have included things such as knowledge of a shared language (e.g., English), of other cultures, and of intercultural communication. Yet, as we have emphasised throughout this book, this is not sufficient and equally important is the ability or the skills to employ this knowledge flexibly. In other words, we need to adapt our communicative practices, including language use, to the context of communication and our interlocutors (i.e.,* *accommodation). At the same time we also need to have the motivation and attitudes, including positive emotions and feelings, towards what can, at times, be quite challenging communication. Many of these ideas are conceptualised through notions such as communicative competence and performance, intercultural communicative competence, and awareness.*

14.1 Communicative competence

The notion of communicative competence has, unsurprisingly, been foundational in trying to understand how people communicate successfully and we have referred to it in a number of places already in this book (see especially Chapter 12.2). Traditionally competence has been viewed as separate from performance, with the latter drawing on the former in actual instances of communication. This competence/performance distinction is often attributed to the Swiss linguist Ferdinand de Saussure, who is considered the 'father' of linguistics. Saussure (1959/2011) distinguished between *langue* and *parole*, with langue referring to the formal, abstract linguistic system and parole to its use. Possibly the most well-known formulation of competence is that by the linguist Noam Chomsky, who, in an attempt to account for how humans acquire language, proposed the notion of formal linguistic competence as perfect knowledge of the language by "an ideal speaker-listener, in a completely homogeneous speech-community" (1965: 3). In other words, competence refers to what it is that a speaker of a language knows in order to be able to communicate as a 'native' speaker of that language. Competence here is an idealised abstraction necessary for theory (Chomsky was not proposing that anyone actually had perfect knowledge of a language as part of a completely homogeneous speech community). This competence is separate from performance, which is the use of the language in concrete situations by individuals and is much messier and far from 'perfect'. Chomsky's abstract notion of linguistic competence has been highly influential, particularly in the field of second-language acquisition (SLA), but has also been heavily criticised in applied linguistics as unrealistic and lacking in relevance for understanding what happens in real-world communication.

In contrast to Chomsky's abstract linguistic competence, the sociolinguist Dell Hymes' (1972) communicative competence has been of greater influence in applied linguistics. Hymes expanded competence beyond Chomsky's linguistic elements to also include sociocultural aspects of communication and blurred the distinction between competence and performance. For Hymes (1972: 281) there are four key aspects of communicative competence:

1. whether something is formally *possible* (this is similar to Chomsky's linguistic competence)
2. whether something is *feasible* (whether what is possible could actually be processed by interlocutors)
3. whether something is *appropriate* (related to social context, what is socially appropriate)
4. whether something is actually *performed* (what has previously been said or written)

It is this approach to communicative competence, focused on real-world communication, connecting linguistic knowledge, sociocultural knowledge and performance, that underpins many of the more recent theories of communicative competence in applied linguistics and intercultural communication. Nonetheless, from the perspective of intercultural communication and Global Englishes there are still some serious limitations to the model (see Chapter 12.2). Hymes' ideas are based on 'native' speakers in stable speech communities. As we have underscored throughout this book, the majority of Global Englishes communication does not involve 'native' speakers (with the category itself questionable) and communities and groupings in intercultural and transcultural communication are fluid and variable. We might question the relevance of appropriateness (aspect 3), since it can be difficult to know in advance what is appropriate in intercultural and transcultural communication and, furthermore, this is often established during the interaction itself. We might also question how reliable a guide what has previously been performed (aspect 4) is, given the adaptability and creativity of intercultural and transcultural communication (see also Chapter 12.1).

Drawing directly on Hymes but addressing the needs of second-language learners and users, Canale and Swain (1980) provide a characterisation of communicative competence which has been hugely influential in language teaching. The original model outlined three areas: grammatical competence, sociolinguistic competence, and strategic competence, with Canale (1983/2013) subsequently adding a fourth element, discourse competence. Grammatical competence is closely related to Chomsky's linguistic competence and Hymes' 'formally possible' and relates to competence in the linguistic system or language. Sociolinguistic competence relates to Hymes' notion of the 'appropriate', i.e., knowledge of what to say/write in a particular social context. The final two elements, discourse competence and strategic competence, are specifically related to the needs of second-language users. Strategic competence in particular focuses on strategies for overcoming communicative difficulties and breakdowns which may be caused by L2 users' lack of linguistic or sociolinguistic competence.

Given the foundational nature of this model in applied linguistics, it has generated a great deal of discussion and criticism, most of which is beyond the scope of this book (see, e.g., Brumfit, 2001; Widdowson, 2012). However, for the purposes of this discussion, it is important to note that although the model is focused on L2 users of a language, they are still expected to conform to the competence of an idealised monolingual 'native' speaker of the language (Canale & Swain, 1980: 12). Moreover, features such as strategic competence are seen from a deficit perspective in which they are used to make up for shortcomings and a lack of competence in other areas on the part of L2 users. This is a very different perspective to that adopted in Global Englishes and intercultural communication research where communicative and **pragmatic strategies** are seen as core competences for *all* participants (often described as **pragmatic competence**), the notion of the 'native' speaker (however it may be defined) is viewed as irrelevant for successful intercultural interactions, and multilingualism rather than monolingualism is regarded as the norm.

In response to these criticisms of monolingual, 'native'-speaker-orientated conceptions of communicative competence, more recent approaches have taken on multilingualism in much more depth. For instance, Vivian Cook (1991; 2002) introduced the notion of multi-competence, which he defines as "knowledge of more than one language in the same mind" (2002: 10), thus placing multilingualism at the core of competence (see also Chapter 12.2). As Cook points out, the majority of people in the world are multilingual not monolingual and so conceptions of communicative competence need to account for competences in multiple languages. Cook explains that "with multi-competence the competence of a monolingual native speaker became in a sense irrelevant; it was the competence of the successful L2 user that mattered" (2008). Similarly, Blommaert (2010) argues that instead of focusing on competences in specific languages we should think of competence in terms of repertoires and resources which allow us to employ a range of linguistic and pragmatic features to achieve communication in specific contexts and for particular purposes. Furthermore, he goes on to suggest that due to the inherent variability in language and communication, "no one knows *all* of a language" (2010: 103; original emphasis) and that partial competence is the norm, as opposed to Chomsky's 'perfect' competence of the idealised 'native' speaker.

In specific relation to Global Englishes, researchers have also been critical of earlier models of communicative competence. For example, Seidlhofer, like Blommaert (2010), also proposes that "competence will always be partial and incomplete" (2011: 89) due to the variable way in which languages such as English are used globally. She argues that Hymes' notions of feasibility, appropriateness, and performance need to be separated from 'native'-speaker communities and connected to the types of communities found in ELF interactions. Seidlhofer believes that "quite different judgements are likely to be made about what is feasible, appropriate to context, and so on ... And indeed here one has to accept that it is likely to be appropriate in many, if not most contexts in which English is currently used, *not* to fully conform to native-speaker conventions" (2011: 91; original emphasis). Likewise, Widdowson writes that "ELF users develop their own construct of the possible as a function of what is feasible and appropriate for their purposes, by exploiting the potential for meaning making inherent in the language" (2012: 21). Indeed, according to Widdowson (2012), it is the potential for meaning-making that is part of all languages that enables users to creatively adapt and change linguistic forms and communicative norms for their own purposes, which in the case of ELF are likely to be very different to 'native'-speaker norms.

In sum, research into multilingualism and Global Englishes shows us that communicative competence needs to account for more than an idealised 'native'-speaker knowledge of a single language. Instead, communicative competence must encompass multiple languages or linguistic (and other) resources and repertoires, as well as acknowledge the constantly variable nature of language use which means competence will always be evolving and incomplete. Alongside this, the sociocultural aspects of language use in diverse and dynamic communities also need to be recognised and it is to this that we now turn.

14.2 Intercultural communicative competence

Within the field of intercultural communication research the notion of intercultural competence has been as central as communicative competence has in applied linguistics. Intercultural competence frameworks are useful in that they typically take a much wider perspective on communication than the narrow linguistic or grammatical focus of communicative competence. For example, Fantini defines intercultural competence as "a complex of abilities needed to perform *effectively* and *appropriately* when interacting with others who are linguistically and culturally different from oneself" (2007: 9; original emphasis). Spitzberg and Changnon (2009), in a review of major models of intercultural competence, identify over 300 concepts and terms used but suggest that they are all underpinned by five broad concepts: motivation, knowledge, skills, contexts, and outcomes. Similarly, Spencer-Oatey and Franklin (2009), in a review of intercultural competence from the varied fields of psychology, communication studies, applied linguistics, foreign-language education, international business, and management studies, also note the wide range of terminology but believe that there is a shared framework underneath them. According to Spencer-Oatey and Franklin, this framework can be reduced to three core components, which they term the "ABC" of intercultural interactional competence (2009: 79). These are affective components (or attitudes), behavioural components (or skills), and cognitive components (or awareness and knowledge). This ABC framework, more commonly referred to in terms of skills, knowledge, and attitudes, has been pervasive in thinking about intercultural competence and intercultural communicative competence and will be returned to later in this chapter. Despite the large number of models of intercultural competence, many have received similar criticisms in terms of simplification of culture and its role in communication (especially earlier cross-cultural models), a lack of empirical evidence or theoretical justification, overly static representations of communication and culture which fail to account for flexibility and adaptation, and, crucially from the perspective of this book, ignoring or simplifying the role of language and multilingualism in intercultural interactions.

An approach which combines the wider scope of intercultural competence but also the more thorough treatment of language from communicative competence is intercultural communicative competence. The best known and most influential model of intercultural communicative competence, or ICC, is that developed by the education scholar Michael Byram (e.g., Byram, 1997; 2008; 2012a; 2021; Byram & Esarte-Sarries, 1991; Byram et al., 1994) and so it will be this model and the research that has built on it that we will focus on here. As Byram explains in combining the two approaches, "[t]he intercultural speaker needs intercultural communicative competence, i.e., both intercultural competence and linguistic/communicative competence, in any task of mediation where two distinct linguacultures are present, and this is something different from and not comparable with the competence of the native speaker" (2012b: 89; Byram & Golubeva, 2020: 74). As is also made clear here, Byram proposes replacing the inappropriate 'native'-speaker model with a model of an "intercultural speaker" who possesses competences different from those of the 'native' speaker. These competences are conceptualised through Byram's (1997) model of ICC in which he draws on the earlier notions of linguistic, sociolinguistic, and discourse competence but adds an extensive intercultural dimension, as shown in Figure 14.1.

Under ICC intercultural competence is further divided into five elements or "savoirs", as Byram terms them. These can be summarised as follows (Byram, 1997: 34, 50–54):

- **attitudes (savoir être)** – relativising the self, valuing others; curiosity and openness, readiness to suspend disbelief about other cultures and beliefs about one's own
- **knowledge (savoirs)** – of self and other, of interaction: individual and societal; of social groups and their products and practices in

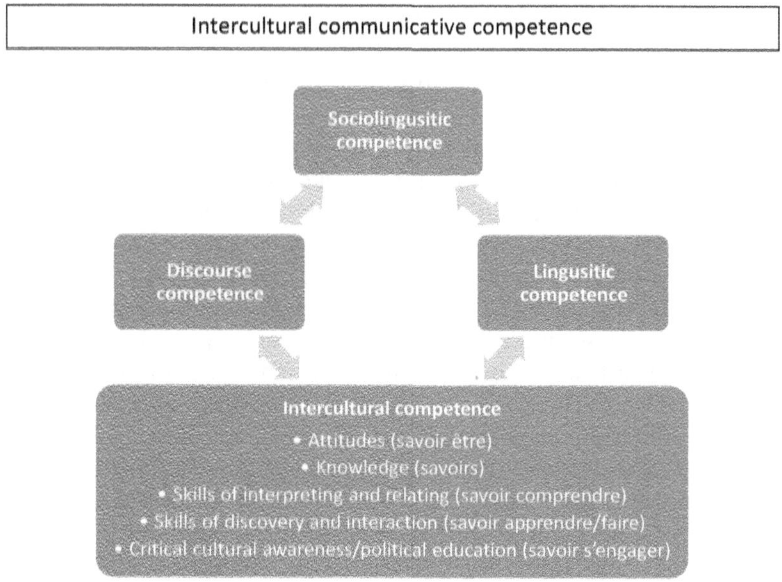

Figure 14.1 Byram's (1997) intercultural communicative competence
(Adapted from Byram, 1997: 73)

one's own and in one's interlocutor's country, and of the general processes of societal and individual interaction

- **skills of interpreting and relating** (**savoir comprendre**) – ability to interpret a document or event from another culture, to explain it and relate it to documents from one's own
- **skills of discovery and interaction** (**savoir apprendre/faire**) – ability to acquire new knowledge of a culture and cultural practices and the ability to operate knowledge, attitudes, and skills under the constraints of real-time communication and interaction
- **critical cultural awareness/political education** (**savoir s'engager**) – an ability to evaluate critically and on the basis of explicit criteria perspectives, practices and products in one's own and other cultures and countries

Critical cultural awareness is viewed by Byram (1997; 2008) as the central component of ICC in enabling the intercultural speaker to be aware of perspectives, practices, and products from their own and other cultures and also being aware of the implicit values that form part of those perspectives, practices, and products. This critical perspective allows the intercultural speaker to relativise their own position so that they can then mediate and negotiate between differences in intercultural communication, drawing upon the attitudes, skills, and knowledge described in the rest of the model. By underscoring the importance of interaction, interpretation, and mediation, ICC also adds a degree of dynamism and adaptability to the model. Furthermore, ICC contains a learning dimension suggesting that ICC can be developed by both the teacher and learner in the classroom, fieldwork (e.g., student exchanges), and independent learning. Indeed, the education aspects of ICC are probably its greatest strength as it has been applied extensively to teaching a wide variety of languages in diverse settings (e.g., Byram & Fleming, 1998; Byram et al., 2001; Roberts et al., 2001; Byram & Grundy, 2003; Alred et al., 2006; Feng et al., 2009).

Despite the clear relevance of this model for understanding and teaching intercultural communication, there are a number of limitations from a Global Englishes and transcultural communication perspective. Most significantly, ICC is focused at the national scale of language and culture. As Byram writes in relation to critical cultural awareness, it is "[a]n ability to evaluate critically and on the basis of explicit criteria perspectives, practices and products in one's own and other *cultures and countries*" (1997: 53; emphasis added). Here cultures are clearly equated with countries (although see Byram, 2021). However, as we have seen throughout this book, such an assumption is problematic. Intercultural and transcultural communication can take place at many different scales from the local to the global, with the nation/country being just one possible cultural scale. The focus on the national may be more relevant as regards teaching and learning languages others than English due to the focus on 'native'-speaker communities and cultures (although we might also wish to question this assumption for any contemporary multilingual and multicultural society). However, it becomes difficult to sustain as regards English and its use as a lingua franca with no set culture or country (Chapter 4.3, 5.5). Furthermore, as Holliday (2011) argues, models such as ICC in correlating culture and country maintain an "intercultural line" in which one's own culture is separated from the culture of the 'other'. Linked to this intercultural line is the assumption that intercultural communicators need to mediate between cultures. In contrast much Global Englishes and intercultural communication research shows cultural practices as much more complex and fluid, often with no clear distinctions or boundaries (Chapter 5). Moreover, from a transcultural communication perspective (Chapter 10), we see interactants moving through and across borders and transcending boundaries rather than being 'between' them (Baker & Sangiamchit, 2019). As we discussed in the examples of Global Englishes in digital communication (Chapter 11), cultural practices and references can be associated with multiple contexts simultaneously, as well as transcending any fixed connections to geographical places, national or otherwise.

Activity 14.2 The native speaker versus the intercultural speaker

One of the major differences between communicative competence and intercultural communicative competence (ICC) is the model of the ideal speaker. In communicative competence, the ideal speaker is a 'native' speaker of the language in a 'native'-speaker community. In ICC, the ideal speaker is an 'intercultural' speaker in intercultural communication. Which of these two models best matches your ideal goal or target when learning and using English? Make some notes on the reasons for your answer. If possible, discuss your answer and reasons with others.

Feedback: *The answer to this question will depend on your personal experiences and goals. However, for English used as a global lingua franca for intercultural and transcultural communication, it is difficult to see the relevance of 'native' English language use associated with Anglophone 'native'-speaker communities. Native-speakerism (Chapter 7.1) is especially problematic as the majority of Global Englishes communication neither involves 'native' English speakers (NESs) nor takes place in Anglophone communities. In fact, as research such as Sweeny and Zhu (2010) has shown, if you communicate like an NES you are less likely to be understood in intercultural communication. The competence of an intercultural speaker is of much more relevance. Even if you are planning to use your English in an Anglophone setting (e.g., for studying or working), many Anglophone countries are multilingual and multicultural with intercultural communication a part of daily life for many. So even here, the competence of an intercultural speaker is likely to be of most relevance (and indeed this is something that NESs also need to learn to interact in intercultural contexts within Anglophone settings, such as international universities and multinational companies).*

14.3 Alternatives to communicative and intercultural communicative competence

As a result of increasing awareness of L2 use as intercultural communication and of the diverse uses of Global Englishes and multilingualism, a number of recent discussions have incorporated more fluid approaches to both language and culture in understanding competence. Kramsch's (2009; 2011) notion of symbolic competence is based on a more critical view of culture than the nationally orientated perspectives in ICC, instead adopting the discourse approach to culture presented in Chapter 1.2. Culture is thus characterised from a poststructuralist perspective in which it is multiple and contested. Symbolic competence becomes more than understanding our own and a cultural 'other'; rather, it is about understanding the complexity of multiple "discourse worlds" (2011: 356) where diverse meanings and interpretations of culture and communication are the norm. Moreover, Kramsch emphasises the central place of reflexivity incorporating the ideological, historic, and aesthetic aspects of intercultural communication and language teaching and learning (2009: 199). Most importantly, multilingualism is fundamental to Kramsch's symbolic competence and it deals with the use of multiple languages, the diverse discourse worlds they create, and the changes to language and culture that multilingual intercultural interaction results in. The symbolic competence of what Kramsch terms "the multilingual subject" is conceptualised through three abilities:

- an ability to understand the symbolic value of symbolic forms and the different cultural memories evoked by different symbol systems
- an ability to draw on the semiotic diversity afforded by multiple languages to reframe ways of seeing familiar events, create alternative realities, and find an appropriate subject position 'between languages', so to speak
- an ability to look both *at* and *through* language and to understand the challenges to the autonomy and integrity of the subject that come from unitary ideologies and a totalizing networked culture (2009: 201)

While there is more in this definition of symbolic competence than can be explained here, key features are not only the ability to take a position "between languages" but also to be able to "look both *at* and *through* language". This suggests an ability or competence similar to that outlined in translanguaging and transcultural communication where boundaries between languages and cultures are recognised but also transgressed and transcended as people move *through*, rather than just *between*, them. Linked to this is the critical stance on "unitary ideologies" and "totalizing networked culture", which advocates an alternative to essentialised descriptions of culture as homogeneous. Such a perspective also indicates a rejection of, or at least a refinement of, Kramsch's own notion of "third places" (1993), which viewed language learners as between their own 'first' language and culture and a 'target' language and culture (Chapter 5.4). As Kramsch herself writes, "the notion of third culture must be seen less as a PLACE than as a symbolic PROCESS of meaning-making that sees beyond the dualities of national languages (L1–L2) and national cultures (C1–C2)" (2011: 355). In keeping with the focus on process, symbolic competence is described as a "dynamic, flexible, and locally contingent competence" (2009: 199). Symbolic competence, thus, goes beyond competence associated with knowledge of the cultural and communicative practices of specific groups and instead outlines a dynamic, contextualised, and critical competence "embracing multiple, changing and conflicting discourse worlds" (Kramsch, 2011: 356). All of these features suggest that symbolic competence would be well-suited for understanding transcultural communication through Global Englishes, although this is not a direction that has been developed by Kramsch.

An approach which directly addresses Global Englishes, multilingualism, and intercultural communication is Canagarajah's (2013) performative competence. As the term suggests, Canagarajah focuses on the actions or performance of communication, rather than the abstract mental representations of language, as envisaged in the earlier discussed notions of communicative competence. In other words, the *how* rather than *what* of communication is emphasised. Performative competence directly draws on ICC (Canagarajah, 2013: 173), in outlining a broad range of skills, attitudes, and knowledge for communication, from social and linguistic awareness, to strategies for the micro-management of specific interactions. However, unlike ICC, performative competence deals specifically with translingual communication and fluid cultural groupings in 'contact zones' (see Chapter 10.2). It is, as Canagarajah explains, "competence for plural language norms and mobile semiotic resources" (2013: 173). This performative competence is, according to Canagarajah, underpinned by the concept of alignment, defined as: "connecting semiotic resources, environmental factors, and human subjects in relation to one's own communicative needs and interests in order to achieve meaning. … translinguals have the ability to align diverse semiotic resources to create meaning and achieve communicative success when words in isolation are inadequate and homogeneous norms are not available in contact zones" (2013: 174). Importantly, Canagarajah (2013: 178) also highlights the role of cooperative dispositions which allow translinguals to develop performative competence. In sum, performative competence goes beyond defined cultures, languages, and communicative norms, emphasises the need for flexibility and awareness of diversity, and, like symbolic competence, puts forward a dynamic contextually based competence.

Turning to Global Englishes research, in addition to the more dynamic, 'non-native' focus on language in communicative competence discussed earlier in this chapter, Global Englishes researchers have also proposed a range of other competences needed for successful communication related primarily to communicative and pragmatic strategies. As Seidlhofer and Widdowson note, rather than any particular use of language, "it may turn out that what is distinctive about ELF lies in the communicative strategies that its speakers use" (2009: 37–38). Although, we would add that these communicative strategies are not unique to ELF and most likely shared with any intercultural interaction or potentially any communication. Importantly, from a Global Englishes perspective these communicative strategies are not viewed as compensating for a lack of proficiency in other areas (as in communicative competence), but rather as a core part of the communicative repertoire of a successful multilingual intercultural communicator. ELF research especially has focused on pragmatic strategies (e.g., Jenkins et al., 2011; Cogo & Dewey, 2012), often conceptualised under the overarching concept of accommodation. Indeed, it was noted early in ELF research (e.g., Firth, 1996; Jenkins, 2000) that despite the 'problems' that were expected in ELF communication due to linguistic and cultural differences, most of the observed interactions appeared successful. This was attributed to the predominantly cooperative disposition of ELF interactions whereby participants made use of communicative and pragmatic strategies to accommodate to each other. Although, it is important to add the caveat that not all ELF interactions are positive and not all interactants accommodate to each other (see Guido, 2012; Jenks, 2018).

As outlined earlier, much of the accommodation takes place through participants adapting and adjusting their pronunciation and language to each other, as well as creatively changing language to fit the purposes and participants in an interaction (e.g., Pitzl's (2009) "we should not wake up any dogs"; see Chapter 6.5). Equally important though for cooperation and accommodation are pragmatic strategies. These include the use of pre-emptive strategies, whereby participants anticipate communicative difficulties and employ strategies such as repetition, clarification, and translation to minimise the risk of mis- and non-understanding (Kaur, 2009; Cogo & Pitzl, 2016). As Jenkins et al. argue, the use of these pre-emptive strategies provides an explanation of why non-understanding is so rarely observed in ELF interactions, since participants do not assume understanding and "speakers engage in a joint effort to monitor understanding at every stage of communication, even before non-understanding has taken place" (2011: 293). When problems do occur, similar strategies such as clarification, self-repair, repetition, reformulation, and translation have been frequently observed (Jenkins et al., 2011; Seidlhofer, 2011; Cogo & Dewey, 2012; Cogo & Pitzl, 2016). At the same time, to help a smooth conversational flow, the strategy of 'let it pass' has been observed where non-understanding is often not indicated immediately, or at all, unless it becomes important later for ensuring understanding (Firth, 1996; Pitzl, 2005). Other strategies used to ensure cooperation and successful communication include supportive turn-taking, simultaneous speech, utterance completion by another speaker, code-switching, and most recently translanguaging (Jenkins et al., 2011; Cogo, 2016). Nonetheless, as with linguistic forms, it is important to note that pragmatic strategies need to be approached as equally variable and fluid in use, with no one particular set of strategies being relevant to all contexts (Baker, 2011; Canagarajah, 2013). Moreover, flexible language and pragmatic strategy use is embedded in a wider range of knowledge, skills, and attitudes related to multilingualism and intercultural and transcultural communication, as proposed in EMF awareness (Chapter 13.3) and intercultural awareness below.

14.4 Intercultural awareness

Intercultural awareness (ICA) is an approach to understanding the knowledge, skills, and attitudes needed for successful communication that has been specifically developed in relation to Global Englishes and ELF. ICA directly builds on the earlier ICC model (Byram, 1997); however, unlike ICC, ICA also incorporates the dynamic perspectives to language and culture of transcultural communication and the critical, flexible approaches to competence discussed above (Kramsch, 2009; 2011; Canagarajah, 2013). ICA is defined as "a conscious understanding of the role culturally based forms, practices and frames of reference can have in intercultural communication, and an ability to put these conceptions into practice in a flexible and context specific manner in communication" (Baker, 2015: 163). Intercultural is chosen rather than cultural awareness (as in ICC's cultural awareness) to emphasise that this conception is focused on awareness of intercultural communication rather than awareness of specific cultures. Transcultural awareness might be a more accurate term, since, as explained in Chapter 10.1, *trans-* is a more appropriate prefix and spatial metaphor than *inter-* for much communication through Global Englishes. However, due to the more common use of the term intercultural and to link ICA to other research in the field, this term has been retained. As with EMF awareness (Chapter 13.3), awareness is used in a holistic sense to refer to knowledge, skills, behaviour, and attitudes and as an alternative to the problematic competence/performance (use) distinction. Unlike ICC and other more essentialist accounts, culture in ICA is not linked to countries or nationalities, nor does it assume an 'our/other' culture distinction. Finally, and similar to symbolic and performative competence, the second part of this definition underscores the importance of flexibility and adaptability in relation to emergent and contextually appropriate communicative practices and sociocultural relations. In other words, ICA is not a 'fixed' set of skills, knowledge, or behaviour but rather something that is dynamic and changeable.

The above definition of ICA can be further expanded into the model of ICA with 12 elements, as seen in Table 14.1. The 12 elements are

Table 14.1 The 12 components of Baker's (2015) intercultural awareness

Level 1: Basic cultural awareness
An awareness of:
1 culture as a set of shared behaviours, beliefs, and values
2 the role culture and context play in any interpretation of meaning
3 our own culturally based behaviour, values, and beliefs and the ability to articulate this
4 others' culturally based behaviour, values, and beliefs and the ability to compare this with our own culturally based behaviour, values, and beliefs

Level 2: Advanced cultural awareness
An awareness of:
5 the relative nature of cultural norms
6 cultural understanding as provisional and open to revision
7 multiple voices or perspectives within any cultural grouping
8 individuals as members of many social groupings including cultural ones
9 common ground between specific cultures as well as an awareness of possibilities for mismatch and miscommunication between specific cultures

Level 3: Intercultural awareness
An awareness of:
10 culturally based frames of reference, forms, and communicative practices as being related both to specific cultures and also as emergent and hybrid in intercultural communication
11 initial interaction in intercultural communication as possibly based on cultural stereotypes or generalisations but an ability to move beyond these through
12 a capacity to negotiate and mediate between different emergent communicative practices and frames of reference based on the above understanding of culture in intercultural communication

(Baker, 2015: 164)

presented in an order which builds from basic cultural awareness (level 1), to cultural awareness (level 2), and finally to the most complex and dynamic level of intercultural awareness (level 3).

In level 1, culture and language are typically conceptualised uncritically at the national scale and orientated to a 'home' culture rather than intercultural communication. As such, they may involve simplistic and stereotyped understandings of culture and its role in communication. Any awareness of other cultures may be centred around generalised or simplistic comparisons. While in intercultural research and education we may want to move beyond such essentialist perspectives, it is important that any model of intercultural awareness or competence can account for them, as they are very common. An instance of level-1 basic cultural awareness is presented in Example 14.1. Here we can see a participant from a study of intercultural awareness and ELF (Baker, 2011: 207) making a generalisation about their (Thai) culture, "every children been taught that you have to work hard in school", and then making a similarly general comparison with another national culture, "I want to know that umm English people pay attention to the (that) stuff".

Example 14.1 Level 1: General comparisons between cultures
Kay: in Thailand everybody umm every children been taught that you have to work hard in school. so you have to get another maybe a high school the good high school and then when you are in high school you have to work hard to go to university ... because going to university is very important ... but umm I would like to know that English people what their opinion about going to university what is the important thing in the world if you cannot go you cannot pass to go to university ... I want to know that umm English people pay attention to the (that) stuff.

(Baker, 2011: 207)

Level 2 moves away from essentialist perspectives to more complex understandings of language, culture, and intercultural communication. Here cultures are seen as diverse and multi-voiced, being made of many different groupings. Furthermore, cultures are recognised as just one of a range of groupings individuals can identify with. There may also be detailed knowledge and experiences of 'other' cultures and intercultural communication, leading to an awareness of the relative nature of cultural norms. In keeping with this more complex view of culture, there is also a recognition of the need to update and revise knowledge of 'other' cultures. Level 2 is, therefore, in many ways similar to Byram's (1997) ICC but, like ICC, it remains limited by an intercultural line (Holliday, 2011) between 'our' and 'other' cultures. The national scale may still be prominent with the complexity of cultural groupings viewed as existing *within* national cultures. The example below (from Baker (2011)) illustrates approaching cultures as relative when discussing cultural products such as movies or music – "you can't really say what is good and what is better" – as well as showing knowledge of different cultures. At the same time, national conceptions of culture are still significant, in this case "English" and "Thai".

Example 14.2 Level 2: Cultures as relative
Oy: Hollywood's better than Thai. I don't think can't really justify what's really better or what good or what's not good and what is (one) English song is better than English music is better than Thai music still the same answer you can't justify that. novels that (tough) because really English and the Thai got different culture and different types of thinking and attitude so you can't really say what is good and what is better.

(Baker, 2011: 207)

Level 3 moves to awareness of the relationships between language, culture, and communication as dynamic, liminal, and emergent, as seen in much Global Englishes research. In particular, it transcends the national scale, or any fixed scale, for culture and language, instead recognising that cultural references and communicative practices in intercultural and transcultural communication may or may not be related to specific cultures. A core element is the ability to negotiate and adapt between different cultural frames of reference and communicative practices, as they emerge in specific examples of intercultural and transcultural communication. Thus, the understanding of culture, language, and communication goes beyond an 'our' and 'other' culture dichotomy and instead, "ICA involves an awareness of cultures, languages and communication which are not correlated and tied to any single native speaker community or even group of communities" (Baker, 2015: 166). As regards Global Englishes, this means that English as a multilingua franca is viewed as resource to express and enact cultural practices and forms that are related to a range of communities from the local to the global, moving between, across, and through scales in fluid ways that often result in emergent and novel cultural practices and forms (Baker, 2015: 166–167). Example 12.3, which you may remember from Chapter 5.4, demonstrates how Nami, when discussing how 'girls' should behave, shows an awareness of Thai cultural norms – "Thai people if you observe" – but also that they are not fixed – "I don't like it because I have my own right". She also goes on to explain how she is aware of different cultural norms "American", "British", and "Thai", but that she does not have to follow any one of them or behave in a fixed way. Rather, she adapts cultural practices for her own purposes – "you should develop your life" – which are not part of any national group – "it's not not like a passion that I want to be like American people ... it's not just the Thai way".

Example 14.3 Level 3: Adapting fluid cultural practices

Nami: oh that's the great up-to-you ... yes that's because Thai people if you observe I think you observe that girls like to say they don't like to make the decision ... everything is just man make a decision and girls aren't allowed to make a decision here in this society and I don't like it because I have my own right to do that too to do that too umm and so that's why I was like making it as a joke.

(Baker, 2009a: 579)

Nami: ... yeah it's not not like a passion that I want to be like American people I want to be like British people it's not like that but it's just the way oh that's interesting ... you should develop your

> life yeah it's not just the Thai way but also the other way that you think that is good from that.
>
> (Baker, 2011: 208)

As with all models, there are, of course, limitations to ICA. First, the three levels and 12 elements, as well as the distinctions between them, are a simplification and abstraction for analytical purposes. They represent complex and infinitely variable phenomena and are unlikely to neatly fit individuals' actual knowledge, awareness, or experiences. Moreover, the relationships between the elements are not shown in the model; they are simply listed and, as such, this does not represent a complete model (for a full account of the ICA model, see Baker, 2015: 163–171). As regards development through the different levels, while people may develop from levels 1 to 3, as outlined here, there is no suggestion that this has to be so. Individuals may at times exhibit awareness at level 2, or even level 3, and at other times revert to more basic level-1 awareness. Some may never progress beyond level 1 or 2. Others may always have an awareness related to level 3, for example, if they were brought up in a multicultural and multilingual environment in which intercultural and transcultural communication is a part of daily life.

Activity 14.3 Intercultural awareness and me

- Where would you put yourself in this ICA model – level 1, 2, or 3? Can you think of any examples from personal experience that illustrate your rating of yourself and the elements of that level?
- Have you experienced any development in your ICA, for example, from levels 1 to 2? Was the development even, or did you move both up and down between the levels (e.g., sometimes showing elements of level 2 and sometimes level 1)?
- Do you think ICA addresses all the knowledge, skills, and attitudes needed for intercultural and transcultural communication? Is there anything you think should be added (or taken away) from the model?

Feedback: *There are obviously no right or wrong answers to these questions and your responses will depend on personal experiences. However, you will probably have noticed some development of ICA as you have gained more experience of intercultural communication in your life. At the same time, you may have found that the development was quite uneven and did not neatly fit into a move from one level to the next (perhaps making it difficult to answer the first question). Again, you may have various ideas about what is missing from this model; however, the model does not really discuss language in any* *detail. You might want to think about the relationship between language learning/development and the development of ICA (for culture in EMF awareness (Ishikawa, 2020a), see Chapter 13.1, 13.3).*

Chapter summary

In this chapter, we considered the knowledge, skills, and attitudes needed for intercultural and transcultural communication through Global Englishes. We began with communicative competence as a central concept in applied linguistics, and looked at the limitations of associating this with a fixed 'native'-speaker model and community. We then moved on to intercultural communicative competence (ICC) as an expansion of communicative competence that accounted for the intercultural dimensions in detail, although we noted the problems of keeping the national scale as prime. Next, we explored more critical and dynamic conceptions of competence, communication, language, and culture, particularly symbolic and performative competence. Finally, we discussed intercultural awareness (ICA) as an approach that combined many of the previous perspectives and was particularly well-suited to the fluid and dynamic relationships between language and culture in transcultural communication and Global Englishes. These approaches are summarised in Table 14.2. We will explore the implications of ICA for teaching and learning in more depth in Chapter 15.

Table 14.2 From communicative competence to intercultural awareness

Approaches	*Main features*	*Examples*
Communicative competence	Focus on linguistic and grammatical competence; sociocultural features are also included (especially Hymes); communication is based on an idealised 'native'-speaker model and homogeneous 'native'-speaker speech community	Chomsky (1965); Hymes (1972); Canale & Swain (1980)
Intercultural communicative competence	Adds an intercultural dimension to communicative competence: • attitudes (savoir être) • knowledge (savoirs) • skills of interpreting and relating (savoir comprendre) • skills of discovery and interaction (savoir apprendre/faire) • critical cultural awareness/political education (savoir s'engager)	Byram (1997; 2021)

(continued)

Table 14.2 Cont.

Approaches	*Main features*	*Examples*
Symbolic competence	Emphasis on multilingualism, critical reflexive perspectives on culture and language; competence is "dynamic, flexible, and locally contingent"	Kramsch (2009)
Performative competence	Translingual communication and fluid cultural groupings in 'contact zones'; focus on *how* not *what* of intercultural communication (process and performance); dynamic contextually based competence	Canagarajah (2013)
Pragmatic competence	Use of pragmatic and other communicative strategies in ELF communication; accommodation as an overarching strategy underpinned by cooperative disposition; strategies include clarification, self-repair, repetition, reformulation, translation, 'let it pass', code-switching, and translanguaging	Jenkins et al. (2011); Cogo & Dewey (2012)
Intercultural awareness (ICA)	Focus on intercultural and transcultural communication and Global Englishes/ ELF; an awareness of the role culturally based forms, practices, and frames of reference can have in intercultural communication, related to multiple scales from local, national, and global but also awareness of culture and language as emergent and not fixed to any one scale; flexible and context-specific awareness	Baker (2011; 2015)

Further reading

Baker, W. (2011). Intercultural awareness: Modelling an understanding of cultures in intercultural communication through English as a lingua franca. *Language and Intercultural Communication*, *11*, 197–214. doi: 10.1080/14708477.2011.577779. The article explains the model of ICA in detail.

Baker, W. (2015). *Culture and identity through English as a lingua franca: Rethinking concepts and goals in intercultural communication.* Berlin: De Gruyter Mouton. Chapter five contains an in-depth discussion of communicative competence, intercultural communicative competence, and the development of intercultural awareness.

Byram, M. (2021). *Teaching and assessing intercultural communicative competence: Revisited* (2nd edn). Clevedon: Multilingual Matters. A comprehensive overview of intercultural communicative competence and its relevance for teaching with updated discussions on key debates on the original text (Byram, 1997).

15 Intercultural language education and Global Englishes

> Education shall be directed to … the strengthening of respect for human rights and fundamental freedoms. It shall promote understanding, tolerance and friendship among all nations, racial or religious groups, and shall further the activities of the United Nations for the maintenance of peace.
>
> (Universal Declaration of Human Rights, Article 26.2)

Introduction

The citation above from the Universal Declaration of Human Rights contains some very ambitious aims for education. However, we think that these are aims that language education is especially well placed to meet. Given the focus on 'other' cultures and intercultural communication, promotion of "understanding, tolerance and friendship among all nations, racial or religious groups" can and should be a goal of the language classroom. Indeed, you may have noticed that many of the aspects of intercultural competence and awareness discussed in the previous chapter appear similar to these aims, including knowledge and understanding of different cultural practices, an ability to relativise our own practices, and positive attitudes to difference and 'others'. Furthermore, due to the role of English as a global language of intercultural and transcultural communication across national, racial, and religious groups, English language teaching (ELT) is the ideal setting to explore these topics. Yet, we wonder how many of these issues and goals have been part of your experience of language education and particularly ELT. As we will see in this chapter, while the intercultural dimensions are firmly established in language teaching theory and increasingly in policy, they have been less well implemented in practice. You will have noticed that we are using the term intercultural education rather than transcultural education, since this is the term most commonly used in the field. However, we think that many of the current approaches under intercultural education are well suited to preparing students for transcultural communication.

We begin this chapter with a discussion of current approaches to intercultural education in language teaching, including limitations around the prevalence of essentialist, stereotyped perspectives. We then outline a number of recent approaches that adopt more complex understandings of culture, language, and intercultural/transcultural communication which are particularly relevant to Global Englishes. Next we return to the concept of intercultural awareness (ICA) (Chapter 14.4) and consider its relevance to teaching practices based on five strands for implementing ICA in the classroom. Then, we introduce the concept of **intercultural citizenship education** as a perspective that combines elements from many of the previous approaches to intercultural education and language teaching and is, we argue, particularly suited to ELT, Global Englishes, and transcultural communication. Finally, we propose a transcultural educational approach and connect this to a summary of the main themes covered in this book. Throughout the chapter, you will have opportunities to reflect on your own experiences and opinions of ELT and intercultural education.

Activity 15.1 Language teaching and culture

Read these four possible approaches to teaching language and culture:

1. language taught as culturally neutral
2. language represents the local culture (classroom, school, community, nation)
3. language represents a 'target' culture, e.g., the US or the UK
4. language as a means of intercultural communication with no fixed cultural associations

Questions

Q1 Which of these have you experienced?
Q2 Which approach do you think is the most useful for you or for others?
Q3 Are there any other approaches to teaching language and culture that you are familiar with?

Feedback: *Your answers to this task will obviously vary depending on your experiences and opinions. However, we would suggest that approach 1 is not actually possible. Even if language is taught as decontextualised sentences in grammar exercises or as vocabulary lists, there is still cultural content whenever you attempt to interpret the meaning of the words or sentences. There is also the cultural context of the classroom, teacher, and students. So we would argue* *that culture is inevitably part of language teaching, whether explicitly addressed or not. However, all of the other approaches are possible, or even a combination of them, as we will explain below.*

15.1 Current approaches to intercultural education in language teaching

As we have seen throughout this book using and learning an additional language is often an intercultural and transcultural experience. Indeed, the **intercultural language education** scholars Liddicoat and Scarino suggest that "language learning is fundamentally engagement in intercultural communication and that the addition of a new language to a person's linguistic repertoire positions that person differently in relation to the world in which they live" (2013: 6). This is not an especially controversial or new perspective and culture has always been a part of language teaching. For instance, literature was an important part of nineteenth-century approaches as a means to understand the 'foreign' culture associated with another language (Risager, 2007). However, there has been an increasing recognition over the previous few decades of the importance of *inter*cultural communication (i.e., not just culture) as part of theory, policy, and, to a lesser extent, practice in language teaching, including in ELT (see Risager, 2007; Baker, 2015).

We can see the integration of culture, language, and the intercultural in many current language education policy documents. Perhaps most significantly, the updated 2018 version of the highly influential Common European Framework of Reference for Languages (CEFR) now includes "pluricultural competence" and in specific relation to education makes multiple references to culture and intercultural dimensions.[1]

> This publication marks a crucial step in the Council of Europe's engagement with language education, which seeks to protect linguistic and cultural diversity, promote plurilingual and intercultural education, reinforce the right to quality education for all, and enhance intercultural dialogue, social inclusion and democracy.
>
> (Emphasis removed)

In the US, "Standards for foreign language learning in the 21st century" (Glisan, 2012) and the Modern Language Association of America (MLA) make extensive references to culture, the relationship between culture, language, and communities, as well as intercultural communication. Similar government documents incorporating intercultural aspects into language education are found in other Anglophone settings such as Australia (Scarino & Liddicoat, 2009) and New Zealand (Newton et al., 2010). Likewise, in Asian settings the Chinese National English Curriculum contains a section on cultural awareness (Ministry of Education, 2011) and in Thailand "language and culture" is one of the four basic strands of the Basic Education Core Curriculum B.E. 2551 (OBEC, 2008). An abnormal case is Japanese national language policy which literally highlights the difference between essentialised Japanese and foreign languages and cultures in primary and secondary English education (Hashimoto, 2013; Ishikawa, 2016a; MEXT, 2020) rather than intercultural communication. Overall, however, cultural and intercultural aspects are increasingly recognised at the policy level globally.

Nonetheless, there are questions about how much the approach to language and culture in such policies goes beyond the national scale and incorporates the complexity and fluidity of multilingual, intercultural, and transcultural perspectives highlighted throughout this book. For example, despite using the term transcultural, the MLA guidelines still make multiple references to 'target' languages and cultures (Mori & Sanuth, 2018), suggesting a more intercultural, rather than transcultural, approach. Additionally, as Liu (2016) discusses in relation to the Chinese national curriculum, there is often a tension between the emphasis on languages for intercultural communication and a perspective that still views language as situated within particular national cultures and the need to conform to associated 'native'-speaker standards (again the speaker category is itself questionable). Moreover, and crucially, there is a frequently noted gap between policy and practice. Thus, the intercultural dimensions in policy are often much less prominent in actual language teaching practices and materials, where they may be marginalised or ignored (Baker, 2015).

Teaching materials are a core part of language teaching and learning and it is vital that the intercultural dimensions are included in ELT materials if they are to be part of classroom practices. Unfortunately, studies have repeatedly shown an over-emphasis on linguistic features of communication, an under-representation of culture and the intercultural in materials, as well as essentialist approaches when culture is included. Three decades of research on leading ELT textbooks comes to similar conclusions about the superficial and stereotyped inclusion of culture and intercultural communication in course books, with the focus remaining on the national scale and static, simplistic 'native'-speaker language and culture connections (Jin & Cortazzi, 1998; Vettorel, 2010; 2018; Rose & Galloway, 2019). Likewise, Gray's (2010) detailed analysis of the cultural content of ELT course books in the previous 40 years revealed a limited range of representations, the absence of locally relevant issues, and a 'native'-speaker focus.

Moreover, even within the focus on Anglophone cultures it is a restricted representation of that world, typically 'white', middle-class, male, and monolingual, presenting an essentialised image of 'other' cultures (Leung, 2005; Hall, 2013; Baker, 2015). To take one example, the bestselling *New Headway* series (e.g., Soars & Soars, 2011) provides a clear case of such stereotypical cultural representations. It is full of touristic images from Anglophone settings, such as Buckingham Palace, which is unlikely to tell us much about the communicative practices and cultures of people living in the UK. Such images are even less relevant to the majority of English learners, who will not be communicating in Anglophone settings or with 'native' English speakers (NESs). Some recent ELT textbooks have adopted a more international perspective, such as the *Global* series (e.g., Clandfield, 2010; 2019), which notably includes examples of 'authentic' interactions with 'non-native' speakers of English. However, even here detailed analysis shows that there is still a focus on 'native' English use and norms, along with Anglophone cultures, with much less interest in Global Englishes and intercultural communication than suggested in the promotion materials (Baker, 2015; Dewey, 2015; Galloway, 2018; Rose & Galloway, 2019). In sum, following Liddicoat and Scarino, we can conclude that "in spite of claims they may have made about their aims and objectives, many approaches to language education have effectively marginalized culture and the intercultural by focusing solely on the linguistic system and the use of materials that are sanitized of cultural complexity" (2013: 47).

Alongside inconsistent language policies and application of those policies, as well as essentialised materials, teaching practices have also been identified as failing to incorporate culture and intercultural communication either systematically or in depth (e.g., Sercu et al., 2005; Young & Sachdev, 2011; Luk, 2012; Driscoll et al., 2013). This is perhaps not surprising given the lack of clear guidance in policy or support from materials. Furthermore, intercultural/transcultural communication and Global Englishes are typically not part of teacher education and training and are rarely part of the tests that teachers are expected to prepare students for (Dewey, 2015; Jenkins & Leung, 2019). Additionally, while intercultural education and ELT research exists (we will discuss some of it later in this chapter), compared to other teaching approaches there has been much less empirical research, particularly on the "uptake and perceived applicability of this [intercultural] approach" (Young & Sachdev, 2011: 83). Subsequently, already-busy teachers often place teaching culture and intercultural communication low on their list of priorities. Even for teachers who are interested in the intercultural dimensions to ELT, the lack of guidance on "uptake" and "applicability" means that it is not always clear to teachers how to integrate them into classroom practices. Again, this results in a marginalisation of intercultural communication, where it often becomes a 'fifth' skill (Kramsch, 1993; 1995) to be dealt with after the other four skills of speaking, listening, writing, and reading and left out if time is short. However, as we have argued throughout this book, the intercultural aspects of communication through Global Englishes are crucial to successful interactions and cannot be ignored or 'bolted on' as a marginal extra in teaching. Despite the difficulties in meaningfully incorporating intercultural/transcultural communication in language education, and ELT specifically, there are approaches that can be adopted, and we will explore some of these in the following section.

15.2 Intercultural education, Global Englishes, and ELT

In this section, we will outline some of the core principles and characteristics of an intercultural approach in ELT that recognises the global role of English. Yet, it is important to note that we are not suggesting that there is a single methodology that will be appropriate in all teaching contexts. Moreover, many of the suggestions here are not unique to Global Englishes and intercultural education but, rather, are principles of good language-teaching practice in general. Indeed, lots of the principles, such as a critical approach to language and pedagogy, expanding communicative competence, removing the 'native' speaker as a model and goal, a shift from products to processes of learning, an increased recognition of multilingualism and interculturality, and a focus on local contexts and needs, are now well accepted in language teaching and learning theory (e.g., Brumfit, 2001; Kumaravadivelu, 2012; Widdowson, 2003). It should also be recognised that many previous approaches to culture and language teaching have, quite rightly, been critiqued as essentialist in following stereotyped nationalist characterisation of culture (as discussed in the previous section and Baker, 2015; Holliday, 2011; Piller, 2017). In contrast, here we move away from a sole focus on the national scale and consider the newer and less explored area of teaching English as a global multilingual franca for transcultural communication.

As discussed in Chapter 14, in intercultural communication research communicative competence is typically expanded beyond linguistic competence to include the knowledge, skills, and attitudes needed for intercultural communication. One of the most influential alternatives to communicative competence is Byram's (1997) intercultural communicative competence (ICC). To summarise what was presented in Chapter 14.2, in ICC, intercultural competence is added to linguistic, sociolinguistic, and discourse competence. This intercultural competence is further divided into five savoirs: attitudes (savoir être), knowledge (savoirs), skills of interpreting and relating (savoir comprendre), skills of discovery and interaction (savor apprendre/faire), and critical cultural awareness/political education (savoir s'engager) (Byram, 1997). ICC provides an alternative to communicative competence that includes intercultural communication in a detailed manner. Importantly, Byram (1997; 2008) offers a systematic approach to classroom practices, curriculum, and assessment in which students develop their understanding of the complex relationship between language and culture as they progress through their L2 learning and use. Furthermore, the pedagogic implications of ICC have been explored in classroom studies in a wide range of settings and languages, often with very positive results (e.g., Byram & Fleming, 1998; Byram et al., 2001; Feng et al., 2009). Yet, as previously suggested, the relevance of ICC to Global Englishes and transcultural communication is limited by its focus on national cultures and languages (even though they are viewed as complex; see Byram, 2021), ignoring lingua franca communication beyond national borders. Moreover, the intercultural line (Holliday, 2011) is prominent in ICC with intercultural communicators viewed as operating between and across bounded named cultures. As emphasised throughout this book, for Global Englishes and transcultural communication it is not always possible to identify cultural practices as related to any specific culture, and boundaries between languages and cultures are frequently transgressed and transcended.

Closely linked to re-thinking and expanding communicative competence is the replacement of the 'native' speaker in language teaching. The competences of an idealised monolingual and monocultural NES are of limited relevance in multilingual and multicultural, intercultural, and transcultural communication (see Chapters 12–14). As such, if the goal of language teaching, especially ELT, is to prepare learners for communication in the language, then a more appropriate model and goal is needed. Alternatives include the intercultural speaker (Byram, 1997; Kramsch, 1998b) with the competences of ICC rather than 'native'-speaker communicative competence. Alongside knowledge of intercultural communication is the development of skills and strategies needed in intercultural interactions such as accommodation and pragmatic competence (Cogo & Dewey, 2012). Equally important, as highlighted by Byram (1997), are positive attitudes to difference, motivation to engage with 'others', and the ability to 'de-centre' and relativise one's own beliefs and practices. These competences and attitudes are connected to the more flexible approaches to language and multilingualism, such as translanguaging and EMF, discussed in Chapters 8 and 9. In combination, all these different elements result in a wider and more holistic understanding of competence going beyond the purely linguistic for intercultural/transcultural communication through Global Englishes and the need for new models for teaching. Yet, this does not necessarily result in a radical change in ELT as in many cases well-educated and experienced local teachers of English will have developed these competences (Chapters 13.3, 14.4). Furthermore, outside the classroom learners will be able to find many local role models of English users who form a more appropriate and realistic target for them. A very recent model for education in general and for language teaching is the intercultural or global citizen, who combines many of the elements outlined here, and we will explain this in more detail later in this chapter.

Intercultural education approaches have frequently shifted the focus of teaching away from final *products* (e.g., knowledge of linguistic forms and functions) to a focus on the *processes* of communication and intercultural interaction (e.g., Liddicoat & Scarino, 2013). This is motivated by the fact that learners can never be prepared with knowledge of all the cultural practices and settings they may encounter in intercultural and transcultural communication and this is especially relevant to Global Englishes. Therefore, learners need to have an awareness of the processes of intercultural and transcultural communication so that they can negotiate the different linguistic and cultural practices they experience. As Canagarajah explains in relation to performative competence (see Chapter 14.3), "competence isn't constituted of the *what*, but of the *how* of communication" (2013: 174). As regards teaching approaches, this means there is no one approach that is most appropriate in all settings and, thus, teaching should be made locally relevant and adapted to learners' purposes and needs. As these needs and purposes are not fixed, so no single set of linguistic forms, cultural practices, or communicative strategies will be appropriate or adequate for all contexts. Canagarajah exemplifies this position in his discussion of teaching strategies: "teaching these strategies explicitly and formulaically for deductive application is distorting. These strategies are situated and practice-based. They cannot be implemented in a product-oriented and a priori manner" (2013: 186). Linguistic and cultural products (e.g., knowledge of grammar, vocabulary, and pronunciation as well as information about other cultures) still have an important place in language teaching; however, this knowledge should not be viewed as the end product. Instead, linguistic and cultural products can be presented as examples to be explored and adapted with all knowledge provisional and continually open to reflection and revision.

Another core theme in intercultural education has been a critical approach to language, culture, and identity and challenging dominant established discourses (e.g., Kramsch, 2009; Holliday, 2011; Piller, 2017; Zhu, 2019). The education scholars Phipps and Guilherme describe a critical pedagogy for intercultural education as "a critical use of language(s), a critical approach to one's own and other cultural backgrounds and a critical view of intercultural interaction" (2004: 3), and propose that this involves reflection, dissent, difference, dialogue, empowerment, action, and hope from both teachers and learners. Similarly, Piller (2017) argues that to avoid reproducing essentialist perspectives, teachers and learners should explore the prevailing discourses of culture, particularly national cultures, and challenge hegemonic views. Additionally, Guilherme (2012; 2020) highlights the importance of reflection in critical pedagogy in which teachers and learners are given time to explore their experiences of intercultural communication and the complexity of culture and language. Finally, critical approaches move beyond reflection and awareness and advocate the importance of action and change in intercultural education. For instance, Liddicoat and Scarino write that: "An intercultural perspective implies the transformational engagement of the learner in the act of learning. The goal of learning is to decenter learners from their preexisting assumptions and practices and to develop an intercultural identity through engagement with an additional culture" (2013: 28–29). In other words, learners are expected to actively *engage* in intercultural communication and *transform* or change themselves in the process. The significance of change and action will be returned to later in this chapter when we discuss intercultural citizenship education.

While all of the above perspectives are commensurable with Global Englishes approaches in ELT and intercultural education, none directly addresses ELF and intercultural/transcultural communication. However, a number of Global Englishes scholars have explicitly considered the links between these different areas. For instance, Hino and Oda (2015) developed a programme for Japanese university students that explored the diversity of English use around the world by making use of global English-language news sources from Asia, Africa, Europe, and the Anglosphere. Through this, students were introduced to both linguistic and cultural diversity in English use. According to Hino and Oda (2015) the programme developed students' intercultural awareness and a sense of identity as members of an international community, as well as being very positively evaluated by students and staff. Galloway (2013), also in a Japanese university, developed a programme in Global Englishes which, similar to Hino and Oda, underscored the diverse sociocultural contexts in which English is used and, crucially, incorporated elements of intercultural awareness. Again, like Hino and Oda, Galloway reported positive feedback from the students and greater understanding of diverse Englishes used for intercultural communication. More recently, Galloway and Rose (2018) and Rose and Galloway (2019) have outlined what they term a **Global Englishes Language Teaching (GELT)** approach which draws together many of the insights from ELF research in relation to ELT pedagogy. As regards intercultural communication, Galloway and Rose (2018: 4–5) suggest replacing fixed NES target cultures with fluid cultures and also viewing students' own cultures as a resource in communication. Similarly, in Chapter 13 we discussed the second author's successful introduction of EMF awareness into language teaching and English-medium instruction (EMI) (Ishikawa, 2020a). Another approach that also makes use of insights from Global Englishes research for ELT practices, but which emphasises the intercultural education dimensions to language teaching, is intercultural awareness (ICA), and we explain this in detail in the next section.

Summary

In this section, we have looked at current approaches to teaching culture and language. We have been critical of many of the materials and practices in ELT for adopting stereotyped and essentialist perspectives on culture. Although there is no single alternative approach, we have identified a number of principles for non-essentialist perspectives on culture, language, and intercultural communication in language teaching with which you should now be familiar. These were:

- expanding communicative competence to intercultural communicative competence (ICC) and awareness (ICA), pragmatic competence, and positive attitudes to difference and 'others'
- removing the 'native' speaker as a model and goal and replacing with the intercultural speaker and intercultural citizen
- a focus on processes of communication, not on linguistic products
- a critical approach to language, culture, and identity that challenges dominant established discourses
- the importance of local contexts and cultures
- recognising the global role of English as a multilingua franca and developing EMF awareness

Activity 15.2 Intercultural education and ELT

Read the quotations below concerning Global Englishes/ELF, intercultural education, and language teaching. Which one best matches your opinions about the choice of communities and cultures in ELT? Discuss your answers in a group if possible.

1. "Some people seem to think that ongoing research projects on language (English) as a lingua franca will result in people beginning to *teach* English as a lingua franca ... In my opinion, this is

very problematic ... We are dealing here with beneficial linguistic experiences and temporary models. But the ultimate aim (the decisive model) for language learning must be a variety (or several) used by native speakers – or near native speakers ... This is because it is important that the ultimate goal for learning is a language that functions as an everyday language in a language community" (Risager, 2007: 197).

2. "It could still be argued that the intercultural speaker of Elf (sic) does not need even this critical approach to British Studies, or the study of any other English-speaking country ... The advantage of focusing on an English-speaking country where English is the subject rather than the medium for other subjects, is that western – especially American and British – cultures are so dominant even where learners will have no need or opportunity to interact with native speakers, that a *critical* study of them and their relationship to learners' own is likely to be more beneficial than to ignore their presence" (Byram, 1997: 114–115).
3. "Given the vast number of ELF users who communicate with each other, it is hard to see the relevance of native speaker target-communities to their communicative practices ... ICA [intercultural awareness] does not deny that national cultures and 'native', 'other' and 'foreign' dichotomies may exist in participants' approaches to intercultural communication ... but it is necessary to recognise that equally they may not and to fully understand the complexity of intercultural communication it is necessary to go beyond such dichotomies" (Baker, 2011: 210).

Feedback: *The first two quotations represent more traditional approaches to culture and language in ELT, i.e., in learning a language you need to learn to use it in the same way as a 'native' speaker and so you should be familiar with the community and culture of those 'native' speakers, in this case US and British culture. However, as we have repeatedly discussed throughout this book, this is not an accurate representation of how English functions as a global language. Given that the majority of English use is by 'non-native' speakers of English outside of Anglophone countries, the relevance of making this the major focus of ELT is questionable, as highlighted in the third quotation. While we agree that learners of English may well have the goal of "a language that functions as an everyday language in a language community" (Risager, 2007: 197), the community or communities of English language users are highly varied. For most learners the most relevant communities of English users are likely to be a mixture of local and global communities (e.g., international students, business people, academics, tourists, professionals, and so forth), not Anglophone communities as conventionally defined.*

15.3 Intercultural awareness and pedagogy

The model of ICA explained in Chapter 14.4 was both an attempt to account for the knowledge, skills, and attitudes needed for successful intercultural and transcultural communication through Global Englishes and a model of intercultural development. As such, the different elements of the model can also be used to inform pedagogic practices. The application of ICA to teaching is organised around five strands: 1. exploring the complexity of local cultures; 2. exploring cultural representations in language-learning materials; 3. exploring cultural representations in the media and arts both in digital and 'traditional' mediums; 4. making use of cultural informants; and 5. engaging in intercultural communication both face-to-face and digitally (Baker, 2015: 195). However, we should stress that the five stands are not presented as a teaching methodology, nor is it proposed that all five will be relevant to all contexts. We suggest that the stands offer broad guidelines for teachers on incorporating intercultural and transcultural communication through Global Englishes into the language classroom. Nonetheless, the details of what to include and what aspects of the recommendations are relevant will depend on local settings and needs. The five strands are explained below.

1. **Exploring the complexity of local cultures.** Through an exploration of their own cultural backgrounds students learn about the diversity and complexity of cultural groupings in their own settings. In doing so students will begin to develop an awareness of the complexity of other cultures too, a crucial aspect of ICA. Even apparently monolingual and monocultural classes typically contain a degree of cultural and linguistic diversity around areas such as different heritage languages, religions, ethnicities, and family backgrounds. These explorations help students to understand that cultures are multi-voiced, and that cultural groupings operate at a range of scales from the local to the national and the global. It should also help to highlight how individuals are members of many different cultural groupings, not only a national culture. Approaches to this strand may include things such as class discussions and mini-ethnographic projects (Byram et al., 2017) describing local communities and cultural groups.
2. **Exploring cultural representations in language-learning materials.** As previously discussed in this chapter, teaching materials and especially textbooks are a central part of language teaching. Therefore, materials offer a prime medium for exploring culture and intercultural communication. However, as also previously highlighted, in ELT the presentation of culture

and the intercultural is frequently limited and essentialist. Yet, even stereotyped materials can be useful in developing ICA if approached critically. Students can explore images of their perceived own and other cultures in materials and consider how well (or not) they reflect their own understanding and experiences. They can also reflect on what has been included and what is missing and why this might be. Through these processes learners can develop the skills needed in ICA to make critical evaluations and comparisons of cultural representations, including their 'own' and 'other' cultures.

3. **Exploring cultural representations in the media and arts both in digital and 'traditional' mediums.** The arts, and particularly literature, have long been used in language teaching as a means of including cultural content of 'target' cultures (e.g., Kramsch, 1993) and recently more diverse, multilingual and multicultural settings (e.g., Kramsch, 2009). Cultural content can also be included from other media sources such as movies, television, radio, and magazines. This can be combined with parallel online digital sources such as news websites, blogs, and podcasts. All of these different mediums can be used to explore cultural content from both Anglophone and non-Anglophone settings that use English (e.g., BBC, Al-Jazeera, NHK) and develop students' awareness of the diverse global roles of English and its links to varied cultural settings (e.g., Hino & Oda, 2015). Furthermore, many online sources provide learners with examples of hybrid and fluid cultural forms and practices that are not connected to any one specific national culture and so can help develop higher levels of ICA. Again, as with materials, it is important that these representations of cultures are explored critically and not just accepted as presented.
4. **Making use of cultural informants.** Non-local and local English teachers with experience of 'other' cultures and intercultural communication can act as 'cultural informants', sharing their experiences and impressions with students. Non-local English teachers can share their own cultural background, provide 'outsider' perspectives on the students' cultures, where the students are in their local setting (i.e., the majority of school ELT classrooms), and discuss their experiences of intercultural communication. Similarly, local English teachers can discuss experiences of 'other' cultures and using English for intercultural communication. In more diverse classrooms (e.g., international language schools), students can act as cultural informants for each other. These experiences and impressions will necessarily be subjective and partial, but as long as they are recognised as

such they provide valuable first-hand accounts of culture and intercultural communication through Global Englishes.

5. **Engaging in intercultural communication both face-to-face and digitally**. Experience of intercultural and transcultural communication and reflection on that experience is a core part of developing ICA (as with EMF awareness in Chapter 13) and where possible should be integrated into language teaching. This can include study abroad and short-term student exchanges with the caveat that there is no need for these to take place in Anglophone settings. Any context where students will have the opportunity to use their English for intercultural communication is relevant. This can include Outer-Circle settings (Chapter 4.1), such as Singapore and Hong Kong, as well as international settings, such as large universities or language schools with diverse populations. In fact, we would argue that international settings (which can include but are not restricted to Anglophone contexts) are most relevant since they provide the multilingual and multicultural environments that are most significant to the development of ICA (see Humphreys & Baker, 2021). There may also be opportunities in the local environment to engage in intercultural communication, for example, in super-diverse urban centres with multilingual and multicultural populations or settings with large numbers of international tourists. However, physical exchanges are expensive and not all settings are diverse enough to provide local opportunities for intercultural communication. Alternative, more accessible experiences of intercultural communication can be brought directly into the classroom through telecollaborative virtual exchanges with language learners in other countries (e.g., O'Dowd, 2011). This can include basic asynchronous email exchanges, blogs, or text-based chat rooms, but also synchronous chat rooms, Voice over Internet Protocol (VoIP), and video, as well as combinations of these in social networking sites such as Facebook. As with EMF awareness, experiences of both face-to-face and digital intercultural and transcultural communication through English provide valuable opportunities to put the knowledge and skills of ICA into practice and develop them further. However, to fully develop ICA (as well as EMF awareness) it is important that space is given in the classroom to reflect on these experiences. Furthermore, even if opportunities for intercultural communication do not exist in the classroom or through exchanges, providing space for reflection allows students to bring their previous experiences to the class for discussion. Development through the stages of

> ICA is often a long-term process that is not necessarily smooth and linear (see Chapter 14.4). Learners need opportunities to explore and discuss their experiences and feelings and to adopt a critical approach to their experiences, considering what was more or less successful.
>
> (Adapted from Baker, 2015: 195–198)

Overall, these five strands provide suggestions for incorporating intercultural and transcultural communication through Global Englishes to develop ICA into classroom practices in a way that makes use of the resources already available in many settings. Depending on what is most relevant and accessible, teachers and students can utilise teaching materials and textbooks, mass media, the internet, the surrounding environment, and their own experiences. Underpinning all these approaches and uses of resources is the necessity for a critical perspective and space for discussion and reflection. While this may seem to be adding extra tasks and complexity to the already-busy language classroom, we would argue that in fact many of these resources are already used by teachers. What we are suggesting here is a more critical and systematic approach to how they are integrated into teaching to better prepare language learners for the use of Global Englishes in dynamic intercultural and transcultural scenarios. In particular, these five strands should help teachers avoid stereotypes and essentialism, as well as de-centre simplistic Anglophone representations of culture that will not be relevant in many contexts.

The relevance of ICA to ELT classrooms has been investigated through a number of empirical studies in a range of settings, including Baker (2012; 2015) in Thailand, Yu and Van Maele (2018) in China, Kusumaningputri and Widodo (2018) in Indonesia, Abdzadeh and Baker (2020) in Iran, and Humphreys and Baker (2021) in Japan. The first author of this book developed a ten-week online course in Global Englishes and intercultural communication/awareness for undergraduate English-language majors at a Thai university (Baker, 2012; 2015). Feedback from teachers and students was mainly very positive, particularly as regards including non-Anglophone cultures, suggesting the relevance and usefulness of Global Englishes and intercultural approaches to ELT. In terms of ICA development, most awareness was at levels 1 and 2 of the model, relating to an understanding of students' own culture and an ability to compare it with other cultures in both essentialist (level 1) and non-essentialist (level 2) ways. However, there was less evidence of the more complex and fluid understanding of culture and language associated with the highest levels of ICA, which may in part have been due to the short nature of the course. Yu and Van Maele (2018) undertook a study that integrated intercultural learning into an English reading course in a Chinese higher-education institution. The model of ICA was used to design the teaching flow and define learning goals. Yu and Van Maele's (2018) findings showed that the course had been successful in fostering cultural awareness at levels 1 and 2, but that more time and structured adjustments would be needed before learners could reach the final ICA level. Kusumaningputri and Widodo's (2018) study set in Indonesian university ELT classes used digital photograph-mediated intercultural tasks to promote students' critical intercultural awareness. Their findings indicated development of students' cultural and intercultural awareness including at more advanced ICA levels in which cultures and cultural identities were seen as fluid and adaptable (Kusumaningputri & Widodo 2018: 59).

Abdzadeh and Baker (2020), drawing on the first author's earlier study (Baker, 2012; 2015), report on a ten-session course focused on implementing and developing cultural awareness (CA) in an Iranian English-language classroom. As with earlier studies, the data suggested that the course aided in developing students' levels of ICA, moving from level 1 in the first half of the course towards level 2 in the second half. However, again similar to previous studies, there was no evidence of level 3 of ICA and, furthermore, due to the limited intercultural experiences of the students, level 3 was not incorporated into the pedagogic design. Nonetheless, the researchers conclude that the study "provides important empirical evidence illustrating the value of systematic instruction of CA [cultural awareness] in students' cultural learning" (Abdzadeh & Baker, 2020: 57). Humphreys and Baker (2021) made use of the ICA model to document intercultural development of Japanese students who took part in English-language short-term study-abroad (SA) programmes. Again, findings showed many students moving from level 1 of ICA to level 2 over the timeframe of the research due to their experiences of SA. While there was some evidence of level 3, it was not clear that it was due to SA rather than previous experience and it only occurred on a few occasions among a minority of students. Importantly, analysis of the findings underscored the significance of multicultural and multilingual SA programmes, typically with large numbers of other international students rather than NESs, for meaningful ICA development. In sum, current research indicates the relevance of ICA in both planning and implementing intercultural pedagogic approaches and as a measure of intercultural development. However, the findings suggest that development is more likely to occur between the lower levels of ICA and intercultural communication rather than at the more complex and dynamic higher levels of transcultural communication. This may be explained by both the basic levels of ICA that students typically demonstrate in these studies and the relatively short nature of many of the ELT programmes investigated.

15.4 Intercultural citizenship education and Global Englishes

The final approach we will consider in this section is **intercultural citizenship** (sometimes referred to as global citizenship and we will use the two terms interchangeably), which combines many of the previous elements of intercultural education, intercultural competence, and intercultural awareness. Intercultural and global citizenships are wide approaches to education in general, rather than specific to any one subject; however, we will argue that they are an especially relevant perspective for language education and Global Englishes in particular as explained below. Intercultural citizenship is conceived as an extension of citizenship that goes beyond national borders and recognises that we are globally connected in many different ways. Key features include responsibility to and participation in communities at a multitude of levels from the local, to the national and the global, with the need to respect and value diversity across these communities (Byram et al., 2017; Gaudelli, 2016; Killick, 2013). In relation to education, due to the influence of globalisation on almost all aspects of the curriculum, intercultural citizenship should be incorporated into all subject areas so that students can better understand and be fully prepared for a globally connected world (Gaudelli, 2016). Nonetheless, the 'foreign' language classroom is a particularly suitable setting to introduce global or intercultural citizenship education because of the focus on 'other' cultures, international connections, and intercultural communication (Byram et al., 2017; Porto et al., 2018). Within language education, Byram's (2008: 187) definition of intercultural citizenship education, below, has been very influential.

1. Causing/facilitating intercultural citizenship experience, and analysis and reflection on it and on the possibility of further social and/or political activity – i.e. activity which involves working with others to achieve an agreed end.
2. Creating learning/change in the individual: cognitive, attitudinal, behavioural change; change in self-perception; change in relationships with Others (i.e. people of a different social group); change that is based in the particular but is related to the universal.

As can be seen in this definition, action is an important part of intercultural citizenship education and language teaching. This is brought about through engagement in intercultural communities and experiences, which in turn leads to change in the individual and their relationships to 'others', resulting in positive action. Thus, intercultural citizenship education incorporates the awareness-raising of earlier accounts of ICC and ICA but further emphasises and extends the behavioural elements through change and action on the part of the student. Intercultural citizenship education is highly relevant to Global Englishes and ELT due to the connections between English and globalisation and its widespread use for intercultural and transcultural communication at multiple scales from the local to the global.

Intercultural citizenship is a new area of research in education in general and especially language education, although a small number of empirical studies are beginning to emerge. Research so far illustrates a range of conceptions of intercultural citizenship. These include 'neo-liberal' approaches which favour global connections for individual gains and networks of global elites (e.g., Aktas et al., 2017), and perspectives with a social justice or 'political' agenda (like Byram's above), which centre on fostering international and intercultural connections for community responsibility across borders and acceptance of diversity and difference (e.g., Byram et al., 2017; Porto et al., 2018), as well as differences based on location and level of education (see Han et al., 2017 in China; Sharkey, 2018 in the US).

To present an example in specific relation to Global Englishes, the first author of this book together with a colleague in China has undertaken a number of studies exploring the relationship between English, ELT, intercultural citizenship, and Chinese international students' experiences in Anglophone international universities (Fang & Baker, 2018; Baker & Fang, 2021). These studies showed that students often had very positive attitudes to intercultural citizenship education and developing an identity as an intercultural or global citizen. Yet, understanding of the concept was quite mixed and for some students was at a superficial level. They focused on essentialised national-level conceptualisations of culture, language, and identity. On the other hand, for other students, particularly those with more experience of studying abroad, many of the concepts associated with intercultural citizenship were familiar. They were able to discuss intercultural citizenship in relation to experiences of other cultures and countries, as well as their ability to use English for intercultural communication as part of a globally connected community. Significantly, many students perceived a strong link between English and intercultural citizenship. Some even equated proficiency in English with being an intercultural citizen due to viewing English as the de facto language for intercultural communication and connections, although a minority of students also viewed multilingualism (not just English) as important for developing intercultural connections and citizenship. However, findings clearly indicated that students' awareness and development of intercultural citizenship was not the result of formal education in ELT or elsewhere. No students reported any intercultural citizenship education, although there were some ad hoc experiences of intercultural communication courses. Students typically felt that ELT courses had not prepared them well for the intercultural aspects of studying abroad, and that this was something they had to work on outside the classroom. Unsurprisingly, given these findings, students wanted to have aspects of intercultural citizenship education incorporated into both general education and ELT.

In terms of how intercultural citizenship education can be implemented in the classroom, suggestions follow from and combine many of the approaches outlined in intercultural education. As already noted, intercultural citizenship is an area that influences all areas of the curriculum and so has implications for all subjects. For example, the higher-education scholar David Killick (2013) proposes that intercultural citizenship should be incorporated across the university curriculum in a consistent and systematic manner. In international universities, there are many opportunities to engage in intercultural interactions with students and staff from diverse backgrounds. Therefore, all students, both 'local' and 'international', should be required to "cross sociocultural boundaries" (Killick, 2013: 730) as part of their educational experience through course-based interactions. Similarly, the first author of this book has argued that given the transcultural nature of many universities, intercultural education and intercultural awareness should be a feature of all university programmes for all students (Baker, 2016). In sum, international universities should incorporate elements of intercultural education and encourage multilingual and multicultural group work across the curriculum in order to foster intercultural citizenship.

Again, as discussed above, due to its focus on other cultures and intercultural communication, language education provides the ideal setting in which to integrate intercultural citizenship education. For general language education this can include the five strands of ICA outlined previously (Baker, 2015) which provide students with the opportunity to both engage in intercultural interactions and to critically reflect on them. A commensurable approach is intercultural group work projects involving mini-ethnographies exploring linguistic and cultural complexity in local communities investigated by Byram et al. (2017). Importantly these mini-ethnographies directly address the aims of intercultural citizenship education by engaging learners in direct action through intercultural interactions with 'others' and 'other' communities. Together with opportunities for intercultural interactions, a critical approach to language should be adopted in the ELT classroom. Learners need time and space to consider the links between language learning/use, intercultural connections, and their identification with intercultural citizenship. Given the global uses of English as a multilingua franca where variability and adaptability are crucial for successful communication, students should be prepared for this multilingual and dynamic approach to using English. The perspectives outlined in ELF pedagogic research are highly relevant (e.g., Crowther & De Costa, 2017; Galloway & Rose, 2018; Rose & Galloway, 2019; Ishikawa, 2020a). These include exposing learners to different varieties and variable uses of English, engaging learners in discussions of who 'owns' English and what constitutes 'proficient' English use, and providing opportunities for learners to use English and other linguistic resources in a variable and adaptable manner. This also entails a move away from potentially negative 'native'-speaker orientations and goals towards an intercultural citizen as a more appropriate alternative model.

Finally, if teachers are expected to integrate intercultural citizenship and its relationship to language learning and use into their teaching practice, then it must be part of teacher education too. Teacher education programmes, both pre-service and in-service, need to incorporate intercultural citizenship education as a core strand in their aims and practices (Osler & Starkey, 2015; Gaudelli, 2016). Within ELT this needs to be combined with the critical approach to English language use outlined in relation to Global Englishes (e.g., Dewey, 2015; see Chapters 4, 8, 9). This perspective on teacher education in ELT also provides teachers with an opportunity to reflect on their own use of English and the development of an intercultural identity. Thus, intercultural citizenship, we argue, provides a meaningful and empowering alternative to the inappropriate model of the idealised NES as teacher.

Activity 15.3 Intercultural awareness in the language classroom

Look at the five areas identified below for developing ICA in the language classroom. Do you think that these are relevant or appropriate to teaching contexts you are familiar with (as a learner or a teacher)? Make notes, in small groups if possible, about how these could be applied to teaching contexts you are familiar with. Do you think there is anything missing from this list?

1. exploring local cultures
2. exploring language-learning materials
3. exploring cultural representations in the media and arts both in digital and 'traditional' mediums
4. cultural informants – non-local English teachers and local English teachers with experience in 'other' cultures
5. taking part in intercultural communication (either face-to-face or virtually)

Feedback: *You will have different answers to this activity depending on your experiences, setting, and opinions. However, we hope that* *you will have experienced some intercultural awareness education in the past. We also hope that some of these suggestions are relevant to your setting. Nonetheless, we also think it is unlikely that all of the five strands are relevant to you, and that there may be things missing from these suggestions.*

15.5 Conclusion and summary: Towards transcultural education

As we have seen throughout this chapter, and this book, the processes of learning and using another language and especially English are inevitably intercultural. It is, therefore, essential that if ELT is to prepare learners for the use of English as a global multilingua franca for intercultural and transcultural communication, intercultural education becomes a core part of pedagogic practices. However, current approaches within ELT are typically ad hoc and superficial with essentialist representations of national cultures and languages. Such stereotyped views of culture and language are as likely to hinder intercultural communication as to help it. Nonetheless, there are alternative approaches, as discussed in this chapter, that more meaningfully incorporate the intercultural aspects of language learning and use. The differences between 'traditional' ELT (to borrow a term from Galloway and Rose, 2018) and more **transculturally orientated ELT**, or **transcultural ELT**, are summarised in Table 15.1.

Table 15.1 Towards transcultural English language education

Traditional ELT	*Transcultural ELT*
National-scale Standard Language ideologies with national language varieties associated with national cultural characterisations	A critical approach to language, culture, and identity that challenges dominant established discourses and recognises the global role of English as a multilingua franca for transcultural communication across and through borders
Communicative competence with a focus on linguistic and grammatical competence	Intercultural communicative competence (ICC) and awareness (ICA) including pragmatic competence and fostering positive attitudes to difference and 'others'
Native-speaker models	The intercultural speaker and intercultural citizen as models
Focus on linguistic products, such as grammar, vocabulary, and pronunciation	Focus on processes of communication and adaptable use of communicative resources including English as a multilingua franca (EMF) awareness
Anglophone methodologies and approaches	Adapting teaching to local contexts and cultures

We focused in detail on two approaches that adopted many of these principles, which were intercultural awareness (ICA) in the classroom and intercultural citizenship education. Although both of these approaches are relatively new, classroom-based research has shown them to be practical and positively received by students and teachers. Through such innovative perspectives on language, culture, and communication in teaching, we believe that ELT can move towards a transcultural stance that will better prepare users of Global Englishes for the diversity and richness of transcultural communication.

In sum, in this book we have set out to illustrate and explore how the use of English as a global multilingua franca for transcultural communication influences our thinking about language, communication, identity, community, culture, learning, and teaching. We began with an outline of core issues in understanding culture, language, and Global Englishes. This entailed a consideration of how we characterise culture and an emphasis on culture as dynamic, varied, and contestable. We also examined the relationship between culture, nations, and globalisation. We highlighted the problems with cultural stereotypes, generalisations, and essentialism. We then turned to the relationship between culture and language, suggesting that they should be viewed as two closely connected but separable concepts. We provided examples of the multitude of different cultural practices and references constructed through global uses of English. We also introduced the ideas of linguistic and cultural flows and of linguistic and cultural repertoires and resources. Next we presented information about global languages in relation to their numbers of L1 speakers, their total numbers of speakers, and geography. We underscored that English is just one of a number of global languages in a multilingual world, and yet the most prominent lingua franca among people with diverse L1, including English. We predicted that it will stay as the world's lingua franca across domains of use, inviting us to question customary concepts, such as target speech community and target culture. We then zoomed in on Global Englishes and different conceptions of them, World Englishes (WE) and English as a lingua franca (ELF), and weighed up the advantages and disadvantages of these different perspectives. We observed that both fields take notice of adaptability of the language, but that the former takes a more nationalistic or a locally minded approach while the latter considers contact among English speakers, typically multilinguals, at a global scale.

In the second part of this book we moved on to more complex and critical approaches to culture, language, and Global Englishes. This started with a contrast between the essentialist approaches of cross-cultural communication research and the more critical perspectives of intercultural communication research. We looked at a number of contemporary approaches to understanding intercultural groupings. We then turned to identity, language, and Global Englishes, adopting a perspective on identity that views it as constructed, multiple, and contestable. We discussed the relationships between identity, difference, and othering. We focused in on the concept of cultural identity as particularly relevant to Global Englishes and transcultural communication. Next we explored the language ideologies surrounding Global Englishes, including native-speakerism, monolingualism, and Standard English, and connected these to ideologies of authenticity and anonymity. Through real-life examples and theoretical discussion, we identified the intricacies of native-speakerism, which entails a number of intertwined fallacies, including méconnaissance or 'ignorant misrecognition' in social experience. We then considered one of the core issues in this book, multilingualism in Global Englishes, and introduced the notion of English as a multilingua franca (EMF) in detail. We also discussed mobile multilingual resources and dynamic multilingual repertoires in the light of multilingualism in EMF. We concluded that multilingualism is observable in *all* global encounters among English users, however covert it may be and without regard to an individual's ability in other languages.

The third part of this book dealt with a range of important contemporary issues and domains in culture, language, and Global Englishes. We started with an exploration of the 'trans' turn in applied linguistics and education research more generally and related this specifically to Global Englishes. This involved a consideration of translanguaging, other contemporary 'trans' perspectives such as transmodality and transculturality, and their relationship to EMF. In line with 'trans' theories, especially translanguaging, we argued for the importance of multilingual, transcultural, and transmodal accommodation to facilitate global communication. We then focused on the relevance of 'trans' perspectives to intercultural communication and provided a detailed outline of another core notion for this book, transcultural communication. This involved a discussion of the move from intercultural communication to transcultural communication, as well as reflection on related notions such as transculturality. We followed this with a reflection on the implications for transcultural education and applied linguistics. We concluded by linking transcultural communication and Global Englishes. We then moved on to one of the most significant newly emerging domains of Global Englishes and transcultural communication use and research, digital communication. We provided a characterisation of digital communication and linked it to multilingualism and Global Englishes. We then looked at digital communication and intercultural/transcultural communication. We also dealt with the important area of social media and social networking sites. Last, we discussed language, identity, and culture through digital transcultural communication. Next we outlined complexity theory in detail as an important current metatheory for understanding many of the approaches taken in the book. We specifically related complexity theory to global communication, Standard English, communicative competence, and language attitudes and awareness. We stressed the situated, emergent nature of communication processes as envisaged by complexity theory and suggested taking a more coherent, holistic approach to considering global communication.

In the fourth and final section we explored the implications of transcultural communication and Global Englishes for teaching and learning culture, language, and Global Englishes. We started with the need for an awareness of 'English-within-multilingualism'. This involved moving from a monolingual construct to multilingual, translanguaging, transcultural, and transmodal reality. We overviewed social representations of English and their implications for language attitudes. We then introduced the notion of EMF awareness and related this to the educational domains of EMI and ELT. We argued that EMF awareness can bridge the convenient fiction of Standard English in ELT with the multilingual reality while integrating attitudinal motivation, cognitive or notional understanding, and communication experience. Next we proposed a reconsideration of the core concept of communicative competence in both language education and intercultural communication. We discussed the move from communicative competence to intercultural communicative competence (ICC) and introduced current alternatives to both these notions. We concluded with a detailed account of intercultural awareness (ICA) in pedagogy as the most relevant conception for transcultural communication through Global Englishes. In the final chapter, already discussed above, we turned our attention to intercultural language education and Global Englishes, and in particular intercultural awareness, intercultural citizenship education, and ELT. We finished by introducing the idea of transcultural ELT and we hope that this book will itself provide an initial example of such a transcultural approach.

Note

1 www.coe.int/en/web/common-european-framework-reference-languages (accessed 30 September 2020).

Further reading

Baker, W. (2015). *Culture and identity through English as a lingua franca: Rethinking concepts and goals in intercultural communication*. Berlin: De Gruyter Mouton. Chapters six and seven discuss intercultural education and ELF, explore the relevance of ICA to teaching, and report on a study of ICA in a Thai university setting.

Baker, W. & Fang, F. (G.) (2018). From English language learners to intercultural citizens: Chinese student sojourners' development of intercultural citizenship in ELT and EMI programmes. *British Council ELT Research Papers*, *18*(4). Retrieved from www.teachingenglish.org.uk/article/english-language-learners-intercultural-citizens (accessed 30 September 2020). An empirical study of Chinese international students before, during, and after study abroad in the UK. This paper draws together intercultural citizenship education, Global Englishes, and ELT.

Rose, H. & Galloway, N. (2019). *Global Englishes for language teaching*. Cambridge: Cambridge University Press. The book provides an overview of the GELT approach that includes a number of the themes recommended here, as well as practical suggestions about how this approach can be investigated in the classroom.

Glossary

Accommodation

Adjusting and adapting communication (including language, communication strategies, multimodality) to your interlocutor and situation. See also **linguistic accommodation**.

Additional language

An individual's language other than their L1. See also **first language(s) (L1)** and **second language(s) (L2)**.

Anonymity/the ideology of anonymity

In the case of language, especially "hegemonic languages in modern society" (Woolard, 2016: 25), this ideology assumes that authority resides in their perceived neutrality and universality as belonging to everyone, not as the belongings of a limited group of speakers. It dictates that there are desirable languages 'out there' for everyone to aim for and 'own' across communicative contexts. See also **authenticity/the ideology of authenticity**.

Applied linguistics

"The theoretical and empirical investigation of real-world problems in which language is a central issue" (Brumfit, 1995: 27).

Authenticity/the ideology of authenticity

In the case of language, this ideology is concerned with how local and vernacular (i.e., associated with a particular group of speakers) a given language or language variety is for it to be real and true. To borrow Woolard's words, "[w]ithin this logic, a speech variety must be perceived as deeply rooted in social and geographic territory in order to have value" (2016: 22). See also **anonymity/the ideology of anonymity**.

Code-switching

Individuals switching or changing between different linguistic 'codes' (languages and language varieties) during an interaction. Examples include US lawyers' strategic switch between African American Vernacular English (AAVE) and 'standard' North American English (Fuller, 1993; Hobbs, 2003).

Codification

Documenting local linguistic features "in a grammar, a lexical or pronouncing dictionary, course books or any other type of reference manual" (Bamgboṣe, 1998: 4) with the help of corpus data. See also **corpus**.

Communicative competence

The linguistic and grammatical competence needed for successful communication, which may also include sociocultural features. Such models of communication are problematic for Global Englishes and intercultural/transcultural communication as they are based on an idealised 'native' speaker and imagined homogeneous 'native'-speaker speech community (Chomsky, 1965; Hymes, 1972; Canale & Swain, 1980).

Communicative contexts

The situations in which communication takes place, i.e., who interactants are, how they are interacting, in what circumstances, and for what purposes.

Communities of practice

Used to describe groupings in non-essentialist terms with a focus on practices in which people come together around 'mutual engagement' in a 'joint endeavour' and in the process develop 'shared repertoires' (Wenger, 1998).

Complex adaptive system (CAS)

A 'system' in which the interaction of individual components or features gives rise to the emergence of more complex aggregate patterns which cannot be reduced or explained according to the individual features. Culture and language, for example, can both be viewed as CASs.

Complexity theory

It is about autonomous complex adaptive systems (CASs), or emergent and ever-changing 'systems', influencing each other in accordance with a diachronically and synchronically variable ecology (e.g., Larsen-Freeman, 1997; 2018). See also **complex adaptive system (CAS)**.

Contact zones

"[S]ocial spaces where disparate cultures meet, clash, and grapple with each other, often in highly asymmetrical relations of domination and subordination" (Pratt, 2008: 7).

Corpus

A large collection of naturally occurring spoken and written texts, e.g., ACE (Asian Corpus of English). https://corpus.eduhk.hk/ace/

Covert multilingual resources

"[T]he influence of the user's multilingual resources on their communication, which nonetheless remains in English ... on the surface" (Cogo, 2018: 358). See also **multilingual resources**.

Cross-cultural communication

The study of the communicative practices of distinct cultural groups independent from interaction (e.g., Japanese communicative practices versus German communicative practices). Comparisons between cultures are typically at the national level. This approach has been criticised for being stereotyped and essentialist.

Cultural identity

Key aspects of cultural identity are race, ethnicity, and nationality. It may also involve identification with diverse groups such as local 'small cultures' (e.g., families, friends), regional, heritage, and diasporic groups, and other globally connected groups (e.g., professions). Cultural identities often involve a complex mix of all these different groups and scales. See also **interculturality**.

Cultural stereotypes

These typically link cultures and nations together and then ascribe a set of stereotyped beliefs, values, and behaviours to all individuals 'within' that culture. These hinder rather than help intercultural communication since nation is just one level of culture and such an ascription ignores both the many other different scales of culture and individual variability within any cultural group. See also **stereotypes**.

Culture

First, culture can be seen as a system of shared products, symbols, discourses, practices, and ideologies among groups of people. Second, these shared products, symbols, discourses, practices, and ideologies and the groupings of people themselves that make up culture are contestable and sites of struggle. Third, the people and shared products, symbols, discourses, practices, and ideologies that make up cultures are constantly in process and changing and hence cannot be fixed and have no clear boundaries.

De facto official language

A language used virtually as a national or regional official language but not established by law. See also the **de jure official language**.

De jure official language

A language established as a national or regional official language by law. See also the **de facto official language**.

Digital communication

"[I]nteractions between people that are mediated by digital communications technology (tools which transmit information in digital form). In practice, this means communication over the internet or GSM (Global System for Mobile Communications, through which SMS text messages are sent), via a range of devices, including desktop computers, laptops, notebooks, tablets and smartphones; and on various media (Facebook, Twitter, Wikipedia)" (Tagg, 2015: 5).

Discourse

Ways of thinking, talking, and writing about particular domains. For instance, we can discuss the discourse of 'gender' or 'education' or 'globalisation'. While discourse and language are closely linked, it is important to stress that they are not the same. So the same discourse can be expressed in many different languages.

Domains (of language use)

Purposes for which languages are used, such as academia, business, and international organisations.

Electronically mediated intercultural communication (EMIC)

The use of multimodal, multilingual, multicultural, and mobile resources in transcultural, translingual, and transmodal digital communication processes (Sangiamchit, 2018; Baker & Sangiamchit, 2019).

English as a foreign language (EFL)

It takes a geographically bounded approach to the English used by Anglophones in association with the English learnt as a school subject and in a context where English is not used or spoken in daily life.

English as an international language (EIL)

Descriptions of global uses of English including English in Kachru's (1992) Expanding Circle. Unlike ELF research there is a focus on describing varieties of English; "once it is (tacitly) decided that English is used, more than one variety of English is often represented in such situations because each speaker brings a variety that he or she is most familiar with" (Matsuda & Friedrich, 2012: 18).

English as a lingua franca (ELF)

"[A]ny use of English among speakers of different first languages for whom English is the communicative medium of choice, and often the only option" (Seidlhofer, 2011: 7; emphasis removed). This includes L1 English speakers. It also includes multilingual speakers of the same L1 (Ishikawa, 2017a: 38).

English as a multilingua franca (EMF)

"Multilingual communication in which English is available as a contact language of choice, but is not necessarily chosen" (Jenkins, 2015b: 73).

English medium instruction (EMI)

The teaching and learning of academic content through English, most often in higher education. It usually refers to settings where English is not the L1 of the institution or setting (i.e., non-Anglophone contexts) but can also refer to international programmes in Anglophone settings where participants (staff and students) have a large variety of L1.

English similect

The contact language between an L1 and English as an additional language within individual minds (Mauranen, 2012). See also **second-order language contact**.

Essentialism

"[P]resuming that there is a universal essence, homogeneity and unity in a particular culture" (Holliday et al., 2017: 1). Essentialist perspectives on culture view it as a physical entity or thing, associate it with a particular place, typically a nation, see the world as divided into different and exclusive cultures with people belonging to only one culture, and believe that culture is the cause and explanation for people's behaviour (Holliday et al., 2017: 3–4). See also **cultural stereotypes**.

Expanding Circle

Countries in which English is used for international communication but does not have an internal role or variety status in Kachru's (1992) three-circles model, e.g., Brazil, China, and Germany. This conception of Expanding Circle uses of English is challenged by ELF researchers. See also **English as a lingua franca (ELF)**.

First language(s) (L1)

People's strongest languages that they learn to speak as children. With more L1 speakers, languages are not just likely to survive in the future, but also likely to have an influence on global communication.

Folk linguistics

A sociolinguistic approach which regards everyone as a folk, whether linguists or non-linguists, and aims to explore people's evaluative repertoires formed and expressed through everyday life (Niedzielski & Preston, 1999/2003; Preston, 2018b).

Global Englishes

The use and users of English outside of the Anglophone world, although Anglophone settings are still included when English is used for intercultural communication. In research it is an umbrella term covering the fields of World Englishes (WE), English as an international language (EIL), and English as a lingua franca (ELF).

Global English language teaching (GELT)

"An approach to English language education that addresses the implications of Global Englishes" (Galloway & Rose, 2015: 254).

Globalisation

Defined as "the spread of transplanetary ... connections between people. From this perspective, globalisation involves reductions in barriers to transworld social contacts. People become more able – physically, legally, linguistically, culturally and psychologically – to engage with each other wherever on earth they might be" (Scholte, 2008: 1478).

Global lingua franca

A lingua franca or a common language at a global scale. English is the currently most prominent global lingua franca among people with diverse L1, including English. See also **lingua franca**.

Identity

A process of orientating towards or being associated with social and cultural groups. In applied linguistics identity is seen as a process rather than a fixed, unitary product or 'thing' and identities are typically described as multiple, negotiable, and contested. Language is viewed as a core aspect of constructing and representing identity. See also **subjectivity/the self**.

Ideologies

Taken-for-granted ideas and beliefs circulating in society to varying extents. These ideas and beliefs often connote moral or political values (e.g., 'right', 'proper', 'standard'). See also **language ideologies**.

Indexical function of language

The nature of language to represent who speakers are. See also the **referential function of language**.

Inner Circle

The original Anglophone countries in Kachru's (1992) three-circles model, e.g., the US, the UK, and Australia.

Intercultural awareness (ICA)

"[A] conscious understanding of the role culturally based forms, practices and frames of reference can have in intercultural communication, and an ability to put these conceptions into practice in a flexible and context specific manner in communication" (Baker, 2015: 163). There is a focus on intercultural and transcultural communication through Global Englishes.

Intercultural citizenship

An extension of citizenship that goes beyond national borders and recognises that we are globally connected in many different ways. Key features include responsibility to and participation in communities at a multitude of levels, from the local to the national and the global, with the need to respect and value diversity across these communities (Byram et al., 2017; Gaudelli, 2016; Killick, 2013). Sometimes also referred to as global citizenship.

Intercultural citizenship education

"[1] causing/facilitating intercultural citizenship experience, and analysis and reflection on it and on the possibility of further social and/or political activity – i.e. activity which involves working with others to achieve an agreed end; [2] creating learning/change in the individual: cognitive, attitudinal, behavioural change; change in self-perception; change in relationships with Others (i.e. people of a different social group); change that is based in the particular but is related to the universal" (Byram, 2008: 187).

Intercultural communication

As a research field it is the study of the communicative practices of distinct cultural or other groups in interaction with each other (e.g., Italians communicating with English). It is communication where cultural and linguistic differences are perceived as relevant to the interaction by participants and/or researchers (Zhu, 2014; 2019; Baker, 2015).

Intercultural communicative competence (ICC)

It adds an intercultural dimension to communicative competence. The intercultural dimension includes: attitudes (savoir être), knowledge (savoirs), skills of interpreting and relating (savoir comprendre), skills of discovery and interaction (savoir apprendre/faire), and critical cultural awareness/political education (savoir s'engager) (Byram, 1997). See also **communicative competence**.

Intercultural competence

The knowledge, skills, and attitudes needed to successfully engage in intercultural communication through an L1. Often distinguished from intercultural communicative competence, which involves the use of an L2. See also **intercultural communicative competence (ICC)**.

Interculturality

A focus on how culture and cultural identities are negotiated and constructed in intercultural interactions. It avoids pre-established assumptions about cultural identifications (Zhu, 2019).

Intercultural language education

The integration of culture, language, and the intercultural in language education in recognition that additional language learning is "fundamentally engagement in intercultural communication" (Liddicoat & Scarino, 2013: 6).

Intranational lingua franca

A lingua franca or a common language within a nation. This can be a national language. Also, it can simultaneously be a lingua franca beyond the nation. See also **lingua franca**.

Language attitudes

While lacking a widely agreed definition, they may be defined "as being identified with a reservoir of evaluative dispositional concepts, directed to a linguistic phenomenon as interpreted through social experience, and underlying observable responses which are constructed situationally" (Ishikawa, 2017b: 243).

Language awareness

"[E]xplicit knowledge about language, and conscious perception and sensitivity in language learning, language teaching and language use" (ALA, n.d.). https://lexically.net/ala/la_defined.htm.

Language-culture nexus

An account of how languages and cultures come together and can also be separated. This can be linguistic flows (e.g., English language), linguacultural flows (L1 use of particular languages associated with the culture in which they are learnt and used), discursive flows (meaning not related to a particular language), and other non-linguistic cultural flows (e.g., music, images) (Risager, 2012: 111; 2020: 120–121). Thus, how particular languages and cultural practices come together is always an empirical question that must be investigated in each instance of communication and cannot be taken for granted. See also **linguistic and cultural flows**.

Language ideologies

Ideologies of language, such as those of native-speakerism (Holliday, 2006; 2018), monolingualism (Blackledge, 2000), and Standard English (Milroy & Milroy, 2012). They usually stem from the social status of language users. As Milroy puts it, "it is not difficult to argue that varieties of language do not actually have prestige in themselves: these varieties acquire prestige when their *speakers* have high prestige" (2001: 532; original emphasis). See also **ideologies**, **native-speakerism/the ideology of native-speakerism**, **monolingualism/monolingual ideology**, **Standard English**, and **Standard English ideology**.

Language varieties

Various local types of languages or dialects with their own conventions of language use. Unlike some uses of the word *dialect*, there is no connotation of being 'provincial' and 'vulgar'. Language changes over time, and develops into different types through mutual interaction from generation to generation (e.g., Gumperz,

2009). Generally speaking, it takes three or more generations for established language varieties to emerge (Mauranen, 2012).

Languaging

The situated act of exerting the meaning potential of linguistic and other semiotic resources to understand and interact with the world.

Lingua franca

A common or shared language among people with diverse L1.

Linguistic accommodation

Adjusting and adapting language use to your interlocutor and situation.

Linguistic and cultural flows

Used to describe the manner in which languages and cultures spread across each other in networks of linguistic and cultural *flows* and come together in variable and complex ways and combinations. Through these flows, cultural and linguistic practices are adapted and changed by their use in different local, but globally connected, contexts and so are in constant processes of transformation (Risager, 2006; Pennycook, 2007). See also the **language-culture nexus** and **transcultural flows**.

Linguistic boundaries

Ideologically imagined border lines between different named languages. As such no one can actually delineate what these boundaries are like.

Linguistic relativity

In its strong form the idea that our language forms our complete culture and worldview. In its weak form the idea that our language influences (but does not limit) how we perceive the world. Both forms propose a strong link between culture and language. Also sometimes referred to as the Sapir-Whorf hypothesis (Whorf, 1939).

Linguistic repertoire

The totality of individually available linguistic resources. See also **linguistic resources**.

Linguistic resources

The different 'bits' of languages that an individual may have acquired or have access to. This does not necessarily correspond to the acquisition of named languages and can result in fragmented, incomplete, or 'truncated' linguistic repertories (Blommaert, 2010). See also **linguistic repertoire**.

Méconnaissance

Bourdieu's (1977) term referring to citizens' 'ignorant misrecognition' through social conditioning (Ishikawa, 2020b). In relation to language, it refers to the situation in which the public fail to recognise the social, historical trajectory of the authority of dominant language use and instead 'recognise' authority as intrinsic in the language use itself.

Metatheory
A theory about theories or notions (e.g., Larsen-Freeman, 2017). As such, it conjoins theories or notions which refer directly to the empirical world.

Monolingualism/monolingual ideology
This ideology imposes the universal value of perceived monolingual thinking and performance on the part of Anglophone speakers even though they are not necessarily monolingual (e.g., Blackledge, 2000). It interprets learning additional languages as the acquisition of one bounded language after another with an individual's multilingual background held in abeyance.

Multi-competence
"[T]he knowledge of more than one language in the same mind" (Cook, 2002: 10).

Multicultural
A grouping or scenario in which participants who are identified with more than one culture are present. This is distinct from multiculturalism. See also **multiculturalism**.

Multiculturalism
A perspective that focuses on different cultural groups existing alongside each other within a society or nation, e.g., South Asian communities in the UK.

Multilanguaging
In the ELF field it refers to linguistic development through accommodation to multilingual English users (Jenkins, 2015b). More precisely, it is the act of learning "to engage in the dynamic exploitation of previously unfamiliar linguistic resources by adapting to a multilingual environment" (Ishikawa, 2017a: 38).

Multilingualism
Knowledge and use of different languages. For individual language users equal proficiency in all languages is not expected and different languages may be used for distinct purposes. In society different languages may be recognised to different degrees in official policies and practices (e.g., schooling, linguistic landscapes).

Multilingual repertoire
The totality of individually available multilingual resources or resources which are associable with multiple named languages. See also **multilingual resources**.

Multilingual resources
The different 'bits' of multiple languages that an individual may simultaneously have acquired or have access to. These recourses are not always categorisable into one particular language. Due to globalisation our linguistic resources become increasingly associable with different languages.

Multilingual, transcultural, and transmodal accommodation
Adjusting and adapting the way we use meaning-making resources and modes according to the situation (Ishikawa, 2021, in press). This entails our conscious understanding of linguistic and cultural roles and effects on interaction as well

as meaning-making affordances beyond language. It also entails our flexible, situationally appropriate interactional practices based on this understanding. The assumption is that we keep the motivational attitudes in these practices, or, put differently, positive feelings and curiosity towards accommodation.

Multimodality

This involves the full range of communication forms or modes for understanding communication and representation. Modes are defined as: "a socially shaped and culturally given resource for meaning making. *Image, writing, layout, music, gesture, speech, moving image, soundtrack* are examples of modes used in representation and communication" (Kress, 2014/2017: 60; original emphasis).

Native (English) speakers

They are considered to be indigenous L1 speakers of the language. This concept itself is questionable, especially in relation to a global lingua franca, which, by definition, is not concerned with particular geographical regions. See also **first language(s) (L1)**.

Native-speakerism/the ideology of native-speakerism

"Native-speakerism is an ideology that upholds the idea that so-called 'native speakers' are the best models and teachers of English because they represent a 'Western culture' from which spring the ideals both of English and of the methodology for teaching it" (Holliday, 2018: 1151).

Non-linear

Not fully predictable from the analysis of any antecedents (Jenkins, 2015b; Larsen-Freeman, 2018)..

Non-native (English) speakers

They are considered not to be indigenous to the language no matter how proficient they may be in the language. See also **native (English) speakers**.

Othering

The process by which we differentiate and distinguish ourselves from 'others' in order to identify with particular groups. This is an inevitable part of identity construction but can lead to stereotyping and essentialism.

Outer Circle

Countries which have developed 'new' varieties of English in Kachru's (1992) three-circles model, largely in post-colonial settings, e.g., Indian English, Kenyan English, and Malaysian English.

Perceptual dialectology

This sociolinguistics research method asks respondents "to label maps [in their own way] with where different dialects are spoken, or to rate various areas (e.g. each state in the US) on how 'correct' and 'pleasant' the language spoken there is" (Lindemann, 2005: 189). The respondents rely on their own perception, but still have to respond geographically.

Performative competence
It deals with translingual communication and fluid cultural groupings in 'contact zones'. A focus is placed on *how* not *what* of intercultural communication (process and performance) as a dynamic contextually based competence (Canagarajah, 2013).

Pragmatic competence
Use of pragmatic and other communicative strategies in ELF communication. Accommodation is an overarching strategy underpinned by cooperative disposition. Strategies include clarification, self-repair, repetition, reformulation or paraphrasing, translation, 'let it pass', code-switching, and translanguaging (Jenkins et al., 2011; Cogo & Dewey, 2012).

Referential function of language
The role of language to deliver, or refer to, what speakers have to say. See also the **indexical function of language**.

Second language(s) (L2)
An individual's first additional language (i.e., L1, L2, L3 …) or all additional languages as commonly used in the field of second-language acquisition. See also **additional language** and **first language(s) (L1)**.

Second-order language contact
Similects (or contact languages at the cognitive level) are contacting each other during interaction, e.g., contact between French and Korean English similects (Mauranen, 2012). See also **English similect**.

Semiotic resources
Meaning-making cues, signs, and symbols with the linguistic as a prime example.

Semiotics
Under the semiotic approach culture is conceived as primarily made up of learned patterns of meaning expressed symbolically: culture "denotes an historically transmitted pattern of meanings embodied in symbols, a system of inherited conceptions expressed in symbolic forms by means of which men communicate, perpetuate, and develop their knowledge about and attitudes toward life" (Geertz, 1973/2000: 89).

Small cultures
Cultures as constructed between small groups of people (e.g., families, classrooms, work places) through shared practices and discourses. A less essentialist and stereotyped perspective than national cultural scales (Holliday, 1999; 2011).

Social networking site (SNS)
"A networked communication platform in which participants 1) have uniquely identifiable profiles that consist of user-supplied content, content provided by other users, and/or system-provided data; 2) can publicly articulate connections that can be viewed and traversed by others; and 3) can consume, produce, and/or interact with streams of user-generated content provided by their connections on the site" (Ellison & Boyd, 2013: 158; emphasis removed).

Sociolinguistics

As its name shows, it enquires into the relationship between language and society; how language functions in different societies and social relationships.

Speech community

A geographical place for a language variety to be used among the population. Each language variety is supposed to have its primary speech community. See also **language varieties**.

Standard English

It is the abstract form of an English variety which is dominant and thus labelled as 'standard' in a country or state (e.g., Milroy & Milroy, 2012). According to Widdowson (1994: 381), its grammar and spelling are most attentively protected for communal, rather than communicative, purposes. Standard English in English language teaching (ELT) is further abstracted and idealised, based on the intuitions of materials writers who are typically 'white', middle-class Anglophones, and is different from the English they actually use for themselves (Leung, 2005; Hall, 2013). See also **Standard English ideology**.

Standard English ideology

It asserts "that a national standard language [in the Inner Circle, or, more narrowly, in the US and the UK] should be valid not only within a particular country but globally" as a variety with "a special and privileged status" (Seidlhofer, 2011: 42–43). See also **Standard Language ideology**.

Standard Language ideology

"[A] bias toward an abstracted, idealized, homogen[e]ous" model, derived from the linguistic practices of the upper-middle class, which is "imposed and maintained by dominant bloc institutions" in countries or states (Lippi-Green, 2012: 67). The identification of any 'standard' "will be a matter of institutional expediency", not a matter of linguistic quality (Seidlhofer, 2011: 46). See also **Standard English ideology**.

Stereotypes

Beliefs about a group of people not based on any personal experience or an over-generalisation based on a small amount of knowledge or experience. Stereotypes tend to be self-perpetuating in that people look for information that confirms their stereotype and ignore information that does not fit their stereotype.

Subjectivity/the self

"[S]ubjectivity focuses on the ways in which the self is formed through the use of language and other symbolic systems, both intrapersonally and interpersonally" (Kramsch, 2009: 25). This is distinct from identity, which focuses on identification with external social or cultural groups. However, the distinction is often blurred in both practice and research.

Symbolic competence

Emphasis on multilingualism, critical reflexive perspectives on culture and language. Competence is "dynamic, flexible, and locally contingent" (Kramsch, 2009: 199).

Target culture

The culture with which we expect to familiarise ourselves. See also **culture**.

Target speech community

The speech community in which we expect to participate. See also **speech community**.

Third places/spaces

From this perspective, cultural references and practices in intercultural communication are seen as occupying a space in between cultures but not the same as, or fixed to, any one culture (Kramsch, 1993; Bhabha, 1994).

Transcultural communication

"[C]ommunication where interactants move through and across, rather than in-between, cultural and linguistic boundaries, thus, 'named' languages and cultures can no longer be taken for granted and in the process borders become blurred, transgressed and transcended" (Baker & Sangiamchit, 2019: 472).

Transcultural competence

The knowledge, skills, and attitudes needed to successfully engage in transcultural communication. See also **intercultural awareness (ICA)** and **transcultural communication**.

Transcultural education

"Transcultural approaches encompass the creation of culturally inclusive teaching and learning environments at the level of the classroom, in curriculum design and pedagogical approaches, through to epistemological plurality of the knowledge base" (Ryan, 2011: 635).

Transcultural English language teaching (ELT)/transculturally oriented ELT

An approach to English language education that incorporates the implications of intercultural and transcultural communication practices and research.

Transcultural flows

Used to describe the relationship between culture and globalisation in which cultural practices and products move around the globe. Also referred to as transnational flows (Risager, 2006). See also **linguistic and cultural flows**.

Transculturality

A multidisciplinary approach that encompasses a wide range of perspectives but generally focuses on how individuals or groups cut across and through cultural borders and create new cultural spaces (similar to third places), e.g., hybridised and adapted cultural practices of diasporic and immigrant communities.

Translanguaging

"[T]he fluid and dynamic practices that transcend the boundaries between named languages, language varieties, and language and other semiotic systems" (Li, 2018: 9). It is also a 'practical theory of language' that views language as "a multilingual, multisemiotic, multisensory, and multimodal resource that human beings use for thinking and for communicating thought" (Li, 2018: 26).

Translanguaging space

"[A] space that is created by and for Translanguaging practices, and a space where language users break down the ideologically laden dichotomies between the macro and the micro, the societal and the individual, and the social and the psychological through interaction" (Li, 2018: 23).

Transmodality/transmodal communication

The processes whereby a range of modes are used simultaneously, with boundaries between modes blurring, and useful distinctions among modes not easily made. See also **multimodality**.

Transnational

The investigation of the relationships between cultures, nations, and globalisation in which national boundaries become more porous and blurred.

Trans theories/the trans turn

A group of more recent theories and perspectives in applied linguistics, sociolinguistics, and social sciences such as the transnational, transcultural, translocal, transpatial, transmodal, and translingual or translanguaging more commonly (Hawkins & Mori, 2018). Typically they involve transcending, transgressing, and transforming boundaries between systems such as languages, modes, cultures, and disciplines. However, they simultaneously recognise that in transcending boundaries, the existence of those boundaries is reaffirmed. Thus, this tension and the power structures that lead to and from the creation of boundaries are also a key part of 'trans' theories.

Virtual spaces

Digital social spaces that are co-constructed between participants, in contrast to places which are based on physical, geographical domains.

World Englishes (WE)

Descriptions of 'new' varieties of English or nativised Englishes mainly in Kachru's (1992) Outer-Circle countries, e.g., Indian English, Kenyan English, Malaysian English, Nigerian English, and Singapore English. This paradigm also involves the three-circles model of English use. See also **Inner Circle**, **Outer Circle**, and **Expanding Circle**.

References

Abdzadeh, Y. & Baker, W. (2020). Cultural awareness in an Iranian English language classroom: A teaching intervention in an interculturally 'conservative' setting. *Journal of English as a Lingua Franca*, 9, 57–80. doi: 10.1515/jelf-2020–2030

Agar, M. (1994). *Language shock: Understanding the culture of conversation*. New York: William Morrow.

Aktas, F., Pitts, K., Richards, J.C., & Silova, I. (2017). Institutionalizing global citizenship: A critical analysis of higher education programs and curricula. *Journal of Studies in International Education*, 21, 65–80. doi: 10.1177/1028315316669815

ALA (Association for Language Awareness). (n.d.). Definition. Association for Language Awareness. Retrieved from https://lexically.net/ala/la_defined.htm (accessed 30 September 2020).

Alharbi, N. (2018). English as a lingua franca in the Gulf Cooperation Council states. In J. Jenkins, W. Baker, & M. Dewey (Eds.), *The Routledge handbook of English as a lingua franca* (pp. 126–137). Abingdon: Routledge.

Alim, H.S. (2009). Straight outta Compton, straight *aus München*: Global linguistic flows, identities, and the politics of language in a global hip hop nation. In H.S. Alim, A. Ibrahim, & A. Pennycook (Eds.), *Global linguistic flows: Hip hop cultures, youth identities, and the politics of language* (pp. 1–22). Abingdon: Routledge.

Allport, G.W. (1935). Attitudes. In C. Murchison (Ed.), *A handbook of social psychology* (pp. 798–844). Worcester, MA: Clark University Press.

Almayez, M. (2019). *The professional identity construction of non-local NNESTs in the Saudi context*. Southampton: University of Southampton PhD thesis.

Alred, G., Byram, M., & Fleming, M. (Eds.). (2006). *Education for intercultural citizenship: Concepts and comparisons*. Clevedon: Multilingual Matters.

Anderson, B. (2006/2016). *Imagined communities: Reflections on the origin and spread of nationalism* (Revised edn). London: Verso.

Androutsopoulos, J. (2014). Languaging when contexts collapse: Audience design in social networking. *Discourse, Context & Media*, 4–5, 62–73. doi: 10.1016/j.dcm.2014.08.006

Appadurai, A. (1996). *Modernity at large: Cultural dimensions of globalization*. Minneapolis, MN: University of Minnesota Press.

Arnold, M. (1869). *Culture and anarchy: An essay in political and social criticism*. London: Smith, Elder and Co.

ASEAN (Association of Southeast Asian Nations). (2008). *The ASEAN Charter*. Jakarta: ASEAN Secretariat. Retrieved from https://asean.org/wp-content/uploads/images/archive/publications/ASEAN-Charter.pdf (accessed 30 September 2020).

Auer, P. (forthcoming). 'Translanguaging' or 'doing languages'? Multilingual practices and the notion of 'codes'. In J. MacSwann (Ed.), *Language(s): Multilingualism and its consequences*. Clevedon: Multilingual Matters.

Baird, R. & Baird, M. (2018). English as a Lingua Franca: Changing 'attitudes'. In J. Jenkins, W. Baker, & M. Dewey (Eds.), *The Routledge handbook of English as a lingua franca* (pp. 531–543). Abingdon: Routledge.

Baird, R., Baker, W., & Kitazawa, M. (2014). The complexity of ELF. *Journal of English as a Lingua Franca*, *3*, 171–196. doi: 10.1515/jelf-2014-0007

Baker, C. (2001). *Foundations of bilingual education and bilingualism* (3rd edn). Clevedon: Multilingual Matters.

Baker, C. & Wright, W.E. (2017). *Foundations of bilingual education and bilingualism* (6th edn). Clevedon: Multilingual Matters.

Baker, W. (2009a). The cultures of English as a lingua franca. *TESOL Quarterly*, *43*, 567–592. doi: 10.1002/j.1545-7249.2009.tb00187.x

Baker, W. (2009b). *Intercultural awareness and intercultural communication through English: An investigation of Thai English language users in higher education*. Southampton: University of Southampton PhD thesis.

Baker, W. (2011). Intercultural awareness: Modelling an understanding of cultures in intercultural communication through English as a lingua franca. *Language and Intercultural Communication*, *11*, 197–214. doi: 10.1080/14708477.2011.577779

Baker, W. (2012). *Using e-learning to develop intercultural awareness in ELT: A critical evaluation in a Thai higher education setting*. London: British Council. Retrieved from www.teachingenglish.org.uk/sites/teacheng/files/B375%20ELTRP%20report%20-%20Baker%20A4%20ONLINE_V5.pdf (accessed 30 September 2020).

Baker, W. (2015). *Culture and identity through English as a lingua franca: Rethinking concepts and goals in intercultural communication*. Berlin: De Gruyter Mouton.

Baker, W. (2016). English as an academic lingua franca and intercultural awareness: Student mobility in the transcultural university. *Language and Intercultural Communication*, *16*, 437–451. doi: 10.1080/14708477.2016.1168053

Baker, W. (2018). English as a lingua franca and intercultural communication. In J. Jenkins, W. Baker, & M. Dewey (Eds.), *The Routledge handbook of English as a lingua franca* (pp. 25–36). Abingdon: Routledge.

Baker, W. & Fang, F. (G.) (2018). From English language learners to intercultural citizens: Chinese student sojourners' development of intercultural citizenship in ELT and EMI programmes. *British Council ELT Research Papers*, *18*(4). Retrieved from www.teachingenglish.org.uk/article/english-language-learners-intercultural-citizens (accessed 30 September 2020).

Baker, W. & Fang, F. (G.) (2021). 'So maybe I'm a global citizen': Developing intercultural citizenship in English medium education. *Language, Culture and Curriculum*, *34*, 1–17. doi: 10.1080/07908318.2020.1748045

Baker, W. & Jenkins, J. (2015). Criticising ELF. *Journal of English as a Lingua Franca*, *4*, 191–198. doi: 10.1515/jelf-2015-0013

Baker, W. & Sangiamchit, C. (2019). Transcultural communication: Language, communication and culture through English as a lingua franca in a social network community. *Language and Intercultural Communication*, *19*, 471–487. doi: 10.1080/14708477.2019.1606230

Ballard, B. & Clanchy, J. (1991). Assessment by misconception: Cultural influences and intellectual traditions. In L. Hamp-Lyons (Ed.), *Assessing second language writing in academic contexts* (pp. 19–35). Norwood, NJ: Ablex.

Bamgboṣe, A. (1998). Torn between the norms: Innovations in world Englishes. *World Englishes*, *17*, 1–14. doi: 10.1111/1467-971X.00078

Banaji, M.R. & Heiphetz, L. (2010). Attitudes. In S.T. Fiske, D.T. Gilbert, & G. Lindzey (Eds.), *Handbook of social psychology* (5th edn, pp. 353–393). Hoboken, NJ: John Wiley & Sons.

Bassili, J.N. & Brown, R.D. (2005/2014). Implicit and explicit attitudes: Research, challenges, and theory. In D. Albarracín, B.T. Johnson, & M.P. Zanna (Eds.), *The handbook of attitudes* (pp. 543–574). London: Psychology Press.

Bauman, Z. (2011). *Culture in a liquid modern world*. Cambridge: Polity.

Baumann, G. (1996). *Contesting culture: Discourses of identity in multi-ethnic London*. Cambridge: Cambridge University Press.

Bayyurt, Y. & Akcan, S. (Eds.). (2015). *Current perspectives on pedagogy for English as a lingua franca*. Berlin: De Gruyter Mouton.

Bell, A. (1984). Language style as audience design. *Language in Society*, *13*, 145–204. doi: 10.1017/S004740450001037X

Bhabha, H.K. (1994). *The location of culture*. London: Routledge.

Bhatt, R.M. (2017). World Englishes and language ideologies. In M. Filppula, J. Klemola, & D. Sharma (Eds.), *The Oxford handbook of World Englishes* (pp. 291–311). Oxford: Oxford University Press.

Billig, M. (1995). *Banal nationalism*. London: Sage.

Björkman, B. (2018). Morphosyntactic variation in spoken English as a lingua franca interactions: Revisiting linguistic variety. In J. Jenkins, W. Baker, & M. Dewey (Eds.), *The Routledge handbook of English as a lingua franca* (pp. 255–266). Abingdon: Routledge.

Blackledge, A. (2000). Monolingual ideologies in multilingual states: Language, hegemony and social justice in Western liberal democracies. *Estudios de Sociolingüística*, *1*(2), 25–45. doi: 10.1558/sols.v1i2.25

Blommaert, J. (2010). *The sociolinguistics of globalization*. Cambridge: Cambridge University Press.

Blommaert, J. (2013). *Ethnography, superdiversity and linguistic landscapes: Chronicles of complexity*. Clevedon: Multilingual Matters.

Blommaert, J. (2016). From mobility to complexity in sociolinguistic theory and method. In N. Coupland (Ed.), *Sociolinguistics: Theoretical debates* (pp. 242–259). Cambridge: Cambridge University Press.

Boas, F. (1911/1986). Language and thought. In J.M. Valdes (Ed.), *Culture bound: Bridging the cultural gap in language teaching* (pp. 5–7). Cambridge: Cambridge University Press.

Bolton, K. (2018). World Englishes and Second Language Acquisition. *World Englishes*, *37*, 5–18. doi: 10.1111/weng.12299

Boonsuk, Y. (2016). *Thai university students, teachers and program administrators, construction of nativeness in English language teaching.* Southampton: University of Southampton PhD thesis.

Bourdieu, P. (1977). *Outline of a theory of practice* (Trans. R. Nice). Cambridge: Cambridge University Press.

Bourdieu, P. (1991). *Language & symbolic power* (Trans. G. Raymond & M. Adamson) (J.B. Thompson (Ed.)). Cambridge: Polity.

Bourdieu, P. & Passeron, J.-C. (1990). *Reproduction in education, society and culture* (Trans. R. Nice) (2nd edn). London: Sage.

Bourdieu, P., Passeron, J.-C., & de Saint Martin, M. (1994). *Academic discourse: Linguistic misunderstanding and professorial power* (Trans. R. Teese). Cambridge: Polity.

Bourdieu, P. & Wacquant, L.J.D. (1992). *An invitation to reflexive sociology.* Chicago, IL: The University of Chicago Press.

boyd, d. (2008). Why youth ♥ social network sites: The role of networked publics in teenage social life. In D. Buckingham (Ed.), *Youth, identity, and digital media* (pp. 119–142). Cambridge, MA: The MIT Press.

boyd, d. & Marwick, A.E. (2011). *Social privacy in networked publics: Teens' attitudes, practices, and strategies* [Paper presentation]. A Decade in Internet Time: Symposium on the Dynamics of the Internet and Society, Oxford. Retrieved from https://papers.ssrn.com/sol3/papers.cfm?abstract_id=1925128 (accessed 30 September 2020).

Brumfit, C. (1995). Teacher professionalism and research. In G. Cook & B. Seidlhofer (Eds.), *Principle & practice in applied linguistics* (pp. 27–41). Oxford: Oxford University Press.

Brumfit, C. (2001). *Individual freedom in language teaching: Helping learners to develop a dialect of their own.* Oxford: Oxford University Press.

Brutt-Griffler, J. (2002). *World English: A study of its development.* Clevedon: Multilingual Matters.

Byram, M. (1997). *Teaching and assessing intercultural communicative competence.* Clevedon: Multilingual Matters.

Byram, M. (2008). *From foreign language education to education for intercultural citizenship: Essays and reflections.* Clevedon: Multilingual Matters.

Byram, M. (2012a). Language awareness and (critical) cultural awareness – Relationships, comparisons and contrasts. *Language Awareness*, *21*, 5–13. doi: 10.1080/09658416.2011.639887

Byram, M. (2012b). Conceptualizing intercultural (communicative) competence and intercultural citizenship. In J. Jackson (Ed.), *The Routledge handbook of language and intercultural communication* (pp. 85–97). Abingdon: Routledge.

Byram, M. (2021). *Teaching and assessing intercultural communicative competence: Revisited* (2nd edn). Clevedon: Multilingual Matters.

Byram, M. & Esarte-Sarries, V. (1991). *Investigating cultural studies in foreign language teaching: A book for teachers.* Clevedon: Multilingual Matters.

Byram, M. & Fleming, M. (Eds.). (1998). *Language learning in intercultural perspective: Approaches through drama and ethnography.* Cambridge: Cambridge University Press.

Byram, M. & Golubeva, I. (2020). Conceptualizing intercultural (communicative) competence and intercultural citizenship. In J. Jackson (Ed.), *The Routledge handbook of language and intercultural communication* (2nd edn, pp. 70–85). Abingdon: Routledge.

Byram, M., Golubeva, I., Han, H., & Wagner, M. (Eds.). (2017). *From principles to practice in education for intercultural citizenship*. Clevedon: Multilingual Matters.

Byram, M. & Grundy, P. (Eds.). (2003). *Context and culture in language teaching and learning*. Clevedon: Multilingual Matters.

Byram, M., Morgan, C., & Colleagues. (1994). *Teaching-and-learning language-and-culture*. Clevedon: Multilingual Matters.

Byram, M., Nichols, A., & Stevens, D. (Eds.). (2001). *Developing intercultural competence in practice*. Clevedon: Multilingual Matters.

Cadwalladr, C. & Graham-Harrison, E. (2018). Revealed: 50 million Facebook profiles harvested for Cambridge Analytica in major data breach, *The Guardian*, 17 March. Retrieved from www.theguardian.com/news/2018/mar/17/cambridge-analytica-facebook-influence-us-election (accessed 30 September 2020).

Campbell, D.T. (1963). Social attitudes and other acquired behavioral dispositions. In S. Koch (Ed.), *Psychology: A study of a science. Investigations of man as socius: Their place in psychology and the social sciences* (pp. 94–172). London: McGraw-Hill.

Canagarajah, S. (2007). Lingua franca English, multilingual communities, and language acquisition. *The Modern Language Journal*, *91*, 923–939. doi: 10.1111/j.1540-4781.2007.00678.x

Canagarajah, S. (2013). *Translingual practice: Global Englishes and cosmopolitan relations*. Abingdon: Routledge.

Canagarajah, S. (2018). Translingual practice as spatial repertoires: Expanding the paradigm beyond structuralist orientations. *Applied Linguistics*, *39*, 31–54. doi: 10.1093/applin/amx041

Canale, M. (1983/2013). From communicative competence to communicative language pedagogy. In J.C. Richards & R.W. Schmidt (Eds.), *Language and communication* (pp. 2–27). Abingdon: Routledge.

Canale, M. & Swain, M. (1980). Theoretical bases of communicative approaches to second language teaching and testing. *Applied Linguistics*, *1*, 1–47. doi: 10.1093/applin/I.1.1

Carey, R. (2013). On the other side: Formulaic organizing chunks in spoken and written academic ELF. *Journal of English as a Lingua Franca*, 2, 207–228. doi: 10.1515/jelf-2013-0013

Carson, J.G. (1992). Becoming biliterate: First language influences. *Journal of Second Language Writing*, *1*, 37–60. doi: 10.1016/1060-3743(92)90019-L

CELF [Center for English as a Lingua Franca]. 2020. English as a lingua franca program at Tamagawa University. *Tamagawa Academy (K-12) & University*. Retrieved from www.tamagawa.jp/en/highereducation/efl.html (accessed 30 September 2020).

Cenoz, J. (2019). Translanguaging pedagogies and English as a lingua franca. *Language Teaching*, *52*, 71–85. doi: 10.1017/S0261444817000246

CGE (Centre for Global Englishes). (2020). Centre for Global Englishes (CGE). University of Southampton. Retrieved from www.southampton.ac.uk/cge/index.page (accessed 30 September 2020).

CHANMINA. (2018). 'Doctor (Official music video)' [Video], 28 September. Retrieved from www.youtube.com/watch?v=xlX8EzRdMl8 (accessed 30 September 2020).

Cheshire, J., Kerswill, P., Fox, S., & Torgersen, E. (2011). Contact, the feature pool and the speech community: The emergence of Multicultural London English. *Journal of Sociolinguistics*, *15*, 151–196. doi: 10.1111/j.1467-9841.2011.00478.x

Chomsky, N. (1965). *Aspects of the theory of syntax*. Cambridge, MA: The MIT Press.

Chukyo University. (2020). Undergraduate schools. Chukyo University. Retrieved from www.chukyo-u.ac.jp/english/under/index.html (accessed 30 September 2020).

CLAIR (Council of Local Authorities for International Relations). (2020). Participating countries. JET (Japan Exchange and Teaching) Programme http://jetprogramme.org/en/countries/ (accessed 30 September 2020).

Clandfield, L. (2010). *Global: Pre-intermediate coursebook*. Oxford: Macmillan Education.

Clandfield, L. (2019). *Global: Pre-intermediate coursebook* (Revised edn). Oxford: Macmillan Education.

Clifford, J. (1992). Traveling cultures. In L. Grossberg, C. Nelson, & P. Treichler (Eds.), *Cultural studies* (pp. 96–116). Abingdon: Routledge.

Cogo, A. (2009). Accommodating difference in ELF conversations: A study of pragmatic strategies. In A. Mauranen & E. Ranta (Eds.), *English as a lingua franca: Studies and findings* (pp. 254–273). Newcastle upon Tyne: Cambridge Scholars.

Cogo, A. (2010). Strategic use and perceptions of English as a Lingua Franca. *Poznań Studies in Contemporary Linguistics*, *46*, 295–312. doi: 10.2478/v10010-010-0013-7

Cogo, A. (2012). ELF and super-diversity: A case study of ELF multilingual practices from a business context. *Journal of English as a Lingua Franca*, *1*, 287–313. doi: 10.1515/jelf-2012-0020

Cogo, A. (2016). Conceptualizing ELF as a translanguaging phenomenon: Covert and overt resources in a transnational workplace. In K. Murata (Ed.), *Waseda Working Papers in ELF* (Vol. 5, pp. 61–76). Tokyo: Waseda ELF Research Group.

Cogo, A. (2018). ELF and multilingualism. In J. Jenkins, W. Baker, & M. Dewey (Eds.), *The Routledge handbook of English as a lingua franca* (pp. 357–368). Abingdon: Routledge.

Cogo, A. & Dewey, M. (2012). *Analysing English as a lingua franca: A corpus-driven investigation*. London: Continuum.

Cogo, A. & Pitzl, M.-L. (2016). Pre-empting and signalling non-understanding in ELF. *ELT Journal*, *70*, 339–345. doi: 10.1093/elt/ccw015

Confucius. (2007). *The analects of Confucius* (Trans. by B. Watson). New York: Columbia University Press.

Connor, U. (1996). *Contrastive rhetoric: Cross-cultural aspects of second-language writing*. Cambridge: Cambridge University Press.

Converse, P.E. (1970). Attitudes and non-attitudes: Continuation of a dialogue. In E.R. Tufte (Ed.), *The quantitative analysis of social problems* (pp. 168–189). London: Addison-Wesley.

Cook, V. (1991). Developing the concept of multi-competence. *Selected Papers on Theoretical and Applied Linguistics*, *5*, 393–404. doi: 10.26262/istal.v5i0.7148

Cook, V. (1999). Going beyond the native speaker in language teaching. *TESOL Quarterly*, *33*, 185–209. doi: 10.2307/3587717

Cook, V. (2002). Background to the L2 user. In V. Cook (Ed.), *Portraits of the L2 user* (pp. 1–28). Clevedon: Multilingual Matters.

Cook, V. (2008). Multi-competence: Black hole or wormhole for second language acquisition research? In Z.H. Han (Ed.), *Understanding second language process* (pp. 16–26). Clevedon: Multilingual Matters.

Cook, V. (2013). Global English: Central or atypical form of SLA? In D. Singleton, J.A. Fishman, L. Aronin, & M.Ó. Laoire (Eds.), *Current multilingualism: A new linguistic dispensation* (pp. 27–44). Berlin: De Gruyter Mouton.

Council of Europe. (2001). *Common European Framework of Reference for Languages: Learning, teaching, assessment*. Cambridge: Cambridge University Press.

Council of Europe. (2018). *Common European Framework of Reference for Languages: Learning, teaching, assessment. Companion volume with new descriptors*. Strasbourg: Council of Europe.

Coupland, N. (2000). Sociolinguistic prevarication about 'standard English'. *Journal of Sociolinguistics*, *4*, 622–634. doi: 10.1111/1467-9481.00133

Coupland, N. (2007). *Style: Language variation and identity*. Cambridge: Cambridge University Press.

Creese, A. & Blackledge, A. (2015). Translanguaging and identity in educational settings. *Annual Review of Applied Linguistics*, *35*, 20–35. doi: 10.1017/S0267190514000233

Crichton, M. (1994/2006). *Disclosure*. London: Arrow Books.

Crowther, D. & De Costa, P.I. (2017). Developing mutual intelligibility and conviviality in the 21st century classroom: Insights from English as a lingua franca and intercultural communication. *TESOL Quarterly*, *51*, 450–460. doi: 10.1002/tesq.341

Crystal, D. (2008). Two thousand million? *English Today*, *24*(1), 3–6. doi: 10.1017/S0266078408000023

Dafouz, E. & Smit, U. (2020). *ROAD-MAPPING English medium education in the internationalised university*. Cham: Palgrave Macmillan.

Dalton-Puffer, C., Kaltenboeck, G., & Smit, U. (1997). Learner attitudes and L2 pronunciation in Austria. *World Englishes*, *16*, 115–128. doi: 10.1111/1467-971X.00052

D'Angelo, J.F. (2005). Educated Japanese English: Expanding oral/aural core vocabulary. *World Englishes*, *24*, 329–349. doi: 10.1111/j.0083-2919.2005.00415.x

D'Angelo, J.F. (2018). The status of ELF in Japan. In J. Jenkins, W. Baker, & M. Dewey (Eds.), *The Routledge handbook of English as a lingua franca* (pp. 165–175). Abingdon: Routledge.

Davies, A. (2013). *Native speakers and native users: Loss and gain*. Cambridge: Cambridge University Press.

Deutscher, G. (2010). *Through the language glass: How words colour your world*. London: William Heinemann.

de Waal, E. (2010). *The hare with amber eyes: A hidden inheritance.* London: Chatto & Windus.

Dewey, M. (2012). Towards a *post-normative* approach: Learning the pedagogy of ELF. *Journal of English as a Lingua Franca, 1*, 141–170. doi: 10.1515/jelf-2012-0007

Dewey, M. (2015). Time to wake up some dogs! Shifting the culture of language in ELT. In Y. Bayyurt & S. Akcan (Eds.), *Current perspectives on pedagogy for English as a lingua franca* (pp. 121–134). Berlin: De Gruyter Mouton.

Doughty, P. (1972). Pupils also use language to live: A defence of a linguistic approach to language study for the classroom. *English in Education, 6*(1), 18–28. doi: 10.1111/j.1754-8845.1972.tb00371.x

Doughty, P. (1979). Language for living: A principled approach to teaching mother tongue. *McGill Journal of Education, 14*, 61–69. Retrieved from https://mje.mcgill.ca/article/view/7254 (accessed 30 September 2020).

Dovchin, S., Sultana, S., & Pennycook, A. (2016). Unequal translingual Englishes in the Asian peripheries. *Asian Englishes, 18*, 92–108. doi: 10.1080/13488678.2016.1171673

Driscoll, P., Earl, J., & Cable, C. (2013). The role and nature of the cultural dimension in primary modern languages. *Language, Culture and Curriculum, 26*, 146–160. doi: 10.1080/07908318.2013.799675

Eagly, A.H. & Chaiken, S. (2007). The advantages of an inclusive definition of attitude. *Social Cognition, 25*, 582–602. doi: 10.1521/soco.2007.25.5.582

Eberhard, D.M., Simons, G.F., & Fennig, C.D. (Eds.). (2019). *Ethnologue: Languages of Africa and Europe; languages of Asia; languages of the Americas and the Pacific* (22nd edn). Dallas, TX: SIL International.

Eberhard, D.M., Simons, G.F., & Fennig, C.D. (Eds.). (2020). *Ethnologue: Languages of the world* (23rd edn, online version). Dallas, TX: SIL International. Retrieved from www.ethnologue.com (accessed 30 September 2020).

Eckert, P. & McConnell-Ginet, S. (1992). Think practically and look locally: Language and gender as community-based practice. *Annual Review of Anthropology, 21*, 461–490. Retrieved from www.jstor.org/stable/2155996 (accessed 30 September 2020).

Eggins, S. & Slade, D. (1997/2004). *Analysing casual conversation.* London: Equinox.

Ehrenreich, S. (2009). English as a lingua franca in multinational corporations – Exploring business communities of practice. In A. Mauranen & E. Ranta (Eds.), *English as a lingua franca: Studies and findings* (pp. 126–151). Newcastle upon Tyne: Cambridge Scholars.

Ehrenreich, S. (2018). Communities of practice and English as a lingua franca. In J. Jenkins, W. Baker, & M. Dewey (Eds.), *The Routledge handbook of English as a lingua franca* (pp. 37–50). Abingdon: Routledge.

Ellison, N.B. & Boyd, D.M. (2013). Sociality through social network sites. In W.H. Dutton (Ed.), *The Oxford handbook of internet studies* (pp. 151–172). Oxford: Oxford University Press.

ETS (Educational Testing Service). (2020a). *2019 report on test takers worldwide: TOEIC® Listening & Reading tests.* Princeton, NJ: Educational

Testing Service. Retrieved from www.iibc-global.org/english/toeic/official_data.html (accessed 30 September 2020).

ETS (Educational Testing Service). (2020b). *2019 report on test takers worldwide: TOEIC® Speaking & Writing tests*. Princeton, NJ: Educational Testing Service. Retrieved from www.iibc-global.org/english/toeic/official_data.html (accessed 30 September 2020).

Evans, B.E. & Imai, T. (2011). 'If we say English, that means America': Japanese students' perceptions of varieties of English. *Language Awareness*, *20*, 315–326. doi: 10.1080/09658416.2011.592590

Everett, D. (2012). *Language: The cultural tool*. London: Profile.

Fang, F. (G.) (2015). *An investigation of attitudes towards English accents at a Chinese university*. Southampton: University of Southampton PhD thesis.

Fang, F. (G.) & Baker, W. (2018). 'A more inclusive mind towards the world': English language teaching and study abroad in China from intercultural citizenship and English as a lingua franca perspectives. *Language Teaching Research*, *22*, 608–624. doi: 10.1177/1362168817718574

Fang, F. (G.) & Ren, W. (2018). Developing students' awareness of Global Englishes. *ELT Journal*, *72*, 384–394. doi: 10.1093/elt/ccy012

Fantini, A. (2007). *Exploring and assessing intercultural competence*. St. Louis, MO: Center for Social Development. Retrieved from https://csd.wustl.edu/07-01/ (accessed 30 September 2020).

Fei, Y. & Weekly, R. (2020). Examining the parameters of translanguaging in the context of Chinese bilinguals' discourse practices. *International Journal of Multilingualism*, Latest Articles. doi: 10.1080/14790718.2020.1742721

Feng, A., Byram, M., & Fleming, M. (Eds.). (2009). *Becoming interculturally competent through education and training*. Clevedon: Multilingual Matters.

Filppula, M., Klemola, J., & Sharma, D. (Eds.). (2017). *The Oxford handbook of World Englishes*. Oxford: Oxford University Press.

Firth, A. (1996). The discursive accomplishment of normality: On 'lingua franca' English and conversation analysis. *Journal of Pragmatics*, *26*, 237–259. doi: 10.1016/0378-2166(96)00014-8

Fox, H. (1994). *Listening to the world: Cultural issues in academic writing*. Urbana, IL: National Council of Teachers of English.

Fuller, J. (1993). Hearing between the lines: Style switching in a courtroom setting. *Pragmatics*, *3*, 29–43. Retrieved from https://journals.linguisticsociety.org/elanguage/pragmatics/article/view/176.html (accessed 30 September 2020).

Galloway, N. (2013). Global Englishes and English Language Teaching (ELT) – Bridging the gap between theory and practice in a Japanese context. *System*, *41*, 786–803. doi: 10.1016/j.system.2013.07.019

Galloway, N. (2018). ELF and ELT teaching materials. In J. Jenkins, W. Baker, & M. Dewey (Eds.), *The Routledge handbook of English as a lingua franca* (pp. 468–480). Abingdon: Routledge.

Galloway, N. & Rose, H. (2013). "They envision going to New York, not Jakarta": The differing attitudes toward ELF of students, teaching assistants, and instructors in an English-medium business program in Japan. *Journal of English as a Lingua Franca*, *2*, 229–253. doi: 10.1515/jelf-2013-0014

Galloway, N. & Rose, H. (2015). *Introducing Global Englishes*. Abingdon: Routledge.

Galloway, N. & Rose, H. (2018). Incorporating Global Englishes into the ELT classroom. *ELT Journal*, 72, 3–14. doi: 10.1093/elt/ccx010

García, O. (2009). *Bilingual education in the 21st century: A global perspective*. Oxford: Wiley-Blackwell.

García, O. (2014). What is translanguaging? Expanded questions and answers for U.S. educators. In S. Hesson, K. Seltzer, & H.H. Woodley (Eds.), *Translanguaging in curriculum and instruction: A CUNY-NYSIEB guide for educators* (pp. 1–13). New York: CUNY-NYSIEB. Retrieved from www.cuny-nysieb.org/translanguaging-resources/translanguaging-guides/ (accessed 30 September 2020).

García, O. & Kleyn, T. (Eds.). (2016). *Translanguaging with multilingual students: Learning from classroom moments*. Abingdon: Routledge.

García, O. & Li, W. (2014). *Translanguaging: Language, bilingualism and education*. Basingstoke: Palgrave Macmillan.

Garrett, P. (2010). *Attitudes to language*. Cambridge: Cambridge University Press.

Gaudelli, W. (2016). *Global citizenship education: Everyday transcendence*. Abingdon: Routledge.

Gee, J.P. (2004). *Situated language and learning: A critique of traditional schooling*. Abingdon: Routledge.

Gee, J.P. (2008). *Social linguistics and literacies: Ideology in discourses* (3rd edn). Abingdon: Routledge.

Gee, J.P. (2015). *Social linguistics and literacies: Ideology in discourses* (5th ed.). Abingdon: Routledge.

Geertz, C. (1973/2000). *The interpretation of cultures*. New York: Basic Books.

Giles, H. & Billings, A.C. (2004). Assessing language attitudes: Speaker evaluation studies. In A. Davies & C. Elder (Eds.), *The handbook of applied linguistics* (pp. 187–209). Oxford: Blackwell.

Gleick, J. (2008). *Chaos: Making a new science* (2nd edn). London: Penguin.

Glisan, E. (2012). National Standards: Research into practice. *Language Teaching*, 45, 515–526. doi: 10.1017/S0261444812000249

Graham, S.L. (2016/2020). Relationality, friendship, and identity in digital communication. In A. Georgakopoulou & T. Spilioti (Eds.), *The Routledge handbook of language and digital communication* (pp. 305–320). Abingdon: Routledge.

Gray, J. (2010). *The construction of English: Culture, consumerism and promotion in the ELT global coursebook*. Basingstoke: Palgrave Macmillan.

Green L.J. (2002). *African American English: A linguistic introduction*. Cambridge: Cambridge University Press.

Greenbaum, S. & Nelson, G. (1996). The International Corpus of English (ICE) project. *World Englishes*, 15, 3–15. doi: 10.1111/j.1467-971X.1996.tb00088.x

Gu, Q. (2009). Editorial. *Language and Intercultural Communication*, 9, 139–143. doi: 10.1080/14708470902748806

Guido, M.G. (2012). ELF authentication and accommodation strategies in crosscultural immigration encounters. *Journal of English as a Lingua Franca*, 1, 219–240. doi: 10.1515/jelf-2012-0017

Guido, M.G. (2018). ELF in migration. In J. Jenkins, W. Baker, & M. Dewey (Eds.), *The Routledge handbook of English as a lingua franca* (pp. 544–555). Abingdon: Routledge.

Guilherme, M. (2012). Critical language and intercultural communication pedagogy. In J. Jackson (Ed.), *The Routledge handbook of language and intercultural communication* (pp. 357–371). Abingdon: Routledge.

Guilherme, M. (2020). Intercultural responsibility: Transnational research and glocal critical citizenship. In J. Jackson (Ed.), *The Routledge handbook of language and intercultural communication* (2nd edn, pp. 343–360). Abingdon: Routledge.

Guilherme, M. & Dietz, G. (2015). Difference in diversity: Multiple perspectives on multicultural, intercultural, and transcultural conceptual complexities. *Journal of Multicultural Discourses*, *10*, 1–21. doi: 10.1080/17447143.2015.1015539

Gumperz, J.J. (1964). Hindi-Punjabi code-switching in Delhi. In H. Lunt (Ed.), *Proceedings of the Ninth International Congress of Linguists* (pp. 1115–1124). The Hague: Mouton.

Gumperz, J.J. (2009). The speech community. In A. Duranti (Ed.), *Linguistic anthropology: A reader* (2nd edn, pp. 66–73). Oxford: Wiley-Blackwell.

Guth, S. & Helm, F. (Eds.). (2010). *Telecollaboration 2.0: Language, literacies and intercultural learning in the 21st century*. Bern: Peter Lang.

Haarmann, H. (1989). *Symbolic values of foreign language use*. Berlin: Mouton de Gruyter.

Hall, C.J. (2013). Cognitive contributions to plurilithic views of English and other languages. *Applied Linguistics*, *34*, 211–231. doi: 10.1093/applin/ams042

Hall, C.J. (2018). Cognitive perspectives on English as a lingua franca. In J. Jenkins, W. Baker, & M. Dewey (Eds.), *The Routledge handbook of English as a lingua franca* (pp. 74–84). Abingdon: Routledge.

Hall, E.T. (1959). *The silent language*. New York: Doubleday.

Hall, E.T. (1966). *The hidden dimension*. New York: Doubleday.

Halliday, M.A.K. (1978). *Language as social semiotic: The social interpretation of language and meaning*. London: Edward Arnold.

Halliday, M.A.K. (2003). *On language and linguistics* (Ed. J.J. Webster). London: Continuum.

Han, H., Li, S., Hongtao, J., & Zhao, Y. (2017). Exploring perceptions of intercultural citizenship among English learners in Chinese universities. In M. Byram, I. Golubeva, H. Han, & M. Wagner (Eds.), *From principles to practice in education for intercultural citizenship* (pp. 25–44). Clevedon: Multilingual Matters.

Hannerz, U. (1996). *Transnational connections: Culture, people, places*. London: Routledge.

Harding, L. & McNamara, T. (2018). Language assessment: The challenge of ELF. In J. Jenkins, W. Baker, & M. Dewey (Eds.), *The Routledge handbook of English as a lingua franca* (pp. 570–582). Abingdon: Routledge.

Harris, R. (1997). From an integrational point of view. In G. Wolf & N. Love (Eds.), *Linguistics inside out: Roy Harris and his critics* (pp. 229–310). Amsterdam: John Benjamins.

Harris, R. (1998). Making sense of communicative competence. In R. Harris & G. Wolf (Eds.), *Integrational linguistics: A first reader* (pp. 27–45). Oxford: Pergamon.

Hashimoto, K. (2013). The Japanisation of English language education: Promotion of the national language within foreign language policy. In J.W. Tollefson (Ed.), *Language policies in education: Critical issues* (2nd edn, pp. 175–190). Abingdon: Routledge.

Hawkins, M.R. (2018). Transmodalities and transnational encounters: Fostering critical cosmopolitan relations. *Applied Linguistics*, *39*, 55–77. doi: 10.1093/applin/amx048

Hawkins, M.R. & Mori, J. (2018). Considering 'trans-' perspectives in language theories and practices. *Applied Linguistics*, *39*, 1–8. doi: 10.1093/applin/amx056

Herring, S.C. (2010). Computer-mediated conversation: Introduction and overview. *Language@Internet*, 7. Retrieved from www.languageatinternet.org/articles/2010/2801 (accessed 30 September 2020).

Herring, S.C. (2013). Discourse in Web 2.0: Familiar, reconfigured, and emergent. In D. Tannen & A.M. Trester (Eds.), *Discourse 2.0: Language and new media* (pp. 1–25). Washington, DC: Georgetown University Press.

Hill, R.J. (1982). *A dictionary of false friends*. London: Macmillan.

Hino, N. (2012). Endonormative models of EIL for the Expanding Circle. In A. Matsuda (Ed.), *Principles and practices of teaching English as an international language* (pp. 28–43). Clevedon: Multilingual Matters.

Hino, N. (2018). *EIL education for the Expanding Circle: A Japanese model*. Abingdon: Routledge.

Hino, N. & Oda, S. (2015). Integrated practice in teaching English as an international language (IPTEIL): A classroom ELF pedagogy in Japan. In Y. Bayyurt & S. Akcan (Eds.), *Current perspectives on pedagogy for English as a lingua franca* (pp. 35–50). Berlin: De Gruyter Mouton.

Hobbs, P. (2003). "Is that what we're here about?": A lawyer's use of impression management in a closing argument at trial. *Discourse & Society*, *14*, 273–290. doi: 10.1177/09579265030143002

Hochberg, J. (2016). *¿Por qué? 101 questions about Spanish*. London: Bloomsbury.

Hofstede, G. (1991). *Cultures and organizations: Software of the mind*. London: McGraw-Hill.

Hofstede, G. (2001). *Culture's consequences: Comparing values, behaviors, institutions, and organizations across nations* (2nd edn). London: Sage.

Hofstede, G., Hofstede, G.J., & Minkov, M. (2010). *Cultures and organizations: Software of the mind – Intercultural cooperation and its importance for survival* (3rd edn). London: McGraw-Hill.

Holland, D. & Quinn, N. (Eds.). (1987). *Cultural models in language and thought*. Cambridge: Cambridge University Press.

Holliday, A. (1999). Small cultures. *Applied Linguistics*, *20*, 237–264. doi: 10.1093/applin/20.2.237

Holliday, A. (2005). *The struggle to teach English as an international language*. Oxford: Oxford University Press.

Holliday, A. (2006). Native-speakerism. *ELT Journal*, *60*, 385–387. doi: 10.1093/elt/ccl030

Holliday, A. (2011). *Intercultural communication and ideology*. London: Sage.

Holliday, A. (2013). *Understanding intercultural communication: Negotiating a grammar of culture*. Abingdon: Routledge.

Holliday, A. (2018). Native-speakerism. In J.I. Liontas, M. DelliCarpini, & TESOL International Association (Eds.), *The TESOL encyclopedia of English language teaching* (Vol. 2, pp. 1151–1157). Oxford: Wiley Blackwell.

Holliday, A. (2019). *Understanding intercultural communication: Negotiating a grammar of culture* (2nd edn). Abingdon: Routledge.

Holliday, A., Kullman, J., & Hyde, M. (2017). *Intercultural communication: An advanced resource book for students* (3rd edn). Abingdon: Routledge.

Honey, J. (1997). *Language is power: The story of standard English and its enemies*. London: Faber & Faber.

Houghton, S.A. & Rivers, D.J. (Eds.). (2013). *Native-speakerism in Japan: Intergroup dynamics in foreign language education*. Clevedon: Multilingual Matters.

House, J. (2014). English as a global lingua franca: A threat to multilingual communication and translation? *Language Teaching*, *47*, 363–376. doi: 10.1017/S0261444812000043

Hülmbauer, C. (2009). "We don't take the right way. We just take the way that we think you will understand" – The shifting relationship between correctness and effectiveness in ELF. In A. Mauranen & E. Ranta (Eds.), *English as a lingua franca: Studies and findings* (pp. 323–347). Newcastle upon Tyne: Cambridge Scholars.

Hülmbauer, C. (2013). From within and without: The virtual and the plurilingual in ELF. *Journal of English as a Lingua Franca*, *2*, 47–73. doi: 10.1515/jelf-2013-0003

Hülmbauer, C. & Seidlhofer, B. (2013). English as a lingua franca in European multilingualism. In A.-C. Berthoud, F. Grin, & G. Lüdi (Eds.), *Exploring the dynamics of multilingualism: The DYLAN project* (pp. 387–406). Amsterdam: John Benjamins.

Humphreys, G. & Baker, W. (2021). Developing intercultural awareness from short-term study abroad: Insights from an interview study of Japanese students. *Language and Intercultural Communication*, Latest Articles. doi: 10.1080/14708477.2020.1860997

Hyde, B. (2002). Japan's emblematic English. *English Today*, *18*(3), 12–16. doi: 10.1017/S0266078402003024

Hymes, D. (1972). On communicative competence. In J.B. Pride & J. Holmes (Eds.), *Sociolinguistics: Selected readings* (pp. 269–293). Harmondsworth: Penguin.

Hyrkstedt, I. & Kalaja, P. (1998). Attitudes toward English and its functions in Finland: A discourse-analytic study. *World Englishes*, *17*, 345–357. doi: 10.1111/1467-971X.00108

Internet World Stats. (2019). Top ten languages in the Internet in millions of users – April 2019. *Internet World Stats: Usage and population statistics*. Retrieved from www.internetworldstats.com/stats7.htm (accessed 30 September 2020).

Internet World Stats. (2020). Internet users distribution in the world – 2020 Q3. *Internet World Stats: Usage and population statistics*. Retrieved from www.internetworldstats.com/stats.htm (accessed 30 September 2020).

Irvine, J.T. & Gal, S. (2000). Language ideology and linguistic differentiation. In P.V. Kroskrity (Ed.), *Regimes of language: Ideologies, polities, and identities* (pp. 35–83). Santa Fe, NM: School of American Research.

Ishikawa, T. (2015). Academic rigour in criticising English as a Lingua Franca. *Englishes in Practice*, 2, 39–48. doi: 10.1515/eip-2015-0002

Ishikawa, T. (2016a). *A study of Japanese university students' attitudes towards their English*. Southampton: University of Southampton PhD thesis.

Ishikawa, T. (2016b). World Englishes and English as a Lingua Franca: Conceptualising the legitimacy of Asian people's English. *Asian Englishes*, *18*, 129–140. doi: 10.1080/13488678.2016.1171672

Ishikawa, T. (2016c). Japanese university students' attitudes towards their English: Open-ended email questionnaire study. In N. Tsantila, J. Mandalios, & M. Ilkos (Eds.), *ELF: Pedagogical and interdisciplinary perspectives* (pp. 87–94). Athens: Deree – The American College of Greece.

Ishikawa, T. (2017a). Conceptualising English as a global contact language. *Englishes in Practice*, 4, 31–49. doi: 10.1515/eip-2017-0002

Ishikawa, T. (2017b). Japanese university students' attitudes towards their English and the possibility of ELF awareness. *Journal of English as a Lingua Franca*, 6, 237–263. doi: 10.1515/jelf-2017-0012

Ishikawa, T. (2017c). Japanese university students' attitudes towards their English: Conversational interview study. In K. Murata (Ed.), *Waseda Working Papers in ELF* (Vol. 6, pp. 110–125). Tokyo: Waseda ELF Research Group.

Ishikawa, T. (2018a). From English native-speakerism to multilingualism: A conceptual note. *JACET ELF SIG Journal*, 2, 9–17. Retrieved from https://jacetelf.wordpress.com/jacet-elf-sig-journal/ (accessed 30 September 2020).

Ishikawa, T. (2018b). Review: The Routledge handbook of English as a lingua franca. *ELT Journal*, 72, 455–458. doi: 10.1093/elt/ccy032

Ishikawa, T. (2020a). EMF awareness in the Japanese EFL/EMI context. *ELT Journal*, 74, 408–417. doi: 10.1093/elt/ccaa037

Ishikawa, T. (2020b). Complexity of English as a Multilingua Franca: Place of monolingual Standard English. In M. Konakahara & K. Tsuchiya (Eds.), *English as a lingua franca in Japan: Towards multilingual practices* (pp. 91–109). Cham: Palgrave Macmillan.

Ishikawa, T. (2020c). Liven up the English classroom with academic learning: Examples from cognitive psychology. *Center for English as a Lingua Franca Journal*, 6, 67–77. doi: 10.15045/ELF_0060107

Ishikawa, T. (2021). Rigour in ELF language attitude research: An example of a conversational interview study. In K. Murata (Ed.), *ELF research methods and approaches to data and analyses: Theoretical and methodological underpinnings* (pp. 258–275). Abingdon: Routledge.

Ishikawa, T. (2021, in press). EMF and translanguaging in the Japanese EMI higher education context. In W. Tsou & W. Baker (Eds.), *English-medium instruction translanguaging practices in Asia: Theories, frameworks and implementation in higher education*. Cham: Springer.

Ishikawa, T. & Jenkins, J. (2019). What is ELF? Introductory questions and answers for ELT professionals. *Center for English as a Lingua Franca Journal*, 5, 1–10. doi: 10.15045/ELF_0050101

Ishikawa, T. & McBride, P. (2019). Doing justice to ELF in ELT: Comments on Toh (2016). *Journal of English as a Lingua Franca*, *8*, 333–345. doi: 10.1515/jelf-2019-2026

Ishikawa, T. & Morán Panero, S. (2016). Exploring language attitudes in ELF research: Contrasting approaches in conversation. *Englishes in Practice*, *3*, 74–109. doi: 101515/eip-2016-0004

Jandt, F.E. (2021). *An introduction to intercultural communication: Identities in a global community* (10th edn). London: Sage.

Japan Science and Technology Agency. (2020). *JREC-IN Portal: Career support portal site for all researchers and research staff who are pioneering innovation.* https://jrecin.jst.go.jp/seek/SeekTop?ln=1 (accessed 30 September 2020).

Javier, E. (2010). The foreign-ness of native speaking teachers of colour. In D. Nunan & J. Choi (Eds.), *Language and culture: Reflective narratives and the emergence of identity* (pp. 97–102). Abingdon: Routledge.

Jenkins, J. (1996). Native speaker, non-native speaker and English as a foreign language: Time for a change. *IATEFL Newsletter*, *131*, 10–11.

Jenkins, J. (2000). *The phonology of English as an International Language: New models, new norms, new goals.* Oxford: Oxford University Press.

Jenkins, J. (2007). *English as a Lingua Franca: Attitude and identity.* Oxford: Oxford University Press.

Jenkins, J. (2011). Accommodating (to) ELF in the international university. *Journal of Pragmatics*, *43*, 926–936. doi: 10.1016/j.pragma.2010.05.011

Jenkins, J. (2014). *English as a Lingua Franca in the international university: The politics of academic English language policy.* Abingdon: Routledge.

Jenkins, J. (2015a). *Global Englishes: A resource book for students* (3rd edn). Abingdon: Routledge.

Jenkins, J. (2015b). Repositioning English and multilingualism in English as a Lingua Franca. *Englishes in Practice*, 2, 49–85. doi: 10.1515/eip-2015-0003

Jenkins, J. (2017). ELF and WE: Competing or complementing paradigms? In E.L. Low & A. Pakir (Eds.), *World Englishes: Rethinking paradigms* (pp. 12–28). Abingdon: Routledge.

Jenkins, J. (2018a). The future of English as a lingua franca? In J. Jenkins, W. Baker, & M. Dewey (Eds.), *The Routledge handbook of English as a lingua franca* (pp. 594–605). Abingdon: Routledge.

Jenkins, J. (2018b). Not English but English-within-multilingualism. In S. Coffey & U. Wingate (Eds.), *New directions for research in foreign language education* (pp. 65–78). Abingdon: Routledge.

Jenkins, J. (2020). Where are we with ELF and language testing? An opinion piece. *ELT Journal*, *74*, 473–479. doi: 10.1093/elt/ccaa045

Jenkins, J., Baker, W., & Dewey, M. (Eds.). (2018). *The Routledge handbook of English as a lingua franca.* Abingdon: Routledge.

Jenkins, J., Cogo, A., & Dewey, M. (2011). Review of developments in research into English as a lingua franca. *Language Teaching*, *44*, 281–315. doi: 10.1017/S0261444811000115

Jenkins, J. & Leung, C. (2019). From mythical 'standard' to standard reality: The need for alternatives to standardized English language tests. *Language Teaching*, *52*, 86–110. doi: 10.1017/s0261444818000307

Jenks, C. (2013). Are you an ELF? The relevance of ELF as an equitable social category in online intercultural communication. *Language and Intercultural Communication*, *13*, 95–108. doi: 10.1080/14708477.2012.748792

Jenks, C. (2018). Uncooperative lingua franca encounters. In J. Jenkins, W. Baker, & M. Dewey (Eds.), *The Routledge handbook of English as a lingua franca* (pp. 279–291). Abingdon: Routledge.

Jensen, R.A. (1993). *Thinking in story: Preaching in a post-literate age*. Lima, OH: CSS Publishing.

Jewitt, C. (Ed.). (2014/2017). *The Routledge handbook of multimodal analysis* (2nd edn). Abingdon: Routledge.

Jin, L.X. & Cortazzi, M. (1998). The culture the learner brings: A bridge or a barrier? In M. Byram & M. Fleming (Eds.), *Language learning in intercultural perspective: Approaches through drama and ethnography* (pp. 98–118). Cambridge: Cambridge University Press.

Johnstone, B. (2016). The sociolinguistics of globalization: Standardization and localization in the context of change. *Annual Review of Linguistics*, *2*, 349–365. doi: 10.1146/annurev-linguistics-011415-040552

Jones, J.F. (1999). From silence to talk: Cross-cultural ideas on students' participation in academic group discussion. *English for Specific Purposes*, *18*, 243–259. doi: 10.1016/S0889-4906(97)00059-8

Joseph, J.E. (2004). *Language and identity: National, ethnic, religious*. Basingstoke: Palgrave Macmillan.

Juan-Garau, M. & Jacob, K. (2015). Developing English learners' transcultural skills through content- and task-based lessons. *System*, *54*, 55–68. doi: 10.1016/j.system.2015.04.017

Kachru, B.B. (1985). Standards, codification and sociolinguistic realism: The English language in the outer circle. In R. Quirk & H.G. Widdowson (Eds.), *English in the world: Teaching and learning the language and literatures* (pp. 11–30). Cambridge: Cambridge University Press.

Kachru, B.B. (1992). Teaching world Englishes. In B.B. Kachru (Ed.), *The other tongue: English across cultures* (2nd edn, pp. 355–365). Urbana, IL: University of Illinois Press.

Kachru, B.B., Kachru, Y., & Nelson, C.L. (Eds.). (2006/2009). *The handbook of world Englishes*. Oxford: Wiley-Blackwell.

Kachru, Y. & Smith, L.E. (2008). *Cultures, contexts, and world Englishes*. Abingdon: Routledge.

Kalocsai, K. (2014). *Communities of practice and English as a lingua franca: A study of students in a Central European context*. Berlin: De Gruyter Mouton.

Kankaanranta, A. & Louhiala-Salminen, L. (2018). ELF in the domain of business – BELF: What does the B stand for? In J. Jenkins, W. Baker, & M. Dewey (Eds.), *The Routledge handbook of English as a lingua franca* (pp. 309–320). Abingdon: Routledge.

Karakaş, A. (2016). *Turkish lecturers' and students' perceptions of English in English-medium instruction universities*. Southampton: University of Southampton PhD thesis.

Kaur, J. (2009). Pre-empting problems of understanding in English as a lingua franca In A. Mauranen & E. Ranta (Eds.), *English as a lingua franca: Studies and findings* (pp. 107–123). Newcastle upon Tyne: Cambridge Scholars.

Ke, I-C. & Cahyani, H. (2014). Learning to become users of English as a Lingua Franca (ELF): How ELF online communication affects Taiwanese learners' beliefs of English. *System*, *46*, 28–38. doi: 10.1016/j.system.2014.07.008

Kemp, S. (2019). Digital 2019: Global digital overview. *DataReportal.* Retrieved from https://datareportal.com/reports/digital-2019-global-digital-overview (accessed 30 September 2020).

Kemp, S. (2020). Digital 2020: Global digital overview. *DataReportal.* Retrieved from https://datareportal.com/reports/digital-2020-global-digital-overview (accessed 30 September 2020).

Kiczkowiak, M. (2018). *Native speakerism in English language teaching: Voices from Poland.* York: University of York PhD thesis.

Killick, D. (2013). Global citizenship, sojourning students and campus communities. *Teaching in Higher Education*, *18*, 721–735. doi: 10.1080/13562517.2013.836087

Kimura, D. & Canagarajah, S. (2018). Translingual practice and ELF. In J. Jenkins, W. Baker, & M. Dewey (Eds.), *The Routledge handbook of English as a lingua franca* (pp. 295–308). Abingdon: Routledge.

Kirkpatrick, A. (2010a). *English as a lingua franca in ASEAN: A multilingual model.* Hong Kong: Hong Kong University Press.

Kirkpatrick, A. (2010b). Researching English as a lingua franca in Asia: The Asian Corpus of English (ACE) project. *Asian Englishes*, *13*, 4–18. doi: 10.1080/13488678.2010.10801269

Kirkpatrick, A. (2012). English as an Asian lingua franca: The 'lingua franca approach' and implications for language education policy. *Journal of English as a Lingua Franca*, *1*, 121–139. doi: 10.1515/jelf-2012-0006

Kitazawa, M. (2013). *Approaching conceptualisations of English in East Asian contexts: Ideas, ideology, and identification.* Southampton: University of Southampton PhD thesis.

Klimpfinger, T. (2009). "She's mixing the two languages together" – Forms and functions of code-switching in English as a lingua franca. In A. Mauranen & E. Ranta (Eds.), *English as a lingua franca: Studies and findings* (pp. 348–371). Newcastle upon Tyne: Cambridge Scholars.

Kobayashi, Y. (2018). *The evolution of English language learners in Japan: Crossing Japan, the West, and South East Asia.* Abingdon: Routledge.

Kramsch, C. (1993). *Context and culture in language teaching.* Oxford: Oxford University Press.

Kramsch, C. (1995). The cultural component of language teaching. *Language, Culture and Curriculum*, *8*, 83–92. doi: 10.1080/07908319509525192

Kramsch, C. (1998a). *Language and culture.* Oxford: Oxford University Press.

Kramsch, C. (1998b). The privilege of the intercultural speaker. In M. Byram & M. Fleming (Eds.), *Language learning in intercultural perspective: Approaches through drama and ethnography* (pp. 16–31). Cambridge: Cambridge University Press.

Kramsch, C. (2009). *The multilingual subject: What foreign language learners say about their experience and why it matters.* Oxford: Oxford University Press.

Kramsch, C. (2011). The symbolic dimensions of the intercultural. *Language Teaching*, *44*, 354–367. doi: 10.1017/S0261444810000431

Kress, G. (2014/2017). What is mode? In C. Jewitt (Ed.), *The Routledge handbook of multimodal analysis* (2nd edn, pp. 60–75). Abingdon: Routledge.
Kress, G. & van Leeuwen, T. (2001). *Multimodal discourse: The modes and media of contemporary communication*. London: Arnold.
Krosnick, J.A., Holbrook, A.L., Berent, M.K., Carson, R.T., Hanemann, W.M., Kopp, R.J., Mitchell, R.C., Presser, S., Ruud, P.A., Smith, V.K., Moody, W.R., Green, M.C., & Conaway, M. (2002). The impact of "no opinion" response options on data quality: Non-attitude reduction or an invitation to satisfice? *Public Opinion Quarterly*, *66*, 371–403. doi: 10.1086/341394
Kubota, R. (1999). Japanese culture constructed by discourses: Implications for applied linguistics research and ELT. *TESOL Quarterly*, *33*, 9–35. doi: 10.2307/3588189
Kubota, R. (2001). Discursive construction of the images of U.S. classrooms. *TESOL Quarterly*, *35*, 9–38. doi: 10.2307/3587858
Kubota, R. (2011). Questioning linguistic instrumentalism: English, neoliberalism, and language tests in Japan. *Linguistics and Education*, 22, 248–260. doi: 10.1016/j.linged.2011.02.002
KUIS. (2020). Los módulos del español de México: Platicando en el español de México. Kanda University of International Studies (KUIS). Retrieved from http://labo.kuis.ac.jp/module/spanish/index.html (accessed 30 September 2020).
KUIS & TUFS. (2020). English modules dialog: Indian English. Greeting someone. Kanda University of International Studies (KUIS) × Tokyo University of Foreign Studies (TUFS). Retrieved from http://labo.kuis.ac.jp/module/module/en_in.html#/en-01 (accessed 30 September 2020).
Kumaravadivelu, B. (2008). *Cultural globalization and language education*. New Haven, CT: Yale University Press.
Kumaravadivelu, B. (2012). *Language teacher education for a global society: A modular model for knowing, analyzing, recognizing, doing, and seeing*. Abingdon: Routledge.
Kumaravadivelu, B. (2016). The decolonial option in English teaching: Can the subaltern act? *TESOL Quarterly*, *50*, 66–85. doi: 10.1002/tesq.202
Kusumaningputri, R. & Widodo, H.P. (2018). Promoting Indonesian university students' critical intercultural awareness in tertiary EAL classrooms: The use of digital photograph-mediated intercultural tasks. *System*, *72*, 49–61. doi: 10.1016/j.system.2017.10.003
Kytölä, S. (2016/2020). Translocality. In A. Georgakopoulou & T. Spilioti (Eds.), *The Routledge handbook of language and digital communication* (pp. 371–388). Abingdon: Routledge.
Larsen-Freeman, D. (1997). Chaos/complexity science and second language acquisition. *Applied Linguistics*, *18*, 141–165. doi: 10.1093/applin/18.2.141
Larsen-Freeman, D. (2017). Complexity theory: The lessons continue. In L. Ortega & Z.-H. Han (Eds.), *Complexity theory and language development: In celebration of Diane Larsen-Freeman* (pp. 11–50). Amsterdam: John Benjamins.
Larsen-Freeman, D. (2018). Complexity and ELF. In J. Jenkins, W. Baker, & M. Dewey (Eds.), *The Routledge handbook of English as a lingua franca* (pp. 51–60). Abingdon: Routledge.

Larsen-Freeman, D. & Cameron, L. (2008). *Complex systems and applied linguistics*. Oxford: Oxford University Press.

Lave, J. & Wenger, E. (1991). *Situated learning: Legitimate peripheral participation*. Cambridge: Cambridge University Press.

Leavitt, J. (2015). Linguistic relativity: Precursors and transformations. In F. Sharifian (Ed.), *The Routledge handbook of language and culture* (pp. 18–30). Abingdon: Routledge.

Lee, E. & Canagarajah, S. (2019). The connection between transcultural dispositions and translingual practices in academic writing. *Journal of Multicultural Discourses*, *14*(1), 14–28. doi: 10.1080/17447143.2018.1501375

Leung, C. (2005). Convivial communication: Recontextualizing communicative competence. *International Journal of Applied Linguistics*, *15*, 119–144. doi: 10.1111/j.1473-4192.2005.00084.x

Leung, C. & Lewkowicz, J. (2018). English language teaching: Pedagogic reconnection with the social dimension. In J. Jenkins, W. Baker, & M. Dewey (Eds.), *The Routledge handbook of English as a lingua franca* (pp. 61–73). Abingdon: Routledge.

Leung, C., Lewkowicz, J., & Jenkins, J. (2016). English for academic purposes: A need for remodelling. *Englishes in Practice*, *3*, 55–73. doi: 10.1515/eip-2016-0003

Lewis, G., Jones, B., & Baker, C. (2012). Translanguaging: Origins and development from school to street and beyond. *Educational Research and Evaluation*, *18*, 641–654. doi: 10.1080/13803611.2012.718488

Li, L. (2015). A Confucian perspective on teaching thinking in China. In R. Wegerif, L. Li, & J.C. Kaufman (Eds.), *The Routledge international handbook of research on teaching thinking* (pp. 45–57). Abingdon: Routledge.

Li, W. (2016). New Chinglish and the Post-Multilingualism challenge: Translanguaging ELF in China. *Journal of English as a Lingua Franca*, *5*, 1–25. doi: 10.1515/jelf-2016-0001

Li, W. (2018). Translanguaging as a practical theory of language. *Applied Linguistics*, *39*, 9–30. doi: 10.1093/applin/amx039

Li, W. (2020). Multilingual English users' linguistic innovation. *World Englishes*, *39*, 236–248. doi: 10.1111/weng.12457

Li, W. & Ho, W.Y. (J.). (2018). Language learning *sans frontiers*: A translanguaging view. *Annual Review of Applied Linguistics*, *38*, 33–59. doi: 10.1017/S0267190518000053

Li, W. & Lin, A.M.Y. (2019). Translanguaging classroom discourse: Pushing limits, breaking boundaries. *Classroom Discourse*, *10*, 209–215. doi: 10.1080/19463014.2019.1635032

Li, W. & Zhu, H. (2013). Diaspora: Multilingual and intercultural communication across time and space. *AILA Review*, *26*, 42–56. doi: 10.1075/aila.26.04wei

Liddicoat, A.J. & Scarino, A. (2013). *Intercultural language teaching and learning*. Oxford: Wiley-Blackwell.

Lindemann, S. (2005). Who speaks "broken English"? US undergraduates' perceptions of non-native English. *International Journal of Applied Linguistics*, *15*, 187–212. doi: 10.1111/j.1473-4192.2005.00087.x

Lippi-Green, R. (2012). *English with an accent: Language, ideology, and discrimination in the United States* (2nd edn). Abingdon: Routledge.

Liu, H. (2016). *Language policy and practice in a Chinese junior high school from global Englishes perspective.* Southampton: University of Southampton PhD thesis.

Love, N. (2004). Cognition and the language myth. *Language Sciences, 26,* 525–544. doi: 10.1016/j.langsci.2004.09.003

Luk, J. (2012). Teachers' ambivalence in integrating culture with EFL teaching in Hong Kong. *Language, Culture and Curriculum, 25,* 249–264. doi: 10.1080/07908318.2012.716849

MacDonald, M.N. (2019). The discourse of 'thirdness' in intercultural studies. *Language and Intercultural Communication, 19,* 93–109. doi: 10.1080/14708477.2019.1544788

Makoni, S. (2003). From misinvention to disinvention of language: Multilingualism and the South African Constitution. In S. Makoni, G. Smitherman, A.F. Ball, & A.K. Spears (Eds.), *Black Linguistics: Language, society, and politics in Africa and the Americas* (pp. 132–151). London: Routledge.

Marlina, R. (2014). The pedagogy of English as an International Language (EIL): More reflections and dialogues. In R. Marlina & R.A. Giri (Eds.), *The pedagogy of English as an international language: Perspectives from scholars, teachers, and students* (pp. 1–19). Cham: Springer.

Marwick, A.E., & boyd, d. (2011). I tweet honestly, I tweet passionately: Twitter users, context collapse, and the imagined audience. *New Media & Society, 13,* 114–133. doi: 10.1177/1461444810365313

Matsuda, A. (2003). The ownership of English in Japanese secondary schools. *World Englishes, 22,* 483–496. doi: 10.1111/j.1467-971X.2003.00314.x

Matsuda, A. & Friedrich, P. (2012). Selecting an instructional variety for an EIL curriculum. In A. Matsuda (Ed.), *Principles and practices of teaching English as an international language* (pp. 17–27). Clevedon: Multilingual Matters.

Mauranen, A. (2003). The corpus of English as lingua franca in academic settings. *TESOL Quarterly, 37,* 513–527. doi: 10.2307/3588402

Mauranen, A. (2012). *Exploring ELF: Academic English shaped by non-native speakers.* Cambridge: Cambridge University Press.

Mauranen, A. (2014). Lingua franca discourse in academic contexts: Shaped by complexity. In J. Flowerdew (Ed.), *Discourse in context* (pp. 225–245). London: Bloomsbury.

Mauranen, A. (2015). What is going on in academic ELF? Findings and implications. In P. Vettorel (Ed.), *New frontiers in teaching and learning English* (pp. 31–52). Newcastle upon Tyne: Cambridge Scholars.

Mauranen, A. (2018a). Conceptualising ELF. In J. Jenkins, W. Baker, & M. Dewey (Eds.), *The Routledge handbook of English as a lingua franca* (pp. 7–24). Abingdon: Routledge.

Mauranen, A. (2018b). Second Language Acquisition, world Englishes, and English as a Lingua Franca (ELF). *World Englishes, 37,* 106–119. doi: 10.1111/weng.12306

May, S. (2014). Contesting metronormativity: Exploring indigenous language dynamism across the urban-rural divide. *Journal of Language, Identity & Education, 13*, 229–235. doi: 10.1080/15348458.2014.939036

McConnell, D.L. (2000). *Importing diversity: Inside Japan's JET Program*. Berkeley, CA: University of California Press.

McKenzie, R.M. (2010). *The social psychology of English as a global language: Attitudes, awareness and identity in the Japanese context*. Dordrecht: Springer.

McKenzie, R.M. & Gilmore, A. (2017). "The people who are out of 'right' English": Japanese university students' social evaluations of English language diversity and the internationalisation of Japanese higher education. *International Journal of Applied Linguistics, 27*, 152–175. doi: 10.1111/ijal.12110

McNamara, T., Morton, J., Storch, N., & Thompson, C. (2018). Students' accounts of their first-year undergraduate academic writing experience: Implications for the use of the CEFR. *Language Assessment Quarterly, 15*, 16–28. doi: 10.1080/15434303.2017.1405420

Meierkord, C. (2012). *Interactions across Englishes: Linguistic choices in local and international contact situations*. Cambridge: Cambridge University Press.

Melchers, G., Shaw, P., & Sundkvist, P. (2019). *World Englishes* (3rd edn). Abingdon: Routledge.

Mesthrie, R. & Bhatt, R.M. (2008). *World Englishes: The study of new linguistic varieties*. Cambridge: Cambridge University Press.

MEXT (Ministry of Education, Culture, Sports, Science and Technology). (2014). 大学における教育内容・方法の改善等について [Concerning the improvement etc. of educational content and teaching methods in universities and colleges (the authors' translation)]. Ministry of Education, Culture, Sports, Science and Technology (MEXT). Retrieved from www.mext.go.jp/a_menu/koutou/daigaku/index.htm. (accessed on 30 September 2020).

MEXT. (2020). 新しい学習指導要領「生きる力」 [New Courses of Study: Ability to live (the authors' translation)]. Ministry of Education, Culture, Sports, Science and Technology (MEXT). Retrieved from www.mext.go.jp/a_menu/shotou/new-cs/index.htm (accessed 30 September 2020).

Miller, J.H. & Page, S.E. (2007). *Complex adaptive systems: An introduction to computational models of social life*. Princeton, NJ: Princeton University Press.

Milroy, J. (2001). Language ideologies and the consequences of standardization. *Journal of Sociolinguistics, 5*, 530–555. doi: 10.1111/1467-9481.00163

Milroy, J. (2007). The ideology of the standard language. In C. Llamas, L. Mullany, & P. Stockwell (Eds.), *The Routledge companion to sociolinguistics* (pp. 133–139). Abingdon: Routledge.

Milroy, J. & Milroy, L. (2012). *Authority in language: Investigating standard English* (4th edn). Abingdon: Routledge.

Ministry of Education (in the People's Republic of China). (2011). *English curriculum standards for compulsory education*. Beijing: People's Education Press.

MLA (Ad Hoc Committee on Foreign Languages). (2007). Foreign languages and higher education: New structures for a changed world. *Profession, 2007*, 234–245. doi: 10.1632/prof.2007.2007.1.234

Modiano, M. (2006/2009). Euro-Englishes. In B.B. Kachru, Y. Kachru, & C.L. Nelson (Eds.), *The handbook of world Englishes* (pp. 223–239). Oxford: Wiley-Blackwell.

Modiano, M. (2017). English in a post-Brexit European Union. *World Englishes, 36*, 313–327. doi: 10.1111/weng.12264

Monceri, F. (2019). Beyond universality: Rethinking transculturality and the transcultural self. *Journal of Multicultural Discourses, 14*, 78–91. doi: 10.1080/17447143.2019.1604715

Morán Panero, S. (2018). Global languages and lingua franca communication. In J. Jenkins, W. Baker, & M. Dewey (Eds.), *The Routledge handbook of English as a lingua franca* (pp. 556–569). Abingdon: Routledge.

Morán Panero, S. (2019). "It's more fashionable to speak it badly": Indexicality and metasemiotic awareness among users of English from the Spanish-speaking world. *Journal of English as a Lingua Franca, 8*, 297–332. doi: 10.1515/jelf-2019-2021

Mori, J. & Sanuth, K.K. (2018). Navigating between a monolingual utopia and translingual realities: Experiences of American learners of Yorùbá as an additional language. *Applied Linguistics, 39*, 78–98. doi: 10.1093/applin/amx042

Mortensen, J. (2013). Notes on English used as a lingua franca as an object of study. *Journal of English as a Lingua Franca, 2*, 25–46. doi: 10.1515/jelf-2013-0002

Mullin, J., Haviland, C.P., & Zenger, A. (2014). Import/export work? Using cross-cultural theories to rethink Englishes, identities, and genres in writing centers. In B. Horner & K. Kopelson (Eds.), *Reworking English in rhetoric and composition: Global interrogations, local interventions* (pp. 150–165). Carbondale, IL: Southern Illinois University Press.

Murata, K. & Iino, M. (2018). EMI in higher education: An ELF perspective. In J. Jenkins, W. Baker, & M. Dewey (Eds.), *The Routledge handbook of English as a lingua franca* (pp. 400–412). Abingdon: Routledge.

Murphy, K.M. (2012). Transmodality and temporality in design interactions. *Journal of Pragmatics, 44*, 1966–1981. doi: 10.1016/j.pragma.2012.08.013

National Portal of India. (2020). Profile. India.gov.in. Retrieved from www.india.gov.in/india-glance/profile (accessed 30 September 2020).

Nelson, C.L., Proshina, Z.G., & Davis, D.R. (Eds.). (2020). *The handbook of world Englishes* (2nd edn). Chichester: Wiley Blackwell.

Newfield, D. (2014/2017). Transformation, transduction and the transmodal moment. In C. Jewitt (Ed.), *The Routledge handbook of multimodal analysis* (2nd edn, pp. 100–113). Abingdon: Routledge.

Newton, J., Yates, E., Shearn, S., & Nowitzki, W. (2010). *Intercultural communicative language teaching: Implications for effective teaching and learning.* Wellington: Ministry of Education.

Nguyen, H.H. (2012). The multilanguaging of a Vietnamese American in South Philadelphia. *Working Papers in Educational Linguistics, 27*(1), 65–85. Retrieved from https://repository.upenn.edu/wpel/vol27/iss1/5 (accessed 30 September 2020).

Niedzielski, N.A. & Preston, D.R. (1999/2003). *Folk linguistics*. Berlin: Mouton De Gruyter.

Norton, B. (2010). Language and identity. In N.H. Hornberger & S.L. McKay (Eds.), *Sociolinguistics and language education* (pp. 349–369). Clevedon: Multilingual Matters.

OBEC (Office of the Basic Education Commission). (2008). *Basic Education Core Curriculum: B.E. 2551*. Bangkok: Ministry of Education. Retrieved from www.ipst.ac.th/index.php (accessed 30 September 2020).

Ochs, E. (2002). Becoming a speaker of culture. In C. Kramsch (Ed.), *Language acquisition and language socialization: Ecological perspectives* (pp. 99–120). London: Continuum.

Oda, M. (2018a). A post-EFL approach to the administration of English language programs. *JACET ELF SIG Journal*, *2*, 32–38. Retrieved from https://jacetelf.wordpress.com/jacet-elf-sig-journal/ (accessed 30 September 2020).

Oda, M. (2018b). Collaboration and collaborative practices. In J.I. Liontas (Ed.), *The TESOL encyclopedia of English language teaching* (Vol. 2, pp. 1022–1027). Oxford: Wiley Blackwell.

Oda, M. (2019). Beyond Global English(es): University English program in transition. In K. Murata (Ed.), *English-medium instruction from an English as a lingua franca perspective: Exploring the higher education context* (pp. 259–270). Abingdon: Routledge.

O'Dowd, R. (2011). Online foreign language interaction: Moving from the periphery to the core of foreign language education? *Language Teaching*, *44*, 368–380. doi: 10.1017/S0261444810000194

Ohmae, K. (1995). *The end of the nation state: The rise of regional economies*. New York: The Free Press.

Osler, A. & Starkey, H. (2015). Education for cosmopolitan citizenship: A framework for language learning. *Argentinian Journal of Applied Linguistics*, *3*(2), 30–39. Retrieved from www.faapi.org.ar/ajal/issues/302/Starkey.html (accessed 30 September 2020).

Ostler, N. (2005/2006). *Empires of the word: A language history of the world*. London: Harper Perennial.

Ostler, N. (2010). *The last lingua franca: English until the return of Babel*. New York: Walker & Company.

Otheguy, R., García, O., & Reid, W. (2015). Clarifying translanguaging and deconstructing named languages: A perspective from linguistics. *Applied Linguistics Review*, *6*, 281–307. doi: 10.1515/applirev-2015-0014

Park, J.-M. (2020). Cherry blossoms must wait, Tokyo governor says, amid supply queues in coronavirus battle. Reuters, 27 March. Retrieved from www.reuters.com/article/us-health-coronavirus-japan/tokyo-residents-stockpile-essentials-to-hunker-down-for-the-weekend-idUSKBN21E0A7 (accessed 30 September 2020).

Parliament of India. (2020). Lok Sabha: House of the People. Parliament of India. Retrieved from https://loksabha.nic.in/ (accessed 30 September 2020).

Pauwels, L. (2012). A multimodal framework for analyzing websites as cultural expressions. *Journal of Computer-Mediated Communication*, *17*, 247–265. doi: 10.1111/j.1083-6101.2012.01572.x

Pavlenko, A. & Blackledge, A. (2004). *Negotiation of identities in multilingual contexts*. Clevedon: Multilingual Matters.

Penny, R. (2002). *A history of the Spanish language* (2nd edn). Cambridge: Cambridge University Press.

Pennycook, A. (2005). Teaching with the flow: Fixity and fluidity in education. *Asia Pacific Journal of Education*, *25*, 29–43. doi: 10.1080/02188790500032491

Pennycook, A. (2007). *Global Englishes and transcultural flows.* Abingdon: Routledge.

Pennycook, A. (2010a). *Language as a local practice.* Abingdon: Routledge.

Pennycook, A. (2010b). The future of Englishes: One, many or none? In A. Kirkpatrick (Ed.), *The Routledge handbook of world Englishes* (pp. 673–687). Abingdon: Routledge.

Pennycook, A. (2011). The sociolinguistics of globalization (review). *Language*, *87*, 884–887. Retrieved from www.jstor.org/stable/41348868 (accessed 30 September 2020).

Pennycook, A. (2020). Translingual entanglements of English. *World Englishes*, *39*, 222–235. doi: 10.1111/weng.12456

Pennycook, A. & Otsuji, E. (2015). *Metrolingualism: Language in the city.* Abingdon: Routledge.

Perez Andrade, G. (2019). *Language ideologies in English Language Teaching: A multiple case study of teacher education programmes in Chile.* Southampton: University of Southampton PhD thesis.

Perloff, R.M. (2021). *The dynamics of persuasion: Communication and attitudes in the 21st century* (7th edn). Abingdon: Routledge.

Petty, R.E., Wegener, D.T., & Fabrigar, L.R. (1997). Attitudes and attitude change. *Annual Review of Psychology*, *48*, 609–647. doi: 10.1146/annurev.psych.48.1.609

Phan, L.H. (2008). *Teaching English as an international language: Identity, resistance and negotiation.* Clevedon: Multilingual Matters.

Phipps, A. & Guilherme, M. (2004). Introduction: Why languages and intercultural communication are never just neutral. In A. Phipps & M. Guilherme (Eds.), *Critical pedagogy: Political approaches to language and intercultural communication* (pp. 1–6). Clevedon: Multilingual Matters.

Pietikäinen, K.S. (2014). ELF couples and automatic code-switching. *Journal of English as a Lingua Franca*, *3*, 1–26. doi: 10.1515/jelf-2014-0001

Pietikäinen, K.S. (2018). Misunderstandings and ensuring understanding in private ELF talk. *Applied Linguistics*, *39*, 188–212. doi: 10.1093/applin/amw005

Piller, I. (2011). *Intercultural communication: A critical introduction.* Edinburgh: Edinburgh University Press.

Piller, I. (2017). *Intercultural communication: A critical introduction* (2nd edn). Edinburgh: Edinburgh University Press.

Pitzl, M.-L. (2005). Non-understanding in English as a lingua franca: Examples from a business context. *Vienna English Working Papers (Views)*, *14*(2), 50–71. Retrieved from https://anglistik.univie.ac.at/research/views/archive/ (accessed 30 September 2020).

Pitzl, M.-L. (2009). "We should not wake up any dogs": Idiom and metaphor in ELF. In A. Mauranen & E. Ranta (Eds.), *English as a lingua franca: Studies and findings* (pp. 298–322). Newcastle upon Tyne: Cambridge Scholars.

Pitzl, M.-L. (2012). Creativity meets convention: Idiom variation and remetaphorization in ELF. *Journal of English as a Lingua Franca*, *1*, 27–55. doi: 10.1515/jelf-2012-0003

Pitzl, M.-L. (2018a). Transient international groups (TIGs): Exploring the group and development dimension of ELF. *Journal of English as a Lingua Franca*, *7*, 25–58. doi: 10.1515/jelf-2018-0002

Pitzl, M.-L. (2018b). *Creativity in English as a lingua franca: Idiom and metaphor*. Berlin: De Gruyter Mouton.

Pitzl, M.-L. (2018c). Creativity, idioms and metaphorical language in ELF. In J. Jenkins, W. Baker, & M. Dewey (Eds.), *The Routledge handbook of English as a lingua franca* (pp. 233–243). Abingdon: Routledge.

Plato. (1999). *Apology* (Trans. B. Jowett) [E-reader version]. Retrieved from www.gutenberg.org/files/1656/1656-h/1656-h.htm (accessed 10 December 2020)

Platt, J., Weber, H., & Ho, M.L. (1984). *The New Englishes*. London: Routledge and Kegan Paul.

Pölzl, U. & Seidlhofer, B. (2006). In and on their own terms: The "habitat factor" in English as a lingua franca interactions. *International Journal of the Sociology of Language*, *2006*(177), 151–176. doi: 10.1515/IJSL.2006.009

Porto, M., Houghton, S.A., & Byram, M. (2018). Intercultural citizenship in the (foreign) language classroom. *Language Teaching Research*, *22*, 484–498. doi: 10.1177/1362168817718580

Potter, J. (1996). Attitudes, social representations and discursive psychology. In M. Wetherell (Ed.), *Identities, groups and social issues* (pp. 119–173). London: Sage.

Potter, J. & Wetherell, M. (1987). *Discourse and social psychology: Beyond attitudes and behaviour*. London: Sage.

Pratt, M.L. (1992). *Imperial eyes: Travel writing and transculturation*. London: Routledge.

Pratt, M.L. (2008). *Imperial eyes: Travel writing and transculturation* (2nd edn). Abingdon: Routledge.

Prescott, C. (2019). *Internet users, UK: 2019. Internet use in the UK annual estimates by age, sex, disability and geographical location*. Newport: Office for National Statistics. Retrieved from www.ons.gov.uk/businessindustryandtrade/itandinternetindustry/bulletins/internetusers/2019 (accessed 30 September 2020).

Preston, D.R. (2010). Variation in language regard. In P. Gilles, J. Scharloth, & E. Ziegler (Eds.), *Variatio delectat: Empirische Evidenzen und theoretische Passungen sprachlicher Variation* (pp. 7–27). Frankfurt am Main: Peter Lang.

Preston, D.R. (2018a). Perceptual dialectology. In C. Boberg, J. Nerbonne, & D. Watt (Eds.), *The handbook of dialectology* (pp. 177–203). Oxford: Wiley Blackwell.

Preston, D.R. (2018b). Folk linguistics and language awareness. In P. Garrett & J.M. Cots (Eds.), *The Routledge handbook of language awareness* (pp. 375–386). Abingdon: Routledge.

Pride, J.B. (Ed.). (1982). *New Englishes*. Rowley, MA: Newbury House.

QS Quacquarelli Symonds. (2020). The world's top 100 universities. QS Top Universities. Retrieved from www.topuniversities.com/student-info/choosing-university/worlds-top-100-universities (accessed 30 September 2020).

Ra, J. (2018). *A study of a multilingual student community's language practices and perceptions at a Korean international university.* Southampton: University of Southampton PhD thesis.

Rampton, B. (1995/2018). *Crossing: Language and ethnicity among adolescents* (3rd edn). Abingdon: Routledge.

Ranta, E. (2006). The 'attractive' progressive – Why use the *-ing* form in English as a lingua franca? *Nordic Journal of English Studies*, *5*(2), 95–116. Retrieved from http://130.241.16.45/ojs/index.php/njes/article/view/64 (accessed 30 September 2020).

Ranta, E. (2010). English in the real world vs. English at school: Finnish English teachers' and students' views. *International Journal of Applied Linguistics*, *20*, 156–177. doi: 10.1111/j.1473-4192.2009.00235.x

Riley, P. (2007). *Language, culture and identity: An ethnolinguistic perspective.* London: Continuum.

Risager, K. (2006). *Language and culture: Global flows and local complexity.* Clevedon: Multilingual Matters.

Risager, K. (2007). *Language and culture pedagogy: From a national to a transnational paradigm.* Clevedon: Multilingual Matters.

Risager, K. (2012). Linguaculture and transnationality: The cultural dimensions of language. In J. Jackson (Ed.), *The Routledge handbook of language and intercultural communication* (pp. 101–115). Abingdon: Routledge.

Risager, K. (2015). Linguaculture: The language–culture nexus in transnational perspective. In F. Sharifian (Ed.), *The Routledge handbook of language and culture* (pp. 87–99). Abingdon: Routledge.

Risager, K. (2020). Linguaculture and transnationality: The cultural dimensions of language. In J. Jackson (Ed.), *The Routledge handbook of language and intercultural communication* (2nd edn, pp. 109–123). Abingdon: Routledge.

Roberts, C., Byram, M., Barro, A., Jordan, S., & Street, B. (2001). *Language learners as ethnographers.* Clevedon: Multilingual Matters.

Rose, H. & Galloway, N. (2019). *Global Englishes for language teaching.* Cambridge: Cambridge University Press.

Rosenberg, M.J. & Hovland, C.I. (1960). Cognitive, affective, and behavioral components of attitudes. In M.J. Rosenberg, C.I. Hovland, W.J. McGuire, R.P. Abelson, & J.W. Brehm (Eds.), *Attitude organization and change: An analysis of consistency among attitude components* (pp. 1–14). New Haven, CT: Yale University Press.

Ryan, E.B., Giles, H., & Sebastian, R.J. (1982). An integrative perspective for the study of attitudes toward language variation. In E.B. Ryan & H. Giles (Eds.), *Attitudes towards language variation: Social and applied contexts* (pp. 1–19). London: Edward Arnold.

Ryan, J. (2011). Teaching and learning for international students: Towards a transcultural approach. *Teachers and Teaching*, *17*, 631–648. doi: 10.1080/13540602.2011.625138

Said, E.W. (1978/2003). *Orientalism.* London: Penguin.

Sangiamchit, C. (2018). ELF in electronically mediated intercultural communication. In J. Jenkins, W. Baker, & M. Dewey (Eds.), *The Routledge handbook of English as a lingua franca* (pp. 345–356). Abingdon: Routledge.

Saraceni, M. (2015). *World Englishes: A critical analysis*. London: Bloomsbury.

Sarup, M. (1996). *Identity, culture and the postmodern world*. Edinburgh: Edinburgh University Press.

Sasayama, S. (2013). Japanese college students' attitudes towards Japan English and American English. *Journal of Multilingual and Multicultural Development*, *34*, 264–278. doi: 10.1080/01434632.2013.767341

Saussure, F. de. (1959/2011). *Course in general linguistics* (Trans. W. Baskin) (P. Meisel & H. Saussy (Eds.)). New York: Columbia University Press.

Scarino, A. & Liddicoat, A.J. (2009). *Teaching and learning languages: A guide*. Melbourne: Curriculum Corporation.

Schneider, E.W. (2007). *Postcolonial English: Varieties around the world*. Cambridge: Cambridge University Press.

Schneider, E.W. (2014). New reflections on the evolutionary dynamics of world Englishes. *World Englishes*, *33*, 9–32. doi: 10.1111/weng.12069

Schneider, E.W. (2020). English in the United States. In C.L. Nelson, Z.G. Proshina, & D.R. Davis (Eds.), *The handbook of world Englishes* (2nd edn, pp. 37–51). Chichester: Wiley Blackwell.

Scholte, J.A. (2008). Defining globalisation. *The World Economy*, *31*, 1471–1502. doi: 10.1111/j.1467-9701.2007.01019.x

Scollon, R. & Scollon, S.W. (2001). Discourse and intercultural communication. In D. Schiffrin, D. Tannen, & H.E. Hamilton (Eds.), *The handbook of discourse analysis* (pp. 538–547). Oxford: Blackwell.

Scollon, R., Scollon, S.W., & Jones, R.H. (2012). *Intercultural communication: A discourse approach* (3rd edn). Oxford: Wiley-Blackwell.

Seargeant, P., Tagg, C., & Ngampramuan, W. (2012). Language choice and addressivity strategies in Thai-English social network interactions. *Journal of Sociolinguistics*, *16*, 510–531. doi: 10.1111/j.1467-9841.2012.00540.x

Seidlhofer, B. (2004). Research perspectives on teaching English as a lingua franca. *Annual Review of Applied Linguistics*, 24, 209–239. doi: 10.1017/S0267190504000145

Seidlhofer, B. (2009). Accommodation and the idiom principle in English as a Lingua Franca. *Intercultural Pragmatics*, 6, 195–215. doi: 10.1515/IPRG.2009.011

Seidlhofer, B. (2011). *Understanding English as a lingua franca*. Oxford: Oxford University Press.

Seidlhofer, B. (2017). English as a lingua franca and multilingualism. In J. Cenoz, D. Gorter, & S. May (Eds.), *Language awareness and multilingualism* (3rd edn, pp. 391–404). Cham: Springer.

Seidlhofer, B. (2018). Standard English and the dynamics of ELF variation. In J. Jenkins, W. Baker, & M. Dewey (Eds.), *The Routledge handbook of English as a lingua franca* (pp. 85–100). Abingdon: Routledge.

Seidlhofer, B. (2019). Tracing themes and trends in ELF research in Japan and beyond. In K. Murata (Ed.), *Waseda Working Papers in ELF* (Vol. 8, pp. 15–22). Tokyo: Waseda ELF Research Group.

Seidlhofer, B. & Jenkins, J. (2003). English as a lingua franca and the politics of property. In C. Mair (Ed.), *The politics of English as a world language: New horizons in postcolonial cultural studies* (pp. 139–154). Amsterdam: Rodopi.

Seidlhofer, B. & Widdowson, H. (2009). Accommodation and the idiom principle in English as a lingua franca. In K. Murata & J. Jenkins (Eds.), *Global Englishes in Asian contexts: Current and future debates* (pp. 26–39). Basingstoke: Palgrave Macmillan.

Sercu, L., Bandura, E., Castro, P., Davcheva, L., Laskaridou, C., Lundgren, U., Méndez García, M. del C., & Ryan, P. (2005). *Foreign language teachers and intercultural competence: An international investigation*. Clevedon: Multilingual Matters.

Shaaban, K. & Ghaith, G. (2002). University students' perceptions of the ethnolinguistic vitality of Arabic, French and English in Lebanon. *Journal of Sociolinguistics*, *6*, 557–574. doi: 10.1111/1467-9481.00201

Sharifian, F. (2011). *Cultural conceptualisations and language: Theoretical framework and applications*. Amsterdam: John Benjamins.

Sharkey, J. (2018). The promising potential role of intercultural citizenship in preparing mainstream teachers for im/migrant populations. *Language Teaching Research*, *22*, 570–589. doi: 10.1177/1362168817718577

Shohamy, E. (2003). Implications of language education policies for language study in schools and universities. *The Modern Language Journal*, *87*, 278–286. Retrieved from www.jstor.org/stable/1193038 (accessed 30 September 2020).

Shohamy, E. (2006). *Language policy: Hidden agendas and new approaches*. Abingdon: Routledge.

Shohamy, E. (2007). Language tests as language policy tools. *Assessment in Education: Principles, Policy & Practice*, *14*, 117–130. doi: 10.1080/09695940701272948

Sifakis, N.C. (2014). ELF awareness as an opportunity for change: A transformative perspective for ESOL teacher education. *Journal of English as a Lingua Franca*, *3*, 317–335. doi: 10.1515/jelf-2014-0019

Sifakis, N.C. (2019). ELF awareness in English language teaching: Principles and processes. *Applied Linguistics*, *40*, 288–306. doi: 10.1093/applin/amx034

Sifakis, N. & Bayyurt, Y. (2018). ELF-aware teaching, learning and teacher development. In J. Jenkins, W. Baker, & M. Dewey (Eds.), *The Routledge handbook of English as a lingua franca* (pp. 456–467). Abingdon: Routledge.

Sifakis, N.C., Lopriore, L., Dewey, M., Bayyurt, Y., Vettorel, P., Cavalheiro, L., Siqueira, D.S.P., & Kordia, S. (2018). ELF-awareness in ELT: Bringing together theory and practice. *Journal of English as a Lingua Franca*, *7*, 155–209. doi: 10.1515/jelf-2018-0008

Slobin, D.I. (1996). From "thought and language" to "thinking for speaking". In J.J. Gumperz & S.C. Levinson (Eds.), *Rethinking linguistic relativity* (pp. 70–96). Cambridge: Cambridge University Press.

Slobin, D. I. (2003). Language and thought online: Cognitive consequences of linguistic relativity. In D. Gentner & S. Goldin-Meadow (Eds.), *Language in mind: Advances in the study of language and thought* (pp. 157–191). Cambridge, MA: The MIT Press.

Smith, H.A., & Segbers, T. (2018). The impact of transculturality on student experience of higher education. *Journal of Experiential Education*, *41*, 75–89. doi: 10.1177/1053825917750406

Smith, L.E. (1976). English as an international auxiliary language. *RELC Journal*, 7(2), 38–42. doi: 10.1177/003368827600700205

Smith, L.E. (2015). English as an international auxiliary language. *Journal of English as a Lingua Franca*, 4, 159–164. doi: 10.1515/jelf-2015-0001

Soars, L. & Soars, J. (2011). *New Headway: Elementary – Student's book* (4th edn). Oxford: Oxford University Press.

Spencer-Oatey, H. & Franklin, P. (2009). *Intercultural interaction: A multidisciplinary approach to intercultural communication*. Basingstoke: Palgrave Macmillan.

Spitzberg, B.H. & Changnon, G. (2009). Conceptualizing intercultural competence. In Deardorff, D.K. (Ed.), *The Sage handbook of intercultural competence* (pp. 2–52). London: Sage.

Stanlaw, J. (2004). *Japanese English: Language and culture contact*. Hong Kong: Hong Kong University Press.

Stavans, I. (2017). The Spanish language in Latin America since independence. *Oxford Research Encyclopedia of Latin American History*, 26 April. Retrieved from https://oxfordre.com/latinamericanhistory/view/10.1093/acrefore/9780199366439.001.0001/acrefore-9780199366439-e-371 (accessed 30 September 2020).

Stenhouse, L. (1975) *An introduction to curriculum research and development*. London: Heinemann.

Street, B.V. (1993). Culture is a verb: Anthropological aspects of language and cultural process. In D. Graddol, L. Thompson, & M. Byram (Eds.), *Language and culture: Papers from the Annual Meeting of the British Association of Applied Linguistics held at Trevelyan College, University of Durham, September 1991* (pp. 23–43). Clevedon: Multilingual Matters.

Sultana, S. (2016). Language and identity in virtual space: Reconceptualisation of ELF. *Journal of Asian Pacific Communication*, 26, 216–237. doi: 10.1075/japc.26.2.03sul

Swain, M. (2006). Languaging, agency and collaboration in advanced second language proficiency. In H. Byrnes (Ed.), *Advanced language learning: The contribution of Halliday and Vygotsky* (pp. 95–108). London: Continuum.

Sweeney, E. & Zhu, H. (2010). Accommodating toward your audience: Do native speakers of English know how to accommodate their communication strategies toward nonnative speakers of English? *International Journal of Business Communication*, 47, 477–504. doi: 10.1177/0021943610377308

Tagg, C. (2015). *Exploring digital communication: Language in action*. Abingdon: Routledge.

Tagg, C. & Seargeant, P. (2012). Writing systems at play in Thai-English online interactions. *Writing Systems Research*, 4, 195–213. doi: 10.1080/17586801.2011.628583

Tagg, C. & Seargeant, P. (2016/2020). Facebook and the discursive construction of the social network. In A. Georgakopoulou & T. Spilioti (Eds.), *The Routledge handbook of language and digital communication* (pp. 339–353). Abingdon: Routledge.

Taguchi, T. (2013). Motivation, attitudes and selves in the Japanese context: A mixed methods approach. In M.T. Apple, D. Da Silva, & T. Fellner (Eds.), *Language learning motivation in Japan* (pp. 169–188). Clevedon: Multilingual Matters.

Tannen, D. (1986/2011). *That's not what I meant! How conversational style makes or breaks relationships*. New York: Harper.

Thibault, P.J. (2017). The reflexivity of human languaging and Nigel Love's two orders of language. *Language Sciences*, *61*, 74–85. doi: 10.1016/j.langsci.2016.09.014

Thompson, C.H. (2011). A *dialogic* approach to the design of a transcultural communication classroom activity for multilingual learners. *Language, Culture and Curriculum*, 24, 207–220. doi: 10.1080/07908318.2011.605140

Toh, G. (2016). Doing justice to an English as a lingua franca paradigm. *Journal of English as a Lingua Franca*, *5*, 355–367. doi: 10.1515/jelf-2016-0024

Tokumoto, M. & Shibata, M. (2011). Asian varieties of English: Attitudes towards pronunciation. *World Englishes*, *30*, 392–408. doi: 10.1111/j.1467-971X.2011.01710.x

Tomalin, B. & Stempleski, S. (1993). *Cultural awareness*. Oxford: Oxford University Press.

Tomasello, M. (2008). *Origins of human communication*. Cambridge, MA: The MIT Press.

Trudgill, P. & Hannah, J. (2017). *International English: A guide to varieties of English around the world* (6th edn). Abingdon: Routledge.

Tylor, E.B. (1871). *Primitive culture: Researches into the development of mythology, philosophy, religion, art, and custom*. London: John Murray.

United Nations. (2020). Official languages. About the UN. Retrieved from www.un.org/en/sections/about-un/official-languages/ (accessed 30 September 2020).

van Lier, L. (2007). Action-based teaching, autonomy and identity. *Innovation in Language Learning and Teaching*, *1*, 46–65. doi: 10.2167/illt42.0

Varis, P. & Wang, X. (2011). Superdiversity on the Internet: A case from China. *Diversities*, *13*(2), 70–83. Retrieved from www.unesco.org/shs/diversities/vol13/issue2/art5 (accessed 30 September 2020).

Vetchinnikova, S. (2015). Usage-based recycling or creative exploitation of the shared code? The case of phraseological patterning. *Journal of English as a Lingua Franca*, *4*, 223–252. doi: 10.1515/jelf-2015-0019

Vettorel, P. (2010). EIL/ELF and representation of culture in textbooks: Only food, fairs, folklore and facts? In C. Gagliardi & A. Maley (Eds.), *EIL, ELF, Global English: Teaching and learning issues* (pp. 153–185). Bern: Peter Lang.

Vettorel, P. (2014). *English as a lingua franca in wider networking: Blogging practices*. Berlin: De Gruyter Mouton.

Vettorel, P. (2018). ELF and communication strategies: Are they taken into account in ELT materials? *RELC Journal*, *49*, 58–73. doi: 10.1177/0033688217746204

Vogel, S. & García, O. (2017). Translanguaging. *Oxford Research Encyclopedia of Education*, 19 December. Retrieved from https://oxfordre.com/education/view/10.1093/acrefore/9780190264093.001.0001/acrefore-9780190264093-e-181 (accessed 30 September 2020).

VOICE (Vienna-Oxford International Corpus of English). (2013). *The Vienna-Oxford International Corpus of English* (version 2.0). Retrieved from www.univie.ac.at/voice/ (accessed 30 September 2020).

Wang, Y. (2013). Non-conformity to ENL norms: A perspective from Chinese English users. *Journal of English as a Lingua Franca*, *2*, 255–282. doi: 10.1515/jelf-2013-0015

Welsch, W. (1999). Transculturality: The puzzling form of cultures today. In M. Featherstone & S. Lash (Eds.), *Spaces of culture: City, nation, world* (pp. 194–213). London: Sage.

Wenger, E. (1998). *Communities of practice: Learning, meaning, and identity.* Cambridge: Cambridge University Press.

Whorf, B. (1939). The relation of habitual thought and behavior to language. In J.B. Carroll (Ed., 1956), *Language, thought, and reality: Selected writings of Benjamin Lee Whorf* (pp. 197–215). Cambridge, MA: The MIT Press.

Widdowson, H.G. (1994). The ownership of English. *TESOL Quarterly*, *28*, 377–389. doi: 10.2307/3587438

Widdowson, H.G. (2003). *Defining issues in English language teaching.* Oxford: Oxford University Press.

Widdowson, H.G. (2012). ELF and the inconvenience of established concepts. *Journal of English as a Lingua Franca*, *1*, 5–26. doi: 10.1515/jelf-2012-0002

Widdowson, H.G. (2015). ELF and the pragmatics of language variation. *Journal of English as a Lingua Franca*, *4*, 359–372. doi: 10.1515/jelf-2015-0027

Wierzbicka, A. (1997). *Understanding cultures through their key words: English, Russian, Polish, German, and Japanese.* Oxford: Oxford University Press.

Wierzbicka, A. (2006). *English: Meaning and culture.* Oxford: Oxford University Press.

Williams, C. (1994). *Arfarniad o ddulliau dysgu ac addysgu yng nghyd-destun addysg uwchradd ddwyieithog [An evaluation of teaching and learning methods in the context of bilingual secondary education]*. Bangor: University of Wales PhD thesis.

Williams, R. (1973). Base and superstructure in Marxist cultural theory. *New Left Review*, *1*(82), 3–16. Retrieved from https://newleftreview.org/issues/I82 (accessed 30 September 2020).

Williams, R. (2015). *Keywords: A vocabulary of culture and society* (new edn). Oxford: Oxford University Press.

Wilson, T.D. & Hodges, S.D. (1992). Attitudes as temporary constructions. In L.L. Martin & A. Tesser (Eds.), *The construction of social judgments* (pp. 37–65). Hove: Lawrence Erlbaum.

Wodak, R. (2002). Aspects of critical discourse analysis. *Zeitschrift für Angewandte Linguistik*, *2002*(36), 5–31. Retrieved from https://userpages.uni-koblenz.de/~diekmann/zfal/zfalarchiv/zfal36_1.pdf (accessed 30 September 2020).

Woolard, K.A. (1992). Language ideology: Issues and approaches. *Pragmatics*, *2*, 235–249. Retrieved from https://journals.linguisticsociety.org/elanguage/pragmatics/issue/view/83.html (accessed 30 September 2020).

Woolard, K.A. (2005). *Language and identity choice in Catalonia: The interplay of contrasting ideologies of linguistic authority* [Paper presentation]. Workshop on Language Ideology and Change in Multilingual Communities,

18 October, San Diego, CA. Retrieved from https://escholarship.org/uc/item/47n938cp (accessed 30 September 2020).

Woolard, K.A. (2016). *Singular and plural: Ideologies of linguistic authority in 21st century Catalonia*. Oxford: Oxford University Press.

Woolard, K.A. & Schieffelin, B.B. (1994). Language ideology. *Annual Review of Anthropology*, *23*, 55–82. doi: 10.1146/annurev.an.23.100194.000415

W3Techs. (2020). W3Techs – World Wide Web technology surveys. Web Technology Surveys. Retrieved from https://w3techs.com/ (accessed 30 November 2020).

Wu, F.H. (2002). Where are you really from? Asian Americans and the perpetual foreigner syndrome. *Civil Rights Journal*, Winter, 14–22. Retrieved from www.usccr.gov/pubs/crj/crj.htm (accessed 30 September 2020).

Würth, M. (2020). The city in mind: Metalinguistic constructions of urban space in Buenos Aires. In A. Lynch (Ed.), *The Routledge handbook of Spanish in the global city* (pp. 141–175). Abingdon: Routledge.

Young, T.J. & Sachdev, I. (2011). Intercultural communicative competence: Exploring English language teachers' beliefs and practices. *Language Awareness*, *20*, 81–98. doi: 10.1080/09658416.2010.540328

Young, T.J. & Sercombe, P. (2010). Communication, discourses and interculturality. *Language and Intercultural Communication*, *10*, 181–188. doi: 10.1080/14708470903348523

Yu, Q. & Van Maele, J. (2018). Fostering intercultural awareness in a Chinese English reading class. *Chinese Journal of Applied Linguistics*, *41*, 357–375. doi: 10.1515/cjal-2018-0027

Zhou, V.X. & Pilcher, N. (2018). 'Intercultural competence' as an intersubjective process: A reply to 'essentialism'. *Language and Intercultural Communication*, *18*, 125–143. doi: 10.1080/14708477.2017.1400510

Zhu, H. (2010). Language socialization and interculturality: Address terms in intergenerational talk in Chinese diasporic families. *Language and Intercultural Communication*, *10*, 189–205. doi: 10.1080/14708470903348531

Zhu, H. (2014). *Exploring intercultural communication: Language in action*. Abingdon: Routledge.

Zhu, H. (2015). Negotiation as the way of engagement in intercultural and lingua franca communication: Frames of reference and Interculturality. *Journal of English as a Lingua Franca*, *4*, 63–90. doi: 10.1515/jelf-2015-0008

Zhu, H. (2019). *Exploring intercultural communication: Language in action* (2nd edn). Abingdon: Routledge.

Zhu, H. & Li, W. (2016). "Where are you really from?": Nationality and Ethnicity Talk (NET) in everyday interactions. *Applied Linguistics Review*, *7*, 449–470. doi: 10.1515/applirev-2016-0020

Zuckerberg, M. (2012). Facebook, Inc.: Registration statement, as filed with the Securities and Exchange Commission on February 1, 2012. Retrieved from www.sec.gov/Archives/edgar/data/1326801/000119312512034517/d287954ds1.htm#toc287954_10 (accessed 30 September 2020).

Index